LEGENDS
OF THE
WORLD

LEGENDS
OF THE
WORLD

Edited by
Richard Cavendish

with illustrations
by Eric Fraser

SCHOCKEN BOOKS · NEW YORK

LIST OF FULL-PAGE ILLUSTRATIONS

First American edition published by Schocken Books 1982
10 9 8 7 6 5 4 3 2 1   82 83 84 85
Copyright © 1982 by Orbis Publishing Limited
Published by agreement with Orbis Publishing Limited, London

Library of Congress Cataloging in Publication Data
Main entry under title:
Legends of the world.
Bibliography: p.
Includes index.
1. Legends. 2. Legends—History and criticism.
I. Cavendish, Richard.
GR79.L43 1982   398.2   82–5525   AACR2

Manufactured in Czechoslovakia
ISBN 0–8052–3805–0

CONTENTS

INTRODUCTION

Legends stand the test of time, better than genuine history does. In Britain every year thousands of people descend on Glastonbury in Somerset and Tintagel in Cornwall. They are drawn by the magic of legend, by nostalgia for a golden age which never existed – the age of King Arthur and the Round Table. A few years ago, archaeologists began digging at Cadbury Castle, an earthwork near Glastonbury in Somerset which may have been the headquarters of the real Arthur, the Dark Age general round whom the legends gathered. Their quiet and dusty excavations were unexpectedly disturbed by hundreds of visitors, who climbed the steep track to the hilltop in search of a link with the heroic world of Camelot. In Spain, during the savage Civil War of the 1930s, both sides clothed themselves in the mantle of El Cid, the great legendary champion of Spanish national identity and pride. He was a fighter of such ferocity that even after he was dead, when his corpse was insulted, his dead hand went to his sword – or so legend has it. The legend of the Virgin of Guadalupe has played a powerful role in the formation of national identity in modern Mexico. At the other side of the globe, in Mongolia, it is still considered not merely ignorant but actually 'un-human' not to know the traditional legends and tales which have been passed down since time immemorial.

The territory of legend has history on one of its borders, myth on another and folk-tale on a third. The frontier zones are vague and shifting, and perhaps no two people will ever agree about precisely where the boundary lines fall. Broadly speaking, however, and allowing for qualifications and exceptions, a legend is first and foremost a story, a narrative. It is an unauthentic or unverifiable story which is handed down by tradition and is accepted in its own milieu as accurate history. Most of the story may be fiction, but it has a foundation of some kind in fact. It is based on people who really lived or places that really existed or events that actually happened, to which tales have clustered and clung. Sometimes the core of fact at the centre of a legend may be no more than a tiny nugget of reality – a word, for instance, as in legends which spring up to explain place names.

Everywhere in the world, legendary stories of what happened in the past have been handed down from generation to generation. They are part of the inherited conglomerate of accepted beliefs, values and attitudes which give a people its identity. These stories consequently provide invaluable evidence about the societies that give birth to

Moses in the rushes, of Jewish legend (page 96)

them, and insights into human nature in general. Hence the wide
range of disciplines — including language and literature, anthropology, history, comparative religion, archaeology, art history, folk
studies — from which the contributors to this collection are drawn.

The book is divided into five sections, spanning the world. These
sections are themselves divided into cultural areas, and separate
chapters deal with each area's legends in the context of their social
and historical background. Some of the cultural areas are sub-
divided. The section on India contains separate treatments of legends
from the major Indian religious systems: Hinduism, Buddhism, and
the Jain and Sikh traditions. Celtic legends are divided into those
from Ireland, Wales and Scotland. The area of Christian Western
Europe has several sub-sections covering the principal legends which
have helped to form the psychological and artistic heritage of the
West: including the tales of the saints, the Arthurian cycle, the *Song
of Roland,* the legends of the siege of Troy and Alexander the Great,
the legends of Atlantis and Faust, and the fabulous stories about the
New World that circulated soon after its discovery.

Legends from different cycles and different parts of the world
often contain striking parallels and similarities, or sometimes
interesting variants. These are brought together in the Comparative
Survey at the end of this book where some of the principal legendary
themes and motifs are classified. Parallels crop up constantly in
stories of the supernatural birth of heroes, for example, and again in
the dangers that beset their childhood. Among the heroes said in
legend to have been exposed to die in infancy, for instance, are
T'ang-seng in China, Genghis Khan in Mongolia, Sargon in Assyria
and Gilgamesh in Babylonia, Moses in Jewish lore, several Celtic
saints, the Indian holy man Kabir, Cyrus the Great and Zoroaster in
Iran, Perseus and Oedipus in Greek legend, Romulus and Remus in
Roman tradition, and the Inca hero Yahuar-Huacac in Peru.

Heroic battles against monsters and titanic evil figures occur
frequently in legends from different societies, whether it is St George
killing the dragon or the Indian hero Rama defeating the demon-
king, Theseus slaying the Minotaur or Prince Yamato in Japanese
legend confronting the Great Serpent. Many stories turn on loves,
hatreds and tensions within a family, on relationships between
parents and children or brothers and sisters. Honour, courage,
loyalty, treachery, revenge, are themes which recur over and over
again, and many legends centre on a tragic conflict of loyalties.

Some legends celebrate the adventures and exploits of great
conquerors, wise kings and formidable warriors. Others are apocryphal tales about founders of religions, saints, mystics and ascetics
— and the same patterns often emerge in these religious legends as in
the tales of secular heroes, the saint being the religious equivalent of
an Achilles, a Galahad or a Cu Chulainn. Then there are stories of

great magicians, sages, artists and craftsmen — Merlin, for instance, or Daedalus. Legends also gather round notorious outlaws, bandits and criminals — from Robin Hood in 'merry England' to Jesse James and Billy the Kid in the American West. They cling not only to people but to places, which may be places with a recognized geography — Rome or Singapore or Istanbul, Mexico City or Glastonbury — or mysterious places believed to be hidden or lost — the lost Garden of Eden, the vanished Atlantis, the elusive golden realm of El Dorado.

Legends are told as good stories, enjoyable in their own right, and so they often describe what ought to have happened instead of what actually did. The peoples of lowland South America, for example, were repeatedly raided and harried by the warlike Caribs of the northeastern coast. Their legends, however, show them craftily turning the tables on the Caribs and trouncing them. Similarly in Russian legend, a disastrous defeat by the Tatars in 1224 is transformed into a Russian victory. The Turks ruled the Balkans and Greece for many centuries and there are numerous legends of heroic resistance to Turkish domination. The great Serbian and Romanian resistance hero is Marko Kraljevic, legend conveniently ignoring the fact that when he was killed in battle in 1395 he was fighting *for* the Turks and *against* his compatriots.

On the other hand, some episodes which did in fact occur in the past gain enormously in significance because they fit into a well-established legendary pattern. An example comes from the life of Muhammad, the prophet of Islam, who made so little headway at first in his home city of Mecca that he went away to the neighbouring town of Medina. A few years later he returned to Mecca in triumph at the head of a conquering army. This conforms to the common legendary theme of the hero who is driven into exile from his own country, his cause apparently lost, but who triumphs against adversity and makes a victorious return.

Each people's traditional history of its past is a *melange* of fact and fiction in which fiction predominates. Where fact leaves off and fiction begins is difficult, and frequently impossible, to determine. That legends are accepted as authentic in their own milieu, however, broadly distinguishes them from folk-tales, which are not told as historically true — though typical folk-tale themes often appear in legends or turn into legends.

Legends are on a different plane from myths, which are imaginative traditions about the nature and destiny of the world, the gods and the human race. In some cases, as in the Bible, a people's account of the past begins with myth — the creation of the world — and then shades over into legends about the founding figures and leaders of the nation and its early history. Legends are set on the human rather than the divine level and the central characters of legends are human beings, not gods, though they are often larger-than-life human beings with superhuman powers.

Traditional stories of the past are handed down for many centuries by word of mouth. Often they are preserved and passed on to each succeeding generation by professional story-tellers, who know the tales by heart and are skilled in their telling: like the Homeridae, the reciters who told Homer's stories in Greece, or the bards who sang of stirring deeds in German chieftains' halls, or the Welsh and Breton minstrels who exported the tales of Arthur from the Celtic fringe to continental Europe.

Sooner or later, the traditional tales are written down. Long narratives about the exploits of a great hero of the past are known as 'epics'. The *Iliad,* the *Aeneid* and *Beowulf* are all epics, with the inherent grandeur of conception and execution which the term implies. In medieval Europe epic poems were fashioned from the legends which had gathered round such figures as Charlemagne, King Arthur and Siegfried. Some countries possess national epics which embody a people's romantic conception of its own history: such as the *Shahname* in Iran or the *Kebra Nagast* in Ethiopia.

Although legends are satisfying tales in their own right, many of them are much more than simple adventure stories. Like myths, they have moral and exemplary purposes. The classical Greek legends were valued in their own time, and immensely influential for centuries afterwards, as examples of the heights and depths of which human nature is capable. Among the Germanic peoples in Europe legends were told to exalt great men and women of the past as examples worthy of emulation. The Arthurian legends showed how men and women could best live their lives in an imperfect world. The word 'legend' was originally applied to stories about Christian saints as figures to be admired and emulated (it comes from Latin *legenda,* meaning 'things to be read').

In some cases legends have been deliberately created and fostered for moral, political or even commercial purposes. Tales of the marvellous feats of Paul Bunyan, the giant lumberjack of American legend, were invented and disseminated to boost the sales of a lumber company in Minnesota. In the East, stories of the Buddha sacrificing himself for animals were told with the conscious intention of inculcating tenderness for all living creatures. The political position of a family is often justified in legends which trace its ancestry back to a god or some towering figure of the past. The Bagratid dynasty in Armenia and Georgia, for example, looked back to King David as the founder of its house, and the rulers of Ethiopia to King Solomon as the ancestor of theirs. The kings of England in the Middle Ages basked in the reflected glory of their legendary descent from Aeneas, the semi-divine hero of Vergil's *Aeneid,* ancestor of the Caesars and forerunner of the greatness of Rome.

In the rough definition of legend given earlier, qualification and exceptions were allowed for. One of them is that in some areas of the world people do not draw the distinctions between legend, history, myth and folk-tale which are customary in the West. In these areas − Papua New Guinea is an example − the whole repertoire of traditional tales is accepted as 'true'. Stories are still told about the past, however, but the legends of some pre-literate societies have a different flavour from those which are most familiar in the West.

Again, although legend has been defined here primarily in terms of narrative, there is a different use of the word which properly finds its place in this collection. Here 'legendary' refers not so much to a story as to superhuman status and glamour. It is in this sense that a person is described as 'a legend in his own lifetime', not because of any particular story told of him but because he has become the focus of special, almost religious admiration and awe. Interesting examples of legendary figures of this kind occur in the chapters on Australia and the United States of America. They demonstrate the continuing human need for larger-than-life figures in a country's past, to help build up a national identity, a shared tradition and pride.

In the end, the ultimate value of great legends lies in their inspiring poetry, their moral values and their attitude to life. It is poetically right for the blinded Samson to bring down the pillars of the Philistine temple upon his enemies and himself, for Robert Bruce to learn a lesson in resolution from the spider, for Roland in his obdurate pride to sound the great horn too late at Rencesvals, for the glory of Arthur and his champions of the Round Table to end in betrayal, destruction and bitter grief. In legend courage, loyalty, generosity and greatness of heart are upheld against cowardice, treachery, meanness and poorness of spirit. The lesson which the supreme heroes of legend and history have to teach is that life need not be petty, that existence can be vivid, exciting and intense, that the limits of human reach and achievement are not as narrow and restricted as they so often seem.

THE FAR EAST

The birth of Buddha in India (page 29)

INDIA

CHAPTER 1
HINDU LEGENDS

Hinduism in one form or another has deeply affected the Indian sub-continent since at least 1500 BC, although elements in it are probably older still. It is hardly a religion as we understand the term through Christianity or Islam, but an accretion of belief and practice around many different focal points. As such, it has engendered a vast body of myths and legends, and the two categories frequently blend into each other. The two most famous Indian epics, for example, the *Mahabharata* and the *Ramayana,* belong largely to myth, but they may contain a core of material based on historical people or events. They relate to so remote a period, however, that their historicity cannot be assessed in any detail.

In the *Mahabharata,* the five Pandava brothers are disinherited by their kinsmen, the hundred Kaurava brothers. In a great battle fought at Kurukshetra near Delhi, said to have lasted for eighteen days, the Pandavas defeat the Kauravas and regain their kingdom. The tale is richly embellished with myth, but archaeological evidence suggests that at least some of the core-story is based on fact. The *Ramayana,* as originally composed, tells how Prince Rama of Ayodhya (modern Oudh) was dispossessed of his Kingdom by his step-mother, Kaikeyi. She desired it for her own son, Bharata, and contrived to have Rama sent into exile. With his wife Sita and his faithful half-brother Lakshmana, Rama wandered for many years in the forest. Sita was abducted by the demon-king Ravana, but Rama and Lakshmana defeated Ravana with the aid of the monkey-army and rescued Sita. They finally returned to Ayodhya, where Bharata had been too righteous to take the throne and had placed the exiled Rama's sandals upon it. Rama was now duly crowned. In all later versions of the story,

Siva and Parvati (page 17)

however, Rama is not a human king but a god, an incarnation on earth of the great god Vishnu, which places the story firmly in the area of myth.

THE KINGS OF MATURAI

The Hindu myths of the gods are principally contained in the *Puranas* (Sanskrit sacred poems of Hindu mythology), but the material often spills over into history or quasi-history: for instance, when a lineage of historical kings includes mythical or legendary ancestors. The Pantiya kings of Maturai are a case in point. The story of Maturai and its kings also provides a classic example of what has been called the 'Little Tradition', the local, minor tradition, interacting with the 'Great Tradition' of mythology: here with the myth of the marriage of the god Siva and his consort Parvati, and their life on Mount Kailasa in the Himalayas.

Maturai is a major religious centre in the south-east of the Indian peninsula and has been an important town since at least the first century AD. The *Purana* relating to its temple of Siva dates from the sixteenth century, but contains themes of a much earlier period. Siva is said to have directed the first Pantiya king as to where Maturai should be built. This king's son begged Siva for a child, and from the flames of the sacrifice he offered a little girl appeared, three years old. She was no ordinary child and, as she grew up, it was seen that she had three breasts. Upon the death of her father, she became queen. Named Tatatakai (Invincible), she fiercely attacked all her suitors until the god Siva appeared. Then, losing her third breast, she laid down her weapons, became peaceable and meek, and was married to him. This marriage can be seen as an analogue to that of Siva and Parvati.

Afterwards Siva ruled Maturai as King Sundara, by which name he is still worshipped there. The subsequent rulers of Maturai were therefore descended from a god and his queen, who later became known as Minakshi. It is she who, as it were, 'fixes' the god into the local tradition. Their child, Ukkira Pantiyan, is identified with Skanda, the son of Siva and Parvati in the Great Tradition. The myth merges into legend as the lineage progresses. Forty-four rulers are listed up to a flood, and the next king re-establishes the city.

One of the best-known stories in this *Purana* is set in the reign of King Vankiya Cutamani, who held a contest among the poets of the literary academy which is said to have existed in Maturai in those days. The following extract is from the version by the missionary William Taylor, published in 1835:

While one named *Terami* was occupied in his usual office of preparing flowers, and putting them on the image of the god, it so happened that the King, *Sudamani,* went one day to one of his flower gardens, and a particular thought occured to him while there, respecting which he resolved on a poetical contest; and hence he tied a sum of gold in a packet, and hung it suspended to the bench of the poets, saying, 'Whichsoever of you shall succeed by a chant in telling me the thought that is in my mind, he shall be rewarded with this packet of gold.' They all attempted, but failed. *Terami,* hearing of this circumstance, paid homage to the god, and said, 'I have long been performing this duty of preparing and robing you with flowers, without establishing myself in life: I am poor, and cannot afford to pay the expenses of marriage; enable me to win this purse of gold.' The god condescended to his request, and put a chant into his hands, which he carried to the collegiate bench; when the poets all said, 'We find no fault with the versification; if it suit the thought in the King's mind, and he approve, you can then take the reward.' The King admitted that the chant contained his thought, and ordered the reward to be given. While *Terami* was just about cutting the string, *Narkiren,* from Kailastri, said, 'Hold! There is a fault in this chant, take it back.' *Terami,* saddened at the disappointment, went to the shrine of the god and said, 'I am ignorant myself of versification, but they say you have given me a defective chant.' The god, being moved, came forth, clothed with all the habiliments of a poet, and coming up to the bench, inquired who found fault with his stanzas? *Narkiren* replied, 'I do.' 'What fault?' 'It is not in the versification, but in the subject.' On this objection being proffered, a discussion arose; and on *Narkiren* manifesting obstinacy, the god opened a little the eye on his forehead, perceptible only to *Narkiren;* who, being infatuated, said, 'If even *Indren* (the god Indra) were to open his thousand eyes, I would not yield.' Whereon the god entirely opened his fiery eye (which burns what it fixes on); and *Narkiren,* perceiving the commencement of combustion, ran away as fast as possible and plunged himself in the golden *lotos* tank, which removes all kind of sin, and there remained to cool at leisure.

The disputed poem is extant and is duly ascribed to Siva. It reveals the King's thought, which was that the tresses of a pretty girl are imbued with a natural fragrance.

THE WIVES OF SUNDARAR

Most of the literary output of ancient and medieval India is religious. From the seventh century AD onwards, indeed, secular literature virtually disappears until the modern period. Far the largest body of legends is formed by stories of the saints.

The very existence upon earth of a saint or philosopher is readily credited to divine intervention. The parents of the famous teacher Sankara, for example, made a pilgrimage to Trichur (in modern Kerala). They were childless, but Siva appeared to them in a dream and told them they could either have several ordinary sons or one special one. They chose the second alternative.

One of the most famous works in Tamil, the principal language of southern India, is the *Periyapuranam,* composed by Cekkilar in the twelfth century and containing the lives of sixty-three saints, worshippers of Siva and undoubtedly historical figures, who probably lived 300 years or more earlier. As with the saints of Christianity or Islam, miracles were ascribed to them and God was believed to intervene in the world on their behalf.

The principal figure among them is Sundarar. In a previous existence, he lived on Mount Kailasa as an attendant upon Siva. There he was attracted to two heavenly maidens, Kamalini and Anintitai. Siva promised that if Sundarar consented to be born on earth and sing his praises there, he would be able to marry them both, for they too would be incarnated on earth. The saint agreed and was duly born. As a child, he was adopted by a local chieftain, who brought him up and in due course arranged a marriage for him. Forgetting his pact with the god, Sundarar agreed and the ceremony began. But an old man came up, brandishing a palm-leaf document as proof of the saint's contract, and stopped the wedding, for the bride was neither of the heavenly girls. Sundarar argued the matter hotly and seized the document and tore it up, which the old man pointed out was proof of his guilty conscience. The saint finally calmed himself and admitted his fault, and the old man, who was of course Siva in disguise, disappeared into his temple at Tiruvenneynallur. There Sundarar poured out his ecstatic first hymn — 'O madman with the moon-girt hair' — for the god had consented to this seeming abuse as a sign of special favour. Sundarar spent the rest of his life in pilgrimage from temple to temple.

Meanwhile, the heavenly Kamalini had been born as a dancing girl named Paravaiyar, in Tiruvarur. During his pilgrimage there, Sundarar saw her, and they fell in love and were married. Continuing his wanderings, Sundarar came to Tiruvottiyur, near Chidambaram, site of the famous cult of Siva as Nataraja, Lord of the Dance. Here he saw the other heavenly maiden, Anintitai, now born as Cankiliyar. She had refused all offers of marriage, saying she would be wedded only to the Lord. To achieve his divine purpose, Siva appeared to her in a dream, and she readily accepted the god's command to marry Sundarar, although the saint was already married. But she made matters difficult by asking the god to order Sundarar to swear to be faithful to her alone. Siva agreed, but said that the oath should not be sworn in the temple but under a tree outside, where it would not be binding! Cankiliyar could not but accept the god's wishes, and she and Sundarar were married. Paravaiyar was furious when she learned of her husband's bigamous alliance, and declared she would rather die than be reunited with him. Sundarar pleaded with the god to intercede with her and Siva, who throughout treats his devotee as a spoilt child, twice went to Paravaiyar and entreated her to forgive the saint. This she did, and Sundarar returned home to Tiruvarur to find the house festively decorated for his homecoming.

Another saint, Kalikkaman, heard of this and was contemptuous of the god for acting as go-between and apparent pander for the wayward Sundarar. As a punishment, Siva inflicted him with a muscular disease and then sent Sundarar to cure him. The angry Kalikkaman swore to die rather than be healed by one who employed the god on so unworthy an errand, but Sundarar arrived and forced his way into the house. Kalikkaman took his sword and killed himself. Horrified, Sundarar seized the weapon and was about to commit suicide himself when Siva restored the other to life, and the two saints were reconciled.

Such was Sundarar's power that when he was prevented by floods from crossing the River Kaveri, he cried out to the river, which parted its waters so that he could cross in safety. On another occasion, when Sundarar was at Avinaci, he heard the sounds of mourning and was told that a five-year-old boy had been seized by a crocodile. Sundarar took the boy's parents to the riverside and sang a hymn in praise of Siva, at which the reptile emerged from the water and disgorged the child, none the worse for his ordeal.

Another motif stressed in the *Periyapuranam* is intense piety and fortitude. A classic example is the tale of Kannappan. He is said to have been in a former birth Arjuna, chief of the Pandava brothers in the *Mahabharata*. He is reborn as a hunter in order to achieve liberation from the cycle of birth and rebirth, the succession of lives to which souls are bound. Going to the Siva temple at Kalahasti, he becomes so enraptured by the god that he worships for thirty days continuously, utterly forgetting his normal routine of hunting, eating and sleeping. To test him Siva causes the eye of the image to bleed as if put out. Kannappan gouges out his own eye to replace it. Then the other eye of the god starts to bleed also. Kannappan desires to replace it with his remaining eye. To guide his hand to the socket on the god's face, since he will by then be blind, he puts his foot in the spot, and then blinds himself. But the god restores his sight, and shortly afterwards he attains liberation. The tale contains a moral about orthodoxy, too, for the priest at the temple, who had been appalled by the hunter Kannappan's offerings of meat to Siva, is compelled to watch while his god accords liberation to the lowly saint.

UNION WITH GOD

The theme of the mystical marriage with God is present in legends from both the north and the south of India, and occurs particularly in devotion to Vishnu and his human incarnation as Krishna. Antal, or Goda, was the daughter of a priest of Vishnu at Srivilliputtur. Secretly, she used to take the garlands to be offered to the god and put them on herself first, so that the god would wear what she had worn. This exchange of garlands is highly significant, as it implies marriage. Her father discovered her, and was full of rage at Antal's apparent blasphemy. Eventually, she entered the shrine of the god and was never seen again.

Antal was a girl, but the theme of mystical union between god and worshipper cuts across sex, for even a male devotee is cast as the bride. In the north, Chaitanya is the supreme example. He was born in 1486 at Nadiya in Bengal, on the banks of the Ganges. From babyhood he showed devotion to Krishna, and is said to have played with a cobra which did him no harm (which recalls the myth of the infant Krishna dancing on the cobra's head). When food or sweets were prepared to be offered to the god, the baby Chaitanya used to cry out for them, as though it was to him that they should be offered. From the age of ten he looked after his widowed mother, and he was brilliant in his studies. At the age of twenty-four he renounced his estate and left home to spread his beliefs as a humble follower of Krishna. He went to the temple of Krishna – in his form as Jagannatha – at Puri (in modern Orissa). He also travelled to the south of India. Returning to Puri, he lived there for more than eighteen years, towards the end of which he would often go into trances. He would even rush into the sea, imagining it to be the River Jumna at Brindaban, a famous centre of the worship of Krishna. One day, in the year 1533, he hastened to the Puri temple, his arms outstretched, and entered Krishna's shrine, the doors of which closed upon him. When they opened again, Chaitanya was nowhere to be seen.

The story of Narasimh Mehta of Gujarat stresses the marriage motif. Born in a village in Saurashtra, he was dumb until a chance meeting with a holy man, who taught him to worship Krishna and the god's beloved, Radha. He grew up so impractical that his family despaired of him. Finally, he went to a Siva temple, where the god appeared to him and directed him to the Krishna shrine at Dvaraka. One night he had a vision of Krishna dancing with his mistresses, the Gopis, and attiring himself in a woman's garb he joined them. Krishna gave him a torch to hold. When it burned away, his hand started to burn, but he was so engrossed in his devotions he did not notice it. The god touched Narasimh's burned hand and it was miraculously cured. He promised Narasimh that whenever he needed help, he should sing a certain *raga*, called Kedar, and Krishna would come to his aid.

When Narasimh returned to his family they scoffed at the whole episode, so he took his wife and children and left. He infuriated those of high caste by singing religious ballads with people of low caste. He got into debt and promised not to sing Kedar again until the money was repaid. On another occasion, he had no cold water to cool his bath; he prayed for rain and it poured at once. The Raja of Junagarh decided to test Narasimh. He was to place a necklace on Krishna's statue in the palace temple, and if the god put the same necklace around Narasimh's neck, his true nature would be acknowledged. When Narasimh put the necklace on the statue, Krishna miraculously repaid the saint's debt so that he was free to sing Kedar. He went to the palace chapel and sang the raga, at which the shrine's doors opened and the necklace was flung about Narasimh's neck. This proved his sanctity and, incidentally, stressed a marriage-like bond between him and the god. Two motifs here emphasize the power of music: Krishna vouchsafes to the saint the raga by which he eventually proves himself, and the saint sings for cold water and rain comes.

No account of the theme of mystical marriage would be complete without a mention of Mirabai, daughter of Rana Ratansingh, ruler of Kurkhi in Rajasthan. She was a contemporary of the great Mughal Emperor, Akbar (1555–1606). As a baby she took seriously her mother's reply to her childish question as to who her husband was: the Lord Krishna. She gave up any play, except adorning the image of the god and dancing and singing before it. In due course she was married to King Bhojraj. For him her frantic love for the god was a trial, but he humoured her, convinced that she was insane. Her fame as a musician spread to the Mughal court at Agra, and Akbar and his musician Tansen visited her in disguise to hear her enraptured singing. It is said that Akbar even touched Mirabai's feet. This was too much for her husband, who banished both her and the statue of her beloved god. She was tempted to commit suicide in the river, but felt herself held back by the god, who commanded her to go to Brindaban, a centre of Krishna devotion north of Agra. In time her husband learned that she was still alive, and received her back. He died some years later, and in her widowhood Mirabai gave herself up entirely to love of God. She went to the great Krishna centre at Dvaraka in Gujarat. At the moment of death she exclaimed: 'I have surrendered myself to you. Till my last breath I will stand at your door, accepting all, Lord, life or death.'

TANSEN THE MUSICIAN

The most famous exponent of the power of music was Tansen, who was born in Gwalior. Childless, his parents had sought the blessing of a sage, Muhammad Gaus, and after this Tansen was born. As a child he learned to mimic the cries of animals and birds, and one day he was heard by a passing holy man, Haridas, who begged Tansen's parents to let him take the boy to Brindaban and teach him music, to which they agreed. After eleven years his parents died, and Tansen went to Muhammad Gaus, who completed his musical training and also introduced him to the Rani of Gwalior, herself a gifted singer. At the court Tansen fell in love with one of the queen's handmaidens, Hushaini, and became a Muslim in order to marry her.

Later, Tansen became court singer to the Maharaja of Rewas. The Emperor Akbar visited the court and was so struck by Tansen's gifts that the Maharaja presented his singer to the Emperor, who settled him in Agra. There he suffered much from the jealousy of the courtiers, who egged him on to sing the raga Dipak (Fiery), in the hope that its power to burn would destroy the singer. Tansen agreed, but taught another raga, Megh (Cloud), to his daughter Sarasvati and her friend Rupavati. Then he began to sing Dipak in court. The air grew warm, the audience was bathed in sweat, the leaves on the trees withered and fell, and the water in the river began to boil. Lamps in the hall lit by themselves, and Tansen felt himself suffocating with the heat. Meanwhile, the two girls desperately sang Megh, calling up a furious thunderstorm and torrential rain, and Tansen rushed out into it. He was ill with fever for a month. The Emperor himself came to his bedside and prayed for his recovery, and Tansen's foes at court were punished. He lived on as court musician, died in 1585, and lies buried in Gwalior.

THE JESTER AND THE THIEVES

As in Europe, buffoons as well as magicians enjoyed an honoured position at court. Probably the most famous of them is Tenali Raman, court jester to King Krishnadeva Raya (1509–29) of Hampi or Vijayanagar. Raman was a country lad, and one day prayed to the many-headed goddess Durga to grant him a boon. When she appeared, he began to laugh, and she indignantly asked him why. He answered that when he had a cold he could not stem the catarrh, so how did she cope, seeing that she had so many noses? The goddess was compelled to laugh, and offered Raman two alternatives: the milk of knowledge or the curds of wealth. Before she could stop him, he snatched both and drank them down. He travelled to the city of Hampi, where he tried to persuade the Rajaguru, the Royal Preceptor, to help him be admitted to court. The guru flatly refused, but one day Raman saw him bathing and hid his clothes. He refused to return them unless the guru carried him into the palace on his back. The guru was forced to agree and carried Raman into the palace, where he became court jester.

Returning home one night, Raman saw thieves lurking near his house, and also remembered that he had still to irrigate his fields. He loudly told his wife that they must hide their valuables down the well. They placed her grinding-stone in a tin trunk and with great effort carried it outdoors and threw it into the well. Seeing this, the foolish thieves were tricked into raising all the water from the well in their eagerness to lay hands on the trunk, and in the process irrigated all Raman's fields. He took pity on them at dawn and came out and sarcastically thanked them.

On another occasion, the King was to witness a special dance-drama and strictly instructed his guards to admit no one, in case the show be disturbed. Finding his way into court barred, Raman told two guards in succession that he was on his way to receive a special present from the King, and promised them half of whatever he was given if they let him in. They allowed him to pass, and once in the King's presence Raman began to belabour the chief actor with a stick. Enraged, the King ordered Raman a hundred lashes. The jester explained that he had an agreement with the guards outside that they should each receive half of whatever the King awarded him. The King was pleased that Raman had exposed the dishonesty of the guards. He rewarded Raman and awarded the guards fifty lashes each.

MAGICAL POWERS

The famous mystic and religious reformer Kabir (1440–1518) was found by his Muslim foster-parents as a baby abandoned beside a river. As he grew up, although a Muslim, he would put the *tilak,* the vermilion mark, upon his forehead and chant the name of the Hindu god Rama. He begged the saint Ramanand to take him as a disciple, which Ramanand finally did. He gave away all his wealth and preached that it was caste and creed which kept men apart, to the consternation of orthodox Hindus and Muslims alike. Finally, Kabir was arrested and brought before the ruler of Delhi, Sikandar Lodi, who sentenced him to death by drowning. Kabir emerged safely from the river. Next, he was to be burned alive in a hut, but he emerged safely from the flames. Finally, an elephant was to trample him to death, but the animal fled in terror, imagining that Kabir was a herd of lions.

Other saints and teachers were credited with magical powers. Madhvacharya, a philosopher of the twelfth century, was once by the sea near Udipi. He saw a ship sinking and by waving his saffron robe he caused the ship to be drawn safely ashore. The ship had sailed from Dvaraka in Gujarat, carrying as ballast the yellow earth of that holy place. Madhvacharya begged for this earth as his reward and took it to the Krishna temple at Udipi, where he immersed it in the tank. A beautiful statue of Krishna floated to the surface upon yellow mud.

Even as a boy, the blind saint Surdas could divine the whereabouts of straying animals. His songs brought Akbar himself to his hut. His descriptions of Krishna were so vivid that sceptics decided to test him. The image of the god was left unadorned one day, but the blind Surdas began to sing of the Lord as being without clothing or ornaments. The critics were silenced.

THE LOST CITIES

Tamil literature contains a flood myth which is connected with a tale of the two 'lost' cities of Tenmaturai and Kapatapuram. The earliest source for this is a work, probably not earlier than the ninth century, attributed to the unfortunate Narkiren whose blasphemy against Siva was noted earlier. The work is mainly concerned with the legend of the three literary academies, of which the third, at Maturai, is the only one likely to have existed. The durations given in Nakkirar's account for the academies are fanciful enough to give one pause: 4440 years, 3700 years and 1850 years. The first and second academies were at Tenmaturai and Kapatapuram, which are both stated to have been destroyed in sea-floods. It is possible that Tenmaturai is the same as Maturai, and that this flood myth and the story of the flood at Maturai are one and the same. As for Kapatapuram, attempts have been made recently to identify it with Tiruccentur, a temple of Skanda on the south-east coast near modern Tuticorin. But there is clearly a mythical element in these stories. The forty-nine poets of the third academy, with Siva as their principal colleague, are worshipped to this day in a special shrine in the temple at Maturai.

THE GREAT KINGS

Another type of legend concerns the deeds of kings who doubtless lived, but who in normal circumstances could hardly have achieved what tradition relates of them. The Himalayas rate highly as a place of pilgrimage and achievement, and a common theme is for a king to make an expedition there and carve his emblem upon the mountains. Kulottunkan I, a Chola king of southern India, for example, is said to have overturned the Himalayas with his axe, and then said: 'Let them be upright again.' On their slopes he carved his emblem of the leaping tiger.

Few kings of ancient India occupy the same position in legend as is held in Europe by an Arthur or a Charlemagne. Probably the closest to them in esteem is the Emperor Asoka (third century BC). He belongs to the Buddhist tradition, but his influence, especially in the matter of his abhorrence of violence, has extended far beyond it. A number of other kings are celebrated as examples of courage and virtuous rule, and perhaps the three most cited in this vein are

Chandragupta Maurya, Vikramaditya and Harsha.

Much of the tradition about Chandragupta (324–313 BC) arose long after his time, but his genuine political importance is clear. He founded the first real empire in northern India, stretching from the border of Persia to the modern Karnataka (Mysore), and completed the driving out of the Greeks after Alexander the Great's incursion. He is said to have had so many enemies that he never slept in the same room two nights running. Typically legendary is the story that he abdicated to become a Jain monk, and fasted to death at the Jain centre of Shravana Belgola, in modern Mysore.

Pataliputra, the modern Patna in Bihar, was Chandragupta's capital, and it was famous again under the Gupta kings in the third century AD. The most celebrated of them was Chandragupta II (376–415), with whom Vikramaditya is generally identified. According to legend, Vikramaditya conquered the whole of India, to which he brought prosperity and peace, and he is famed as a virtuous, brave and just ruler. As a Prince, he slew a lion single-handed. He relinquished the succession to the Kingdom to his elder brother, correctly, but against his father's dying wish. His father's foresight was proved, however, for the brother, Ramagupta, turned out to be a weakling who was even prepared to trade his Queen, Dhruva Devi, to the Sakas (Scythians) in return for peace. Vikramaditya dressed up as a woman and rode to the camp of the Sakas in a palanquin. Gaining access to the Saka King, he wounded him so severely that the Saka troops surrendered to Vikramaditya, who now revealed who he was. Ramagupta, ashamed, plotted to kill his brother and attacked him in bed one night, but was himself slain. His widow, Dhruva Devi, married Vikramaditya, who had defended her honour.

Harsah (606–48) reigned at Sthanvisvara (modern Thanesar) in the foothills of the Himalayas, and his rule is well documented by the poet Bana and by a Chinese traveller to India, Hsuan Tsang. Harsha drove out the Huns. He destroyed the King of Malwa, who sought to take Harsha's Kingdom and had abducted his sister, Rayjasri. She had escaped, and was at last found in the mountains just as she was about to commit suicide. Harsha almost lost a battle with a King of the Deccan, Pulakesin. He is said to have owned no less than 60 000 war elephants, but in the manner of Asoka he turned away from violence and war, and sought peace and prosperity for his kingdom. While Hsuan Tsang was at Harsha's court, a seminar on religions was held in which the Chinese visitor participated. The King and Queen gave all the royal treasure away to the scholars and the people. One man was left out, and Harsha borrowed a shawl from his sister, so that he could give the poor man what he himself was wearing.

This tradition of royal chivalry and liberality descended into medieval and modern times, and became infused with themes of patriotism and independence. Sivaji (1627–80) is one of the great hero-kings of Maharashtra. He rebelled against the Mughal ruler Aurangzeb. His ability to vanish into the forests and rocks of the hills around Poona was legendary. He was lured by Aurangzeb to the court at Agra, and he and his son were held virtual prisoners there. Sivaji feigned illness, at the same time arranging for hampers of sweetmeats to be sent out of the palace every day for distribution to the poor. One day, Sivaji and his son hid in the baskets and escaped. He was crowned at Raigarh and though he ruled for only five years, he established a lasting kingdom in Maharashtra.

Two heroines of the nineteenth century added patriotism to the royal tradition, the ranis of Kittur and Jhansi. The first was besieged by the British at Kittur in 1824. Taken prisoner, she regretted that she had not died in battle. The rani of Jhansi is perhaps the most compelling figure in the Mutiny of 1857. She had come up the hard way, having had to contend with family intrigues and with aggression against her by other Rajput states. She died fighting the British and was cremated on the battlefield.

In modern times, the disappearance of Subhas Chandra Bose, leader of the Indian National Army which sided with the Japanese in the Second World War, set off the same type of speculation that surrounded the fates of some of the Nazi leaders in Germany: was he dead or not? Sought by the British and Americans after the surrender of Japan, in August 1945 he boarded a Japanese plane for an unknown destination. The plane and its passengers were never seen again, and rumours circulated that Bose was not dead.

The fact that such speculations still thrive emphasizes that Hindu tradition stems from a living faith that is continuously revitalized in one way or another. It is Hinduism which has given to the people of India, from the Himalayas to Cape Comorin, a sense of identity, and in this process legend has played an ample part.

INDIA

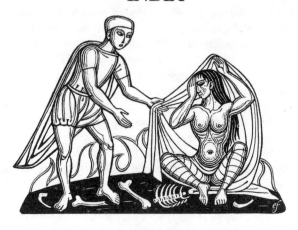

CHAPTER 2

BUDDHIST LEGENDS

Buddhist tradition is rich in stories of all kinds. Some of these are folk-tales which come from a period earlier than the rise of Buddhism in the sixth century BC. These old tales have been adapted for Buddhist purposes and many of them are now presented as stories about the previous existences of the Buddha and of Buddhist saints. Such stories are generally known as *Jatakas,* 'stories of (former) births', but they are not Buddhist in origin and sometimes have only a very superficial Buddhist gloss upon them.

However, even in the case of stories which originated in a Buddhist milieu and appear to have been concerned in their earliest form with Buddhist characters, it cannot be assumed that all material of the Jataka kind has been excluded. In the form in which Buddhist legends about the Buddha and the early Buddhists have come to us, there are features which appear to the modern reader to be incredible, certainly unverifiable and probably unhistorical. What is historical and what is not is as difficult to determine in the case of Buddhist legends as it is in most others. In Buddhist tradition there is a special name for this type of story: *avadana.* The word means 'a noteworthy deed' and, while it sometimes has a bad sense, is used more often in a good sense, to mean a story about 'a heroic deed' or 'a moral feat'.

THE BUDDHA'S LIFE IN LEGENDS

The most notable of Buddhist legends are those concerning the Buddha. This usually means the person who lived in northern India in the sixth century BC, who is sometimes known also by his given name of Gautama. Because of its central place in Buddhist tradition, the

Upagupta and the courtesan (page 33)

story of the Buddha's life has been embellished and re-embellished with all kinds of miraculous elements intended to enhance the honorific quality of the story.

Embellishments of this kind clustered round his birth and early life, for example. It was said that his mother, Queen Maya, though married, was still a virgin when she conceived him. She dreamed that she was carried up into the Himalayas, where the future Buddha in the form of a snow-white elephant entered her body through her right side. She told the dream to her husband and his court, and it was prophesied that she would bear a child who would be either a great ruler or a Buddha. Maya carried the child for ten months. He emerged from her side, without causing her pain. On the same day was born the tree beneath which he would attain enlightenment at Bodh Gaya. As soon as the child was born he took seven steps, so taking possession of the world, and lotuses blossomed where he trod. Maya died seven days afterwards, entrusting him to her sister. When he was taken to the temple the statues of the gods bowed down to him. He was brought up in seclusion in his father's palace, shielded from the real world outside, and married his cousin, the beautiful Yasodhara, winning her by defeating her other suitors in trials of strength and skill, including an archery contest. She bore him a son. It was only after this that Gautama decided to leave his home and family, and go out into the world to seek the truth.

Some of the features of stories of this kind do not inspire in a modern reader a strong confidence in the historical veracity of the narrative. After the Buddha's enlightenment at Bodh Gaya and the beginning of his career as a teacher of the new doctrines he had discovered, he was eating his meal one evening and resting beside a lake in the Himalayas when he decided to go to Sri Lanka, to teach there. He immediately did so, arriving by air and hovering overhead where a great gathering of spirits of the island was taking place. He thereupon struck terror into their hearts by rain and storm and darkness. This, it seems, was intended to announce his presence and induce the spirits to provide him a place among them where he could sit down.

Such is the story as it is told in the *Mahavamsa,* a collection of legends which was made in Sri Lanka. The nucleus of the story must obviously have been formed originally in India. But it is interesting that no complete and continuous story of the Buddha's life, from his birth to his passing, was produced until about six centuries after the event. The first continuous biography was the work of an Indian Buddhist poet, Ashvaghosha, in the first century of the Christian era. What had existed until then were accounts of varying lengths (some very long) of particular episodes or periods of the Buddha's life. The last weeks of his life seem to have inspired some of the earliest of these accounts, though how early it is not possible to say. One of the best known, 'the narrative concerning the Great Decease' *(Maha-Parinibbana-Sutta),* contains some material which may well have originated with the Buddha himself, notably the farewell words to his disciples. But elsewhere in this same narrative, as it now exists, the Buddha is represented as performing miracles like a magician, and we are told also of an earthquake accompanying the words with which he announced his imminent decease. Thus a figure who teaches a realistic and naturalistic philosophy in many of the utterances attributed to him, had nevertheless in the course of a century or two already become the subject of a supernaturalistic story.

The same kind of development can be observed in the various versions of the encounters of the Buddha with Mara the Evil One, who attempted to prevent his enlightenment at Bodh Gaya. In some versions the Buddha recalls certain significant occasions in the past when Mara approached him (usually in disguise, which the Buddha always saw through at once) and put certain ideas to him, which the Buddha immediately rejected; whereupon Mara withdrew, disconsolate. In other versions there is an elaborate description of Mara's three 'daughters', who were used, in vain, to try to deflect the Buddha from his path, and of a great army of virtually cosmic dimensions with which Mara attempted to frighten the Buddha into submission. They too were defeated, and fled in all directions. The place became a vast deserted battlefield, with rocks, logs and trees strewn everywhere, while a rain of sweet-scented flowers descended from heaven upon the victorious Buddha.

Thus, there is now only the *legend* of the Buddha, to whichever of the traditions or texts we turn. The historical figure is inextricably interwoven with what is legendary.

THE BUDDHA AND THE PLAGUE

The period between the Buddha's enlightenment and his decease at the age of eighty was rich in episodes and events connected with his constant travels throughout the cities of the central plain of the Ganges, events which, as in the case of any great and famous teacher, would have been remembered, recounted, treasured, and eventually hallowed as part of the tradition concerning a man who was not as other men are. What piety began by embellishing, popular demand for wonders and miracles succeeded in transforming almost entirely into a divine legend, a process which was facilitated and encouraged by the later, more metaphysical developments of Buddhist thought.

A fair example of the multitude of legends concerning the Buddha is one which tells how he cured the people of a certain city of an epidemic disease. The disease was regarded as the work of demons and it had caused many deaths in the city of Vaishali. Various appeals for help had been made by the citizens to certain other great teachers. 'They sent for Kashyapa Purana, saying: "Come, a demonic plague has broken out among the people of Vaishali. If you come it will be allayed." Kashyapa Purana came to Vaishali but failed to allay the plague, and the people reflected, "Kashyapa has come, but the demonic plague has not been allayed."'

Kashyapa Purana was the teacher of a rival philosophy to that taught by the Buddha. Six such rival teachers are frequently mentioned in the early Buddhist tradition, and the significance of their names in this legend would immediately have been recognized by the hearers of the story. Each of the six was in turn invited by the people of Vaishali to come and allay the demonic plague, and each in turn came, and failed to do so. We are then told that 'some dead kinsmen of these people of Vaishali had been reborn among the devas (good spirits), and some of these called to the people of Vaishali, saying: "Those who have been summoned by you are not experts; they do not speak as experts, nor are they able to allay the demonic plague that rages among the people of Vaishali. Now here is the Buddha, the Exalted One, who has appeared after incalculable ages, one who is perfectly enlightened, who is possessed of the insight that comes from perfect knowledge, who has great magic power and great majesty, who is all-knowing and all-seeing. Whenever he stays in a meadow on the outskirts of a village, all disease and strife, all riot, calamity and trouble in that village are stayed. Summon him, and when he comes the demonic plague that rages among the people of Vaishali will be allayed."'

Accordingly a citizen named Tomara, who was a learned courtier and had a great following and retinue (that is, a *very* important person), was asked by the people to go to Rajgir, in Bihar, where the Buddha was staying at the invitation of the King of the country of Magadha. He was to offer the Buddha the homage of the people of Vaishali, to enquire after his health and well-being, and then to tell him of the plague in Vaishali and to say, 'Well would it be if the Exalted One who is beneficent and benevolent would come and bring mercy to Vaishali.'

Tomara set out with 'a fitting escort riding in fine carriages', and eventually came to the Bamboo Grove at Rajgir, where the Buddha was preaching to 'five hundred monks and several thousands of other people'. When Tomara was able to deliver his message, the Buddha agreed to travel to Vaishali, provided the King of Magadha gave his permission. The King consented, and proposed to escort the Buddha to the frontier to meet the people of Vaishali. The frontier between the two countries was the River Ganges and the legend makes much of the elaborate arrangements which were made, to prepare the road to the Ganges and make it level, sprinkled and swept, carpeted, and strewn with flowers. The whole event is presented in the manner of the preparations for the visit of a great universal monarch. Entertainment in the form of 'mimes, dancers, athletes, wrestlers and musicians' was provided, and rest places along the way, with food and drink for the great retinue that would accompany the Buddha, together with an array of chariots with banners and pennants, and the sound of 'drums, tabours, cymbals and trumpets'.

The legend continues in this manner, with a description of the pontoon bridge which was built across the Ganges (which is very wide at this point) and the many other preparations which had to be made. It would be out of keeping with the intention of the narrative for the modern reader to ask jokingly why the Buddha could not have gone by air, as he did to Sri Lanka, and thus have arrived earlier and saved many lives. It would also be contrary to the underlying theme to expect that the Buddha might have issued a supernatural fiat by means of his magical powers and healed the suffering people of Vaishali from a distance. When at long last the legend tells of the arrival of the Buddha and his retinue of monks at Vaishali, after many intervening stories of the cure of sickness by Buddhas of previous ages in the world's history, the legend states baldly, almost as the expression of the obvious: 'So in due course the Exalted One reached Vaishali. There he brought well-being both to those within and to those without Vaishali.'[1]

LEGEND AND REALITY

Behind the general grandiloquence of the legend as it comes to us in this Sanskrit version, certain features of the historical scene in the India of the Buddha's day can be discerned. Amid the growth of urban life, and the emergence of great monarchies extending their power across the Ganges plain and engulfing the older, simpler life of the villages in vast and much less personal systems, the individual in many places was ill at ease in the new world of that day (as so often before and since) and was asking basic questions about the nature and purpose of human existence. A number of different new philosophies had arisen which attempted to provide answers to these questions, and these are conventionally referred to in Buddhist tradition as seven in number, the philosophy of Buddha being the seventh, and, it was claimed, able more satisfactorily and surely than any other to bring men peace, serenity and health.

The effect upon a village, tribe or country of adherence to Buddhist norms and values can fairly be said to have been, as the legend claims, an amelioration in the general social condition of the people, the replacement of older aggressive attitudes by more peaceable ones, and even an improvement in general physical conditions. It is still the practice for people, in Burma for example, to resort to the monastery when they need medical help. There is thus a general truth which the legend rests upon, that the coming of the Buddha, representing the coming of Buddhist monks, means the staying of 'disease and strife, riot, calamity and trouble'.

UPAGUPTA AND THE COURTESAN

Another type of legend concerns the Buddhist hero, or saint, and usually provides the Buddhist listener with a model of attitudes and conduct which he or she may emulate. An example is the story of the young merchant Upagupta of the town of Mathura. Upagupta followed his father's profession and was well known for his honesty and politeness. He was a good-looking young man and he attracted a famous courtesan of Mathura, who sent him an invitation to come and see her. Upagupta declined, and thinking that her usual fee of 500 gold coins was too high for him she sent him a further message, saying that she wanted no money from him but only love. Upagupta sent back the reply: 'Sister, it is not yet time for you to see me.' Some years later the courtesan was visited by a rich client at a time when she was entertaining someone less wealthy and desirable. Out of greed, she had her poorer client murdered and his body hidden, so that she was free to receive the rich client. The murder was discovered and the king ordered the courtesan to be disfigured and expelled from the town.

Hideous and wretched, the courtesan lived at the place where dead bodies were burned and where no one came. Hearing of this, the merchant Upagupta reflected that now was the time for him to accept the invitation she had once sent him. He set off to the burning place. Seeing him coming, the maidservant who had stayed with the courtesan said to her mistress: 'Upagupta whom you once invited is coming to see you. Surely he wants enjoyment!' The courtesan, lamenting her disfigured body and mutilated face, bade her maid-servant bandage her limbs quickly, in order to hide at least some of her unsightliness, and when Upagupta came she said: 'When this body of mine enchanted even the gods with its beauty you did not come, my friend! How can you come now? How can this disfigured and marred body attract you?' Upagupta replied: 'Lust have I none! Alas, even the most lustful shall give up lust when he sees the end which is the flesh's fate.' He urged her to think of the merciful Lord (the Buddha), whose mercy would extend even to her. 'Who is there to take you across this ocean of affliction except him who is the fountain-spring of compassion? Take refuge in him with all your heart; he is the Lord of the lowliest and the lost.' Having said this, Upagupta stayed with her and nursed her with great devotion until she died. The legend says that the courtesan attained peace before she died, and the true vision of things. Upagupta himself soon afterwards left his life as a merchant and was ordained as a Buddhist monk.

This story, which inspired the Indian poet Rabindranath Tagore to give it modern expression, illustrates the nature of a Buddhist legend; it is an *avadana,* 'a noteworthy deed', 'a moral feat'. Moreover it is attributed to a renowned historical figure, for Upagupta the monk became the Buddhist preceptor of the great Emperor Asoka (third century BC). The story is not merely idealistic, for it exemplifies the general attitude of Buddhist monks towards women, that although feelings of sexual attraction may deflect a monk from his serious purpose, women are nevertheless to be respected as sisters or mothers, and are to be helped without hesitation whenever they encounter misfortune or suffering.[2]

The legend in its present form comes from the later Sanskrit literature of Buddhism, but embodies material from a source of the second or first century BC. It forms part of a collection bearing the name of the Emperor Asoka, containing the story of his conversion to Buddhism and his subsequent turning away from aggressive, expansionist policies to the peaceful promotion of Buddhist ethical values throughout his empire. The collection also includes legends which tell of Asoka's cruelty before he became a Buddhist, the effect upon him of his brother's life as a Buddhist, the effect upon a minister of state of Asoka's own life as a Buddhist, and Asoka's last days. Having given away all his valuable possessions as gifts for the support of the monks of his kingdom, he died in poverty, but possessed of 'the treasure of the realm of spirit that is neither wasted nor robbed', as the legend says. It is doubtful whether these legends of Asoka have any solid historical foundation, except in so far as they illustrate the quality of life of a man who has been called the greatest of all the followers of Buddha, and who, in the many stone inscriptions throughout his empire (discovered in modern times) gave evidence of the existence in ancient India of an emperor whom Buddhism had profoundly affected and who, however legendary he may have become, is also undoubtedly historical.

INDIA

CHAPTER 3

JAIN AND SIKH LEGENDS

Jainism is in many ways similar to Buddhism. The founders of both religions were contemporary with each other and came from the same area of India, and perhaps it is not surprising that some of the legends associated with both founders are similar. The founder of Jainism was Vardhamana, also called Mahavira. He is believed to have been born in about 599 BC, though some Jains date him sixty years earlier. He was the son of a chieftain and at the age of thirty, on the death of his parents, he devoted himself to a life of rigorous asceticism. After thirteen years he obtained full enlightenment, or omniscience. He spent the rest of his life teaching and died, unseen by anyone, at the age of seventy-two.

THE LIFE OF MAHAVIRA

It is said that before Mahavira was born, his mother, Trisala, had a series of auspicious dreams foretelling the greatness of the child she was to bear. She first dreamed of a white elephant, then of a white bull, then of a white lion. Next she saw the goddess of wealth in a dream, which was followed by a dream in which she smelled the fragrance of flowers. Then she dreamed of the full moon shining all over the universe and next of the sun, red and radiating. Some Jains say that in her eighth and ninth dreams she saw the golden banner of the god Indra and a golden pitcher, others that she saw a pair of fish sporting – a sign of happiness – and then two pitchers. Next she

Mahavira and the herdsmen (page 36)

dreamt of a lake full of lotus flowers attended by bees and beetles. In the eleventh dream she saw the ocean of celestial milk, and in the twelfth a celestial palace in which gods played music. This was followed by a vase of precious stones, and then a sacred fire fed by clarified butter. Some Jains add two more dreams, making sixteen in all, one of a throne studded with rubies and diamonds, and the final one of a celestial king.

The wise men of the court interpreted these dreams to mean that Trisala's child would be either a great ruler or a world teacher. A similar story is told of the Buddha, but an unusual twist to the Jain legend is that Mahavira was not conceived by Trisala but by another woman, Devananda, the wife of a Brahmin. The gods, however, transferred the embryo to Trisala to prevent Mahavira being born into a Brahmin household. (The Jains rejected the Brahminical religion of that time.) From the moment Mahavira was transferred to Trisala's womb, her family's fortunes changed, improving day by day, and so they named the child Vardhamana (Increasing).

His other name, Mahavira, was given him by the gods after an episode in a garden, when a god, seeking to test the child's strength of mind, raised him high into the air. Vardhamana was not frightened but reacted by beating the god on the chest. The god quickly put him down and henceforth he became known as Mahavira (Great Hero).

Legend also surrounds Mahavira's enlightenment. After tearing out his hair to prove his contempt for pain, he sat for two-and-a-half days beneath a tree, taking neither food nor water. Nearly all the gods witnessed the supreme moment of his enlightenment, after which they carried him in a golden palanquin to a special five-tiered throne. Before mounting it he discarded the robes which Indra, king of the gods, had given him. One sect of Jains disputes this, however, saying that Mahavira meditated naked.

There are many stories illustrating Mahavira's indifference to the world and its passions and feelings. In one he is taunted by herdsmen, who burn his feet and drive nails into his ears without disturbing his meditation. On another occasion he was nearly strangled but offered no resistance, and eventually Indra came to his aid and saved him.

A remarkable story surrounds Mahavira's death. Seated on a diamond throne, illuminated by supernatural light, he preached to all the rulers of the world for six days continuously. When he came to his last words, everyone present fell asleep. When they awoke, they found him still sitting in the meditation posture, but dead. Thus Mahavira slipped away from this world, unseen by anyone. There are other legends associated with him, especially stories of his previous lives which are similar to, though less impressive than, the Buddhist *Jatakas*.

THE SIKH GURUS

Sikhism is a comparatively modern religion, formulated in the late fifteenth and early sixteenth centuries. The early leaders of the Sikhs were called Gurus, or Teachers, and the founder of Sikhism was Guru Nanak (1460–1539), who developed his ideas from both Hindu and Muslim thought. Stories grew up about him of the kind which cling to celebrated religious teachers. It was said that his future greatness was predicted at his birth and there were tales of his precocity as a child. Before he was a year old, he was able to sit in the meditation posture. There were also many improving tales which pithily conveyed the essence of his teaching. When he visited Mecca, he lay down near the Kaaba, the dwelling-place of God, with his feet pointing to it. Reproved by a Muslim for this disrespect toward the house of God, Nanak asked the man to point his feet in whatever direction the house of God was not. The man pulled his feet round and as he moved them, the Kaaba moved too.

There is a famous story, which may well be true, about the tenth Guru, Gobind Singh (1666–1708), who was largely responsible for the transformation of the Sikh community into a military brotherhood, renowned for its fighting qualities. Gathering the Sikhs together, he told them that the times required supreme loyalty to their leader. He drew his sword and asked for volunteers who would give him their heads. After a long silence, one Sikh volunteered and was led into the Guru's tent, from which Gobind Singh presently reappeared, alone and with blood on his sword. The same thing happened four times more, and then the Guru reappeared with all five volunteers, unharmed. Some Sikhs say that the blood on the sword came from a goat, others that the Guru had beheaded the volunteers and restored them to life again. In either version the point of the story is the courage and devotion required of the faithful Sikh.

CHAPTER 4
TIBET

The principal Tibetan legends can be grouped in two categories: religious and ancestral. In both cases the term 'legend' is used here from a Western viewpoint, for what we call a legend may be regarded by Tibetan standards as a piece of history or biography. A vast number of religious legends found their way into Tibet following the introduction of Buddhism from India in the seventh century AD. Legends describing the origin of historical Tibetan dynasties and celebrating the deeds of their founders tend to play a social and political role. An example is the epic cycle of Ge-sar, King of Ling, a heroic ruler with magical powers. Sent to earth by the gods, he destroyed evil demons who had devastated Ling and killed many of its people. Ling was a small kingdom between Tibet and China, and the dynasty which ruled Ling down to 1959 fostered the saga of Ge-sar to support its own position.

By the mid-thirteenth century political power in Tibet had passed from kings to the Buddhist monastic order of the Sakya. However, lay power was restored for a time by a member of one of the great families of Tibet, Byang-chub rGyal-mtshan (1302−64). In his time legends celebrating the early kings of Tibet were used to promote the principle of royal rule. To this period can be traced the legendary account of how the Chinese Princess Wen Cheng went to Tibet to be married to its first great historical King, Srong-btsan-sgam-po (*c.* 609−49). This King was a successful military commander and his presence on the Chinese borders was viewed with apprehension by the T'ang government of China, which won his friendship by granting him a Chinese princess as a bride in the year 641. There were already historical accounts of his reign, but the later legend is largely unhistorical.

Padmasambhava (page 42)

THE WINNING OF THE CHINESE PRINCESS

According to the legend, when Srong-btsan-sgam-po reached the age of sixteen, having heard that the Chinese Emperor had a beautiful and talented daughter, Princess Wen Cheng, he dispatched his minister sGar-ba to China, with 100 horsemen and rich gifts, to ask for her hand. After overcoming countless difficulties on the way, sGar-ba and his suite arrived at the T'ang capital, Ch'ang-an. Four other countries had also sent ministers to ask for the Princess in marriage and the Emperor decided to give his daughter to the wisest of the five ministers, and to test them accordingly. As a first test, they were asked to draw a silken thread through a piece of jade which had a hole turning and twisting in nine directions. sGar-ba won this contest by tying the silk thread round the waist of a large ant and sending it through the hole.

For the second test, the Emperor sent for 100 mares and 100 foals, and then asked the five ministers to pair the foals with their mothers. The other four ministers tried to solve the problem by studying the colours of the hair and the characteristics of the animals. The Tibetan minister was helped by a groom, who had heard of the prowess and wisdom of King Srong-btsan-sgam-po and who was greatly impressed by his minister's modesty. Following his advice, sGar-ba had all the foals kept inside the stables with fodder but no water. When he let them go the following day each foal, being very thirsty, started looking for its mother to suckle from her. So sGar-ba won the second contest.

As a third test the Emperor gave each of the ministers 100 jugs of wine and 100 sheep, and asked them to drink all of the wine, eat all the mutton and tan all the skins in one day. The other ministers and their attendants immediately started slaughtering the sheep and then began to drink the wine. Not only were they drunk before they could eat the mutton, but they also left the court grounds in a gruesome state, with blood and wool everywhere. sGar-ba, on the other hand, instructed his horsemen to slaughter the sheep, and then divided them into two teams: one would eat and drink, and the other would dress the hides. The result was that not only did sGar-ba's men soon complete their task, but they were not drunk and they left the grounds clear.

For the fourth test the Emperor summoned the five ministers suddenly, by the beating of drums in the middle of the night. Then he ordered them to go back to their quarters, to see who would reach them first. As the Tibetan minister had marked his way with signs beforehand, he reached his lodgings sooner than the other ministers, who had been in such a hurry to arrive first at the Emperor's palace that they had hardly noticed the crossroads on the way. The Emperor and the other four ministers rejoiced at sGar-ba's wisdom and thought he deserved to to take the Princess to Tibet. However, the Emperor wished to test the ministers once more. They had to recognize Wen Cheng among 2500 beautifully dressed and bejewelled young ladies. All the ministers were at their wits' end, but sGar-ba remembered the landlady of the inn telling him that she had once been a servant to the Princess. He secretly sought her help and because she had heard that the King of Tibet was young and handsome, and found also that sGar-ba was a man of pleasant disposition, she described the appearance of the Princess in detail. sGar-ba won that contest too, and the Emperor let his daughter go to Tibet with a large number of craftsmen and a rich dowry, including household utensils, medicines, books on arts and crafts, an orchestra, musical instruments, silkworm eggs, grain seeds and a statue of the Buddha. When Wen Cheng reached Lhassa a sumptuous wedding took place, after which Srong-btsan-sgam-po and the Chinese Princess loved each other for ever and ruled the country hand in hand. The Chinese craftsmen introduced a number of new skills and the Princess and the King together started spreading the Buddhist doctrine.

This account can hardly be regarded as historical, and there is a discrepancy between the date when the King was given his Chinese wife, according to historical evidence, and his age when he asked for her hand according to the legend. Besides ministering to Tibetan pride and glorifying a royal and national ideal, the story acknowledges the important role played by the sGar-ba family during the period of monarchy. It also reveals the values of a farming and stock-raising society, where practical skills such as tending horses, tanning, or finding one's bearings in vast territories unsurveyed to this day, are highly esteemed. The tests set by the Chinese Emperor are not abstract puzzles or riddles, nor do they have the philosophical or religious connotations that might be expected in this kind of plot. They are meant to ascertain the practical intelligence of the protagonists, from the Tibetan standpoint. Finally, the list of items allegedly borrowed from the Chinese suggests a great respect for the Chinese civilization of the T'ang period, when arts and sciences reached new heights.

TALES OF THE BUDDHA

Tibetan religious legends include moral tales, hagiographies — lives of holy beings who may or may not have existed historically — and stories about the miraculous foundation of holy places. The moral legends derive ultimately from the religious tales of story-tellers in India before the introduction of Buddhism to Tibet. Among them the Tibetan translations of the so-called Jataka tales, legendary accounts of the 550 previous lives of the Buddha, which were originally told to illustrate Buddhist moral precepts. A few Sanskrit collections of these tales were translated into Tibetan and included in the Kanjur (the Tibetan Buddhist scriptures). One of the principles they inculcate is tenderness for all living beings, exemplified by the very popular legends of the Buddha's self-sacrifice. As a prince he killed himself to feed a starving tigress, as a hare he offered his body to appease the hunger of an ascetic, and as a monkey or a deer he saved his herd by giving up his own life. Although the tales came originally from India and drew abundantly on the rich heritage of Indian folklore and literature, they are presented as incidents in the previous lives of the historical Buddha and Tibetans regard them as actual events, though in fact they were deliberately created to serve a religious purpose.

The same thing is true of the romantic biography of the Buddha himself *(Lalita-vistara),* which is also included in the Kanjur. Like all versions of the life of the Buddha, this legendary account assumes that he was the son of a king, a detail now generally accepted as being unhistorical. The legend says that he was born miraculously from the side of Queen Maya of the Sakyas, after having entered her womb with the appearance of an elephant. The child then took seven steps in the direction of each cardinal point and declared that he would reach the highest Nirvana, that he would be the first of all living beings, that this would be his last rebirth, and that he would cross the ocean of existence. A stream of cold water and a stream of warm water fell on his head and washed him, while on the spot where he had been born a spring appeared, in which his mother washed. Other legendary episodes refer to the Buddha's extraordinary strength and power: as a child, still in his nurse's arms, with one finger he pulled a golden bowl which 500 elephants could not move from its place; the statue of a god bowed down at his feet; after staying three months in the realm of the gods he returned to the earth down a staircase of lapis lazuli, followed by Hindu deities. Brahma with his godly retinue descended a golden stair to the Buddha's right, and Indra with his own suite of gods descended a crystal stair on the Buddha's left.

THE FOUNDER OF BON

Buddha's hagiography provided the model for the later fabricated life of gShen-rab, a legendary figure who is regarded as the founder of Bon, the second religion of Tibet. The account of gShen-rab's birth and life is related in a Bon religious text, the *gZer-mig.* There the miraculous conception of the hero is operated by two rays of light, a white one entering the top of his father's head, and a red one entering the top of his mother's. The first one, in the form of an arrow, represents the male component (sperm); the second, in the form of a spindle, represents the female component (blood). According to an earlier version, gShen-rab himself appeared in the form of a rainbow.

It is interesting that Tibetan mythology also sees the origin of the first legendary kings in the sky, to which they were attached by a cord that enabled each of them to spend the day on earth and the night in heaven, and eventually to disappear into the sky at the end of his reign.

PADMASAMBHAVA

This kind of hagiography reached a peak with the *Padma-thang-yig,* a legendary account of the life of Padmasambhava, better known to the Tibetans as Guru Rin-po-che, the patron of the rNying-ma-pa order of Tibetan Buddhism, which regards him as a second Buddha after the historical Buddha. The amount of legendary material that proliferated around this famous Indian yogin is so vast as to raise doubts about his historical existence. He is said to have been invited to Tibet by King Khri-srong-lde'u-bstan in about 779, on the recommendation of the celebrated Indian teacher Santarakshita. However, this might well be a later fabrication intended to give authority to the teachings put forward by his followers, and it is possible that Padmasambhava was not a historical person at all and merely represents an ideal of holy man and magician. Even his country of origin is uncertain, though it has been suggested that he came from the region of Swat (Pakistan).

The sage's miraculous birth is indicated by his name, which means 'Born from a Lotus Flower', and an idea of the content of his hagiography can be gathered from the following episode which gives an account of his deeds in Sahor (the former Punjab, now Himachal Pradesh, India) and of the magic creation of the Padma-mtsho lake at Riwalsar. The Tibetan temple now standing on the bank of the lake bears witness to the immense popularity which Padmasambhava still enjoys. The episode also illustrates the theme of the origin of a holy place.

Knowing that the time had come to give religious instruction to the sister of Santarakshita, Princess Mandarava of Sahor, Padmasambhava flew on a cloud to her retreat. While the Princess and her attendants were out in the garden they saw a smiling youth sitting in a rainbow. The air was filled with the sound of cymbals and the scent of incense. Overcome with joy, Mandarava and her attendants lost consciousness. Padmasambhava revived them by emanating red, white and blue rays of light, and landed in the garden, where all the nuns bowed before him. Then Mandarava invited him into the monastery to expound the Buddhist doctrine, and Padmasambhava instructed her and her followers in three kinds of yoga. A cowherd who had seen Padmasambhava's arrival and activity in the nunnery reported that Mandarava was living with a young man and was not as virtuous as they had taken her to be. When the King heard the accusation he ordered the monastery to be forcibly entered and the young man to be seized. After Padmasambhava had been taken and bound with ropes, the King punished his daughter, Mandarava, by sentencing her to be confined naked in a pit filled with thorns for twenty-five years. A cover was put over the pit so that she could not see the sky. The King also ordered that the two chief nuns should be confined in the monastery in such a manner that they could no longer hear the voice of a man. Soldiers took Padmasambhava, stripped him naked, spat upon him, assaulted him, stoned him, tied his hands behind his back, placed a rope around his neck, and bound him to a stake at the junction of three roads. Seventeen thousand people were ordered each to fetch a small bundle of wood and a small measure of oil. After a long roll of black cloth soaked in the oil had been wrapped around Padmasambhava, they heaped leaves and wood on him and poured oil on top. The pyre was as high as a mountain and when it was kindled the smoke hid the sun and the sky.

After the satisfied multitude had dispersed to their homes a great sound was heard, as of an earthquake. All the deities of the Buddha came to Padmasambhava's aid. Some created a lake, some cast the wood aside, some unrolled the oil-soaked cloth, some fanned him. A week later, the King realized that smoke was still coming from the pyre, which should have been reduced to ashes by this time. He thought he might have made a mistake, and he sent his ministers to investigate. To their astonishment, the ministers saw a lake, all the wood aflame. At the centre of the lake there had risen a lotus blossom upon which sat a beautiful child with an aura, apparently about eight years old, his face covered with a dew-like perspiration. Eight maidens of the same appearance as Mandarava attended him

When the King heard this he took it all to be a dream. He went to the lake himself and walked around it, rubbing his eyes to be sure he was awake. The child cried out, accusing him of attempting to kill a Buddha and scolding him for being unreligious and dominated by the five passions of lust, anger, sloth, jealousy and selfishness. The King made humble repentance, recognized in Padmasambhava the Buddha of the past, present and future, and offered himself and his Kingdom to him. Padmasambhava accepted the King's repentance and expained that he knew neither pleasure nor pain and that the fire could not burn his inexhaustible body of bliss. However, Mandarava refused to come out of the thorn-filled pit when the King sent for her. Not until the King went to the Princess himself and explained everything did she return to the palace. The King clad Padmasambhava in royal garments, placed jewels and a head-dress like a crown upon him, and gave him both Mandarava and the Kingdom.[1]

The popularity of Padmasambhava, not only as the founder of the rNying-ma-pa order but also as an archetype of magician and holy man among Tibetans in general, is shown by his numerous legendary traces in Ladakh, western Tibet, Sikkim and Bhutan: footprints in rocks, caves in which he meditated, and so on. The success of his legend is accounted for by the Tibetan fondness for fantastic tales and paranormal phenomena. Such legends, indeed, were born of the necessity for making a serious religious message understandable to Tibetan folk, who could only be impressed by displays of magic which could match and rival those of their own ancient religion.

CHAPTER 5

MONGOLIA

Legends, myths and oral chronicles of history are important parts of Mongolian culture. Even during the period of the Mongolian Empire, from the twelfth to the fourteenth centuries, the great mass of Mongols, outside the aristocracy, could not read or write. In later centuries, when the Mongols were converted to Buddhism, the Tibetan written language became important in religious circles, but popular culture was an oral culture, a mixture of native Mongolian themes and elements from Tibet, China and Central Asia.

The Mongolians today, living in the Mongolian People's Republic and in China and the Soviet Union, share a common way of life based on pastoralism, and a common language. The dialects are mutually understandable and many legendary themes are common to all groups. Regional variations are only now becoming apparent, as the oral culture is gradually recorded. All the young people can read and write today, but the older generations are still rooted in the oral culture. It is considered uncultured, even literally 'un-human', to be unable to sing folk songs and recite genealogies, riddles and wise sayings. Every group of Mongols, every family, has old men and women who can recite oral epics which may take hours, even days, to perform.

GESER KHAN

The best known and loved Mongolian epic is the history of Geser Khan, ruler of the Ten Regions of the World. The Buddhist Church disapproved of it and would have preferred the Mongols to know nothing but edifying stories about Buddhist saints and forget their many epics, especially the saga of Geser Khan. But they did precisely the opposite. More and more new songs appeared, woven around the

Geser Khan and the black-spotted tiger (page 46)

heroic king, son of the god-king Khormusta, who sent him down to earth to put an end to injustice and evil. Accompanied by his thirty-three heroes, Geser Khan undertook this duty. The more popular the legend became, the more tasks Geser undertook, and perhaps even today more adventures are being added to his campaigns.

One of Geser's tasks, in the Chahar (Inner Mongolian) version of the epic, is to track down the wild and dangerous black-spotted tiger, to free the world of this menace. Geser sets out with his thirty-three knights and his brother, Dshasa Shikir. Geser, who has the power of sorcery, turns himself into a tiger. He appears in this form before his heroes and warns them of the strength and gigantic size of the real tiger and the terrible deeds committed by the monster, which has already eaten many thousands of creatures. When Dshasa catches sight of the tiger in the distance, the men spur on their horses to advance, but the horses refuse to move so much as one step farther towards it.

Geser now turns himself into a horse and leads the horses forward. They gallop towards the tiger, which emits ear-splitting roars. It grows dark. Geser can no longer hold the reins in his hand, but his magic powers triumph over the tiger's and it grows light again. At full gallop, Geser rides into the tiger's great maw. After he has delivered a short, fervent prayer to Buddha, the eight dragon-kings appear, riding on golden rams, to help him against the tiger. Geser kills it, but meanwhile the thirty-three heroes, frightened by the tiger, have left Geser in the lurch. Dshasa, reproaching himself for deserting Geser, rides back to find him. At last they meet, overjoyed at the reunion. Geser instructs Dshasa not to destroy the giant tiger's skin, as it can be used to provide armour and tent-coverings for many thousands of warriors. After the warriors have received their shares of the tiger's flesh, they all ride back to Geser's wife, Rogmo goa, who prepares a feast in celebration.

Another passage describes a duel between Buidung, who is a companion of Geser Khan, and an enemy knight who possesses magical powers. They galloped towards each other and struck so that the sparks flew. Buidung cut off the enemy knight's right arm, but he was far from having conquered him. However often he struck his opponent the latter was not in the least affected, but when the magic knight retaliated, Buidung's skin and face, hands and legs, were covered in blood:

> Buidung ceased bringing him down,
> Shot arrows, sitting on his horse.
> Hit by an arrow, the magic knight said:
> 'More I cannot bear;'
> Turned his grey horse three times into powder,

Put it in his pocket for the bolt of fire.
Transformed his own body,
Appeared now as a mottled brown snake, and said:
'I will entwine myself round Buidung's neck!' ...

It is becoming generally accepted that the Geser epic has its origins in the border area between Mongolia and Tibet. The theory that it originated in Tibet has become more plausible now that a manuscript has been found translated from Tibetan in the seventeenth century. But many of the adventures of Geser must have been the product of the fertile imagination of the Mongols themselves. His adventures took place in the Mongol steppes and mountains, and themes from other sagas were transferred to him. He became so revered a figure among the Mongols that one legend describes him as 'the same person' as the Emperor of China, and despite the protests of the Buddhist lamas he was also regarded as the god of riders, warriors and herds.

GENGHIS KHAN: LEGEND AND HISTORY

Mongol epics were partly sung, partly recited and partly related in prose, the singer accompanying himself on a horse-headed fiddle. The sung parts had a more strictly poetical form and metre than the recited parts, but even the latter were regulated by rules of parallelism, so that lines repeat one another with only a few regular changes of word. For example, in the epic called 'Three-year-old Bullock Red Hero':

Although it was intended to catch him with a pole-lasso,
he was not caught,
Although it was intended to catch him with clever tricks,
he was not caught.

This kind of repetition occurs in all Mongolian legends of the epic genre. When the reciter reaches the word *gene* (it is said), the listeners take part by saying in unison, *Dzaa!* (Yes! Agreed!).

Another important series of Mongolian legends concern historical figures, glorious princes *(khans)* and emperors *(khagans),* wise lamas and powerful living Buddhas *(khutukhtus).* The most widespread are legends about Genghis Khan, the great military leader of the early Mongols at the turn of the twelfth and thirteenth centuries. Here is one such legend from western Mongolia:

Some say that Genghis-Khan was a god *(burkhan),* and some that he was a prince. They say he was a son of the sky, who came down to earth and lay under a tree. Near this tree there was another, and both trees leaned together and joined at the top. From one of the branches sap dripped out and fell into the mouth of the child, and this is what kept him alive. At this time the Khan of the Dzhungars (west Mongols) died with no heir. The officials gathered together to choose a Khan but they could not come to any agreement, because everyone wished to become Khan. Therefore they decided to choose a Khan from outside their own circle and they chose this child.

There is clear influence here of the Buddhist practice of choosing holders of religious office by magical signs ascribed to a child, which has the advantage of averting the emergence of powerful hereditary dynasties, since each child is chosen from different, 'magically' determined surroundings. In fact, of course, Mongolian history was not like this. Genghis Khan came from a famous lineage, the Borzhigid, and his descendants, 'the Golden Clan', became the aristocratic rulers of Mongolia.

The legend shows how mixed up history becomes when each group adapts it to its own purposes. Genghis Khan was never 'chosen' by the western Mongols. He conquered them. And, in fact, the group of western Mongols mentioned in the legend, the Dzhungars, did not come into existence under this name until several centuries after Genghis' death. But every Mongol group likes to link its history to the famous Emperor in one way or another. The Khori Buryat Mongols, for example, trace their descent from Genghis Khan's daughter.

In many legends Genghis acquires the characteristics of a god and a creator. Like Geser, he is supposed in some versions to be the son of Khormusta-tengri, a sky-god whose name goes back to ancient Persian mythology. In some versions Genghis himself is a cosmological creator:

> Shingit-khan (Genghis-Khan) had four sons. The oldest was the Dalai-lama, the second was Amy-gylyn-khan, the third was Talden-khan. They had in their kingdom all the dead who had been criminals or thieves. The fourth son was Tsagan-khan. The eternal snow on the peak of Mount Munko-sagan is the spittle of Genghis which he spat when he was smoking his pipe; the ashes from his pipe formed the bare rocky peak of Mount Bayan-ula. The hill called Yangit, lying to the east of Munko-sagan, is the button from the hat which Shingit-khan left there.

In many parts of Mongolia there was a religious cult of Genghis Khan. Even in the present century the cult was important enough in the Chinese province of Inner Mongolia for the Chinese government to go some way towards supporting it in order not to offend

Mongolian nationalist feelings. A cult-centre, a kind of mausoleum, was built in the steppes, containing battle-standards, tents and other objects supposed to have belonged to the famous hero. The pro-Soviet government of the Mongolian People's Republic took the opposite attitude. They proclaimed Genghis to have been a purely destructive tyrant, and a projected issue of stamps to commemorate the great leader was forbidden in 1962.

THE BULL-ANCESTOR

Many Mongolian legends are about animals which turn into people and back again. In the more outlying areas, where the clan system survived the impact of changing empires and governments, these animals had the function of totems. Each was associated with a clan, usually as an ancestor. One well-known example of this is the bull-ancestor, Bukha-Noyon, of the Bulagat clan of the Buryat Mongols. The story goes that a famous prince had a daughter who became pregnant by a bull. Her father accused her of immorality, and in shame she locked the child in an iron cradle and cast it into Lake Baikal. It was found on the bank by a female shaman who brought up the child. He was Bulagat, the founder of the clan.

Even here, the motifs were adapted to the obsession with Genghis Khan. One of the stories about Genghis current among the Buryats went as follows:

A khan had two wives. The younger one bore a child, but the older one was barren. The younger wrote to her husband who was away, but the older wife got hold of the letter and substituted another saying that what had been born was not a child but a wild animal. The khan wrote back, 'Leave it till I get back.' But the older wife got hold of this letter too, and she substituted another saying, 'Put it in a cradle closed up with pitch and throw it into the lake.' The cradle floated on the water and came to the bank. Shingis kicked and the cradle opened. He got out of the cradle. Just at that moment a lark was singing, 'Shin, shhin!' That is why they called him Shingis (Genghis).

For the Mongols, Geser and Genghis and Bkha-Noyon were all part of 'history', which was linked to the present day in a continuous sequence. The sequence was genealogical, for people traced their descent from these legendary figures. In this way of thinking, time was measured by generations, not by years or centuries. Even today, many Buryat Mongols can trace their genealogies back twenty-five generations or so, to legendary figures such as Bukha-Noyon. But Mongols were probably always conscious of other ways of thinking about time. The cyclical view of history, common to China, Tibet and

Central Asia, embodied in the twelve-animal cycle of lunar years, was known in Mongolia from early times. By the eighteenth century, western notions of linear time had also made some impact. The Buryats have interesting chronicles in which they tried to correlate the legendary and historical ways of thinking, giving dates, for example, to princes and princesses whose lives were imbued with magic.

LEGENDS AND EVERYDAY LIFE

Many of these 'historical' legends also have the function of explaining place names and linking geographical sites with mythical events. Such places were thought to be the homes of spirits, the 'masters' of the place, without whose blessing no inhabitant of the region could live in prosperity. Thus Bukha-Noyon, bull ancestor of the Bulagat, walked over the land; where he urinated there grew thick forests of cedar, where he pawed the ground there emerged a valley, and so on. All of these places are named by the Buryats, although each group tends to designate different places as the sacred sites. Bukha-Noyon had nine sons, each of whom lived after his death on the summit of a different mountain in the Lake Baikal region. There are nine sons in every version, but the mountains chosen vary from group to group.

Other legends simply have the function of conveying an understanding of the symbolic aspects of everyday life. The Mongols, living mainly in treeless steppes, burn dried dung on their fires. But in one place they clearly came across some coal, as the following legend shows:

In the Uydzin-Gun district, in the Bain-Ulan hills, there is a place with plentiful water. This was Genghis Khan's wintering place. It is strewn with black stones. These are greatly respected as the dung of Genghis Khan's sheep. They burn these stones, and the smoke is good for sick cattle.

There are legends attached to almost every aspect of Mongolian everyday life. Why do lamas not wear trousers? Why do Russians have round eyes? How was writing invented? Who are the ancestors of domestic animals? What are the ingredients of alcohol? All of these questions have answers. The legends are funny, quick-witted, and aptly metaphoric: how else would they be remembered? They tell us a great deal about the Mongol way of thinking, but in order for an outsider to understand them, it is really necessary to be present when the stories are told; only then is it possible to understand the irony which these 'everyday legends' usually embody. Here, for example is a story about the origin of writing:

Tangut writing was invented by the famous lamas Dzhebtsun-Tsambu Khutukhtu and Arybdzhan Zaya Pandita. But for a long time no-one knew how to invent Mongolian writing. While the lamas were praying and holding whole temple services for the gift of writing, an old woman went to the temple carrying an *edrin* (a wooden stick with notches cut in one side, used for working sheep-skins and making them soft). This must be a sign, thought the lamas; the white sheep-skin is the paper, the marks made by the *edrin* are the letters. And they took these marks and made Mongolian writing.

The point of this is that Mongol writing is being mocked. No one has less status in Mongol society than old women, no occupation is seen as more boring than softening sheep-skins. The high lamas and their knowledge of writing *should* be objects of intense respect, but are they? The bearers of the oral culture, the ordinary herdsmen, have their own methods of derisive retaliation.

CHAPTER 6

CHINA

Although China has a written history going back more than 3000 years, we are very inadequately furnished with early Chinese legends and myths. Records which appear to contain concepts dating from the remote past have to be treated with the utmost caution. The formation of China as we know it was a long process, during which the northern peoples expanded into the south, until the Middle Kingdom, as the Chinese call it, was united for the first time in the third century BC. There were written records which incorporated new materials as the Chinese moved southwards, but in 213 BC a political decision led to a great burning of all books except technical manuals. The decree was reversed twenty-two years later, but the scholars who reconstructed the books which had been destroyed did so in such a way as to reinforce their own position and to emphasize the hierarchical nature of Chinese society, in which scholars had a high status as advisers to the sovereign. Agnostic puritanism was the order of the day, for these were 'old, learned, respectable bald-heads' who edited and annotated the material which had been remembered from the past and explained in terms of political virtue poems and songs which belonged with spring sowing and love-making, harvest and fertility rites. One such song commemorates the gathering of orchids in the springtime in the state of Cheng.

THE ORCHIDS OF CHANG

In the state of Cheng, whose songs Confucius described as licentious, the Rivers Chen and Wei meet at the foot of Mount Tu-liang. On the river banks there flourishes an orchid, efficacious against poison and an antidote to evil influences, which is called the fragrance of Tu-liang. When the eastern winds have melted the ice and the peach

Emperor Chu Hung-wu and barber Lü Tung-Pin (page 59)

trees blossom, the people of Cheng invoke the higher spirits and the boys and girls gather orchids. When the Chen and the Wei overflow their banks, the boys and the girls come to the orchid beds. Over the Wei there are fair green fields. The boys and the girls take their pleasure together, and the girls are given a flower as a token.

Now the Duke of Cheng had a junior wife named Yen Chi. One night she dreamed that an ancestor gave her an orchid, saying. 'Make a child with this; his royal fragrance will gain him recognition as a prince.' When the Duke of Cheng took her into his bed, he gave her an orchid. Being of junior rank, she asked that, should she bear a son, the orchid should be a proof of his princely heritage. To this the Duke agreed, and when she gave birth to a son he was given the name Lan, orchid. In due course he became Duke Mu Lan of Cheng. When he fell ill, he told his ministers, 'When the orchid withers, I, who owe my being to it, will die.' And in the tenth month, when the orchids are cut, he died.

THE FOAM OF THE DRAGONS

Many Chinese legends involve dragons, of which there were two kinds, *chiao* and *lung*. Both were essentially aquatic, but the latter spent part of the year in the sky. The first type of dragon looked like a snake with the head of a tiger and the bellow of a bull. It lived in rivers and streams, where it would trap men in its fetid saliva and suck their blood from their armpits. The second type, on the other hand, was generally beneficent and had the power to leave the water in the spring and mount to Heaven, where it spent the summer as a rain-maker.

Certain men were said to have the power to train these beasts, and it was believed that the emperors of the early dynasties were given dragons by the Ruler of Heaven to draw their chariots. Some said that the Hsia dynasty had two dragons, while the Shang dynasty was granted a third and the Chou dynasty a fourth. Among the ancestors of the Fan family was Liu-lei, whose title was Yu-lung, dragon-driver. He lived at the time of the Emperor Ch'ung-chia of the Hsia dynasty (traditionally 2000–1520 BC), who was given two pairs of dragons by the Ruler of Heaven. One pair came from the Yellow River and the other from the Han. One of the females died and Liu-lei pickled her flesh and fed it to the Emperor. He developed a taste for the meat and Liu-lei fled, fearing that he would not be able to maintain the supply. Some say that it was at this time that the dynasty lapsed into vicious decadence.

It was then that two dragons appeared at the Hsia palace, claiming to be princes of the state of Pao. The Emperor ordered the tortoise-shell oracle to be consulted. Should the dragons be killed? Or driven away? Or kept? Or should they be asked for some of the foam from their mouths? The oracle having approved the last course, a piece of cloth and a written petition were presented to the dragons, who withdrew after leaving some foam on the cloth. This was then enclosed in a chest, which was passed from the Hsia dynasty to the Shang dynasty and thence to the Chou dynasty until, in the time of Emperor Hsuan, the chest was rashly opened. The foam surged through the palace and nothing would restrain it. The Emperor ordered his wives to oppose it naked, with objurgations and imprecations, at which the foam changed into a black lizard, or some say a tortoise, rushed into the women's quarters and fecundated a seven-year-old child. At the age of fifteen, 'without having a husband, she gave birth; stricken with fear she exposed the child'. As the baby lay crying on a path she was found by a man and his wife, for whom the Emperor's soldiers were searching as it had been revealed that they posed a threat to the dynasty. They took the child to Pao, where she grew up and was given the name Pao-ssu (Ssu was the family name of the Hsia dynasty). Later she was given to Emperor Yu, the successor to Hsuan. The Emperor she destroyed, and she almost encompassed the destruction of the dynasty as well.

THE FLOATING MONK

Not all encounters with dragons were so dangerous. The best known of the later stories concerns a certain Ch'en Kuang-jui, father of T'ang-seng, the 'floating monk', the legendary name of Hsuan Tsang, the famous Buddhist pilgrim who travelled to India in the seventh century AD in search of Buddhist scriptures, which he brought back to China.

Ch'en's wife was sick and, as the cook prepared to kill a carp to make broth for her, Ch'en noticed that the fish was weeping. He ordered the cook to cut only three scales from the fish for the broth, and to return the creature to the water. This was done and Ch'en's wife recovered. Shortly afterwards Ch'en was posted to the south and took passage on a ship with his pregnant wife. The captain, a pirate, threw Ch'en overboard and ordered the wife into his bed. But she pleaded her belly. Ch'en meanwhile had been caught as he fell into the water by a handsome youth, who took him to a crystal palace under the sea and thanked him effusively for saving his life. Ch'en was astonished, for he thought it was his own life that had been saved. The youth explained that he was the third son of the Dragon King and had gone swimming in the form of a carp, the very fish who had been spared by Ch'en's cook. During a stay of ten days in the palace the Dragon King offered Ch'en gold and silver, but Ch'en, advised by the third son, asked for a small box that stood on the King's table. The King was displeased, but could not refuse. Then the King's son took Ch'en back to his home at Mount Lingchou in Chekiang, where Ch'en opened the box. It contained three flower-vessels which produced beautiful maidens, who announced themselves as the daughters of the Dragon King. All became wives of Ch'en and each bore him a son.

Meanwhile the pirate had assumed Ch'en Kuang-jui's name as well as his wife, and had taken up his post in the south. After three months the woman gave birth to a son. She wrapped him in a red and white silk cloth and placed him in a wooden bucket together with a letter written in her own blood, setting out his history. She dropped the bucket into the River Yangtze, where it was finally discovered by a monk on a rocky islet, who heard the baby crying. He reared the infant as a disciple, giving him the name T'ang-seng (Floating Monk).

T'ang-seng's mother continued to resist the pirate, pleading ill health. T'ang-seng himself, mocked as an orphan by the other novices, was told his history by his master, who had magic powers and knew that the boy's father was alive in Chekiang. T'ang-seng set off to find his mother, and identified himself to her by means of the letter in blood, at the same time telling her that her husband was still alive. She thereupon sent him to find his father. This he did, and Ch'en obtained troops from the Emperor to kill the pirate and free his wife, whom he brought home to join T'ang-seng.

After a time T'ang-seng went about his travels as a monk. The three grandsons of the Dragon King sought posts in the celestial bureaucracy. The youngest, sent to Heaven to make enquiries, was told that they were to become the San Kuan, the Three Officials, and was appointed Inspector of Heaven on the spot. When he failed to return, the middle grandson went to find him and was made Inspector of Waters. The eldest, arriving last, found that only the most junior post as Inspector of Earth was left. This he was forced to accept, but the redness of his eyes is a reminder of his anger at the slight.

RECRUITS TO THE CELESTIAL BUREAUCRACY

Just as China was ruled by an emperor who was served by a vast bureaucracy, which depended for its recruits on a system of public examinations, so heaven too was ruled by the August Personage of Jade, Yu-ti, with the assistance of a celestial civil service whose ministers and officials dealt with every aspect of life in heaven and on earth. Meritorious human beings, on death, might be appointed to places in the heavenly service and subsequently earn promotion. The case of two cousins, Liu Ch'en and Yuan Chao, furnishes an example.

The two boys, who lived in the T'ian-t'ai mountains of Chekiang during the Later Han dynasty (AD 25–220), went one spring day to fetch water. The countryside was so beautiful that they left their buckets by the stream and wandered off along a path which, after many a twist and turn, brought them to the entrance of a cave where two spirits were sitting playing chess. As the boys stood and watched they saw that a white hare was springing up and down beside the players. As it rose in the air, the flowers around the cave entrance blossomed; as it returned to the earth the flowers withered. At last the chess game was finished and the spirits asked the boys how long they had been there. They replied, a few hours, and turned to retrace their steps, but the spirits urged them to stay, saying that no one would recognize them at home. The boys did not understand and insisted on leaving, so the spirits gave them a piece of reed, telling them that if they found everything changed at home, they should come back to the cave. It would open for them if the reed was pointed at it.

When the boys reached the stream, everything had changed. They could not find their buckets and the banks of the stream were overgrown. They entered the village, but could not find their homes. They questioned two old men with white hair, who said that they were descendants of Liu Ch'en and Yuan Chao in the seventh generation. The boys replied that this was impossible since they were the two young men in question. The old men called out in alarm and the villagers came running and beat the youths for upsetting their elders. The boys fled in dismay and sought the cave, which was closed when they found it. They then realized that in their flight they had lost the reed. They banged on the rock in despair but it did not open. Finally they banged their heads against the rock and died.

The August Personage of Jade had pity on them and made Liu Ch'en god of good luck and Yuan Chao god of ill luck. The mountain itself became famous as a result and, later on, the Buddhists built many monasteries there.

THE LOYANG BRIDGE

Chess was a favourite pastime of spirits and other immortals, including those who helped to construct the bridge which crosses the River Loyang at Ch'uan-chou in Fukien, where the sea-tide meets the land-waters. Matters are made more complicated by the fact that when the Ruler of Heaven disposed of his human body he split it with his magic sword and his entrails fell into the river at Ch'uan-chou. There they turned into a tortoise and a snake, which behaved maliciously towards human beings (perhaps because together they represent the deity of the North, a notoriously dangerous direction).

Before there was a bridge the river was crossed by ferry. In the time of Emperer Shen-tsung, a thousand years ago, the two reptiles sent high winds and waves to attack a boat in mid-channel. Suddenly a voice was heard, saying, 'Spirits, respect the scholar Ts'ai who is in the boat!' The waters at once grew calm and the passengers found that one of their number, a pregnant woman, belonged to the Ts'ai family. She vowed that should she give birth to a son who became a scholar, she would dedicate him to build a bridge over the Loyang.

In due course she bore a son, Ts'ai Hsiang, who in time passed the state examinations in the highest grade. His mother told him of her vow and he at once agreed to undertake the task. There was a problem, however, because at that time no one was allowed to be appointed as an official in his own province, and Ts'ai Hsiang was a native of Fukien. Fortunately the chief eunuch was Ts'ai Hsiang's friend and he found a way round the difficulty. He wrote with sweetened water on a banana leaf the characters reading 'Let Ts'ai Hsiang officiate in his own town', and dropped the leaf in the garden where the Emperor was due to walk. To the Emperor's amazement, ants were attracted by the sweetness and settled on the characters, which could then be plainly read. As the Emperor deciphered the message, the chief eunuch handed him a decree making Ts'ai Hsiang governor of Ch'uan-chou, and the scholar was duly appointed.

Much study convinced the scholar that the waves and currents made it impossible to establish the footings for the bridge. He therefore wrote a letter to the Dragon King, and then asked, 'Who can go into the sea to deliver this?' Among his servants was a drunkard whose name, Hsia Te-hai, means Able-to-enter-the-sea. So he at once replied, 'I am Able-to-enter-the-sea', and was instructed, to his horror, to go to the Dragon King's realm in the ocean and return within three days with an answer to the scholar's letter. The penalty for failure would be 300 lashes. Like other despairing men, Hsia Te-hai sought refuge in drink, finally stumbling along the river bank, intending to plunge into the water and end it all. He tripped and fell unconscious.

Next morning, when he awoke, he felt in his pocket and found that the scholar's letter had been replaced by another. A miracle had taken place and he hurried back to the governor's office. There Ts'ai Hsiang opened and read the reply, which consisted of a single character meaning vinegar but which, as a scholar of the highest grade, he was able to interpret as an order from the Dragon King to install the footings at the hour *yu* on the twenty-first day.

Great quantities of building material were prepared and, while this was going on, Ts'ai Hsiang engaged eight strangers who volunteered, to do the work without pay. Most people thought that the number was insufficient and, worse still, the men did nothing but sit on the river bank playing chess. In reply to criticism they simply said that it was a lot of fuss about very little and that anyway it was not yet the hour *yu,* even if the twenty-first day had arrived.

Certainly the tide seemed less violent, the stream flowed more slowly. Suddenly the river dried up; a whirlwind engulfed the chess-players; sand and stones were everywhere; even the sun was hidden. When the upheaval had died away, it was seen that the stone footings were in place and the eight strangers had vanished. They must have been the Eight Immortals (Taoist holy men who had gained immortality). Even so, much remained to be done and a large work force was engaged to complete the upper works of the bridge. Ts'ai Hsiang had also appointed a committee of fifteen to supervise the work; among their members was a monk called I-po, a Buddhist who did much to improve the design of the bridge. He was able to contribute in another, more remarkable way. The great number of workmen used vast quantities of wood to prepare their food and this led to shortages. When these occurred, I-po would stick his foot into the stove and the food would be cooked more quickly than usual by the flames he created. After the bridge was finished he flew to heaven. His body is preserved in a temple north of Ch'uan-chou.

Despite the help of the Immortals and of I-po and the expenditure of all Ts'ai Hsiang's funds, as well as the donations of many benefactors, resources to complete the work were still insufficient. Then it was the turn of the compassionate goddess Kuan Yin. She appeared as a beautiful woman, sailed up the River Loyang in a boat and invited men to throw money at her. She would marry any man whose coin hit her, but the coins of those who missed would be used for the construction expenses. All the rich young men of Ch'uan-chou and the surrounding districts tried their best; the coins fell like snow but none was successful. However, the Immortal Lü Tung-pin, who happened to be flying overhead, saw what was going on and caused a coin thrown by a fruit-seller to touch the robe of the goddess. The fruit-seller was overjoyed at the prospect of so beautiful a bride but ship and goddess vanished as he rushed forward to claim her. He fell into the river and was drowned. The goddess, hearing that there was a shortage of fish for the people working there, turned the fruit-seller's body into shoals of tiny, silvery fish. These can be seen to this day in the River Loyang near the bridge which Ts'ai Hsiang built in fulfilment of his mother's vow.

In the time of the Emperor Ch'ien-lung the Loyang Bridge was improved by a man called Li Wu in fulfilment of another vow. He had been falsely accused and was on his way to Peking for judgment. It was high tide and the waters soaked him as the cart in which he was travelling as prisoner crossed the Loyang Bridge. If he were acquitted, he vowed, he would raise the parapets by a metre (or three feet). Thanks to the help of a Taoist saint and the intervention of the Empress he was able to prove that he had been falsely accused. On his return to Fukien he engaged workmen to undertake the work. Those who had mocked at his vow, believing him guilty and as good as dead, since he had been accused of planning a revolt, were forced to contribute their fortunes to the work.

LÜ TUNG-PIN

At the building of the Loyang Bridge, the mischievous intervention of Lü Tung-pin led to the death of an innocent fruit-seller. But he is the patron saint of barbers, for he saved many of their guild from death. The first Ming Emperor, Chu Hung-wu (fourteenth century AD), suffered from a disease of the skin. Each day a barber called at the palace to shave him, but none succeeded without causing him pain and each in turn was executed. The guild of barbers addressed a petition to the August Personage of Jade imploring his help, for otherwise there would soon be no barbers left. Lü Tung-pin, who has a magic sword, was sent to earth where he took on the guise of a barber, transforming his sword into a razor. He went to the palace and shaved the Emperor. Far from causing him pain, Lü Tung-pin's razor cured the Emperor's affliction. That is why the barbers of China make offerings to Lü Tung-pin, on the fourteenth day of the fourth month, as the deity of barbers in the celestial bureaucracy.

Lü Tung-pin once transformed himself into a beggar with a pustulous leg to test the resolution of an ascetic who was thought to be ready to fly to heaven. The test consisted of sucking the festering sores clean and the ascetic proved equal to the task. The form taken by Lü on that occasion resembles that of his constant companion, Li T'ieh-kuai, Iron-Crutch Li. The latter owed his unfortunate frame to a lack of faith on the part of one of his disciples. He went off on a magical journey, leaving his body to be watched over by the student. Unfortunately, at the end of seven days the young man thought his master dead and buried the body. When Li returned he had to enter the first available body, a beggar with festering sores.

A MAGIC BANQUET

The interventions of immortals in human affairs took curious forms on occasion. The family Ts'ai had an experience of this when one of their number, with the members of his household, was entertaining the great adept Wang Yuan. While he was there, Miss Ma appeared, a pretty girl of eighteen or nineteen, with her hair in a chignon on top of her head so that the end fell to the level of her waist. All the family saw her. Wang Yuan rose to greet her and the two of them provided a banquet from nowhere. The serving dishes were all of gold and silver, and the savour of the food spread through the house and the courtyards. When the preserved meat was served in slices it was revealed that it was unicorn flesh. At last rice was brought in. Miss Ma threw it on the ground, saying that she did so to purify it, but when it was picked up the grains of rice had turned into powdered cinnabar. Wang Yuan told the family that Miss Ma was still young, but that he was too old for that sort of legerdemain, which was not very amusing.

He announced that he would serve them with wine from the Heavenly Banquet. This was so strong that they could not drink it — it burned their guts. It had to be mixed with ten parts of water and even then, a quarter of a pint of the mixture made the family drunk.

THE SWORDS OF FAN WEN

Magic swords are a familiar theme in Chinese legends and two of them play a major role in the history of a change of dynasty in a kingdom on the southernmost boundary of China, at the time when the northern and central areas of Vietnam formed part of the Empire. There, in the province of Jihnan, lived a barbarian chief called Fan the Hammer, who had a slave named Fan Wen.

One day when Fan Wen was pasturing sheep on the banks of a mountain stream, he found two carp. He hid them and later took them home, hoping to eat them on his own. His master learned of this and ordered Wen to produce them. Wen, who was ashamed and frightened, said that there were no fish, only two whetstones. His master went to the place where they were hidden and saw that there were indeed two stones. Wen realized that they were of a special value and that the carp had transformed themselves into iron ore. He took them up into the mountains, smelted the iron and forged two swords. Then he raised the blades towards the Great Dyke of Stone, the Annamite Chain, and uttered a prayer. 'The carp transformed themselves into stone; the swords have been made from the smelting of the iron. If they indeed have magic power, let the stone be cleft, let the Dyke be broken. If this be achieved, I shall become the ruler of the realm. If the swords cannot split the rock, they are powerless.' He moved towards the mountain chain, the blades clove the Great Dyke.

Fan Wen's master sent him on a trading voyage which took him to China, where he learned many things. In the time of the Chin Emperor Min-ti he went south to the Kingdom of Lin-i, to the south of Jihnan. There he taught the King, Fan I, to build ramparts and ditches, to manufacture weapons of offence and defence, and to draw up stategic plans. The King placed his trust in Fan Wen and made him commander-in-chief of the forces of Lin-i. Fan Wen then cast doubt on the loyalty of the Crown Prince, who fled abroad. King Fan I died and Fan Wen went to fetch the Crown Prince home from the foreign land where he was living. During the return voyage Fan Wen introduced poison into a coconut and gave it to the Prince, who drank it. Then he came to Lin-i and used the army to enforce his enthronement as King. The Queens and concubines of the dead King were shut in a high tower. Those who accepted Fan Wen as King were taken into his harem, while the rest were left to die of hunger and thirst. The swords were transmitted with the succession to the heirs of Fan Wen. The clefts in the Great Dyke can still be seen.

CHAPTER 7
JAPAN

Japan is a treasure-house of myths and legends. While its mythology is drawn mainly from the nature-based Shinto religion, much of its rich store of legend draws its inspiration directly or indirectly from Buddhism. The legends are principally the stories of heroes and heroines, historical personages, religious leaders and the places and events connected with them. They have provided stories and epics which have found a firm place in the hearts and the literature of the Japanese.

History and fiction often merge in these stories to create epic legends as great as the tales of King Arthur and the knights of the Round Table. In Japan, the principal heroes are the samurai, the traditional warrior class, who from the twelfth century were the real rulers of Japan, the power behind the throne. Historical figures, however, provided the basis for legend long before the ascendancy of the samurai. In the early years of the first millennium AD the division between myth and legend is far from distinct, and gods and men are hardly distinguishable from each other. Indeed it is this celestial ancestry that forms the basis of Japanese tradition and the lineage of the emperors, who traced their descent from the goddess of the sun, Amaterasu. The first Emperor of Japan is supposed to have been the great-great-grandson of the goddess. This is related in the Nihongi, the chronicles of Japan from the earliest times up to AD 697, and the Kojiki, the 'Record of Ancient Matters', both written early in the eighth century.

THE EXPLOITS OF PRINCE YAMATO

Typical examples of the blending of myth and legend, fact and fiction, are the stories of Yamato Date, the father of the Emperor Chai (AD

Yamato and Iwato-hime (page 63)

192—200). There are several versions, some of them more fantastic than others. The character of Prince Yamato appears to be a composite one, for his stories almost certainly embody the exploits of a number of historical personages. The legends show him as a transitional figure between gods and heroes. While being entirely human physically, he finds no difficulty whatever in battling with monsters. He is portrayed as a brave warrior, almost the archetype for the later samurai tradition. The comparison with the legends of King Arthur is compelling and he, like Arthur, has a special sword, but unlike the knights of the Arthurian tales, Yamato totally lacks the element of romantic chivalry.

His story starts with a violent episode in which, enraged by his elder brother's late attendance at dinner, he slaughters him. This does not please his father, the Emperor Keiko, who decides that Yamato would be better employed in destroying his enemies, rather than his family, and sends him off to deal with them. It is at this point that Yamato visits the great Shrine of Ise, where his aunt, who is the high priestess, gives him the sacred sword Cloud Cluster, which he takes with him on his adventures. In his first adventure, however, he does not rely on the sword's miraculous powers but on his own craftiness. Arriving at the heavily guarded home of an enemy, he observed that it was being prepared for a feast. Seeing this as a way of entry, he disguised himself as a young maiden and joined the celebrations. He seated himself between his two targets, cleverly tricked them into becoming stupendously drunk, and then drew his sword, which he had concealed in his costume, and slew them both.

On another occasion, on his way home, he took the opportunity to put down the local ruler of Izumo province. Again it was cunning and trickery, rather than superb swordsmanship or valour, which won the day. He first established a friendship with his enemy and then made a wooden copy of Cloud Cluster, which he wore instead of the real sword. This having been done, he took the chance one day to join his enemy for a swim. They took off their swords and left them on the bank of the river, and when they came out, Yamato suggested that they might exchange swords as a sign of friendship, after which they might have a friendly duel. This they did, but the friendly duel soon turned into a fight for life or death, as the enemy realized that he had been tricked and that his sword was only of wood. Thus fell yet another of Yamato's foes.

Another version says they exchanged swords before going into the river, as it was their practice to go armed even when swimming. When they came out, Yamato challenged his enemy to a friendly fight. He readily accepted, but found it impossible to remove his sword from its scabbard, because the wood had swollen while in the water. Yamato quickly drew his enemy's sword and decapitated him, thus having the satisfaction of killing his opponent with his opponent's own sword.

YAMATO AND THE SERPENT

These early stories do not paint Yamato Date in very pleasing colours, but his personality seems to change in the later tales in which he appears as a wandering hero, aided by his sword Cloud Cluster. In one of them he is confronted by an apparition of the Great Serpent. This creature had been killed by the god Susano-o, who had taken Cloud Cluster from the monster's tail, after which the sword had come in time to the Shrine of Ise. The serpent demanded the return of the sword, but Yamato simply ignored the apparition and continued on his journey.

Yamato was not totally violent, for on his journey he fell in love with a beautiful girl, Iwato-hime. Eventually freeing himself from the chains of love, he continued on his way. Then follows an exciting episode in which his enemies trick him into joining them in a stag-hunt and set fire to the vegetation, hoping to burn him alive. However, Yamato draws his trusty sword and hacks his way through the burning bushes and escapes. This gave his sword another name, Kusanagi no Tsurugi, 'grass-mowing sword'. He returned to his love, Iwato-hime, but after a while he left her again, leaving the sword behind as a memento, hung on the branches of a mulberry tree.

No longer protected by his sacred sword, Yamato once more encountered the apparition of the evil serpent. Again he tried to ignore the monster and pass it by, but when he leaped over the serpent's body his foot touched it, and he was struck by a fever which rapidly spread throughout his body. As he lay dying, Iwato-hime joined him at his bedside, for she had not stayed at home, but had secretly followed him. When he died it is said that he changed into a white bird. Another version recounts that after he was buried a white bird flew out of his burial mound. He was reburied and again the white bird was sighted flying from his burial mound. The white bird in this case can perhaps be compared with the black raven seen after King Arthur's death. Legends wherever they occur often have common traits. Like Arthur, Yamato Date is thought to have some historical basis. The story of Yamato, a warrior against evil, dying in tragic circumstances, became the basis of many Japanese samurai legends, and indeed is perhaps the basis of the very idea of the samurai as a heroic individual warrior.

THE SAMURAI

Yamato's daughter-in-law was the Empress Jingo. She too is the subject of legend, for she is supposed to have led the invasion of Korea in AD 200. This date is almost as uncertain as the events, for it is said that she carried her unborn son for three years during the campaign. After subjugating Korea, she returned to Japan where her

son, the future Emperor Ojin, was born. He later became deified as
the Shinto god of war, Hachiman. This again brings us back to the
samurai, for Hachiman was the patron deity of the Minamoto, one of
the two samurai groups who fought each other for supremacy in the
twelfth century. The wars between the two sides have become
a legendary saga of glorious heroism and tragedy, two qualities close
to the Japanese heart. The Gempei Wars have been likened to the
Wars of the Roses in England, for the standard of the Minamoto was
red, while that of their opponents, the Taira, was white.

The heroes of these and later times provide some of the most
colourful legends of Japan. They are heroes of Bushi-do and Giri, the
Japanese qualities of honour, moral obligation and loyalty, embodied
in their heroic actions, complete disregard for death and contempt for
life at any price. The heroes themselves are in some cases as
mythological as they are legendary, Issun-Boshi or 'Little One-Inch',
for example, or Momotaro, another small hero who was born from
a peach.

Heroes of a more historical nature were still involved in battles
with phantoms and serpents, who were the traditional enemies of
heroes, and their actions are often no less fantastic than those of their
mythological colleagues. Perhaps the most heroic character is
Yoshitsune, whose exploits form the basis of Noh drama.

YOSHITSUNE AND BENKEI

Minamoto Yoritomo was the victor of the Gempei Wars, the conflict
between the Minamoto and the Taira clans of the samurai. He
became the first shogun, or commander-in-chief, of the Japanese
army. As a child he had been spared execution by the Taira, but was
banished to the peninsula of Izu. He was under lenient supervision,
however, and was able to train in the art of warfare, and he eventually
raised an army against the Taira. Yoritomo himself was a plain and
staid character. It is his brother, Minamoto Yoshitsune, who has the
most romantic and mysterious legends told of him. He is the subject
of numerous books, poems and plays and in him there is a note of
chivalry. It is said that Yoshitsune learned the art of sword-fighting
and warfare from the Tengu, small goblin-like creatures, half-man
and half-bird, who inhabited the highlands. This happened while he
was supposedly being instructed in the more placid arts of the
priesthood.

When he was fifteen, he left the monastery to prove himself as
a warrior. He had a number of skirmishes with bandits, and he also
seduced the daughter of a Taira lord by serenading her with his flute
outside her window. He had a two-fold interest in her — her beauty,
and the fact that she could help him read a Chinese book on the art of
warfare.

Yoshitsune's name is linked with that of Benkei, a larger-than-life figure, who himself has many legends to his name. They were brought together, during Yoshitsune's journey, on the Gojo bridge in Kyoto. The meeting between these two has become one of the best-known legends of Japan. Benkei was a boisterous, massive fellow, enamoured of the art of swordsmanship. He was a warrior priest, rather like a combination of Friar Tuck and Little John, for he had established himself as a kind of one-man monastery, but could not resist the thrill of war. Benkei had always been an exceptional character for, like many Japanese heroes, he had overstayed his time in his mother's womb. He is said to have been born after three years, as a big boy with long hair and a full set of teeth.

By the time that Yoshitsune met Benkei on the Gojo bridge, Benkei was already well advanced in his hobby of sword collecting. He had acquired nearly 1000 specimens, trophies of battles won. He had placed himself on the bridge with the intention of attacking the next traveller who had a fine sword. Yoshitsune had a magnificent sword, and so there took place on the Gojo bridge one of the most dazzling battles ever fought between two men. Yoshitsune, aided by his supernatural allies the Tengu, outmanoeuvred Benkei, who realized that he had met his match. He surrendered and established a strong bond of frienship with Yoshitsune, a relationship that was to last from that time on. Their names are linked together in several legends of the Gempei Wars. Many of these stories are related in the Heike Monogatari.

After a number of skirmishes, Yoshitsune conducted a maritime battle against the Taira. The battle of Dan-no-ura ended in the utter defeat of the Taira and in one of the most tragic mass suicides in the history of the samurai. Even today it is said that the ghosts of the Taira still haunt the waters of Dan-no-ura, and sailors and peasants claim to have seen ghostly apparitions of armies trying in vain to remove the stain of their defeat. The battle marked the end of the Gempei Wars. Minamoto Yoritomo was made shogun by the new Emperor in 1192, and became in effect the ruler of Japan. The shogunate was not handed back until 1868, remaining hereditarily in the hands of the Minamoto.

Yoritomo became jealous of Yoshitsune and hunted him throughout Japan. During this period, with his trusty friend Benkei, Yoshitsune encountered both earthly and supernatural opponents. Eventually Yoritomo's forces caught up with him, and there followed a tragic last stand, in which Benkei fought off the shogun's samurai so that Yoshitsune could commit suicide. Benkei continued to fight for so long that it seemed to his enemies that he was invincible, and it was only by accident that a samurai found out that in fact he had been dead for some time, and was simply a standing target. One legend has it that Yoshitsune did not really die but escaped to the mainland of

Asia, where he joined the Mongols and took the name of Genghis
Khan.

THE FORTY-SEVEN RONIN

Not all legends of the samurai are old for one of the most popular, the
story of the forty-seven ronin, is quite recent, belonging to the
eighteenth century. A ronin is a wandering, masterless samurai. This
is again a tale of honour, for in 1702 two daimyo (provincial
noblemen) were chosen by the Tokugawa shogun to entertain an
emissary from the Imperial court in Kyoto. Being unskilled in the
protocol of the court, they were given lessons by a certain Kira
Kozuke-no-Suke, who expected to be well paid in return.
Kozuke-no-Suke was not satisfied by the gifts given him by one of the
daimyo, Asano by name, and he therefore despised and insulted him.
During one session of instruction Kozuke-no-Suke goaded Asano so
much that Asano lost his temper and tried to stab him. He was not
successful, and as the attack had occurred in the shogun's palace, he
was sentenced to commit hara-kiri, which he duly did. The main
events of the story take place after the suicide, for Asano's samurai,
forty-seven of them, were now masterless. They did not avenge their
master's death at once, but made careful plans, always seeming to be
drunk and wanton, caring about nothing, never appearing together so
as to avoid suspicion. At last, on the evening of 14 December 1703
during a snow-storm, they stormed Kuzuke-no-Suke's mansion.
There was a great fight and many defenders were killed or ran away.
Kuzuke-no-Suke himself was found hiding in a storehouse and was
given the opportunity to commit hara-kiri, but he did not have the
courage. One of the ronin cut off his head with the very same dagger
that Asano had used to kill himself.

Although this was a great act of samurai loyalty, such actions were
at that time against the law. The ronin committed mass hara-kiri and
were buried together near the grave of Asano. They are today
extremely popular legendary heroes, and their story has been the
subject of a major Japanese film. Legends are continually being
created and the samurai spirit identified in actions that have occurred
during the twentieth century.

HOLY MEN

The samurai were supporters of Zen Buddhism, so that in an indirect
way these heroic legends are Buddhist in inspiration. Zen thought not
only coloured their actions, but was itself coloured by them. There are
many legends associated with the founders of various Buddhist sects
in Japan, including the Indian Zen master Bodhi Dharma and later
Japanese masters such as Hakuin. Other historical but also legendary

characters are Kobodashi (Kobo Daishi or Kukai), founder of the Shingon sect of Buddhism, Dengiodashi, founder of Tendai Buddhism, and Nichiren, founder of the Nichiren sect.

The legends of Kobodashi are both prolific and fantastic. He is said to have been born with his hands clasped together in prayer. He is supposed to have worked numerous miracles as he went around the country disguised as a travelling beggar. Many of these miracles are linked with water in some way, as rivers which no longer drown people, for example, and he is described creating wells by striking the ground with his staff. During his meditations he was sometimes disturbed by dragons and sea-monsters, but he was not perturbed and drove them away with magic words and by spitting light at them from the evening star! He was a great sculptor and is alleged to have carved a figure in grey basalt of Jizo, the Buddhist guardian of souls, in a single night. When he died at the age of sixty, he was said to be merely awaiting the coming of the future Buddha, Minoku. He is still waiting at the Koya-san Monastery, near Nara, where he is buried.

In Japanese legends almost anyone of importance is supposed to have had a miraculous birth, or death, or both. The Buddhist monk Nichiren is no exception, for he was conceived as a result of his mother dreaming of the sun falling on a lotus flower. He was no mythical being, however, for he was born in 1222. Having displeased the authorities by his activities, he was condemned to death but was spared after the executioner's sword had failed to decapitate him. There is a similar story about the Buddhist saint En no Shokaku, who made his executioner's sword snap by magic and then, suddenly acquiring the ability to fly, escaped, never to be seen again.

Most Japanese legends were handed down by word of mouth before they came to be written down, in chronicles such as the Nihongi and the Koji-ki. They have provided the inspiration for numerous epic works, poems and Noh plays, and have been recorded and illustrated in *makemono,* or hand-scrolls. They are living testaments to a rich and fascinating period in Japanese history.

CHAPTER 8
BURMA

Burma has been a Buddhist country for centuries, and was one of the first to which Buddhism spread from India. The Burmese claim that the new faith was brought to their country by two merchants, Tapussa and Bhallika. This tradition reflects the undoubted importance of the merchant community in the support and dissemination of Buddhism. According to Sri Lankan sources, two missionaries, Sona and Uttara, were sent by Asoka, the great Buddhist emperor of India in the third century BC, to 'the golden country', which may have been Burma.

Whatever the truth of the matter, a major factor in the success of Buddhism in Burma was the support which it received from Burmese kings. This is reflected in the story of King Duttabaung. Long before the Buddha's time, so the chronicles relate, an Indian prince had come to Burma with his army and founded a city at Tagaung in the north. Later, in the fifth year after his Enlightenment, the Buddha, accompanied by his friend Ananda and a group of disciples, flew to Mount Hpo-u in Burma. There a mole scraped earth together with his snout and made obeisance to the Buddha, who smiled at the sight. When Ananda asked him why he smiled, the Buddha replied that in the 101st year after he attained Nirvana the mole would become a man called Duttabaung, who would found a great city and a kingdom, setting up a palace and a royal umbrella and reigning as king. 'From the time of this King, Ananda, shall my religion be manifest in Burma.' The story goes on to tell how, through a long series of remarkable events and with the assistance of the gods, the prophecy was fulfilled.

THE STORY OF KING DUTTABAUNG

The border lands of Tagaung were ravaged by a giant boar, so tall that when it crossed the River Irawadi the skin of its belly was not

Indra, the master mason (page 71)

made wet. The King sent his heir to kill the boar, which he did after a long pursuit, but then, rather than return home, he stayed in the forest. He became a hermit and attained mystical powers. He used to urinate in a hollow in a rock and a young doe, drinking his urine, became pregnant and gave birth to a girl. The child's crying frightened the doe, who fled, and drew the attention of the hermit. He realized what had occurred and in confirmation of his paternity milk flowed from his first and middle fingers so that the child could suckle. The hermit named her Bedayi. She was very beautiful, and when she was seventeen the hermit kept her away all day by ordering her to fill a bamboo tube with water by using a gourd which had no hole in it.

Now at the time when the King's heir had left to hunt the boar, the Queen of Tagaung had given birth to two blind boys. The King ordered them to be done away with, but the Queen hid them. At the end of nineteen years, however, the King discovered that they were still alive and ordered them to be killed at once. The Queen could no longer disobey, but she claimed that she wished them to die out of her sight. She had them placed on a raft on which she had secretly stored food, and the raft was launched on the river. One day the raft struck an overhanging acacia tree and the ogress who lived in the tree dropped on to the raft, where she stole food. The Princes caught the ogress and prepared to kill her. She offered to cure their blindness, which she did with medicines provided by the great spirits who recognized that the brothers would found a dynasty which would uphold the religion of the Buddha for ever. When they had recovered their sight, the Princes continued to the place where their uncle was living as a hermit, and saw Bedayi drawing water. They laughed at her and with their sword cut off the top of the gourd, emptied out its contents and gave it back to Bedayi. She at once filled her tube and told her father what had happened. Calling the young men, he learned their story and soon Bedayi married the first-born Prince.

At this time the Queen of the Pyu sought the help of the hermit against her enemies and he advised her to take his son-in-law to be King of the Pyu. To this she agreed and he ruled over the Pyu with Bedayi and the Pyu Queen as his two Queens. The latter gave birth to a daughter, and died shortly afterwards. When Bedayi was three months with child the King himself died. Bedayi married his younger brother, who became King in his stead, and she gave birth to a Prince who was called Duttabaung.

After thirty-five years it became dark as night for seven days and at the end of this time the King died. Then the great gods, the Seven Exalted Ones, held a council, remembering the Buddha's prophecy, and Indra, the King of the Gods, chose a piece of pleasant flat land, stood at the centre of it and described a circle by means of a rope, Within this circle was erected the city of Shriksetra, with thirty-two great gates and thirty-two lesser gates, turreted and battlemented walls, ditches and moats and a golden palace. And this was on Sunday, the first waxing of the moon in the month of Tagu in the 101st year after the Buddha attained Nirvana.

There were three mansions, of seven, nine and eleven storeys, built by the spirits, where the King could pass the rainy season, the hot season and the cold season. And all the work took seven days. When it was finished, Indra took Duttabaung and installed him on the golden throne, where he was anointed as King. His two Queens were the daughter of the Pyu Queen and the Nagini Besandi, one of the nagas, the serpent-spirits. As he walked, the earth sank under his feet until Indra caused each step to fall upon an iron plate. The god gave the King a lance, Areindama, with which he demanded tribute from the kings of India, from the lands of the demons and from the nagas. For it was a flying lance, to which he would attach a letter and cast it from the mountain top, and it would hang above the head of the tributary king until the proper amount had been paid.

Duttabaung also had a great bell and a great drum, at the sound of which tributary kings would beg for mercy. Hundreds of kings sent him their virgin daughters and the finest of their elephants and their horses, with gold and silver, precious jewels and the most beautiful of cloths. And he had 360 white elephants, while the black ones numbered 36 million. Each day he provided for 3000 holy ones, followers of the Lord Buddha, who were his teachers. He built eleven pagodas over relics of the Buddha, and helped by the 3000 holy ones he prepared a code of laws for future kings and the benefit of all beings.

Now a certain woman gave a small piece of land to a holy one. This the King seized and at once Areindama ceased to fly and the great bell and the great drum would no longer sound. Then the holy ones told the King that this had befallen because he had seized the land. He ordered it to be restored, but this restitution was in vain. Since he could no longer send out the lance to gather tribute, he set out himself to the land of India on a ship which the nagas gave him. There he collected tribute, until he came to the Kingdom of Pantwa, where the Queen took a foul garment and by magic turned it into a cloth with which the unsuspecting Duttabaung wiped his face. At once the auspicious mole in the centre of his forehead shrivelled and the Nagini Besandi left him. In his sorrow the King returned home, but on the voyage he spat directly into the ocean instead of into the royal spittoon. The nagas were angry and, the *karma* of his good deeds being expended, they carried him in the ship to the land of the nagas. This was in his 105th year, after he had reigned for seventy years.

THE BUILDING OF THE SHWEZIGON PAGODA

Another legend in which a pious king upholds Buddhism is the story of the building of the great Shwezigon Pagoda. Besides Buddhism, the Burmese had an old religion of their own, the cult of spirits called nats, thirty-seven of them by later accounts. During the Pagan dynasty (eleventh to thirteenth centuries AD) attempts were made to unify the two religons, as the story recounts.

Among the pagodas built by King Duttabaung was one to house the Buddha's forehead-band which the King had obtained. There it remained for many centuries until King Anawratha sacked the city of Shriksetra and destroyed the pagoda. He took the relic and placed it on the back of a white elephant and carried it off to Pagan. Once there, he consulted the great teacher Shin Arahan and the relic was placed again upon the back of a white elephant, which was set to walk. It walked until it knelt on a sandbank and the King was sad, for he intended a foundation so that the religion would last for 5000 years. But Indra appeared to him in a dream and assured him that the sandbank would be made solid with rock clamped round with iron. So then the King was glad and began the work. And when the relic-chamber was ready the relic itself ascended into the sky and prophesied that the King would in due course become an enlightened one himself. The King embraced the jewelled casket in joy and then, on Shin Arahan's advice, made a gold image of a man embracing a jewelled relic and enshrined it in the relic-chamber. Then, after many vicissitudes, the King obtained a tooth relic from Sri Lanka. This too was enshrined in the Shwezigon and miraculously multiplied to produce four more teeth, which were enshrined elsewhere. But he completed no more than the three terraces of the pagoda itself. When King Kyanzittha came to the throne, Shin Arahan advised him to complete the work.

The new King ordered the rocks of Mount Tuywin to be hewn into blocks three spans long and one span wide. Then he drew up all his soldiers in two lines facing one another, from the mountain to the Shwezigon, and they passed the ashlar from hand to hand. The men suffered much from the heat of the sun, so the King planted tamarind seeds along either row and made a vow: 'If I am worthy to receive the relics of the Lord, let the seeds sprout now to give shade!' And in a single night the tamarinds grew enough to shelter the soldiers.

Indra appeared as a master mason to split the rocks and when the mortar of mud would not set he made mortar with lime and fresh milk. The King then bought 1000 pails of milk a day, paying with silver. During daylight men built one circle of the spire; at night spirits built two rings. Indra made a figure of a lion for the south-east corner and covered the whole pagoda with plaster which was eight hands thick. In seven months and seven days the whole work was finished. It is said that Indra himself regularly visited the pagoda.

And the King drew up a list of the nats, the spirits of the Kingdom of Burma, and placed it in the pagoda. And a shrine for the Thirty-Seven Nats was made on the north-east corner of the platform of the Shwezigon Pagoda so that the spirits might be brought within the religion whose coming to Burma the Lord Buddha had foretold.

THE MAHAGIRI NATS

In the time of King Thinlikyaung there lived a man called Nga Tinde, the son of Nga Tindaw the blacksmith of Tagaung. He was famous for his strength, and it was said that he could wrench out the tusk of a fully grown male elephant. Knowledge of this came to the King who, thinking that Nga Tinde would destroy his prosperity, ordered his ministers to seize and lose him, for this was the royal phrase for having a man put to death. Nga Tinde fled to a distant land where he lived in the forest. This increased the King's fear, so that he took Nga Tinde's younger sister, who was very beautiful, as his Queen. And after some time he said: 'Your brother is a man of might. Send for him and I will make him the governor of a city.' This she did, and her brother returned, but when he came to Tagaung the King had him seized by guile and bound to a champak tree. Then charcoal was heaped around the tree and bellows were applied to the fire. And the Queen said, 'My brother is dying because of me.' And she descended into the fire. It is said that the King clutched at her hair which was piled up on her head, thus saving her head and face, but her body was burned with her brother.

Nga Tinde and his sister became spirits and lived in the champak tree and any living creature, whether man or beast, which entered the area over which the shadow of the tree fell died. Then the tree was uprooted and cast into the Irawadi. And after many days it drifted ashore at the city of Pagan, and from the trunk of the tree two images were made in the form of human heads, which were placed in a shrine on Mount Popa. (Some say that they were placed in shrines outside the great pillars of the Tharaba Gate at Pagan.) Once a year everyone from King to villager went to make offerings to the spirits of the great mountain, the Mahagiri Nats. They were given offerings of alcohol, white buffalo, white oxen and white goats until the time of King Bayinnaung, King of Pegu, when he annexed the Kingdom of Pagan, for such offerings were not in accordance with the laws of the Buddha.

Earlier, King Kyanzittha, who had received much aid from the Mahagiri Nats, ordered that every household in Burma should hang up a coconut in honour of them. The coconut hangs on the south-east house-post and is replaced when the stem breaks, usually after about four months. At this time the brother, who has become the pre-eminent household spirit, is given offerings of bananas, palm sugar, rice, sandalwood and pickled tea leaves. Men say that the coconut was chosen as the proper gift to the Mahagiri Nats because its cool juice assuages the pain caused by the fire in which they died.

At the time of his stay in the forest, Nga Tinde had met the daughter of a serpent who was worshipping a footprint of the Buddha. He married her and she produced two eggs, which were found and taken home by a hermit. They hatched out as two boys who, when they grew up, became famous as wrestlers. The news of their skill reached King Duttabaung of Shriksetra, who feared they might be a threat to him. He had them brought to court and set them to fight one another. One was killed in the contest, at which the other died of grief. They too became nats, as did their mother when she heard of the death of Nga Tinde. Another of Nga Tinde's sisters was intended as a bride for King Duttabaung, but his Queens and concubines feared that she would become the favourite wife because of her outstanding beauty. They persuaded the ministers to tell the King that she would be unable to enter the city gates because of her enormous size. A house was therefore built for her outside the walls and there she waited for the King, supporting herelf by weaving. At last, when the king failed to appear to consummate the marriage, she died disconsolate. She also became a nat.

Many of the nats were said to have met violent ends in their earthly lives, usually at the hands of kings whose wrath they had incurred, justly or unjustly. The legend of Nga Tinde and his sister also reflects the tension which existed between the cult of the nats and Burmese Buddhism.

CHAPTER 9

INDONESIA AND MALAYSIA

The thousands of islands which make up Indonesia are rich in myths and legends, many of which exhibit common themes testifying to an underlying cultural unity. Over the past 2000 years, however, the islands have been profoundly influenced by concepts, beliefs and elements of material culture coming from abroad. These have been generally welcomed, and indeed have been given a special status precisely because of their foreign origin. Particularly in Java, Sumatra and Bali, they are connected with legendary figures. Those reflecting Hindu and Buddhist influences from the Indian subcontinent are attributed to Aji Saka, a culture-bringer whose name actually derives from the Shaka era (starting in AD 78) of a northern-Indian calendrical system. Islamic influences are associated with Sultan Rum, the ruler of the Ottoman Empire, while the Dutch, whose colonial influence lasted for some 350 years, are surprisingly linked with Alexander the Great, in the guise of Sakender the merchant.

Indonesia is now predominantly Muslim, but the earlier influences persist, with others from China and eastern Asia, and colour every aspect of life. There is a very strong sense of historical continuity, which can also be seen in the courtly tradition of Malaysia, with its strong Indonesian links. The stories that follow have been chosen, from a still relatively unknown wealth of material, to illustrate something of this cultural pattern.

MPU BARADA AND THE WITCH

Hinduism was carried to Indonesia in the early centuries of the Christian era, largely by Indian merchants. Local kings adopted the religion, and the island of Bali has preserved its own variety of Hinduism to this day. The story of Mpu Barada and the witch

The God Brahme with Endok and child (page 76)

Mahendradatta is typical of Hindu piety. It begins with Dharmodayana, King of Bali. By his wife Mahendradatta he had a son, Erlangga, who became ruler of the Javanese Kingdom of Daha. Dharmodayana suspected the Queen of witchcraft and she was banished into the forest. She had a daughter, Ratna Menggali, who was famed for her beauty, but none dared to marry her, her mother being a witch.

When Dharmodayana died his widow sought power from the goddess Durga to destroy Erlangga's Kingdom, because he had failed to prevent his father from taking a second wife and because none of his nobles would marry Ratna Menggali. By the fervour of her worship Mahendradatta gained the consent of Durga and that night she danced in a cemetery with her disciples to the music of a great gong. The very next day pestilence struck the land while the widow danced at the crossroads. Erlangga sent soldiers to kill her, but she was unharmed by their krisses (daggers) and fire from her eyes, ears, mouth and nostrils destroyed them. Then the widow called her disciples and bade them dance in turn. She sat in the middle of them and took a fresh corpse, which she brought back to life. She cradled it in her arms like a mother with her child. Then she cut its head and the blood flowed as an offering to Durga. The widow made a garland from the entrails of the corpse and danced before the goddess so that the pestilence might spread more widely and enter the royal palace itself.

Then the King sought the aid of Mpu Barada, whose magic power was famous throughout the world. Mpu Barada sent his son Bahula to ask for Ratna Menggali in marriage. The witch gladly consented but, once they were wed, Bahula questioned his bride about her mother's witchcraft and discovered that she had learned her magic from an old book. He persuaded Ratna Menggali to show it to him and then, while she was busy with the affairs of the house, he flew back to his father with the book. Mpu Barada read it, committing each page to memory, for he recognized at once that the book itself was good and that the witch had turned it to evil purposes by reading each of its pages from right to left. Then Mpu Barada went with Bahula throughout the devastated Kingdom, curing the sick and, by means of the book, raising from the dead those whose bodies had not yet decayed.

Meanwhile Durga had warned the witch that the end of her power was near. So when Mpu Barada came to the place where she was, the witch asked him for religious instruction. He answered that he would instruct her, but that death alone would free her from sin: he could not free her. Angered, she sought to destroy the sage, that her sins might be the greater, swearing to kill him as she killed the banyan tree by which they stood. And at her glance the tree burst into flames and was consumed. Then Mpu Barada with one spell restored the tree. And when the fire spurted from the eyes, ears, mouth and nostrils of the witch, Mpu Barada was unharmed and, in his turn, he uttered a spell by which the witch was at once destroyed. Then, in his compassion, he restored her to life in order that she might receive absolution. Thus prepared for death, she made obeisance to Mpu Barada and the path to the heaven of the goddess was revealed to her.

THE FATAL KRIS

In another story, also with a Hindu background, the Hindu gods determine the fate of dynasties. The gods met in council and resolved that a new ruler was required in Java. Accordingly, the god Brahme descended to earth and impregnated Endok, the wife of Gajahpara, as she took his food to the rice fields. After that she had no further relations with her husband. When the child, Ken Angrok, was born he manifested many signs of his mysterious origin, both as an infant, when he emitted a strange light, and later when he went to school. Finally he was sent to study with the brahmin Lohgawe. One day, when Queen Dedes was descending from a wagonette when she was picnicking, her sarong was displaced and Ken Angrok saw that her vulva glowed. He asked his teacher the significance of this and was told that whoever married such a woman would become a world-ruler.

Ken Angrok resolved to win the Queen for himself. A special kris would be needed if her husband, the King, was to be removed, for he was a mighty man. A smith called Mpu Gandring alone could make such a weapon. Angrok went to find the smith and ordered a kris, saying that it must be ready in five months. Gandring said that a special kris would take twelve months, but Angrok paid no attention and, returning after five months, demanded the weapon. Gandring said that he was working on it but it was not finished. In fury Angrok seized it and stabbed the smith. As he died, the smith said, 'With that kris shall Angrok, his children and his children's children perish, seven kings in all.' And Ken Angrok grieved. But he returned to Tumapel, where the King's palace was, and wore his new kris.

Now the King had a favourite, who was friendly with Angrok, and he persuaded Angrok to lend him the kris, which he in turn wore while he served the King. Consequently, when the King was found dead one morning with the kris through his heart, the favourite was put to death, no one knowing that Angrok had recovered it and used it to kill the King. Angrok married Dedes, who was with child by the dead King, and became King of Tumapel. In due course Dedes bore the dead King's child. Her pregnancy had not stopped her sleeping with Angrok, to whom she subsequently bore three sons and a daughter. One day the son of the former King learned from his mother of the history of the kris and of his father's death. He then asked Angrok for the kris, as an heirloom, and with it he killed

Angrok. He in his turn was killed with the same kris and the slaughter continued until the prophecy of Mpu Gandring, the blacksmith and sword-maker, had been fulfilled and the gods in council brought about another change of dynasty in the island of Java.

THE MERCHANT SAKENDER

That the power of such women did not die with Queen Dedes is shown by a story which explains how the Dutch achieved dominion in Java. There was a Princess of Pajajaran, an incarnation of the goddess Durga, who was the wife of the Prince of Jakarta. He was unable to have intercourse with her because of the flames that issued from her vagina. He offered her to his overlord, the ruler of Ceribon, who was no more successful. He then passed her on to the Sultan of Mataram, the suzerain of both Jakarta and Ceribon, but he also failed. The Princess was then exiled to Odrus island, which had been bought for three cannon by Sakender the merchant, a manifestation of Alexander the Great. Sakender quelled the flames with a magic ointment and fathered a son called Jan-Kung. The son is explained as Jan Coen, who was actually the first governor-general of the Netherlands East India Company. The story makes him heir to the Indies through the lineage of Alexander the Great and the goddess who embodies kingship.

THE ENTHRONEMENT OF RADEN PATAH

Another legend deals with the coming of Islam. The last Hindu King of Majapahit was Brawijaya. His son, Raden Patah, had been living in Sumatra, but he returned to East Java, where he received instruction in Islam. Raden Patah refused an invitation to court, saying that fear of God made it impossible for him to pledge loyalty to an infidel. He therefore set up a base at Bintara and, after the propriety of a son attacking his father had been discussed by the Raden's counsellors, who advised in his favour, he moved with his army, equipped with many magic weapons, against King Brawijaya's capital. He appeared at the head of his men on the great open space which lay before the royal palace in its walled enclosure. When the King saw his son arrayed against him he flew up to heaven with all the troops that had remained loyal to him. And at that very moment an object like a ball of fire, with a flash like lightning and a terrible sound of thunder, came out of the palace and fell to earth at Bintara. This sacred light was the light of royalty. Then Raden Patah went into the empty palace and took the royal emblems, among them the sacred gong Seka Delima, and the sacred saddle and bridle, and returned to Bintara, which was to be the new capital. Some say that he also carried off the assembly hall of carved wood and erected it as the verandah at the front of the mosque of Demak, as Bintara became known. That is why, to this day, the mosques of Java have a verandah.

Every time Raden Patah, who wore the costume of a Muslim pilgrim, tried to take his place on the throne he was prevented by illness, and sometimes he fell unconscious. He consulted his most senior spiritual adviser, Sunan Kalijaga, one of the bringers of Islam to Java, who advised him to seek the permission of his father to mount the throne. The Prince went off to look for his father, disguised as a member of a troupe of masked dancers. Finally, he found Brawijaya and his whole court, installed on the summit of Gunung Lawu, a sacred mountain in Central Java. Asked to perform, Raden Patah put on the mask of a giant and danced before the audience. He was thus able to approach Brawijaya and kiss his knee in homage, at the same time seeking permission to rule. This was granted on condition that he abandoned the dress of a Muslim pilgrim and wore the costume proper to a Javanese royal prince. Provided he observed the customs of Javanese royalty he would be able to ascend the throne, and he could practise Islam on his own account. This he duly did.

THE DYNASTY OF MATARAM

The teacher Sunan Kalijaga was much concerned with the prosperity of Javanese dynasties. His next major task was to preside over the founding of the sixteenth-century dynasty of Mataram. Long after Raden Patah's time, Java was in a turmoil of civil strife. A prince named Senapati was told by a star, which spoke with a human voice, that he was to become ruler. He went to Parang Tritis on the south coast and as he stood on the shore in prayer, the waters of the sea boiled and the fish began to die. Rara Kidul, the goddess of the southern ocean, came and paid reverence to Senapati, telling him that all the spirits of Java would recognize him as their overlord and he would be the father of the rulers of Java. Then she took him to her underwater palace, where they made love for three days and three nights.

Senapati returned to Parang Tritis, where he found Sunan Kalijaga, who demanded to see his palace. When the teacher saw that the palace was not walled, he reproved Senapati, saying: 'That is not good. Men will say that you are presumptuous, trusting in your magic powers and invincibility. Buffalo and cattle without byres naturally wander off in all directions. One should tether them firmly, shut them in at night and let them graze under supervision, placing them under the protection of Allah. How much more then should you protect your house with a surrounding wall. Make the people of the region of Mataram make bricks each dry season and when it is finished, build there a city with a population of many sorts of men.' Then the teacher took a coconut shell filled with water and sprinkled it in a circle while muttering prayers. And he said, 'When you build the wall of the city, let that be its line.'

THE FOUNDING OF SINGAPORE AND MALACCA

This is the story which the chronicler received from his father and his forebears, assembling all the stories of the men of bygone days. He tells how the lineage of the Malay kings goes back to Sri Tri Buana, who was himself a descendant of Raja Iskandar Zhu'l Qarnain, Alexander the Great, the Two-Horned.

The city of Palembang stands on the Muara Tatang, on whose upper reaches was another river called Melayu, where two widows had rice fields on the slopes of a hill. One night when the rice was ripe they saw a glow on the hillside and the following morning they found that the rice grains had turned to gold, the leaves to silver and the stalks to an alloy of the two metals. The crest of the hill had also turned to gold. And there were three beautiful youths wearing jewelled crowns and riding on white elephants. Being questioned, they said that they were of the lineage of King Solomon and descendants of Iskandar Zhu'l Qarnain. The King of Palembang had the youths brought to his city, where people came from far and wide to see them. One was taken to Andelus and was made raja of Menengkabau; the second became raja of Tanjong Pura in northern Sumatra; the third remained in Palembang and became its ruler with the name Sri Tri Buana. The former King served as his first minister, while his daughter, the Princess Wan Sendari, became Sri Tri Buana's wife.

After a while Sri Tri Buana announced that he was going to look for a site to found a city. And they set out, the King in a boat of gold, the Queen in one of silver, and the first minister and the war-chiefs in their own boats, a fleet so great that the sea seemed to be nothing but ships. When they reached Riau, its Queen sent to enquire the age of the newcomer, thinking to make him her husband; but finding him too young, she adopted him as her son and heir. After some time Sri Tri Buana wished to travel again and, despite the misgivings of his adopted mother, a fleet was equipped and he set off. When they reached Tanjong Bemian, the King went ashore to hunt. He pursued a deer to the top of a high rock from which, looking across the water, he saw a great stretch of sand like a sheet of white cloth. It was called Temasek, and they embarked and sailed there, but on the way the ship began to fill with water and could only be saved after everything, including the crown, had been thrown overboard.

Again Sri Tri Buana went hunting. And they saw an animal which moved very fast: its body was red, its head black and its breast white. The first minister said that he had heard that in ancient times the *singa*

had such a form. It must therefore have been a lion. Then Sri Tri
Buana sent to tell the Queen of Riau that they would stay in Temasek
and asked her to send men, elephants and horses so that he might
found a city. She sent numberless men and horses and elephants, and
he founded a city which he called Singapura, Lion City, to which
foreigners resorted in great numbers and its fame and greatness
became known throughout the world.

After a century, the then ruler, Sri Sultan Iskandar Shah,
humiliated one of his treasury officials, who invited the men of Java to
attack Singapura. After a siege of several days the officer opened the
gates of the fort and the Javanese entered. The sultan fled, going
slowly northwards, until he reached the Bertam River. One day, as he
stood under a tree when out hunting, one of his hounds was kicked by
a mouse-deer. And Sultan Iskandar Shah said: 'This is a good place;
even the mouse-deer are pugnacious. It would be good to build a city
here.' And his chiefs agreed. Then the sultan asked the name of the
tree under which he was standing ; on learning that it was *malaka* he
gave orders for a city to be built with that name and there he ruled for
twenty years until his death.

THE MIDDLE EAST

Gilgamesh and the Bull of Heaven in Mesopotamia (page 93)

CHAPTER 10
EGYPT

The legends of ancient Egypt provide an insight, not otherwise easily obtainable, into the minds of a people long since gone and a way of life which flourished for thousands of years. They are colourful, sometimes exciting and often amusing, and recall the brave deeds and adventures of kings and courtiers, and the wise sayings and prophecies of sages and magicians. Some stories are couched in terms which indicate that they were composed and used for propagandist purposes, to spread a convincing message throughout the towns and villages where public story-tellers spun their tales.

One story recounts events which are set in the period immediately before the rise of the cult of the sun in the Fifth Dynasty (about 2480–2340 BC), although the account was written long after this. At the royal court of Cheops, the builder of the Great Pyramid at Gizeh, the King demands that his sons relate the wonderful deeds performed by the magicians of olden times. The Princes regale him with these stories and then Prince Hardedef, a famous sage, brings a contemporary magician to the palace. In the great pillared hall he demonstrates his skill by reuniting the severed heads and bodies of various creatures by means of magic.

The narrative now turns to the main purpose of the tale — to justify the claim of the Fifth Dynasty kings to rule Egypt, although they were not direct descendants of Cheops. Desiring knowledge which will ensure the security of his own pyramid, Cheops asks the magician to divulge the whereabouts of the sacred locks of the god Thoth. Dedi, the magician, tells him that the eldest son of an unknown woman will bring them to him, and reveals that in preference to Cheops' own descendants the sun-god Re will set on the throne the three sons whom the god has begotten on this woman, named Red-dedet, who is the wife of a priest of Re. These sons will become the first rulers of the

Wenamun receiving his ship from Smendes (page 87)

Fifth Dynasty, and the story here asserts their divine origin.

Cheops is dismayed, although Dedi assures him that his own son and grandson, Chephren and Mycerinus (the builders of the other pyramids at Gizeh), will both rule before the new Dynasty is installed. The tale now describes in some detail the birth of the divine triplets to Red-dedet, assisted by various goddesses. Re tells the attendant deities of the good deeds which these pious kings will perform for him.

Although the story embodies several historical inaccuracies, it would nevertheless have conveyed to its listeners, in an amusing and light-hearted manner, the divine origin of the Fifth Dynasty kings, their selection by Re, their pious devotion to him and the supremacy of the solar cult which these kings fostered.

THE STORY OF SINUHE

Another example of the use of a legend to convince the populace of their ruler's benign and well-intentioned nature is the Story of Sinuhe, probably composed in the Middle Kingdom (*c.* 1900 BC) but still popular in the New Kingdom (*c.* 1575–1087 BC). Although the story-line is simple, it is a fine product of the story-teller's art and was acclaimed as a classic of Egyptian literature.

The hero, Sinuhe, enjoys a position of great influence at the court of Amenammes I (the founder of the Twelfth Dynasty). However, the King dies, and word is sent to his son, Sesostris, who is returning from subduing Libyan tribes to the west. There appears to have been some threat to his succession from a rival claimant, and this seems to reflect an accurate picture of the times for, although the story does not mention it, Amenemmes I was probably murdered by court officials. Sinuhe's role in this is unclear but, fearful of the consequences of the King's death, he leaves Egypt, fleeing first to the area near modern Cairo and then reaching the isthmus of Suez. A brief account of his travels is given and he finally arrives in Upper Retenu (Palestine), where the local prince invites him to stay and gives him good land and his daughter's hand in marriage.

Sinuhe prospers and his children flourish, but as old age approaches he longs to return to Egypt and to ensure his burial there. The King of Egypt – the same Sesostris from whom he fled – hears of his plight and sends him presents. The royal children write to him and Sesostris begs him to return so that he may eventually receive an appropriate burial in Egypt. In his reply Sinuhe lavishly praises his King and is at a loss to explain his stupidity in leaving Egypt. He hands over his possessions to his children in Retenu and goes home, where he is received by the King and the royal family. Terror overcomes him in the presence of Sesostris, and his unshaven, unkempt appearance, acceptable among the Beduin in Retenu, causes much comment from the Queen and her family. However, Sinuhe is treated most graciously. He is led from the palace and bathed, anointed and clothed in a manner befitting an Egyptian. A house is built for him and Sesostris grants him a tomb in the vicinity of his own pyramid, which will be equipped with the finest funerary goods and staffed by priests. Because of the forgiveness and mercy of his King, Sinuhe can look forward to eternal joy in the afterlife.

THE PROPHECY OF NEFERTI

The Egyptians sometimes made use of a 'prophecy' to justify a king's claim to the throne. This would appear to foretell the brave deeds of a future king, but in fact the 'prophecy' was written during that king's reign. Amenemmes I, mentioned in the Story of Sinuhe, was such a ruler. He was of non-royal descent and was probably the vizier of the previous King, and conspired against him to gain the throne. A legend known as the Prophecy of Neferti is preserved in a papyrus of a later date, but it describes events which must have occurred in the reign of Amenemmes or shortly afterwards.

In this 'prophecy' the action is set in the reign of Snefru, an earlier King. Sitting with his court, he asks his officials to find a sage who can provide some diversion. The name of Neferti, a priest of Bubastis, is suggested and he is brought to the palace. The King asks him to foretell the future and he puts his predictions in writing. He vividly describes the terrible events which will come to pass – drought, famine, sandstorms, the entry of the Beduin into Egypt, internal strife and upheaval. However, although these occurrences are projected into the future, there is every probability that they reflect conditions immediately before the composition of the poem, in the troubled times of the First Intermediate Period (*c.* 2200 BC). The prophecy tells of a saviour who will appear in the person of Ameni, the son of a woman of Nubia; he will drive out the invaders and restore order in Egypt. This Ameni is Amenemmes I and the story attempts to justify his rule of Egypt, although in reality he had usurped the throne.

The Prophecy of Neferti and the Story of Sinuhe provide interesting reflections of this troubled period and throw light on internal conditions and the King's need to be portrayed as a legitimate, benign and non-tyrannical ruler.

THE TAKING OF JOPPA

Other tales simply regale the audience with feats of bravery or narrate adventurous travels. One recalls an incident in the wars waged by Tuthmosis III (about 1450 BC). It occurs in a later papyrus and centres around the skill of his general Thutii, who was remembered by later generations. He had been unsuccessfully besieging the port of

Joppa in Palestine and finally had to resort to guile. He invited the Prince of Joppa to meet him for a conference outside the city and told him that he would surrender and hand over his wife and children. The Prince then asked to see the club of Tuthmosis III, which Thutii showed him, and then promptly hit the Prince over the head with it and made him captive.

In the meantime Egyptian soldiers were hidden in sacks, with fetters and handcuffs, and other soldiers were ordered to carry them into the city and release them there. The Egyptians informed the Prince's charioteer that his master instructed him to go to his wife and tell her of Thutii's surrender and that tribute was to be sent into the city. The gates of Joppa were then opened to admit the 'tribute' (the sacks concealing the soldiers). Once inside, the sack-bearers released their comrades, who seized and fettered the townspeople. Thus Joppa was taken and General Thutii could report his success to Tuthmosis in Egypt.

WENAMUN'S MISSION

From the later period there is an account of the travels of Wenamun, a temple official who lived about 1085 BC. Egypt was no longer a great power with influence abroad and was internally divided between different political factions. The tale traces Wenamun's adventures when he is sent on a quest for cedar wood from Lebanon to restore the state barque of Amun, god of Thebes. The various petty rulers in Egypt raise the money and, to support their request for the wood, an image of the god, known as Amun of the Road, is sent with Wenamun to Byblos.

Smendes, the ruler of northern Egypt, provides Wenamun with a ship and he sails for Dor on the Palestinian coast, where he meets with misfortune when one of his sailors runs off with the money intended for the purchase of the wood. Since the thief is not one of his subjects, the local prince refuses to help. Wenamun continues his journey. He encounters some Zakar tribesmen, from whom he steals a bag of silver to recompense himself for his loss, and goes on to Byblos. The Prince of Byblos is displeased with the theft of the Zakar people's money and queries the validity of the Egyptian's mission. He is scathing about Wenamun's request and recalls the heavily laden ships which earlier Egyptian kings sent to Byblos to obtain wood. It is only too obvious that Egypt is no longer honoured and esteemed by her trading neighbours.

Eventually, contact is made with Smendes, who agrees to advance money to Wenamun. The Prince of Byblos agrees to send some of the wood, but asks Wenamun to leave immediately. Wenamun goes to the shore where the timber is stacked ready for departure. There he sees eleven ships approaching, carrying the Zakar people who intend to take him prisoner for his theft. He begs the Prince of Byblos for help. The Prince tells the Zakar that he cannot himself capture the god's messenger, but that he will send him away so that they can pursue him. Wenamun puts to sea and somehow eludes his pursuers. He finally reaches another kingdom (probably Cyprus) where he has further adventures, but unfortunately the papyrus breaks off here and the outcome of his mission is unknown.

CHAPTER 11
MESOPOTAMIA

Ancient Mesopotamia, which corresponds approximately to modern
Iraq, comprised the lands of Sumer and Babylonia in the south and
Assyria in the north. The earliest people in the area of whom much is
known were the Sumerians, who had settled in southern
Mesopotamia by about 3500 BC. The golden age of Mesopotamian
legend was the following period, from about 3000 to 2000 BC, close to
the beginning of recorded history. The legends are almost exclusively
concerned with the quasi-historical achievements and adventures of
the kings of two renowned early dynasties of cities in Babylonia: the
Sumerian First Dynasty of Uruk and the later Semitic Dynasty of
Agade.

The legends have survived in two languages. Those about the
Kings of Uruk were composed primarily in Sumerian, and those of
the Kings of Agade in Akkadian, a Semitic tongue which gradually
replaced Sumerian as the spoken language of Mesopotamia during
the period from 3000 to 2000 BC. Although Sumerian consequently
became a 'dead' language, it went on being used for hundreds of years
for scholarly and religious purposes.

Mesopotamian literature was preserved and transmitted by scribes
writing on clay tablets in the wedge-shaped cuneiform script which
finally fell out of use in the late centuries BC. The earliest extensive
archives of literary texts are in Sumerian and date from about 2000
BC, though probably composed rather earlier. The same period saw
the first extensive recording of a distinctive Akkadian literature, most
of which has survived in copies of much later date – from the library
of King Assurbanipal (seventh century BC) at Nineveh. Akkadian
literature probably owed a considerable debt to Sumerian literature,
but it is often difficult to determine the degree and, sometimes the
direction of influence operating between the two.

Enmerkar and the sacks of barley (page 90)

ENMERKAR AND LUGALBANDA

The First Dynasty of Uruk (Erech in the Bible), a city of southern
Babylonia, ruled from approximately the twenty-eighth to the
twenty-sixth centuries BC. Three of its early kings were celebrated in
legend — Enmerkar, Lugalbanda and Gilgamesh, who were later
credited with fabulously long reigns, of 420, 1200 and 126 years
respectively. The legends about Enmerkar and Lugalbanda have
a common background, in confrontations between the city of Uruk
and the city of Aratta in Iran, east of the Zagros Mountains. The two
cities were uneasy trading partners, Uruk being rich in grain and
Aratta in precious stones and metals.

Two separate stories tell how Enmerkar, the second King of the
First Dynasty of Uruk, and the Lord of Aratta each strove to drive the
other into submission, not by might of arms but in battles of wit,
cunning and magic. In the first tale, 'Enmerkar and the Lord of
Aratta', Aratta is suffering from famine, but Enmerkar dispatches an
envoy to demand building materials and craftsmen from the stricken
city. The lord of Aratta sends back a spirited refusal and challenges
Enmerkar to an apparently impossible task: to transport barley in
open-weave net sacks by donkey along the mountain route to Aratta.
Enmerkar, however, following the advice of Nisaba, the goddess of
grain, craftily waters the grain and allows it to germinate, so that it
does not pour out of the net sacks. Further similar challenges of
a riddling kind pass between the two rulers, until eventually
a compromise is reached. It is agreed that Aratta will provide Uruk
with building materials and Uruk will send food to Aratta.

In the second tale, 'Enmerkar and Ensuhkeshdanna', the Lord of
Aratta, Ensuhkeshdanna, opens hostilities, demanding that Enmerkar recognize him as overlord. Enmerkar indignantly refuses,
whereupon an Arattan magician boasts that he can bring Uruk to heel
by supernatural means. He succeeds in causing famine in Uruk, by
drying up the milk of the livestock, but he is ultimately outwitted by
two shepherds, aided by an old crone, Mother Sagburru. She kills the
magician and throws his corpse into the River Euphrates. On hearing
of this, Ensuhkeshdanna throws in his hand and sends a grovelling
submission to Enmerkar.

Both these stories celebrate successes for Uruk, aided by
supernatural forces. There is also a lengthy tale, surviving in two
parts, about Lugalbanda, the third King of the Uruk dynasty,
Enmerkar's eventual successor. Again, the story concerns a power
struggle between Uruk and Aratta, this time carried on by military
means. In the first part of the story, Enmerkar sends an army against
Aratta, led by Lugalbanda's seven brothers. Lugalbanda falls ill on
the dangerous journey through the mountains and his brothers leave
him for dead. Reviving and finding himself abandoned, he prays

piteously to the gods for strength to complete the journey. Here the text breaks.

In the second part, Lugalbanda travels to the mountain home of the mythical Anzu-eagle, hoping the bird will help him to rejoin the army. On arriving, he finds that the Anzu-eagle is away from the nest, so he feeds the young chicks and then decks them out with ornaments. When Anzu returns, he is overwhelmed with gratitude and offers Lugalbanda a choice of blessings – power, a kingdom, invincible weapons. Lugalbanda refuses them all, asking only for the ability to run fast and tirelessly. His wish is granted and he is thus able to rejoin the army, which now sets siege to Aratta, where it meets fierce resistance. After a year's siege, a warrior is needed to return to Uruk and ask help from the goddess Inanna. Lugalbanda volunteers to make the hazardous journey alone. This arouses general admiration but, unknown to the others, he has the Anzu-eagle's blessing and so he makes the journey safely. The goddess Inanna tells Lugalbanda how the magic weapon is to be forged, by whose means alone Aratta can be captured. Here the tale ends, pointing forward to a happy outcome for Uruk.

LEGENDS OF GILGAMESH

Of all Mesopotamian rulers, Gilgamesh, the fifth King of Uruk, achieved the most enduring fame. The earliest tales about him are in Sumerian and he was later celebrated in an extensive and magnificent Akkadian epic. His renown extended beyond Mesopotamia and throughout the ancient Near East. Versions of the Akkadian epic in the Hittite and Hurrian languages have been found, fragmentarily preserved, in the Hittite capital of Boghazkoy in Anatolia.

Numerous stories became associated with Gilgamesh as time went by, including one about his birth, reported by Aelian, a Roman writer of the second century AD. According to this legend, the Babylonian king was told that his daughter's son would seize the kingdom from him. He consequently shut the girl up in the citadel and had her closely guarded, but she became pregnant by an obscure man and gave birth to a son. Her guards, fearing the king's rage, threw the baby off the walls of the citadel, to kill him, but as he fell he was saved by an eagle, which caught him on its back and put him gently down in an orchard. The keeper of the orchard, seeing the child's beauty, loved him and brought him up. He grew up to be Gilgamesh. The story has many parallels in legends about other heroes.

The Sumerian tales of Gilgamesh do not form a unified epic, but a cycle of disparate tales. Some are legendary sagas and others are closer to myth. A pervasive theme is Gilgamesh's quest for immortality.

The most realistic and 'historical' of the stories is the short tale of

'Gilgamesh and Agga of Kish'. Like the Enmerkar and Lugalbanda tales, its theme is one of conflict between cities. King Agga of Kish, a city in northern Babylonia, demands the submission of Uruk. Against the advice of the city elders, Gilgamesh decides to resist. Agga besieges Uruk, to such effect that Gilgamesh seeks volunteers to go out and treat with him. The first two volunteers are overwhelmed. Then Gilgamesh himself ascends the city wall to confront Agga face to face. At the sight of him, Agga is confounded and abandons the siege, and the rulers are eventually reconciled.

The story of 'Gilgamesh and Huwawa', surviving in versions of varying length, describes an expedition against the monstrous Huwawa, guardian of the Cedar Forest (probably located in the Amanus Mountains on the Syria-Turkey border). Gilgamesh resolves that since immortality is denied to mankind he will at least carve an immortal name for himself through heroic exploits. Aided by the sun god, Shamash, he sets out with his servant Enkidu and an escort of troops to make the arduous journey to the Cedar Forest. After a hard struggle against Huwawa, Gilgamesh overpowers him and ties him up, but then he is filled with pity on hearing Huwawa's laments. Enkidu urges him not to relent, because Huwawa could prevent their safe return to Uruk. Huwawa taunts Gilgamesh with taking counsel from a mere 'servant', at which the enraged Enkidu chops off Huwawa's head. Gilgamesh and Enkidu return triumphantly to Uruk and go to the temple of the god Enlil. The god, however, is angry at Huwawa's slaughter and curses the heroes. (This episode was incorporated in the Akkadian epic of Gilgamesh, with some significant variations.)

There is a poorly preserved tale, 'Gilgamesh, Enkidu and the Bull of Heaven', in which the goddess of Uruk, Inanna, is enraged with Gilgamesh, for reasons that are not clear. She demands from her father, the sky god, the Bull of Heaven with which to punish Gilgamesh. However, he and Enkidu manage to kill the ferocious bull. (This episode was also included in the Akkadian epic.) Another tale, 'Gilgamesh, Enkidu and the Underworld', is really a myth rather than a legend. It relates how Enkidu is trapped in the underworld and is released for a last meeting with Gilgamesh, during which he describes what happens after death.

'THE EPIC OF GILGAMESH'

This great poem is one of the longest Akkadian compositions (around 3000 lines) and one of the most impressive literary achievements of the ancient world. It incorporates two of the Sumerian tales, but it includes many incidents not found in Sumerian to forge a unified epic transcending the Sumerian in scope and narrative power. Its appeal is timeless and universal, for it treats of the joy of friendship, the anguish of bereavement and the dread of death. The earliest texts date from about 1800 BC, but the epic is better known in the slightly different version from Assurbanipal's library. It is still not possible to reconstruct the entire tale.

In this version Gilgamesh is one-third human and two-thirds divine, his mother being the goddess Ninsun. His divine part gives him the thirst for immortality; the fatal human third ensures that he will not attain it. At the outset the dynamic young King is tyrannizing over his subjects in Uruk, who complain to the gods. The gods decide to create a creature who is part-man and part-beast, named Enkidu, as a foil for Gilgamesh's superabundant energies. In all respects Enkidu is the opposite of Gilgamesh, the civilized city-dweller. Born and reared in the desert, Enkidu is ignorant of human society. His whole body is covered with hair and he lives happily with the wild animals, eating grass. His existence is reported to Gilgamesh, who sends a prostitute to seduce and tame this wild being. Her task accomplished, she leads him to Uruk, introducing him on the way to civilized eating customs and the wearing of clothing. On their first meeting, Gilgamesh and Enkidu fight fiercely, like maddened bulls. But they admire each other's strength and courage, and they form an enduring friendship.

The plan of the gods succeeds, however, because Gilgamesh is determined to win immortal fame for himself and his new friend. Together they go to the Cedar Forest, to attack its terrible supernatural guardian, Huwawa. They make their way to the centre of the forest. Gilgamesh cuts down a cedar tree with an axe, at which the monster Huwawa himself appears. Gilgamesh is terrified and calls out to Shamash, the sun god, who sends eight great winds which hold Huwawa fast. Huwawa begs for mercy, but Gilgamesh and Enkidu cut off his head.

On their triumphant return to Uruk, Ishtar, the goddess of love, is filled with desire for Gilgamesh. He rejects her overtures, making caustic remarks about her behaviour to past lovers. The insulted goddess demands from her father that the Bull of Heaven be released to rampage through Uruk. The bull slaughters hundreds of Urukmen with its breath, until Enkidu seizes it and the heroes kill the bull with a sword. The goddess Ishtar goes up on the city wall and curses Gilgamesh, but Enkidu tears off the bull's leg and flings it in Ishtar's face, telling her he would do the same to her if he could catch her.

Retribution follows. In emergency session the gods decree Enkidu's death. He dies slowly, in anguish and bitterness of spirit. Gilgamesh mourns his dead friend 'like a lioness deprived of her cubs'. Then, maddened with grief and obsessed with the fear of his own future death, he throws off his royal robes, abandons his

Kingdom and goes out into the desert in search of the secret of eternal life.

He determines to seek out Ut-napishtim (the counterpart of Noah in the Bible), who dwells 'in the distance, at the mouth of the rivers'. His arduous journey lies through strange, perpetually dark mountain ranges. On reaching the sea, he meets Siduri, the divine ale-wife, in her magic garden. She lectures him on the folly of his quest: 'When the gods created mankind, they appointed death for mankind. Life they kept in their own hands.' She advises him to be content with ordinary human pleasures – a loving wife, children, a full belly – to eat, drink and be merry, in effect. Unpersuaded, he rows across the Waters of Death to Ut-napishtim's island. There Ut-napishtim relates to him the story of the Great Flood, which the gods sent to destroy mankind, and how he alone was warned by the god Ea to build a ship, and so was spared and was subsequently granted immortality. But the gods will never again favour a mortal thus, and Gilgamesh must accept the fate of mankind. As Gilgamesh sorrowfully departs, Ut-napishtim tells him that at the bottom of the sea there grows a magic plant. If he can obtain it, it will make him young again. Gilgamesh ties heavy stones to his feet and descends to the bottom of the sea. He seizes the plant, but even this consolation prize is denied him, for the plant is stolen from him by a snake, which sloughs its skin as it glides away. At last he realizes the futility of his quest and returns to Uruk a sadder man but a wiser king.

LEGENDS OF AGADE

The legends of the Semitic Dynasty of Agade, of the twenty-fourth to the twenty-second centuries BC, centre on its two most prominent rulers, Sargon and his grandson, Naram-Sin. It is not surprising that Sargon achieved legendary status, for with his reign history changed scale. He founded the city of Agade in northern Babylonia, subdued the old Sumerian cities and carved out an empire, gaining mastery of the Persian Gulf with its valuable trade routes, of Syria, of the mountainous regions east of Babylonia and of Assyria. Some of the legends are in the form of autobiography: a narrative allegedly penned by the King himself, but in reality composed some time after his death. Though based on authentic tradition, they incorporate legendary and fabulous elements.

In a tale known only from late copies (first millennium BC), Sargon recounts the story of his early life. His mother, a priestess, bore him in secret and cast him into the river in a reed basket. He was found by a drawer of water, who reared him as his own son. The legend has obvious affinities with tales of the unpromising birth of other heroes, most strikingly Moses.

'The King of Battle', a popular saga also known to the Hittites, tells how Sargon undertook the long and difficult journey to Purushkhanda, in eastern Anatolia, after a merchant colony there had requested his aid against an oppressive ruler. This ruler, Nur-Dagan, was confident that the difficult terrain would keep Sargon away. Just as he was expressing this hope, Sargon stormed up with his troops and Nur-Dagan was overcome. Instead of pressing his advantage Sargon took his leisure in the town for over three years, to the disgust of his troops, who urged him to demolish the walls of the city and take booty as befitted a true conqueror. At length Sargon took their advice.

The Cuthaean legend of Naram-Sin, versions of which were again current in Hittite, is so called because it was first inscribed, allegedly by Naram-Sin himself, on a stele deposited in a temple in Cuthah, in northern Babylonia, so that future monarchs might benefit from the King's unfortunate experience. Naram-Sin was confronted by a formidable coalition of warriors 'with the faces of ravens', led by seventeen kings. He disregarded the express advice of the gods, revealed through oracles, not to march against them, asking contemptuously: 'What lion ever observed oracles? What wolf ever consulted a dream-priestess?' In consequence his army suffered annihilating defeats for three years running. The chastened King thenceforth gave due weight to divine counsel and desisted from warfare. The story is another object-lesson in the necessity of obeying the will of the gods, and the limitations of being human.

JEWISH LEGENDS

Jewish legends constitute a very large and fascinating body of material. Besides legends contained in the Bible, there are the numerous stories which grew up around the Bible, amplifying its characters and incidents. There are also legends about later figures and events – including non-Jewish characters such as Alexander the Great and Nero as well as Jewish leaders, teachers and mystics.

The distinction between what is historical and what is legendary in the Bible itself is often hard to draw. It is not sufficient merely to point to the element of the miraculous as being legendary, for what appeared miraculous to the narrator may frequently have a natural explanation in modern scientific terms. There is, however, a strong probability that a legendary element is sometimes present in the Bible. A good example is the story of the infancy of Moses. It has many parallels elsewhere and is therefore likely to represent a common theme in the portrayal of a hero in legend, rather than a historical fact.

MOSES AND PHARAOH'S DAUGHTER

According to the story (Exodus 1 & 2), while the Israelites were living in subjection in Egypt, Pharaoh decreed that all their male babies were to be thrown into the Nile. This was because he feared their growing numbers. When Moses was born, his mother hid him for three months and finally put him in a basket of bulrushes, which she laid among the reeds at the bank of the river. His sister Miriam waited nearby to see what would happen. Pharaoh's daughter, coming to bathe, found the child and took pity on him. She allowed him to be suckled by his own mother, at Miriam's quick-witted suggestion, and then brought him up in the palace.

Samson and Delilah (page 98)

There is a clear parallel with the story of Sargon of Agade (see MESOPOTAMIA). His birth was concealed and his mother cast him into a river in a basket of bulrushes, but he was rescued by a stranger and grew up to be a great ruler. Sargon's father was said to be unknown, but the secrecy of the birth points to a liaison with a noble or royal personage, or even with a god. The legend may have influenced the story of Moses, but since parallels to the basket-in-a-river theme have been found in oriental sources, it may have a psychological origin.

Many legendary heroes are exposed to die as infants. Freud believed that such stories arise from the day-dreaming of adolescents, who imagine that their humdrum parents are only foster-parents and that they are really the offspring of some much more glamorous figure, who wished to destroy them as infants, but with whom they will one day be reconciled. This explanation, however, does not fit the story of Moses, whose real parents are portrayed as lowly Israelites, with whom he is eventually reunited. Others have suggested that stories of a river-ordeal for infants arise from a primitive custom of testing the legitimacy of babies by throwing them into a river. Where an infant whose father was unknown nevertheless survived the test, his begetting would be ascribed to a god. Many such conjectures are possible, but the main point is surely that a story of a miraculous escape from danger in infancy enhances the status of a great leader and surrounds him with an aura of special destiny. A strong parallel can be seen between the infancy story of Moses and that of Jesus, whose life is endangered by the decree of King Herod. This is almost certainly due to direct influence by the Moses legend on the Jesus legend.

SAMSON AND DELILAH

While Moses may be regarded as a historical figure whose portrayal in the Bible contains many legendary features, the story of Samson is almost entirely legendary. Even here, however, there is a substratum of historical fact in the border warfare, combined with considerable social and commercial intercourse, between the Israelites and Philistines in the late twelfth or early eleventh century BC. In these circumstances (similar to the centuries of border warfare betweeen England and Scotland), the exploits of a local hero were exaggerated into a saga of supernatural proportions, while retaining the earthiness of its origin in popular tales. Thus the story of Samson, of all the biographies in the historical books of the Bible, is the least moralized or theological. An attempt was made to bring it into line with sacred history by having Samson's birth announced by an angel and by portraying him as dedicated to God from birth (Judges 13), but the attempt was hardly sustained. In general Samson is a rollicking folk-hero, who pays little attention to spirituality and has much in common with the uninhibited heroes of Greek legend.

Samson, like Hercules, has superhuman strength, which for a long time enables him to survive the Philistine attacks on his life, partly occasioned by his exploits among Philistine women. The first of these is 'the woman of Timnah', whom he marries against his parents' wishes and in contravention of Jewish law. At his wedding-feast he poses a riddle to his Philistine guests, but his bride betrays the secret of the riddle to them. In his fury Samson kills thirty Philistines and devastates the Philistine fields by letting loose 300 foxes with firebrands tied to their tails. Then his own people bind Samson with ropes and hand him over to the Philistines, but Samson bursts his bonds and slaughters 1000 of the Philistines with the jawbone of an ass. Later, he is surrounded while sleeping with a prostitute in Gaza, but he escapes, uprooting the city gates and taking them with him.

Samson's third involvement with a Philistine woman, however, proves his downfall. This is the famous Delilah, who is bribed by the Philistine leaders to discover the secret of Samson's strength. After three unsuccessful attempts, she cajoles him into revealing that his strength depends on his long hair and will leave him if his hair is cut off. Putting him to sleep, the treacherous Delilah has his head shaved and Samson is so weak that the Philistines capture him, blind him and set him to work at the mill in the prison in Gaza. Gradually, however, his strength returns as his hair grows again, and when the Philistines put him on display at a festival in their chief temple he seizes the pillars and brings the temple down, killing himself and the 3000 spectators.

This dramatic and romantic story has been a source of literary and artistic inspiration in Western culture (as in Milton's *Samson Agonistes*), but Samson is untypical of the heroes of the Bible. He is a lone figure, performing exploits for his own satisfaction, rather than for his people or for their mission. He is the only example in the Bible of a hero admired for his physical qualities, exaggerated in legendary fashion. The tendency elsewhere is to ascribe great physical strength to the enemies of Israel, and give the credit for their defeat to God.

DAVID AND SOLOMON

Such a figure is the Philistine giant Goliath, whose defeat by the boy David is one of the most celebrated of Biblical stories (I Samuel 17). The tale almost certainly belongs to the category of legend, rather than historical reality. The reason for this conclusion is not the gigantic stature of Goliath, which does not pass the bounds of credibility, but that the defeat of Goliath is ascribed elsewhere in the Bible to another person, Elhanan (II Samuel 21 : 19). It seems very likely that the feat was transferred to David to enhance his glory and was also credited to his boyhood to make his victory even more marvellous. In general, however, the story of David is not legendary in character, but a sober historical chronicle, though obviously written from the angle of a supporter of David and his claim to the throne. The Goliath story is thus a case of a mere heightening of a predominantly factual biography.

A similar heightening can be seen in the biography of Solomon, whose reign proliferates into wondrous legends only in post-biblical literature. The Bible itself describes him in restrained terms as a successful and wealthy monarch. Only in the portrayal of his wisdom is a legendary element introduced, as in the famous story of his wise judgment (I Kings 3). Two women disputed before him over which was the mother of a baby. The King ordered a sword to be fetched and the child to be cut in two, one half being given to one woman and the other half to the other. At this the real mother gave up her claim, while the other woman agread to the King's plan. Then Solomon said, 'Give the child to the merciful woman. She is its mother.' There is a parallel to this story in Indian legend.

PROPHETS AND PATRIARCHS

The most purely legendary stories in the Bible are those about the deeds of the prophets, especially Elijah and Elisha. The accounts of miraculous healing may well be based on fact, but Elijah's ascent to heaven in a chariot of fire (II Kings 2) is the type of legend which signalizes people's reluctance to believe that their beloved heroes really died in the normal way (King Arthur is another example). Similarly, there are many parallels to the miracle ascribed to Elisha in which a single flask of oil fills a whole roomful of vessels, in order to save a poor widow from her creditor (II Kings 4). Such stories are regularly told about people of high religious stature.

A type of legend frequently found in the Bible concerns the origin of a place-name or a local landmark. A striking salt pillar in the area of the Dead Sea was explained by the story of Lot's wife. She disobeyed the angel's order not to look back when escaping from the destruction of Sodom and Gomorrah, and was turned into a pillar of salt (Genesis 19). The origin of Babylonia (Babel) was found in the world *balal,* 'to confuse', and the legend arose that it was there that the division of mankind into mutually unintelligible language-groups occurred, as punishment for trying to storm heaven (Genesis 11).

The early part of the Bible story, up to the time of the patriarchs, is legendary in another sense. It is an attempt to fill in a large stretch of remote time for which scanty data existed. The account of the creation of the world belongs to mythology rather than legend, but after the creation the role of mythology is very small, since the nature of Israelite monotheism did not allow it. It is on the human scale of

legend that the period before the Flood is reconstructed, evidently
with the help of Kenite records (the Kenites being the clan into which
Moses married). A succession of generations is given, in which the
patriarchs who lived before the Flood are given lives of awesome
length, averaging 1000 years each (though compared with corresponding Egyptian and Babylonian records, these ages are very
short).

It is hinted that one patriarch, Enoch, was translated to heaven
before his time (Genesis 5 : 22, 24), which later gave rise to
a voluminous body of legend, but in general the account is free of
supernatural wonders and represents a sober attempt at history. The
story of the Flood itself, though possibly based on a real-life disaster,
has many parallels in other cultures. The stories of the patriarchs
Abraham, Isaac and Jacob are again kept on a factual level, apart
from a few miraculous embellishments. The story of the angel
preventing Abraham from sacrificing Isaac (Genesis 22) validates the
shift from human sacrifice to animal sacrifice. One of the functions of
legend is illustrated here: to explain and support the institutions of
a community or, even more important, to justify a change in the
institutions. It may be that Abraham in pre-biblical versions was
a god, not a man (both his name, meaning 'high father', and
archaeological evidence suggest this). If so, we have an example of
the biblical tendency to convert myth into legend by humanizing
stories of the gods. This tendency can be found in other cultures too,
but it is especially characteristic of Israelite culture because of its
abolition of polytheism.

The interventions of God in the stories of the patriarchs and in
later biblical history cannot be classed as either myth or legend. They
belong to 'sacred history', in which an overall theological theme is
traced through the whole of history.

LEGENDS BASED ON THE BIBLE

The most substantial body of Jewish legends consists of elaborations
and amplifications of the events and characters of the Bible. These
elaborations, very different in tone from the pervading realism of the
Bible itself, show a high degree of imagination and fantasy. They
often fix on an ambiguity or a gap in the Bible story and have the
function of answering the questions of those who studied the Bible
with loving attention. Often they illustrate the art of the story-tellers,
who added details to the biblical narrative to increase its dramatic
effectiveness. Sometimes the legends have an air of being more
primitive than the Bible itself, preserving the earlier form of stories
which were given a more civilized character in the biblical books. In
general, these post-biblical legends are the product of folk-culture,
though they were collected into anthologies by scholars who added

their own contribution.

The two main sources of these tales are, first, the Apocrypha, Pseudepigrapha and Hellenistic writings, dating in written form from about 200 BC to AD 100; and, second, the writings of the rabbis, a huge body of work compiled over many centuries and known collectively as the Midrash (mainly narrative) and Talmud (mainly law, but rich in narrative material). This second source did not reach written form before AD 250 and is found in collections made as late as AD 1000.

The Apocrypha and Pseudepigrapha were writings which were intended to be regarded as sacred, but which were rejected by mainstream Judaism as heretical in tendency. They circulated among small unorthodox Jewish groups and were eventually treated as semi-canonical by the Christian Church. The substantial measure of agreement between these writings and the rabbinic writings shows that the latter are based on early material. The Apocrypha and Pseudepigrapha, however, have a tendency towards the reintroduction of mythology, especially of dualistic myths involving evil powers, a tendency which accounts for the rejection of this literature by the anti-mythological mainstream. The Hellenistic secular writings, on the other hand, notably the historical works of Josephus (first century AD), presented no religious challenge but were neglected as unimportant by mainstream Judaism. They provide some interesting legends based on the Bible and not found in other sources.

ENOCH, CAIN AND ISAIAH

An example of non-rabbinical development of a legend based on the Bible is the case of Enoch, mentioned earlier. The Bible merely says laconically, 'And Enoch walked with God: and he was not; for God took him.' On this basis the Book of Enoch and several other pseudepigraphic works erect a full picture of Enoch. While on earth, he was the inventor of writing, mathematics and astronomy. After his translation to heaven he acquired knowledge of all secrets, and eventually was made into an angel. Rabbinical sources decry this legend, but it is found on the edges of rabbinic literature too, and became quite prominent again in late Midrashic collections. The Enoch legend's association with Christianity and its representation of Enoch as a semi-divine figure made the rabbis hostile to it, but this hostility eventually evaporated.

In the Enoch theme legend melts into mythology, with the elevation of Enoch from earthly status. Examples of legends proper abound, however, in the non-rabbinical writings. For example, the Book of Jubilees fills a biblical gap by telling us about the death of Cain. 'His house fell on him and he died in the midst of his house, and he was killed by its stones; for with a stone he killed Abel, and by a stone was he killed in righteous judgment.' This passage also supplies a legendary detail about the method by which Cain killed Abel.

As we shall see, the Midrash supplies an entirely different story about the death of Cain. Often, however, the legends in non-rabbinic and rabbinic literature are almost identical. For example, *The Martyrdom of Isaiah,* a pseudepigraphic work, tells the legend of Isaiah's death at the hands of the tyrant Menasseh, who caused the prophet to be sawn in half with a wood saw while hiding in a tree. The same legend is found in the Midrash and Talmud, but the rabbis were certainly not acquainted with the pseudepigraphic work, which was not part of their tradition and was preserved in Western Christian circles (in Greek, Latin and Ethiopic versions). There may be a reference, too, to this legend in the New Testament, where among those who suffered for their faith are mentioned some who 'were sawn in two' (Hebrews 11 : 37).

MOSES IN ETHIOPIA

In the non-religious Hellenistic literature an interesting legendary supplement to the biblical biography of Moses is found in the writings of the historian Josephus. It tells how Moses, before taking up the cause of the oppressed Israelites, waged war successfully as the general of the Egyptians against Ethiopia, which had previously come near to conquering Egypt. Moses led his army on a detour through a land thought to be impassable because of its multitude of serpents, but he cleverly took with him thousands of ibis-birds, which his soldiers carried in baskets. When the birds were released they quickly cleared away the serpents and Moses took the enemy by surprise and defeated them in battle. He then advanced to besiege the Ethiopian capital, Saba, which was impregnable, being surrounded by rivers. However, Tharbis, the daughter of the King of Ethiopia, saw Moses from a distance, fell in love with him and sent her servant to offer to betray the city if he would marry her. Moses agreed, took the city, married the Princess and led the Egyptians home again victorious.

This story is hardly in the spirit of the Bible and bears the marks of Hellenistic romancing. It can be traced back to a Jewish-Hellenistic writer called Artapanos, who may have invented it (though in his version Moses did not acquire an Ethiopian bride). It was evidently invented to fill part of the large gap in the biography of Moses in the Bible, between his youth in Egypt and his arrival to demand from Pharaoh the release of the Israelites, when he is declared to have been eighty years old (Exodus 7 : 7). The story also explains the text that asserts that Moses had an Ethiopian wife (Numbers 12 : 1). Apart from a very late Midrash, the rabbinic sources do not contain the legend of Moses's campaign in Ethiopia.

THE DEATH OF CAIN

It is in the rabbinic writings that the largest body of legends about the Bible is to be found. These legends show a quaint fancifulness and Oriental exuberance reminiscent of *The Arabian Nights*. It should be noted that although these stories have a kind of canonical status among adherents of Talmudic Judaism, they are not believed in a fully literal sense. They are regarded as 'Aggada', the aspect of the rabbinic writings on which no firm juridical conclusions can he based and which everyone is at liberty to understand and expound in his own way, whether literal, metaphorical or mystical.

The rabbinic version of the death of Cain (found in Midrash Tanhuma) is far more complex and imaginative than the story quoted earlier from the Book of Jubilees. The Midrash is based on the cryptic verses in (Genesis 4:23-4) about Lamech, who cries to his two wives: 'I have slain a man to my wounding, and a young man to my hurt. If Cain shall be avenged sevenfold, truly Lamech seventy and seven-fold.' The Midrash explains that Lamech was blind, but he neverthe-less used to go hunting, guided by his son Tubal Cain. One day Tubal Cain saw the horn of what seemed to be an animal in the distance and guided his father to shoot it. On coming up with the quarry, however, he found a dead man with a horn growing from his forehead. Lamech, informed of this, realized that he had shot his own forebear, Cain, the horn being the 'sign' or 'mark' that God had put upon Cain after the murder of Abel. This fulfilled a prophecy that Cain would pay for the murder with his own life after seven generations. Lamech was so distressed at having killed Cain that he clapped his hands together with great force and thus unfortunately killed his son Tubal Cain too, who was standing near him. At evening his two wives came to find him and he excused himself for the double killing by saying, 'I have slain a man (Cain) to my wounding (meaning, to my great grief), and a young man (Tubal Cain) to my hurt.'

This story is evidently concerned with exegesis, the interpretation of scripture. It explains Lamech's enigmatic speech, ignoring the poetic device of parallelism involved which, rightly interpreted, refers to only one killing. It interprets God's pronouncement to Cain (Genesis 4 : 15), usually taken to mean that if anyone kills Cain vengeance will be taken on him sevenfold, to mean that vengeance will be taken on Cain himself after seven generations. The story was prompted by Lamech's remark about Cain being avenged sevenfold. Yet despite these exegetical purposes, the story has an authentically primitive aura and was probably adapted to exegesis rather than arising wholly from it. The motif of the blind man killing an awesome quarry by mischievous or mistaken direction from another person appears elsewhere in mythology, notably in the Norse story of the god Balder being killed by the blind Hother at the direction of Loki.

Here then we have a not untypical kind of rabbinic legend, compounded of mythical elements shaped by exegetical needs. The story passed from the Midrash into Christian lore and became a popular theme for representation in Christian art (for example, in one of the windows of the Sainte-Chapelle in Paris).

THE DRUNKENNESS OF NOAH

A similar adaptation of what was originally a mythological motif to form a Midrashic legend occurs in the rabbinical story of the drunkenness of Noah. In the Bible (Genesis 9), the sin of Ham was failing to avert his eyes when his father Noah became uncovered while drunk. On awakening, Noah cursed him and his son Canaan with the prediction that they would become slaves to Ham's brothers Shem and Japhet. The Midrash, however, states that the sin of Ham was a much cruder one. He came across his father helplessly drunk and took the opportunity to castrate him. Furthermore, Noah was at the time having intercourse with his wife, and this was what occasioned Ham's action. Ham was afraid that a new brother might be born, with whom he would have to share his portion of the world. The reason why Canaan, who was Ham's fourth son, was also cursed was that Ham had prevented Noah from having a fourth son.

Here again, exegetical aims are evident. Why was Ham cursed for an apparently trivial offence? What is meant by saying that Noah was 'uncovered within his tent' (the consonantal reading is actually 'within *her* tent')? Why was Canaan included in the curse? The rabbinical legend answers these questions, but the content of the story goes beyond mere exegesis and clearly has an ancient folk-origin. It reminds us of such primitive myths as the castration of the Greek god Uranus by his son Cronus. The Bible itself has purified the story of its savage content, but the Midrashic version is a return of the censored.

In both Bible and Midrash the story also has a politico-religious aim, in that it justifies the Israelite conquest of the land of Canaan. There was never any racialist motive in the tale, however. The Canaanites, against whom the story was primarily aimed, were white. One nation descended from Ham was black, the Ethiopians, but the curse of Ham was never applied to them until certain Christian apologists thought of this allegedly biblical justification for anti-black racialism.

GIANTS AND SOLOMON'S RING

Many rabbinical legends arise not from exegesis or myth, but from sheer imaginative exuberance. In the Bible, King Og of Bashan is a gigantic and fearsome warrior, who was defeated by Moses in battle.

'For only Og king of Bashan remained of the remnant of giants; behold his bedstead was a bedstead of iron; is it not in Rabbath of the children of Ammon? Nine cubits was the length thereof, and four cubits the breadth of it, after the cubit of a man' (Deuteronomy 3 : 11). (A cubit was the length of a forearm.) This verse occasioned some breath-taking rabbinical elaborations. The Bible's dimensions make Og about 3.3 metres (11 feet) tall, but the rabbis turned him into an enormous giant capable of uprooting mountains. One story, about the single combat between Og and Moses, says that Moses, who was ten cubits tall, took an axe ten cubits long, jumped ten cubits in the air and struck Og a fatal blow on the ankle!

Exaggeration of this kind was applied even to figures not described as giants in the Bible. Rabbah bar Hanah, the renowned traveller, who corresponds in the Talmud to Sinbad the Sailor, told how once when he was travelling in the desert he found the bodies of the Israelites who died there in the time of Moses. They were lying on their backs and they were so huge that his companion was able to ride his camel under the raised knee of one of the corpses.

A good example of the elaboration of a Bible story into a body of legend is the rabbinical treatment of King Solomon, the builder of the Temple. The Talmud tells how Solomon learned that Asmodeus, the King of the Demons, knew the secret of the shamir, the magic worm that splits rocks, which was needed to shape the stones of the Temple, for no iron implement might be used on them. Benaiah the son of Jehoiada, Solomon's chief warrior, was sent to fetch Asmodeus and managed to capture him by tricking him into drunkenness and by using a ring on which the Name of God was engraved. Asmodeus now became Solomon's slave and taught him how to obtain the shamir from its owner, the Angel of the Sea. After the Temple was completed, however, Asmodeus contrived to trick Solomon into lending him the magic ring. The tables were now turned, Asmodeus had power over Solomon and he hurled the King far away from Jerusalem. He them assumed the appearance and identity of Solomon and reigned in Jerusalem himself. Solomon became a beggar and no one believed his assertions that he was the King. After three years, however, he managed to recover the ring and regain his throne.

There are clearly many folk-tale elements in this story and tales of this kind were regarded merely as wondrous stories. They did not command the respect belonging to genuine legend, which embodies a perception of the significance of the figure concerned in the culture as a whole.

THE ASCENT OF MOSES

A story which meets this requirement is a tale about Moses, found in the Babylonian Talmud. At the time when Moses ascended to heaven, he found God tying crowns to the letters of the Torah (the Law). Moses said, 'Master of the Universe, why are you doing this?' God replied, 'There will be a man at the end of many generations, Akiba ben Joseph by name, who will derive laws plentifully from each branch of these crowns.' Moses said, 'Master of the Universe, show me this man.' Upon this, God transported Moses through time to a lecture by Rabbi Akiba (who lived in the first and second centuries AD). Moses took his place in the back row of the students but, to his great dismay, he could not understand what Akiba was talking about. Presently however, one of the students asked, 'Rabbi, how do you know that point?', upon which Akiba replied, 'It is a tradition of Moses from Mount Sinai.' On hearing this, Moses was comforted. This legend says something about progress and continuity in a religious culture. It is a story about Moses, but it is also about the rabbinic movement which, by its ability to create such legends, evinces its sense of historic mission, combining tradition with innovation.

The ascent of Moses to heaven was a well-established legend, perhaps current even in biblical times. According to the Bible, 'Moses entered into the midst of the cloud' (Exodus 24 : 18), meaning the cloud which covered Mount Sinai during the giving of the Law. It was a natural exercise of the legend-making faculty to say that this cloud carried Moses up to heaven. There he was accosted by a destroying angel, whom he vanquished, but he almost succumbed to a higher angel called Hadarniel, whose every word was accompanied by 12 000 flashes of lightning. Hadarniel, however, was rebuked by a voice from God and escorted Moses to a higher stage. Moses then passed through many other dangers until he reached the throne of God. This story was later used as the basis of a similar legend about Muhammad.

ALEXANDER THE GREAT

Besides legends about biblical characters, the rabbinical literature contains a wealth of stories about figures of later times. One of them is Alexander the Great, whose personality and deeds were a focus of legend in many different cultures. Rabbinical legends are favourable to him, on the whole, portraying him as just in his dealings with the Jews and as deeply impressed by the Jewish religion. One such story tells how Alexander visited Jerusalem and met the High Priest, Simon the Just. To the surprise of his attendant noblemen, Alexander bowed low before the High Priest. Alexander explained that Simon's appearance was familiar to him, as he had seen a vision of a supernatural figure of the same appearance fighting on his side in a crucial battle. This story in the Talmud has a parallel in Josephus, who says that a vision of the High Priest appeared to Alexander while he was still in Macedonia and encouraged him to set out on his career of world conquest. Such legends reassured the Jews of their own central importance despite the Greek rise to world power. Even the mighty Alexander, whom many nations worshipped as a god, was the instrument of the God whose Temple stood in Jerusalem. At the same time there was a foundation of fact in the stories, in that Alexander did treat the Jews and Judaism with respect.

On the other hand, some of the rabbinical stories about Alexander have a satirical intent, showing the hollowness of his dream of world power. One of them tells how Alexander visited a kingdom called Cassia, beyond the Mountains of Darkness, where true principles of honesty and justice prevailed. While Alexander was sitting with the King, two men brought a law-suit to be judged. One had sold the other a ruin, in which treasure had subsequently been found. The buyer wished to return the treasure to the vendor, saying he had bought only the ruin, not the treasure. The vendor disputed this, saying that he had sold the ruin and everything in it. The King settled the dispute by arranging a marriage between the vendor's son and the buyer's daughter. Alexander was amazed at the whole transaction and the King asked him, 'How would you have arranged the matter in your country?' Said Alexander, 'Both men would have been put to death and the treasure confiscated for the royal treasury.' After more conversation of this kind, the King asked Alexander, 'Does it rain in your land?' 'Yes.' 'Does the sun shine over you?' 'Yes.' 'Are there animals in your land?' 'Yes.' 'Then it must be for their sake that the sun shines and the rain falls.' In another story the King sets before Alexander at a banquet bread, meat, poultry and vegetables made of gold, saying that if he loves gold so much he ought to eat it.

Other great non-Jewish figures of the Greco-Roman world appear in rabbinical legends. The Emperor Titus is called 'Titus the Wicked' in the Talmud because he destroyed the Temple in AD 70. According to one legend, on his way back to Rome by sea he was threatened by Nabshol, the spirit of the storm. Titus said, 'I know you have been sent by the God of the Jews, whose power is only at sea where he destroyed the Egyptians. I challenge him to fight me by land.' At this the storm subsided, but when Titus landed, a gnat entered his nostril and kept him in torment for seven years until he died. The Emperor Nero, on the other hand, is highly regarded. A legend says that he was unwilling to fulfil the doom of Jerusalem and therefore resigned his throne and became a convert to Judaism. This story builds on a rumour that Nero did not die but mysteriously disappeared.

LEGENDS OF THE RABBIS

Many of the rabbinical legends are about the rabbis themselves. Some of them were charismatic figures, credited with powers of healing and rain-making, through their efficacious prayers to God. Hanina ben Dosa, for example, was famous for his miraculous cures and other miracles were associated with him. On one occasion, while he was at prayer, a scorpion bit him. Hanina continued his prayer as if nothing had happened and suffered no ill effects, but the scorpion was found dead. A saying became current: 'Woe to the man who is bitten by a scorpion, but woe to the scorpion that has bitten Hanina ben Dosa.'

A charming story about Hanina is that, as he was very poor, his wife asked him to pray to God for financial help. When he did so, a hand appeared and gave him one leg of a golden table. That night he dreamed that he heard a voice which said, 'In the World to Come, the righteous will eat at tables with three legs, but you will eat at a table with only two legs.' He told this dream to his wife, who said, 'Are you content that everyone else should eat at a three-legged table, and we should eat at a two-legged table?' Said he, 'What shall I do?' Said she, 'Pray that the golden leg should be taken back again.' He did, and it was, which (it was taught) was a greater miracle than the first.

Another charismatic called Honi, who was renowned for his ability to pray successfully for rain, was dissatisfied on one occasion with God's slowness to respond. He drew a circle and stationed himself in it, saying that he would not move from it until rain fell. Rain promptly fell in torrents, but Honi, still not satisfied, refused to move until it fell in a more moderate fashion. Because of this feat he became known as Honi the Circle-Maker, though some of the rabbis rather disapproved of his high-handed manner of prayer.

Another type of story might be called the anti-miracle legend. The best-known example concerns Rabbi Eliezer, a much-revered teacher who was nevertheless often outvoted in the council of rabbis. One day, when outvoted, he resorted to miracles to prove his point. 'If I am right,' he said, 'may the stream outside this building prove it.' Upon this the stream changed its direction of flow from east to west. Rabbi Joshua, however, stood up and said. 'One cannot derive a legal conclusion from the flow of a stream.' Rabbi Eliezer then performed other miracles, to no avail. At last he said, 'If I am right, may a voice from heaven declare me to be right.' A voice from heaven immediately did, but Rabbi Joshua declared the voice to be out of order. Later, Rabbi Nathan had a visit from the prophet Elijah and asked him, 'What did God think when the rabbis ruled Him out of order?' Elijah replied, 'He laughed and said, "My children have defeated Me."'

This legend graphically expresses the Talmudic rabbis' belief that God had delivered his Law to human beings, to develop by their own intellect and moral sense without interruption or influence by divine intervention. Despite the many stories of the rabbis' miracles, their legal discussions are based on nothing but solid argument. One rabbi,

Johanan ben Dabahai, tried to win his point by saying that he had heard his view of the matter from the the Ministering Angels, but was sternly overruled. The rabbis believed in miracles and in Ministering Angels, but wished to keep them in their place. The Talmudic legends about the rabbis are the product of a vigorous religious movement full of characters impressive enough to attract legends, but determined to avoid any cult of personality inimical to its basic egalitarianism and humanism.

THE ERA OF PERSECUTION

During the Middle Ages and on into modern times the Jews lived in exile and were often persecuted, especially in Christian lands. Most of the legends that now arose among them consequently concerned miraculous deliverance from persecution and massacre, representing the wish-fulfilment of people frequently subjected to such treatment in reality. Many of these legends were collected in a sixteenth-century compilation, written in Yiddish known as the *Maase-buch*. One of the accusations made against Jews was that they murdered Christian children in evil rituals. This vicious slander sometimes led to the massacre of an entire community and many legends centre round it. An example is a tale about Rabbi Kalonymos of Jerusalem. The enemies of the Jews, angry because the Governor pursued a just policy, devised a plot. They kidnapped and killed the Governor's son and blamed the murder on the Jews. The boy's body was discovered in the synagogue and the Governor threatened to destroy the whole Jewish community unless the culprit was handed over. After fervent prayer, Rabbi Kalonymos wrote the Name of God on a piece of paper and placed it on the dead child's forehead. The boy came back to life and pointed out the three men, non-Jews, who had murdered him.

The most famous of all European Jewish legends, the tale of the Golem, was inspired by fear of the 'ritual murder' accusation. The story is that a famous sixteenth-century rabbi, Judah Loew of Prague, prayed to God to provide him with a means of defence against the accusation, and was told to make a human image of clay. He and two companions did so and by mystic formulas brought the image to life. This golem, or artificial man, was called Joseph. He was preternaturally strong and was utterly obedient to his master. He could be made invisible and his task was to go about and watch for people carrying sacks, who might be intending to hide a dead Christian child in a Jewish home as a prelude to an accusation of ritual murder. When he found such a person, the Golem would tie him up and hand him over to the authorities.

Another type of legend, that of the Jewish pope, shows a desire for protection by high Christian authorities. According to one story, Rabbi Simeon of Mayence had a son called Elhanan, who was captured as a child and handed over to the Church. In time he rose to be pope, but he discovered his origin and longed to be reunited with his father. He sent a letter to the Bishop of Mayence, asking him to prevent the practice of the Jewish religion, and as he expected, a deputation of Jews headed by Rabbi Simeon came from Mayence to plead with him. The pope then revealed his identity to his father in private, rescinded his letter and issued decrees favourable to the Jews instead. Later he disappeared and returned to Judaism. In another story, the Jew who became pope was fond of playing chess but could not find worthy opponents. He heard that a certain rabbi was an excellent player and invited him to a match. The rabbi was astonished when the pope played a move which the rabbi had taught to his long-lost son, and this led to mutual recognition.

The trauma of exile contributed to the popularity of the legend of the ten lost tribes, who were carried away into exile by the Assyrians in the eighth century BC but were said to have retained their identity. The Midrash speaks of the River Sambatyon, which borders the territory of the lost tribes and which is turbulent during the week but rests on the sabbath. In the Middle Ages certain impostors, notably Eldad ha-Dani and David Reubeni, claimed to be members of the lost tribes who had travelled to Europe. Sometimes the legend was to the effect that the lost tribes were extremely powerful and were organized in a war-like kingdom somewhere in Africa. This gave oppressed European Jews some hope of assistance, and indeed was at times believed by Christian authorities sufficiently to temper their treatment of the Jews.

Another comforting type of legend involved Elijah. The prophet was thought to have escaped death and there are many stories in the Midrash and Talmud of his wanderings in the world to help Jews in trouble. These legends proliferated in the Middle Ages until Elijah became the chief legendary hero of biblical provenance, overshadowing even Solomon. In many of the stories Elijah has become a purely imaginary folk-hero who rights wrongs, but one of them concerns the historical figure of Mayer Amschel Rothschild, the eighteenth-century founder of the great Rothschild dynasty. The Rothschild fortune is said to have begun when Mayer Amschel, in return for a good deed, was given by Elijah an inexhaustible barrel of oil.

KABBALISTIC LEGENDS

The legend of the Golem was partly a product of the mystical movement known as Kabbalism, which reached its full form in the *Zohar,* a mystical work composed in Spain in the thirteenth century. It contains a new type of legend about the rabbis of the Talmud, who are portrayed as Kabbalistic mystics. An example is a story about Rabbi Eleazar, the son of the chief figure in the *Zohar,* Rabbi

Simeon. Seated with his disciples one day, Eleazar saw a serpent gliding by. He told the serpent to go back, because the man it had come to kill had repented, and ordered it to kill some unrepentant sinner instead. He explained to his disciples that such a messenger of evil can only be turned back by giving him another similar task. He then led his incredulous disciples to a place where they found a dead man lying with the serpent coiled round him and nearby a purse of gold. Along came a sorrowing Jew, saying that his purse had been stolen. It contained gold belonging to a poor man, who was saving it for his daughter's marriage. Eleazar showed him the purse, which he recognized as his own, and he praised Eleazar as a holy saint.

This type of story extols the mystical powers of the rabbis, who are transmuted into Kabbalistic masters, and so the Kabbalists themselves are extolled. Compared with the earlier Talmudic legends, they have a forced, factitious air and they spring from a small sect, rather than from the Jewish community as a whole.

THE HASIDIC MOVEMENT

More authentic folk-products are the legends attached to Hasidism, a movement that arose in Eastern Europe in the eighteenth century. Kabbalism was the chief theoretical influence on it, but it was no longer an esoteric mysticism but a doctrine affecting the whole community, to whom the Hasidic masters, the Zaddikim, brought a universal message. The telling of stories was an important aspect of Hasidism and the huge fund of stories to which the movement gave rise is one of Judaism's greatest religious legacies. Most of them are anecdotes or parables, but some are genuine legends, not merely aggrandizing the various Zaddikim of whom they are told, but illuminating the ideas for which they stood, as filtered through the minds of the people.

The founder of Hasidism, Rabbi Israel Baal-Shem Tov, was the hero of countless legends of healings and other miraculous feats, including walking over a river on his girdle, but there is an earthy quality about the stories that differentiates them from those in the *Zohar*. One tells how the Baal-Shem Tov was riding in a carriage one day, smoking his famous long pipe. Some soldiers riding by snatched the pipe from his mouth and rode away. The rabbi was undisturbed, but after some time he told his servant to ride in the direction the soldiers had taken. He did and found them sitting on their horses by the wayside, fast asleep. He took the pipe back to his master.

A picturesque legend, deriving ultimately from the Talmud but given a special development by the Hasidic story-tellers, is that there are always thirty-six hidden saints in the world. It is their merit which prevents the world from being destroyed. There are many stories of a meeting between one of the Hasidic masters and one of the hidden saints, who shunned all public notice. The concept of the hidden saint acted as a corrective to any tendency of the Zaddikim to take undue pride in their own fame.

However, many legends told of the mystic powers of the Zaddikim, including their ability to read a man's sins in his face or to divine his previous existences (the doctrine of reincarnation being prominent in Hasidism). This type of story was part of Hasidism's legacy from later Kabbalism. The Zaddikim were also credited with powers of exorcism. It was believed that the soul of a dead sinner might invade the body of a living person, and the Zaddikim could expel such a soul and enable it to find rest. These stories have no roots in Talmudic tradition and derive from non-Jewish folklore.

Since the advent of Hasidism, which is still active and still productive of legends, there has been no other Jewish movement providing legends with miraculous content. Legends can occur without such content, however, and tend to develop wherever great men or events occur. Many legends have appeared in such secular movements as Zionism, and while it is the historian's duty to sift fact from fiction, the ineradicable tendency of the human mind to create legends out of a sense of awe and admiration has its own value.

CHAPTER 13

THE ISLAMIC WORLD

The Islamic world extends from Morocco in the west to Indonesia in the east, enclosing an area of some 25 million square kilometres (or 10 million square miles), a population of up to 500 millions, some 35 countries and half a dozen major religious faiths apart from Islam itself. The legends of this vast area include persons, places and narratives whose origins are far earlier than the Islamic era and which therefore cannot be said to be Islamic in the proper sense of the word. An obvious example is the Iranian national epic (see IRAN), which nevertheless impinges on the body of legend to be found in Islamic Iran. To disentangle Islamic from non-Islamic would be a daunting task, and the legends covered here are either current over more than one cultural or political division of the whole Islamic complex, or have in some other way gained an importance that overrides geographical or linguistic barriers. They come primarily from the central linguistic areas of Arabic (including the Arabian peninsula, Iraq, Syria, Lebanon, Jordan, Palestine, Egypt and North Africa), Persian (Iran, Afghanistan, Tajikistan) and Turkish (Turkey, some of the Caucasian lands and certain of the Central Asian countries, such as Turkmenistan and Uzbekistan).

The one common heritage that is shared by all the Islamic countries is the Koran, the Word of God revealed to the Prophet Muhammad during the early years of the seventh century AD. Many of the figures who appear in the Koran are those already known to the Judaeo-Christian world through the Old and New Testaments (although some elements can be seen to have come from apocryphal works), but even to these the Koran, and still more its Muslim commentators, have given a special Islamic colouring. The story of Adam is an example.

God creating Adam (page 114)

THE LEGEND OF ADAM

According to Islamic legend, God moulded Adam's body from dust of many colours from different parts of the earth. The lifeless mould lay for 120 years between Mecca and Taif, and during this period an angel, later known as Iblis or Satan, crept into it and left a black spot. Then God breathed his Holy Spirit into the body, brought Adam to life and set him above all the angels. Only Iblis refused to bow down before him, and was expelled from Paradise.

The story of the temptation follows in outline the biblical version, but with elaborations. For example, Paradise is said to have been guarded by the peacock, to whom Iblis, seeking entry in order to take his revenge on Adam, offered to teach the spell granting eternal life. The peacock consulted the serpent, who contrived to take Iblis into the Garden of Eden in his mouth. When the sin of Adam and Eve was discovered, their shell-like covering dropped away, except for their finger-nails and toe-nails. After the expulsion Adam fell to earth on Mount Sarandib (Adam's Peak in Sri Lanka), where his footprint can still be seen on a rock. It was the highest mountain on earth, and Adam was originally so tall that his head reached the first heaven, the sun burned off his hair, and he talked with the angels. Then God reduced his height to 60 cubits (roughly 30 metres or 100 feet), or some say 60 leagues. Eve fell at Jedda in Arabia, Iblis at Multan in India, the serpent at Isfahan in Iran, and the peacock in India.

Adam lived for 200 to 300 years at Sarandib, where the angel Gabriel taught him farming, spinning and weaving, mining, medicine, music and geometry. Finally God accepted his repentance, made a covenant with him, and sent him to Mecca, where he had set up for Adam a house (the Ka'ba) carved out of a ruby, into which was set a white stone. There he was reunited with Eve.

ABRAHAM AND ISHMAEL

After Adam's death God continued to send prophets to guide men into the right path. Their names and numbers vary in different traditions — some say there were as many as 72 000 — but Seth, Idris (Enoch) and Noah are included in all lists. Among those peculiar to Muslim tradition is Salih, who was sent to the people of Thamud. Salih was challenged by the idolaters to prove the omnipotence of his God by producing a red pregnant camel from a rock, a miracle that God performed for him. The camel lived for thirty years as protector of Salih and his people, but was then killed by certain members of the tribe, while its foal was pursued in vain to the top of a mountain where it disappeared. Thereafter, God, having warned Salih to escape, destroyed the people of Thamud in an earthquake.

The next major prophet brings us back to the Bible story. Abraham was born in the days of the tyrannical King Nimrod, who had been warned by an astrologer that he would be destroyed by a boy to be born during a certain year. Nimrod gave orders for all new-born boys to be killed, to the number of 100 000, and decreed that all the men should immediately leave the city, leaving the women behind. However his vizier Azar returned to the city for some purpose, and there saw Nuna (Usha), by whom 'his passion was inflamed'. When Abraham was born, Nuna hid him in a cave outside the city. He sucked milk from one finger, and honey from another, and grew as much in one day as a normal child in one month. After fifteen years in hiding, Abraham came out of the cave and saw in turn Venus, the moon and the sun, each of whom he thought to be his Lord, until they set. At last he recognized the True God, and went to the city, where he preached against the idols. Nimrod had him hurled into a great fire; but on looking down from his palace wall, he saw that the fire had turned cold, and that Abraham was sitting in the midst of a garden talking with an angel.

After defeating Nimrod's army with the aid of a swarm of mosquitoes, Abraham left the city, and his various adventures – the affair of Sarah and the Pharaoh of Egypt, the story of Lot and the Cities of the Plain – are much as in the Bible. Islamic tradition is more interested in the destiny of Hagar, as the mother of Ishmael, the ancestor of the Arabs. Sarah's jealousy of Hagar compelled Abraham to take her and her new-born son to the Meccan desert, where with the help of an angel they discovered the well of Zemzen, round which Mecca was later built. Abraham visited them from time to time, and together they rebuilt the Ka'ba, washed away during the Flood, and replaced in it the original White Stone, now black because of the sins of men who had touched it. In Islamic tradition the sacrifice of Isaac is transferred to the person of Ishmael. Episodes and actions in the story of Hagar and Ishmael are cited as the origin of rituals and ceremonies used in the Pilgrimage to Mecca up to the present day.

THE TWO-HORNED ONE

The mysterious figure of Dhu'l-Qarnain, the Two-Horned One, is mentioned in the Koran without other identification, but is generally assumed to be the same as Alexander the Great. Certainly so much of the widespread Alexander legend, of which versions exist throughout the Islamic world, has been attached to the name of the Two-Horned One, that it would be impossible to disentangle the two. It is interesting that the conqueror, originally cursed in Iranian Zoroastrian tradition as destroyer of the Mazdean faith, had come by Islamic times to be regarded as a chivalrous and heroic figure, possibly because of a desire on the part of the Iranian aristocracy to legitimize his and so their own position by attributing Achaemenid descent to him. To this end it was claimed that Alexander was really the son, not of Philip of Macedon, but of the Persian King Darab, whose half-brother, Dara (Darius III), Alexander subsequently overthrew, marrying his daughter Roushanak (Roxana).

The Islamic Alexander Legend, however, is less concerned with his historical conquest of Persia and overthrow of the Achaemeniads than with what was believed to be his world-wide divine mission to spread acceptance of the One God. In pursuit of this mission he is said to have travelled throughout the world from Spain to China, encountering many wonderful sights and adventures on the way. One Islamic interpolation is the account of his pilgrimage to the Ka'ba at Mecca, but the two most popular episodes concern the building of the wall against Gog and Magog, and the journey through the Land of Darkness to the Spring of Life. The savage people of Gog and Magog descended from Japhet who inhabited a mountainous area to the north. They were said to be two cubits in height (about 1 metre or 3 feet), to go naked, and to have two huge ears, on one of which they slept, using the other for a cover. In response to pleas from the peoples living below them Alexander built a barrier of iron and brass across the gap in the mountains from which they were wont to emerge. It was believed that every night the people of Gog and Magog licked the barrier until it was as thin as an eggshell; they then left it, saying, 'Tomorrow we shall break through!' But because they did not add, 'If God wills!', they found next day that it was as thick as ever. However, they will burst through on the Day of Judgment, drink up all the waters of the Tigris and the Euphrates, and slaughter all the inhabitants of the earth.

Alexander sought to discover the secret of eternal life, and learned from Adam's will that God had created a spring behind Mount Qaf (the mountain barrier surrounding the earth) in the Land of Darkness. Its water was whiter than milk, colder than ice, sweeter than honey, softer than butter, sweeter-smelling than musk. Alexander's army, under the command of his vizier Khidr, marched into the Land of Darkness, taking with them the mares and she-asses and tethering their foals at the edge, so that the mothers would instinctively find their way back to them. Khidr found the spring, washed and drank, and gained eternal life, but when he sought to show Alexander the place, he was unable to find it again. The story of Alexander's journey became a favourite theme of Persian Sufi poetry, his world-wide travels and adventures serving to symbolize the Sufi Path. (Sufism is the mystical tradition of Islam.)

KHIDR AND MOSES

The mysterious Khidr, who drank of the Water of Life and became immortal, is next met in the company of Moses. Sometimes identified with Elias (Elijah) or Jirjis (St George), the name Khidr associates him with the colour green as the Green Man, and it is said that the rock on which he was accustomed to pray turned green.

Moses one day set out to look for Khidr, and was guided to him by a dried fish, brought for his meal, which miraculously came alive when it fell into a stream emanating from the Spring of Life. Khidr agreed rather reluctantly to accept Moses as a pupil, but warned him that he would not have the patience to listen, and that he must on no account question anything that he did. They boarded a boat manned by fishermen, and Khidr knocked a hole in it. They came to a village, and Khidr killed a young boy. At the next village they were refused hospitality, but Khidr nevertheless went out of his way to repair a ruined wall.

Moses could not contain himself any longer, and asked Khidr why he should do these strange actions. Khidr rebuked him and sent him away; but before doing so he explained that a tyrannical king was about to confiscate all sound boats, that the boy was an unbelieving son of pious parents who were destined to have another better one, while the wall concealed a treasure belonging to two orphans for whom it was to be kept safe until they were old enough to take charge of it. In Sufi doctrine Khidr is the embodiment of love and the manifestation of reason. He is Guide to the true Sufi Path, and will often appear to Sufi adepts, either in dreams or in the flesh, to direct them along the way.

KING SOLOMON

The name of Solomon (Sulaiman) is widely revered throughout the Islamic world. God granted him royalty, wisdom and prophecy, and gave him dominion over demons, men, beasts, birds and the wind. He possessed a carpet 500 leagues in length (a league is usually calculated at about 5 kilometres or 3 miles), on which the wind would carry himself and his thousand wives and concubines wherever he wished. The Jinn (beings of fire) were forced to work for him, constructing shrines, palaces, and costly statues and vessels. Among his possessions were a magic mirror in which he could see the whole world, a magic ring inscribed with the Most Great Name of God, and a throne of rubies guarded by four lions and four vultures. He was once deprived of his power for forty days. He used to hand his magic ring for safe-keeping to one of his concubines while he was performing his ablutions. On one occasion a demon named Sakhr assumed his shape and deceived the concubine into giving him the ring, and Solomon was obliged to go down to the sea-shore and work as a fisherman. Meanwhile his ministers soon suspected from the false Solomon's actions that he was not what he appeared to be, and by reciting the Book of God drove him from the throne. Sakhr threw the ring into the sea, and after forty days it was swallowed by a fish, which was caught by Solomon, who was thus enabled to recover his throne.

Solomon's propensity for boasting and the penances inflicted on him by God are illustrated in other stories. Once he was so engrossed in admiring his 1000 horses that he missed the hour of afternoon prayer (it must be remembered that Muslims believe all their religious observances to have been laid down and practised from the beginning, and merely forgotten by those who lapsed from the True Faith, until it was revived by the Seal of the Prophets, Muhammad). In remorse Solomon cut off the horses' heads and limbs or, following a less harsh version, he symbolically sacrificed them and devoted them all to the service of God in war against the infidels. In either event, God accepted his repentance and moved the sun back, so that Solomon could complete his prayers at the right time.

No account of Solomon would be complete without the story of his meeting with Bilqis, the Queen of Sheba. Solomon learned from his messenger, the hoopoe, of Bilqis' beauty, wealth and wisdom, and sent the bird back with a letter summoning the Queen to the worship of the True God. Bilqis replied with presents and questions; Solomon answered the latter with Gabriel's help and rejected the presents. Bilqis, intrigued, decided to visit Solomon. Rumour had it that the Queen, for all her beauty, had hairy legs, and to test the truth of this Solomon had constructed before his palace a pavement of crystal with water flowing beneath. Bilqis thought it was a pool of water, and raised her skirts in order to pass through it. The story about the hair on her legs turned out to be true, but Solomon invented a depilatory (the first ever used), and then married her.

The body of traditon incorporated into Islamic religious legend is drawn mainly from Jewish sources. But Jesus is also recognized as one of the Prophets, and there are many stories told of His miracles.

LEGENDS OF MUHAMMAD

From the beginning of the Islamic era we are dealing with wholly historical characters. This fact has not prevented the growth of legendary and supernatural material around the bare bones of the historical facts, as a look at the traditional accounts of the life of the Prophet himself will show. Coming later in time than any of the other founders of great religions, Muhammad's life was recorded in accurate detail by his followers, and it is this perhaps that accounts for the fact that most of the obviously legendary material is concerned with his early childhood. On the night of his birth, it is said, idols and thrones were overturned, the towers of the Persian emperor's palace and the great arch at Ctesiphon collapsed, the sacred fire in the great Zoroastrian temple in Fars was extinguished, and the lake of Saveh was dried up. His mother was visited by Pharaoh's daughter, Mary the mother of Jesus, and other holy women, who helped with the delivery, while angels washed the baby and wrapped him in silk.

Tradition has it that Muhammad was brought up by a Bedouin foster-mother, and this may well be historically true, for such a practice was common among Arab families of noble descent, such as that into which Muhammad was born. It was during this time, so the story goes, that he experienced the event that was to mark him out for all time as the last and greatest of the prophets. While he was sleeping in the pasture-grounds near Mecca, three angels appeared and proceeded to weigh him against one man, ten, a hundred, a thousand, and finally the whole of mankind. Muhammad outweighed them all, and by this they knew that he was the destined prophet. Then they opened his side and took out his heart, and washed it in a golden bowl so as to remove the black spot placed in all men by Satan. Then with a gold seal-ring they marked him between the shoulders with the seal of prophet-hood.

It was not until the age of forty-eight that Muhammad received, through Gabriel, the first revelation from God (Sura 96 of the Koran), and so started his mission. Since the Prophet was an ordinary human being without any attributes of divinity, orthodox Muslims will not accept the miraculous and supernatural powers that are given to him in popular lore. The story of the Night Journey to Paradise is referred to in one chapter of the Koran (Sura 17, entitled 'The Night Journey'), which says: 'Glory be to Him Who carried His servant by night from the sacred temple to the temple that is more remote...' Whether this refers to an actual journey or to a dream, there is general agreement that the sacred temple is the Ka'ba and the more remote one the temple in Jerusalem (which title indeed it bears to this day). Later pious tradition has expanded this meagre statement to include a journey mounted on a magical winged horse, Buraq, which had the head of a woman and the tail of a peacock, during which Muhammad soared through the seven heavens, received a glimpse of hell, and was finally admitted to the presence of God.

The Hijra or Flight from Mecca to Medina, on the other hand, is of unquestionable historical authenticity, having taken place in AD 622, but tradition has added various miraculous events that facilitated the Prophet's escape from his enemies, including invisibility, the sudden conversion of a pursuer, and the like. On the first night Muhammad and his companion Abu Bakr (later the first Caliph or successor to the Prophet) took refuge in a cave on Mount Thaur. After they had entered, a spider wove its web across the entrance and a pigeon laid its eggs there, while a thornbush sprang up and concealed the opening. At the back of the cave Abu Bakr found a spring of water, 'whiter than milk, colder than snow, and sweeter than honey'. He washed in it, and all the pains of travel were removed. Another version says that a doorway opened at the back of the cave, and through it Abu Bakr saw a great sea and a boat with sails set.

THE DEATH OF HUSAIN

The orthodox Muslim rejection of miracles has not hindered the growth of a great body of supernatural lore around not only the Prophet but also the early Caliphs and other figures of the early Islamic period. Much of it is concerned with the great cleavage in Islam between the Sunnis and the Shi'ites, between the majority who — at least in the early days — believed in the elective principle for the selection of the Prophet's successors, and the minority who held that the divine inspiration passed down the Prophet's line through his daughter Fatima and her husband, Muhammad's cousin Ali. The events of this tragic split in the unity of Islam are commemorated in Shi'ite countries up to the present day, often in the form of dramatized re-enactments. The central episode around which these plays are grouped is the martyrdom of the Prophet's grandson Husain. In 680 Husain was invited by a group of supporters in Kufa to join them with a view to challenging the legitimacy of the Damascus Caliph, Yazid. But on his arrival in Iraq he found that the promised support did not exist, and most of his followers melted away. Meanwhile Yazid ordered the Syrian troops in Iraq to prevent Husain from reaching Kufa, and finally to bring him dead or alive to Damascus. The little band was surrounded on the plain of Kerbela and massacred one by one, and the women and children taken captive to Damascus.

Around this simple framework have been woven elaborations ranging from the factual to the fanciful and the miraculous. Typical episodes tell of the martyrdom of Husain's companions and relations, of which one of the most moving is the wedding on the field of battle of Husain's daughter Fatima to her cousin Qasim, who was immediately afterwards killed in battle. Another martyr was Husain's brother Abbas, whose hand was cut off during the fighting, a tragedy symbolized by the 'hand of Abbas' over many Shi'ite mosques, shrines and processions in Iran and elsewhere. An angel Futrus (Peter?), and Ja'far, son of Za'far, King of the Jinn (beings of fire), both offered their services, but Husain rejected such celestial aid, for it was his destiny to be sacrificed for the redemption of the whole Islamic community — an important Shi'ite doctrine entirely alien to Sunnism.

A constant theme of the plays is the cruelty and harshness of the Syrian troops. Their leaders, the Caliph Yazid, the governor of Iraq Ubaidallah, the commander of the army at Kerbela Omar ibn Sa'd, and above all the infamous Shimr, the actual killer of Husain, are painted in the blackest colours. For the Iranians, however, another element in the story is of equal importance. Husain's wife, generally known as Umm Laila, is held to have been Shahrbanu, daughter of the last Sasanid monarch of Iran, Yezdegerd III. Her surviving son, Ali Zainalabedin, who was too ill to participate in the fighting, continued the line of Imams, descendants of the Prophet, from whom the legitimacy of the Shi'ite hierarchy is derived. By linking his mother to the deposed Iranian royal house, the two hereditary principles of divine inspiration and royal aura are combined. After the battle, it is said that Husain's spirit sent his blood-stained horse back to the tents, where Shahrbanu mounted it and, aided by her husband's ghost, escaped from the field and hid in a cave at Rayy, near the present-day Tehran. There she was found by her brother and taken to safety.

SUFI SAINTS

Another major strand in the religious life of Islam is Sufism, whose hagiology provides many examples of saints with abnormal and even supernatural powers. Among these one of the most interesting is Ibrahim son of Adham, who was said to have been King of Balkh and a ruler of immense wealth and power. One night he heard a man walking on the roof of his palace, who on being challenged said that he was looking for his camel. 'Fool!' retorted the king, 'do you expect to find a camel on the roof?' 'Heedless one!' replied the man, 'do you expect to find God by wearing silken clothes and lying on a golden couch?' After other mysterious warnings the secrets of heaven were opened to Ibrahim, he threw off his jewelled robes and took up the life of a wandering beggar, learning many secrets from the immortal Khidr and performing wonders and miracles.

The theme of the king who abandons his throne in order to become a mendicant preacher is identical with the story of the Buddha, and some scholars have identified Ibrahim with him. But the Buddha story is also found in Islamic tradition, and indeed in the West, as the story of Barlaam and Josaphat (the latter name being derived by a distortion of spelling from Budasaf = Bodhisattva). In this version a king of India, wishing to conceal from his son the facts of human misery, confined him in a palace where he would see neither poverty, nor sickness, neither old age nor death. But by chance some of this was revealed to him, and an ascetic, Bilauhar (= Barlaam), completed his conversion. In spite of his father's efforts to lure him back, he renounced his throne and followed the path of holiness and asceticism for the rest of his life.

Hasan of Basra, by trade a jeweller, is known to have lived from 642 to 728, and after a religious experience gave up his occupation and became one of the founders of Islamic Sufism. Among the many stories about him, one tells how he tried to persuade Simeon, a Zoroastrian neighbour on his deathbed, to accept Islam. Simeon was put off by the daily sight of Muslims engaged in worldly pursuits, but Hasan convinced him that, while they would all go to hell, Simeon's life-long worship of fire would avail him nothing against hell-fire, whereas God could ordain that Muslims would be unharmed. And to prove his point he placed his hand in the fire, and it was unharmed. Simeon agreed to become a Muslim if Hasan would give him a witnessed document that God would not punish him. He was buried with the paper in his hand, and that night Hasan dreamt that he saw Simeon in Paradise. 'God has greatly favoured me,' he said, 'and so I have no further need of your paper.' When Hasan woke, he found the paper in his hand. 'O God!' he exclaimed, 'you have admitted to Your presence a fire-worshipper of seventy years because he uttered a single phrase of submission at the end of his life. How then can You exclude me, a believer for seventy years?'

TALES OF KINGS

Islamic legend is not concerned solely with religious traditions, and there is a considerable body of secular literature. Some of this centres round historical figures, rulers like the Sasanid King Anushirvan the Just, the Caliph Harun al-Rashid, or the Safavid monarch Shah Abbas. Indeed it is not unusual to find essentially the same stories told about more than one of these, always designed to emphasize the ruler's justice and concern for the well-being of his people. Of Anushirvan it was said that there was a chain hanging outside his palace, and a petitioner had only to pull on this and his plea would be heard personally by the King. One day the chain was heard to jangle, but there was no one outside. The chain jangled again, and a third time, and it was then observed that a donkey was rubbing against it. Anushirvan ordered the case to be investigated, and it was found that the donkey was indeed being maltreated by its owner, who was duly punished by the justice-loving monarch.

The Arabian Nights stories, which show Harun roaming Baghdad at night in disguise in order to ensure the well-being of his people, are typical of another group in this category. Of a somewhat different character is the legend of the Sasanid King Khosrou Parviz, his love for the Armenian Princess Shirin, and his rivalry with the engineer Farhad, whom he exiled by commissioning him to cut a passage through the mountains at Bisitum in north-west Iran and whom he finally drove to suicide by sending him false news of Shirin's death. There are other romantic epics of this character woven around the names of kings — Bahram and the Seven Princesses, Shiruya, Mahmud and Ayyaz, to mention only a few. Most of these have no more than the slenderest historical basis.

ANTAR AND ABLA

Perhaps more nearly historical are the tribal histories, of which that of the Bani Hilal is well-known and typical. Even here, strict history seems to have been distorted by the need to weave the story around the person of a hero, in this case one Barakat, known as Abu Zaid, the swarthy and ill-favoured son of the Amir Rizq, who refused to acknowledge him and sent him and his mother away in disgust. The whole story is immensely long and complex, and involves the migration of the tribe from Arabia to Tunis, with numerous adventures on the way, in all of which Abu Zaid plays an active and heroic part, figuring as the saviour of the tribe on many occasions until he finally gains the chieftainship.

Rather similar, but with probably a greater admixture of fiction, is the legend of Antar. That there was such a person seems probable, for we have a famous poem by one Antara which was among those hung in pre-Islamic times in the Ka'ba, and this even mentions the name of Antar's beloved Abla. Like Abu Zaid, Antar was black and ugly; he early showed signs of exceptional strength and heroism, fighting successfully with a dog and a wolf while yet in his cradle. Later he fell in love with his cousin Abla, but her parents refused the match because he was the son of a slave-woman. In spite of his heroic deeds, aided by his horse Abjar and his sword Dhami (we repeatedly meet such descriptions as 'Antar's sword split his vizor in twain, and it penetrated even to his thighs, down to the back of the horse; and the rider and the horse fell in four parts'), Abla's father refused to change his mind, and contracted Abla to another. The story continues in this vein, with kidnappings, rescues, betrothals and counter-betrothals, rivalries, battles and raids, until at last Antar and Abla are united. The whole story is a blend of pre-Islamic legend, Islamic elements, Iranian epic, and even in some places hints of the Crusades. Another epic in the same vein is the story of Saif son of Dhu Yazan, which symbolizes the struggle between the pagan Arabs and the Ethiopians, but with an admixture of Islamic elements, even though the story is set in pre-Islamic times. Both these epics, though they have been written down, have been preserved primarily in oral tradition.

THE SON OF THE BLIND MAN

In the northern belt of the Islamic world, stretching from Central Asia to Anatolia, the popular hero is a Robin Hood-like character known as Kuroghli, the Son of the Blind Man. It is said that there actually was a seventeenth-century brigand of that name in Khorasan. According to the legend, he was the leader of a band of 777 brigands known as Dali (mad), whose headquarters was a mountain fortress called Chamli Bil. From this vantage-point he engaged in many daring exploits, aided by his wonderful horse Qirat and his companions Ayvaz, son of a butcher, Demircioghli, Dali Mehtar, and many others. The stories in the cycle tell of his fights with his enemies, robbing of caravans, kidnapping of beautiful women; all of them emphasize his recklessness and courage, his generosity, and his enormous appetite and capacity for wine. He is often depicted in the guise of a guitar-playing *ashiq* (minstrel), a device that enables the story-teller to introduce poetry and song into his narration.

Like many other legends, the Kuroghli cycle is still very much alive and open to topical modification and embellishment. In one Central Asian version with an Islamic colouring Kuroghli is said to enjoy the special protection of Khidr, and even to be a reincarnation of the Prophet's son-in-law Ali. During the 1920s episodes were added against the background of the Basmachi movement, the anti-Soviet rising briefly active in the Turkish-speaking parts of Central Asia after the 1916 Revolution. Generally speaking Kuroghli is the type of the noble and generous rebel, enemy of the rich, protector of the poor, and challenger of authority.

HATIM THE GENEROUS

A rather different personality who is at the centre of another cycle of tales is Hatim, said to have been chief of the Arabian tribe of Tai during the sixth century AD. Indeed there is a well-attested story of the Prophet Muhammad's kindness to his son and daughter, which seems to set him in a historical context. Nevertheless Hatim became a figure proverbial for generosity. It was said that as a baby he would refuse to suck his mother's breast unless another child was fed at the other breast at the same time. By contrast, his younger brother would keep his hand on her other breast to prevent any other child from sharing her milk. On one occasion the Emperor of Byzantium sent an envoy to purchase from Hatim his favourite horse. Hatim, having no other means of entertainment and without waiting to hear the purpose of his visitor's mission, slaughtered the horse to provide a banquet.

In Iran Hatim is the central figure in a cycle of romantic adventure stories which have little direct bearing on the theme of generosity, except to the extent that Hatim generously volunteered to help a young suitor for the hand of a beautiful girl, who had stipulated that she would marry only the man who successfully carried out seven quests. Hatim carried out the quests, which led him into all kinds of dangerous situations, having first secured the girl's agreement that, if he were successful, he might bestow her on whom he wished.

CHAPTER 14

IRAN

As in many other countries and cultures, the ancient Iranian legends were handed on by word of mouth long before they came to be written down. Many of them are the products of court poetry, extolling the magnificence of monarchs and the prowess of warriors. The interpreter of the past and commentator on the present in ancient Iran was not a scholar writing in his study but the minstrel who entertained king and commoners alike. There was evidently a body of tradition which the minstrels passed on and to which the best of each generation added. What has survived the ravages of time and Muslim persecution is the material which the priests incorporated into the written religious tradition, and the stories that were blended into the great national epic, the *Shahname*. Most of the legends, consequently, have either a religious or a national theme.

CYRUS THE GREAT

Royal legends served to idealize great kings and to support the authority of the crown, and one figure around whom legend grew was Cyrus the Great, the founder of the Achaemenid Empire, who ruled from 549 to 530 B C. He came from the tribe of the Persians in the south-west. He first subdued the various other tribes in Iran, including the Medes who dominated most of the west, and united the country under a single authority for the first time. He than extended his influence east to India and west through Babylon to Asia Minor, and was remembered not only by Iranians but by other subject peoples as a model ruler.

The legends about him have come to us mainly from Greek sources. Herodotus, 'the father of history', who lived in Asia Minor in the fifth century B C and was technically a Persian subject, tells an

Rustom chasing Akvan – disguised as a wild ass (page 133)

interesting story about the boyhood of the future emperor. His mother, Mandane, was the daughter of a Median King, Astyages, who married her to a Persian of good family named Cambyses. When Mandane became pregnant, Astyages dreamed that a vine grew from her genitals and spread over Asia. He consulted the priests, who interpreted the dream to mean that his daughter would bear a son who would usurp his throne. When the boy was born, Astyages gave him to his trusted kinsman Harpagus, telling him to take the child home with him and kill him.

Harpagus took the child home, but could not bring himself to carry out the murder. He gave the baby to a herdsman named Mitradates and ordered him to leave the child to die in the mountains. Mitradates realized who the child was and at the entreaty of his wife, Cyno, he kept the baby at home and exposed the body of his own child, who had been born dead that day. Cyrus was brought up by Mitradates and Cyno but when he was ten years old his true identity was discovered. One day he was playing at being a king with the village children and he had the son of a noble Mede whipped for disobedience. The story reached the ears of Astyages, who sent for Cyrus and demanded why he had impudently mistreated the son of a distinguished citizen. Cyrus retorted with such authority that the boy merited punishment for disobeying a king that Astyages guessed who he was.

Astyages extracted the truth from the herdsman and confronted Harpagus with it, to the astonishment of Harpagus, who believed that the Prince was dead. The King, then had Harpagus' thirteen-year-old son butchered. His flesh was roasted and served up to his unwitting father at a feast. It was only when the boy's head, hands and feet were shown to Harpagus on a silver dish that he realized how the King had punished him for his disobedience.

Astyages then turned his attention to Cyrus, but the priests said that because the dream had been fulfilled when Cyrus took the role of king in the children's game, Astyages need have no fear of him. The King thus felt secure and sent the Prince to his parents (Mandane and Cambyses) in Persia. According to Herodotus, when Cyrus explained to them how he had been saved by Mitradates and Cyno, the name Cyno, which means 'bitch', suggested to them a way of creating a legend about the miraculous preservation of their son. They set the story going that a bitch had found him in the mountains and had suckled him.

THE DEEDS OF ARDASHIR

Stories of this kind are told about great kings and prophets all over the world, and the motif of the dream is meant to imply that God or the mysterious power of fate was at work in Cyrus's rise to power. The story appears to have influenced legends about more than one subsequent Iranian king, including Ardashir, the founder of the Sasanian Empire. The Achaemenid Empire was brought to an end by the invasion of Alexander the Great in 331 BC. Alexander was succeeded by a Greek dynasty, the Seleucids, but this period of foreign domination did not last long. By the next century a Parthian dynasty from the north-east of Iran had begun to emerge and their rule lasted until the third century of the Christian era, when they were overthrown by Ardashir, who was a Persian.

Ardashir wished to give his successful rebellion an aura of respectability. He presented it to his contemporaries and to posterity as a divinely ordained reassertion of the traditional Persian culture of the Achaemenids. He had a relief carved at the sacred Achaemenid site of Naqsh-i Rustam, showing God bestowing the kingship on him and representing his defeat of the Parthian King as the triumph of good over evil. The same point is made in a legend, surviving in the *Karnarmag-i-Ardashir* (the Book of the Deeds of Ardashir).

In this story Ardashir is the son of a Persian shepherd, Sasan, who is descended from the last Achaemenid King, Darius III. His future greatness is foretold in dreams. He is brought up in obscurity, but his precocious brilliance attracts the attention of the Parthian King, Shah Ardaban, who invites him to court. There Ardashir's skill at polo, chess, riding and in battle arouses the jealousy of the Parthian Crown Prince, who has him unfairly excluded from the royal hunt. Shah Ardaban's favourite maiden now falls passionately in love with Ardashir and spends her nights with him after the Shah has fallen asleep. She presently tells him that the court astrologers have predicted from the stars the rise of a new ruler and that any male court attendant who flees from the Shah in the next three days will achieve victory, greatness and kingship. At this Ardashir promptly leaves court with the girl and they ride away to Persia.

Ardaban, mindful of the predictions, gives chase, enquiring of villagers on the way for news of the fugitives. He is told that they have been seen passing through like a violent wind and followed by a large, swift ram. A priest tells Ardaban that the ram is the symbol of the royal Iranian glory. The Shah now gathers an army against Ardashir, but the outcome of the struggle is inevitable, because Ardashir has the royal glory with him. Thus the new Sasanian dynasty is founded, named after Ardashir's father.

This legend obviously contains little accurate historical detail about the Sasanian rebellion, but by the use of such motifs as the prophetic dreams, the astrologers' predictions and the symbol of the ram the story is used to convey the propaganda that Ardashir's rise to power was 'written in the stars' and inspired and supported by God. There are other versions of the emergence of the Sasanians, including a more prosaic official one given in royal inscriptions, but this legendary account was the popular form transmitted by the minstrels and thereby incorporated in the national epic tradition.

VIS AND RAMIN

Not all royal legends have political implications. The romance *Visramiani,* the story of Vis and Ramin, has all the marks of a popular tale often and lovingly told by minstrels. It opens with Shah Mobad's magnificent celebration of the New Year feast. Among the women present was Shahro, a lady of some years, but whose beauty could still turn men's heads. Shah Mobad was so impressed that he made her swear an oath to marry her daughter to him, for he believed that the fruit would be like the seed. As Shahro had no daughter and at her age did not expect to have one, she agreed. Years later, however, she gave birth to a daughter, Vis.

Shahro had forgotten the oath. She decided that no man in the world was fit for her daughter except her own son, so she married them. While the wedding was being celebrated, a messenger came from the Shah, demanding the hand of Shahro's daughter. Shahro was distraught that she had forgotten her oath and Vis was outraged that she had lost her brother and husband even before the marriage had been consummated. Wagon trains of treasure failed to soften Vis's feelings against the love-sick Mobad, who took her to his palace, where he was 'as merry as a hungry lion which is set to guard a herd of wild asses', but the grieving Vis became as thin as a needle and as yellow as saffron. She persuaded her nurse, who had tended her from childhood, to use sorcery to bind the Shah's virility. The nurse did, making a talisman and hiding it for a month as a temporary measure, but a flood washed the magic charm away. Mobad's virility was now bound for all time, and Vis, though twice married, remained a virgin.

The handsome young brother of the Shah, Ramin, had been burning with passion for the Queen from the first day he saw her. After much pleading, he persuaded the nurse to convey his ardent love to the Queen, but she was as virtuous as she was beautiful and rebuffed his advances. The old nurse now again used her magic, but this time to entice the Queen to find excitement in the person and ardour of the Prince. So at last, when Shah Mobad was away, the nurse showed Ramin to the Queen's bedchamber. 'Then they lay down together, they spoke to each other of grief past and of joy. In the pleasures of love Vis lay on her side like the chief among sovereigns, and Ramin, like the sun and moon, embraced her neck. If angels had seen, surely they would not have perceived which was fairer, nor whether one or two lay there. Their couch was filled with roses and jewels...'

Mobad subsequently learned that his brother and his wife were deceiving him. Over the years he alternated between moods of rage and forgiveness, revenge and kindness, as Vis and Ramin, despite their protestations of repentance, were carried away by their ardour and consummated their passion whenever the Shah was away. Although Mobad's love for his brother kept his wrath in check, the situation was obviously dangerous and a friend of Ramin's urged him to go away, far from court, and find a new mistress. Ramin took this advice and on his travels fell deeply in love with 'a maid like the sun'. Her name was Gul. 'In form and beauty she was without blemish. She was flower of the spring, gladdening the heart, scattering grief; a doer of righteousness, a ravisher of the heart in a moment, sovereign of beauties, skilfully attracting youth.'

Ramin and Gul were married, and Ramin wrote to Vis saying that he was weary of her. Vis was heartbroken, but in time Ramin grew tired of Gul. He left his wife, to whom he had promised a lifetime's devotion, and returned to Vis. At her instigation he plotted to overthrow his brother, Mobad. Ramin raised an army, but the night before the decisive battle a boar ran amok in the royal camp and gored Mobad to death. Ramin consequently came to the throne without having to kill his brother. He now married Vis and they lived together happily as King and Queen for eighty-three years.

Visramiani is not a legend of political significance or religious concern, but a story of true love following a path that does not run smooth. Both lovers act dishonourably and their faults and faithlessness are openly pilloried, but in the end, like all good love-stories, it is a tale with a happy ending. Behind the plot lies a strong sense of fate. The lovers frequently cry out that their fate is black and wretched, and the narrator interjects similar reflections. 'However much one may try Fate, it is always thus, that its joy is not without pain. Its rose is thorny and its joy is troublous; love is mischance and its profit is loss.' It is because Vis and Ramin are seen as helpless in the grip of fate that their faithlessness is not so damnable. They are imprisoned in a situation of misery throughout much of the story.

'THE BOOK OF KINGS'

The minstrels of ancient Iran blended the religious and the secular, local and national, eastern and western Iranian traditions in their stories. During the Sasanian period the medley of epics and sagas was welded into a national legend, a work carried out mainly by the learned class, the priests, which gave the whole something of a religious hue. The major Sasanian production of this kind, the *Khwaday Namag,* has not survived, but it and and other lost works were synthesized and given an artistic unity in the *Shahname* (the Book of Kings). This epic poem tells the story of Iran and her monarchs from the creation of the world down to the Muslim invasion in the year 636. It was completed early in the eleventh century by an author who took the poetic pseudonym of Firdausi, 'the Paradisal'. He was formally a Muslim, but his religion sat rather lightly on him and he was a more fervent supporter of his nation than of Islam. What appealed to him was the courage and loyalty of a hero in defence of the national glory and the royal crown, in battles against enemies within and without, particularly in the shape of the great national foe, Turan, to the north.

The content of the *Shahname* can be conveniently divided into four parts: the early chapters transform the Zoroastrian myths of creation and primordial time into a legendary account of the earliest phase of the world; second, a variety of legends from different Iranian tribal traditions is woven into an unhistorical but popular account of the nation's history; third comes a brief account of the Achaemenid and Parthian empires; fourth is the lengthy and lovingly told story of the Sasanians. It is the first two parts which are of most interest here, but as they occupy many volumes, this account of them is necessarily highly selective.

THE EARLIEST TIMES

In the *Shahname* the first man of Zoroastrian mythology, Gayomard, becomes the first King. He is said to have ruled benevolently from his mountain-throne for thirty years and to have begun the process of introducing civilization. In the reigns of his sons metals were discovered, fire was first produced and worshipped, animals were tamed and demons subjugated. The fourth King, Jamshid, is considered to be the prototype of all good kings, at least in his early days. He organized society by instituting what Iranians regard as the four basic classes of men, under the king – priests, warriors, scribes and artisans. The demons he set to labour under men. Thus was order imposed at all levels.

Jamshid also found new metals, new lands, and drugs to give men health. His throne was glorious, like the sun, and because of his magnificence the famous Achaemenid palace of Persepolis is popularly known as 'the throne of Jamshid'. But his is a sad case of 'how are the mighty fallen'. He became puffed up with pride and set himself up as God, demanding that the people worship him as the Creator. As he demanded this, the halo of sovereignty left him.

THE DRAGON KING

The story now turns from Iran, where all these Kings had lived, to the court of an Arab Prince, Merdas. He had a son named Zahhak (from the Zoroastrian demonic figure, Azi Dahaka). Zahhak was a youth of high courage, swift in action and bold, until one day the Devil appeared at court, in the guise of an old man, and led the young prince astray. Under this evil influence Zahhak killed his own father and took his crown. The Devil disguised himself as a cook and led Zahhak into eating meat, and so into the sin of taking animal life. With deceitful flattery the 'cook' asked to kiss the shoulders of the mighty Prince. To Zahhak's horror and shame, two black snakes grew from his shoulders and thereafter needed human brains each day for their food.

As Jamshid's glory diminished in Iran, so Zahhak's might grew, and the Iranian nobles came to seek his protection for their land. Zahak, the 'Dragon King', journeyed as swift as the wind, took the Iranian crown and had Jamshid sawn in two. He then ruled for 1000 years in the land of the Shahs, 1000 years of oppression, when virtue was humiliated, sorcery esteemed, truth hid itself and evil flourished.

Zahhak foresaw his overthrow by the great hero Faridun and to prevent this he raised an enormous demonic army and issued a proclamation affirming his regal virtue. None dared deny or oppose him, until a humble blacksmith named Kava came to press his case at court for the release of his wrongly imprisoned son, declaring, 'Although you have a dragon's form, you are the King and it is your duty to let me have justice in this thing' (an interesting reflection of what Iranians consider any king's duty to be). Zahhak recognized the justice of the case and released the blacksmith's son, but in return asked him to sign the proclamation. The brave and righteous blacksmith refused and damned the nobles for agreeing to the proclamation. He gathered an army for Faridun from the market-place and made for him an ox-headed mace, the hero's traditional weapon, which is still to this day the Zoroastrian symbol of the priesthood. Eventually, Faridun and Zahhak fought in single combat in the Dragon King's palace in Jerusalem. The hero advanced upon Zahhak with the speed of a storm and dealt him a blow with the mace that shattered his helmet. An angel warned Faridun that Zahhak's time was not yet come and he must not be killed, so Faridun bound him in a cave on Mount Demavend and ascended the throne himself.

Already, the duty of the King is made clear. He must provide for the physical needs of his subjects. He should establish order in society and keep evil forces in subjection, and he should give justice to all, however lowly, but he is not to think of himself as a god. There is also an insight into the Iranian view of their own land and of other races. The first kings were universal monarchs, ruling all men without division into kingdoms. Until Jamshid fell, all ruled from Iran, the centre of the world. The Arabs, who brought to Iran not only Islam but also military defeat and persecution, Firdausi considered to be an honourable race by nature, but perverted by the Devil.

After he had ruled the world well, Faridun divided his global empire between his sons. To the eldest, Salm, he gave the whole of the western world, to the second, Tur, he gave the east, and to the youngest, Eraj, he gave Iran. The older brothers were jealous of Eraj, because he had been given the most treasured of all possessions, and they plotted and carried out his murder. According to Firdausi, this murder of the first Iranian King lies at the heart of all the wars, bitterness and enmity between Iran and her neighbours.

THE VALIANT RUSTOM

It is at this point that some of the diverse tribal legends of ancient heroes are introduced. The most famous of them is Rustom, celebrated in ancient and modern Iran for his courage, strength and loyalty. His exploits are figured in many Persian miniatures and are often on the lips of Iranians, whose staple literary diet has included the *Shahname,* especially in the twentieth century.

The story of Rustom begins with his father, Zal. Zal was rejected at birth by his own father because he had white hair, which was interpreted to mean that he was the progeny of the Devil. The infant Zal was therefore left in the open to die, but the Simurgh bird, a popular mythological figure in Iran, carried him to her nest and there reared him into a goodly youth. When Zal's father heard of this, he recovered his son from the Simurgh. Later, when Zal was travelling in the east, he fell in love with, and married, a princess from Kabul. When she conceived, it was discovered that she was descended from the evil Zahhak, which meant that the delivery of the child would be attended with great danger. Zal sought the aid of the Simurgh, who declared: 'The child will not come into existence by the ordinary birth. Bring me a poniard of tempered steel and a man of percipient heart versed in incantation. Let the girl be given a drug to stupefy her and to dull fear or anxiety in her mind; then keep guard while the clairvoyant recites his incantations and so watch until the lion boy leaves the vessel which contains him. The wizard will pierce the frame of the young woman without her awareness of any pain and will draw the lion child out of her, covering her flank with blood, and will sew together the part he has cut.'

When Rustom was born, in this manner, he needed ten foster-mothers to nourish him, and when he was weaned, he ate as much as five children. He grew to the height of eight men, as tall as a noble cypress. One of his most famous exploits was his first. The King's white elephant ran amok, killing several men. The sleeping Rustom was awakened by the shouting. Grasping his father's ox-headed mace, he knocked the head off a gateman who tried to block his way and ran out to confront the wild beast. It was raging like the Nile in flood, but Rustom, roaring like a lion, attacked it fearlessly and killed it with one blow of his mace.

The mighty hero's strength was destined for a lifetime's service to his nation. As he told his father: 'I am not the man for luxury and wine-cups. These shoulders and these long fingers did not win their strength for a career of ease... when I cover my breast with armour the world will have reason to fear my quiverful... when my lance goes into battle, even a stone will have its heart drenched in blood.' With his horse Raksh, whose strength was that of an elephant, whose speed equalled that of any racing camel, and who was a lion for courage, Rustom was the ideal Iranian warrior, fighting in support of King and Country. Among his numerous heroic feats, he overcame a ferocious lion, travelled across a poison-aired and waterless desert, fought a dragon and killed a sorceress and a Great White Demon.

In one battle the warrior ruler of Bidad, Kafur, whose food was the flesh of children, led the assault on the Iranian forces. He let fly a sword at Rustom as if it was an arrow, but Rustom warded it off with his shield. Then Rustom dodged Kafur's lasso and struck Kafur a blow which crushed his head, his helmet and his shoulders together, so that his brains gushed out of his nostrils.

One of Rustom's most famous fights was with the demon Akvan, who had taken the form of an onager (wild ass). The 'elephant-bodied hero' set off in chase, but each time he slung an arrow to shoot the onager it vanished. After a pursuit of a day and a night, Rustom lay down by a stream and fell asleep. Akvan now changed himself into a storm-wind, approached the hero and dug up the earth all around him, raising him on this bed of earth to the skies. On waking, Rustom was afraid. Tauntingly the demon asked him whether he preferred to be thrown into the sea or onto a mountain. Realizing that Akvan would do the opposite of what he asked, Rustom chose the mountain, at which the demon threw him into the sea. While falling towards the ocean, the hero drew his sword and when he landed in the water he swam with his left arm and leg, while fending off the monsters which attacked him. Gaining land, he set off in pursuit of the demon once more, and when he found him, he caught him in his lasso and brought his axe down on the demon's head with the strength of a wild elephant, crushing head, brain and shoulders into one mass.

Rustom eventually died as a result of the intrigues of his own younger brother, who was in league with the King of Kabul. During a hunt, they led Rustom to fall into a concealed pit, filled with sharp knives and pointed sticks. Dying from his wounds, the 'lion-bodied warrior' raised the strength to shoot an arrow with such force that it pierced the tree behind which his murderous brother was hiding and killed him.

In his battles on behalf of the Iranian crown, Rustom is the great example of the fearless courage, resourcefulness, determination and loyalty which all Iranians should show to their monarch. Yet the cycle of Rustom stories fits somewhat uneasily into the *Shahname*. They evidently come from a different tradition from many of the other stories, and Firdausi or his source seems to have welded the extremely popular Rustom legend into a structure where it had no natural place. It is generally thought that Rustom was an East Iranian, or Saka, hero. Whatever his origin his bravery and strength are a legend in Iran.

THE LEGEND OF ZOROASTER

There are a number of Iranian legends about holy men, but none so important as the story of Zoroaster, the great prophet of ancient Iran. There is no doubt that Zoroaster lived (his dates are uncertain, but probably about 1500 BC) but, as in all religions, generations of followers have added to the bare bones of the prophet's story legendary details which stimulate religious emotion and elevate him as the great example for men to follow. The legendary account of Zoroaster's life evidently began to develop before the Achaemenid period, but is mainly elaborated in texts of the tenth and thirteenth centuries.

Zoroaster was a man, not a god, but he was not as other men are. His birth was miraculous; it was part of the divinely ordained plan for history. His coming was foretold to a number of holy beings, first to the archetypal bull, the source of all animal life. The soul of this bull protested to the Creator that it had no protector from the ravages of men. When it was shown the heavenly self of the prophet to come, however, it was content to return to the earth to nourish men. Zoroaster's coming was also foretold to Jamshid.

The divine glory which settled on kings also settled on the prophet. It came from the world of light to the sun, thence to the moon and stars, before descending to Zoroaster's future home. His expectant mother, a virgin who had conceived him through drinking the sacred haoma liquid, was so radiant with the child's glory that her father thought she was bewitched and drove her from home. At Zoroaster's birth the whole of the Good Creation rejoiced. Whereas ordinary children cry, he laughed. The demons were terror-struck. They inspired his father to try to burn the baby on a fire, but the firewood would not light. Then he laid the child in the path of a stampeding herd of cattle, but the leading white bull stood over him to protect him from the others' hooves. Similarly, when the baby was laid in the path of stampeding horses, the leading white stallion stood guard over him. Next he was put in the lair of a she-wolf, but intead of killing the infant the wolf accepted him as one of her cubs and a ewe came to suckle him.

From infancy the child conversed with God and as he grew up he showed the wisdom and devotion which characterized his later mission. Once a priest who worshipped false gods came to the family home and was asked by the prophet's parents to recite prayers before the meal. Zoroaster, being wholly opposed to false religion, objected and incurred the wrath of the old priest — who was struck dead as he left the house.

The young Zoroaster was taught by a wise old man. As a young man he spent days meditating in a desert cave in silent solitude. When he was thirty he had the first of his eight visions, which were spread over a period of ten years. The message he brought to men was at first rejected and the prophet was disconsolate. The demons returned to the offensive and sought to seduce him into worshipping them, but in vain. Zoroaster was resolute in the faith, steadfast in his recital of the prayers and faithful in his practice of the rituals.

At last Zoroaster made his first convert, his cousin. Then, two years later, he visited the court of King Vishtasp. The court was a centre of superstition and magic. For three days Zoroaster disputed with the King's 'wise men' and his perceptive powers were obviously beginning to impress the monarch. Fearing the loss of their prestige and influence, the wicked priests plotted against Zoroaster and had him imprisoned on a charge of necromancy. While the prophet was in prison, the King's favourite horse fell ill and its legs drew up into its body. When all efforts to cure it failed, Zoroaster offered to heal it on four conditions: first, that the King must accept Zoroaster's religion; second, that the war-like Prince, Isfandiyar, must fight for the religion; third, that the Queen must accept the religion; and fourth, that the identity of the plotters must be revealed. As each condition was accepted, so one of the horse's legs was restored, until the animal was perfectly healthy again.

With the royal court converted, Zoroaster's teaching became the religion of the realm, and began its march across continents, and down the centuries. With royal support the heavenly teaching became known and the miraculous powers of the prophet were seen by men. The prophet lived on at court as a royal adviser until he was murdered when he was seventy-seven, killed at the altar by the hand of an invader.

The legend is as popular among Zoroastrians as it has ever been. Zoroaster's mission is seen as the turning-point in history. His birth is regarded as the beginning of the era in which good is triumphant, for with the Good Religion revealed to men the defeat of evil is assured. The point of the legends about the assaults of evil is that the follower of the Good Religion cannot expect the way to be easy. Like the prophet before him, the worshipper should stand fast in the religion, regardless of the trials and temptations that beset him. The troubles of the prophet foreshadow those of his later followers. Like him, they must be courageous, resolute and resolved.

CHAPTER 15

ARMENIA AND GEORGIA

The mighty range of the Caucasus Mountains extends for more than 965 kilometres (or 600 miles), from the Black Sea to the shores of the Caspian. Marking the boundary between Europe and Asia, it serves as a barrier between the world of Russia and the Central Asian steppes to the north and the world of ancient Near Eastern civilizations to the south. This barrier has often been breached, by the migration of barbarian peoples from north to south in ancient times, and again with the Russian conquest of the Caucasus and eastern Armenia in modern times.

Since classical times, the Caucasus and Armenia have been associated with important myths and legends, which have been diffused all over the world. Mount Ararat, some 320 kilometres (or 200 miles) to the south of the Caucasus range, is the legendary resting place of Noah's Ark. Mount Elbruz in the Caucasus, according to one tradition, is the peak on which the Titan Prometheus was fettered. Jason and the Argonauts carried off the Golden Fleece from Colchis, in what is now western Georgia. In the nineteenth century, Charles Kingsley described the awe inspired by the Caucasus Mountains when he voiced the emotions of Jason and his shipmates as they sailed eastwards across the Black Sea and approached the land of Colchis. 'And at day dawn they looked eastward, and midway between the sea and the sky, they saw white snow peaks hanging, glittering sharp and bright above the clouds. And they knew that they were come to Caucasus, at the end of all the earth: Caucasus the highest of all mountains, the father of the rivers of the east.'

Many ancient races and tribes still inhabit the Caucasus and the Armenian plateau of eastern Anatolia. As many as fifty different languages and dialects are spoken in this vast and, in parts, inaccessible region. The most important indigenous literary lan-

King Artashes captures the Princess Satenik (page 138)

guages of the area are Georgian and Armenian, and it is through them that we shall approach the body of legends associated with this historic part of the world.

LEGENDS OF NATIONAL ORIGINS

A series of fascinating legends about ancient Armenia is contained in the history of Armenia by Moses of Khorene, a writer now usually assigned to the eighth century AD. The Armenians call their land Hayastan, and their nation Hayk. Moses tells of the heroic exploits of Hayk, the legendary ancestor of the Armenian people. Hayk was a descendant of Noah's son Japheth. After the destruction of the Tower of Babel, Hayk revolted against the Titan Bel and led his family and followers from Mesopotamia to the north, towards mighty Ararat. On the way, Hayk subdued a mountain district, which he gave as an appanage to his grandson Armenak, son of Cadmus. Later on, he built a village called Haykashen, which means 'built by Hayk'. The Titan Bel then invaded Armenia, and a great battle took place close to the 'salt water lake' — Lake Van. Hayk was a skilled marksman and shot Bel through the chest with an arrow, whereupon Bel's forces fled for their lives.

Moses of Khorene continues his story in detail right up to the fifth century AD. The historical narrative is interspersed with legendary elements of great interest. Georgian chroniclers of medieval times also composed legends about the ancestor of the Georgians, whose name was Kartlos. The Georgians call themselves Kartvelebi and their country Sakartvelo. The figure of Kartlos, a descendant of Noah, is purely imaginary, and he remains rather colourless and conventional.

TALES OF ARMENIAN KINGS

There are some ancient Armenian poems, known as the *Songs of Koghten,* which are fragments of epic sagas celebrating the deeds of Armenian kings, particularly Artashes and his son Artavazd. Artashes (Artaxerxes in Persian, Araxias in Greek) reigned from 190 to 159 BC, and founded the Artaxiad dynasty. One beautiful poetic legend tells of the romance between Artashes and the lovely Princess Satenik, daughter of the King of the Alans, an Iranian people from North Caucasia. Artashes captures Satenik's brother in battle and completely routs the Alan army. The Alans retreat northwards beyond the River Mtkvari (Kura). Satenik comes down to the river bank and calls to the Armenian monarch:

> I appeal to you, O valiant Artashes,
> You who have conquered the brave nation of the Alans.

Come now, listen to the plea of the bright-eyed Princess of the
Alans,

    Send the youth back to us.
It is not fitting for heroes to wreak vengeance
By slaying the sons of other heroes in their wrath;
Still less to keep them as slaves in durance vile,
    Thus starting up a perpetual feud
Between the men of two valiant nations!

The gallant Artashes is smitten with passion for this Princess, as
beautiful as she is wise. But the Alan King rejects his suit, whereupon
Artashes mounts his black charger, crosses the River Kura like
a swift-winged eagle, and lassoes the Alan Princess with his
gold-ringed leather belt. Her resistance is but a token one. Artashes
carries her off in triumph to the Armenian camp and a magnificient
wedding follows. The people sing:

    Golden showers rained down when Artashes became
a bridegroom;
    Showers of pearls rained down when Satenik became a bride.

Five centuries later in Armenian history, comes the story of King
Arshak II and his dauntless consort Queen Parantsem, who reigned
from AD 351 to 367. This was a time of merciless pressure from
the Sasanian dynasty of Persia, headed then by King Shapur II
(309–79), whose ambition was to abolish Armenia's independence
and impose the Zoroastrian religion on a people only recently
converted to Christianity.

    The saga of King Arshak II and his struggle against the Persians for
freedom was made into a magnificent opera by Tigran Chuhajian
(1837–98) and in Soviet times the tale of Arshak II was treated as
a symbolical legend by the ill-fated poet Osip Mandelstam. Mandelstam's adaptation of the legend[1] forms part of his last work to be
published by the Soviet authorities, before the poet's arrest and
subsequent death from starvation and ill treatment in Siberia in 1938.
Into his travel narrative, Mandelstam inserts a fragment rich in
allegory, in which he conjures up the image of King Arshak sitting in
a filthy dungeon in the Persian state prison – the fortress of Aniush,
otherwise known as the Castle of Oblivion – and saying to himself
'...The Assyrian has hold of my heart.' In this allusion to 'the
Assyrian' there is an interesting double allegory. In King Arshak's
despairing mind, the Assyrian represents King Shapur (Shapukh),
latest of a long line of infidel invaders who subjugated Armenia over
the years. But, for Mandelstam, reference to 'the Assyrian' conjured
up the baleful, philistine image of Stalin, the Georgian dictator. This
was a nickname which Mandelstam used repeatedly in his poems, to

Stalin's great irritation — and eventually to Mandelstam's doom.

Later in this same poetic fragment, Mandelstam introduces another episode from the Arshak legend — that of the faithful retainer Drastamat, who seeks out his imprisoned lord and cheers him up with the songs of minstrels, just as Blondel does for Richard the Lion-Hearted some centuries later.

GEORGIAN LEGENDARY HISTORY

In Georgia, the national chronicle known as *Kartlis tskhovreba* (the Life of Georgia) is also replete with legendary episodes. The beginning of royal power in Georgia is connected with the name of Alexander the Great, who never invaded Georgia at all, but who is credited in the Caucasus and Near East with all manner of mighty feats and the construction of famous buildings. Alexander the Great is said to have delegated the administration of Georgia to a tyrannical relative of his named Azon — very likely a confusion with the name Jason, of Argonaut fame. The oppressed Georgians finally revolted under the lead of Parnavaz, a descendant of Kartlos, the ancestor of the Kartvelian or Georgian nation. After expelling Azon and his Greek mercenaries, Parnavaz was — according to the national legend — recognized as legitimate ruler of Georgian Iberia, and set up his capital at Mtskheta on the River Kura. This story relates to the early third century BC, when the Georgian monarchy of Iberia was going through a formative period.

In the early Christian period in Georgia, the outstanding semi-legendary figure is King Vakhtang Gorgaslan (Vakhtang the Wolf-Lion). Vakhtang's reign occupies the second half of the fifth century AD. He was undoubtedly a historical ruler, and he is credited with the establishment of Tiflis (Tbilisi) as capital of Georgia in the year 458. The life of Vakhtang composed in the ninth century by Juansher Juansheriani also ascribes to the monarch many legendary feats of arms, including vast conquests in Byzantium, Iran and Central Asia.

No Georgian sovereign has inspired more legends than Queen Tamar, daughter and co-ruler of King Giorgi III, who reigned on her own from 1184 until her death in 1213. Here again, Tamar was an authentic historical figure. Her valour and beauty kindled the lively imagination of her fellow countrymen. Just as Queen Elizabeth is supposed to have slept in every English mansion existing in the sixteenth century, Queen Tamar is credited with either building or dwelling in every Georgian feudal castle of any importance.

It is an irritating fact that a ballad by Lermontov (1814–41), supported by the musical genius of the composer Balakirev (1837–1910), has created the image of an entirely different and wholly imaginary Tamar figure. This is a kind of 'Tamar–Turandot'

— a royal harlot dwelling in a castle high up in the Caucasus range. She lures in a fresh lover every night and, inevitably, casts her exhausted nocturnal admirer over the cliff as dawn breaks over Mount Kazbek.

LEGENDARY ANCESTRY

The Bagratid dynasty, to which the historical Queen Tamar belonged, created its own legend — that of the family's descent from King David and King Solomon of Israel. The Bagratids, who reigned in both Georgia and Armenia, were really local Caucasian dynasts, hailing from south-western Georgia. To reinforce their claim to kinship with Jesus Christ, through descent from King David, the Georgian Bagratid kings incorporated into their coat of arms David's sling and harp, and the seamless tunic of Christ.

Not to be outdone, the Armenian kings of Vaspurakan (a large area of southern Armenia, around Lake Van) claimed descent from an Assyrian king, Sennacherib. They relied on a passage in the Second Book of Kings (II Kings 19 : 37): 'And it came to pass, as he [Sennacherib] was worshipping in the house of Nisroch his god, that Adrammelech and Sharezer his sons smote him with the sword; and they escaped into the land of Armenia...' The last king of the Ardsruni dynasty of Vaspurakan, during the early years of the eleventh century, actually assumed the name Senekerim, which is the Armenian form of Sennacherib. Even more exotic was the legendary pedigree of the Armenian princely family of the Mamikonians: they affirmed that one of their ancestors was a Chinese prince, and claimed to be related to the Emperors of China.

FETTERED TITANS

The Caucasus is associated with the ancient myth of Prometheus, the fettered demigod, punished by the gods for giving to mortals the secret of divine fire. There is a local Georgian variant of this myth, involving the rather unsympathetic figure of the Titan Amiran, who is a loud-mouthed braggart, eventually chained to a rock by Christ. If Amiran ever gets loose, it will mean the end of the world. The same belief attaches to the legendary Armenian king Artavazd, who is supposed to be chained in a cavern deep inside Mount Ararat.

One might expect to find somewhere in the Caucasus a friendly fettered Titan, whose liberation would benefit mankind instead of destroying it. After all, the archetypal legend of Frederick Barbarossa in his cave points towards universal redemption rather than universal destruction, as the ultimate aim and aspiration of the imprisoned hero.

There is, indeed, a 'benevolent Titan' legend in the Caucasus — in the story of Abrskil, a hero of the Abkhazians, who lived close to the Black Sea in what is now the Abkhazian Autonomous Soviet Socialist Republic. One version of the Abrskil legend depicts him as a friend of the human race, who communicated to mankind the secrets of the heavens, as did Prometheus. When clinging jungle lianas and bracken choke the crops, Abrskil clears the ground for men to cultivate. Abrskil's superhuman powers and his services to mankind arouse the jealousy of Almighty God, who commands angels to chain him in a cavern. A black hound gnaws away at Abrskil's chain, but when the links become as thin as thread, a maiden sitting on guard notifies an evil witch, who reinforces the chain with her magic wand.

If some bold mortal ventures into Abrskil's gloomy cavern, the Titan will cry out: 'Turn back! Only tell me first, do bracken and weeds still grow upon the earth? Are there still brambles and thorn bushes? Do wicked men still oppress the weak?' 'Yes,' the visitor sadly replies. The chain rattles and the hero groans: 'Alas, not yet does happiness reign in my native land, no peace is there yet for man upon the earth.'

SAINTS AND HOLY PERSONAGES

Armenia and Georgia are among the very oldest Christian nations in the world. Armenia was converted to Christianity under King Tiridates III in or about the year 301, and Georgia followed suit during the reign of King Mirian, about 330. Legends of saints and hermits abound in both Armenia and Georgia. In most cases, the saints themselves are authentic personages, but their life stories have been embroidered with picturesque detail.

Pride of place in Armenian national tradition belongs to St Gregory the Illuminator and his successful mission to convert the land to Christianity. Gregory is portrayed as a scion of a Parthian princely family. His father is said to have murdered the father of the Armenian King Tiridates III, about AD 238.

The young Gregory grew up in exile, in Cappadocia, but returned to Armenia towards the end of the third century and began to preach the Gospel. Tiridates identified him, subjected him to gruesome tortures, and cast him into a dungeon where Greogory languished for fifteen years. A charitable widow kept him alive with food.

King Tiridates meanwhile ruled tyrannically at Vagharshapat, where he martyred a group of thirty-seven Christian virgins, who had refused to enter the royal harem. Their leaders, Hripsime and Gaiane, are revered among the chief saints of the Armenian Apostolic Church. By divine retribution, Tiridates was deprived of his reason, and grovelled around on the floor like a wild beast (as did King Nebuchadnezzar in the Old Testament). The King's conversion restored his health and sanity.

What St Gregory is for the Armenians, St Nino represents for the Georgians. The Church of Georgia − unlike that of Armenia − adheres to the Eastern Orthodox family of Churches, which also embraces those of Russia, Greece, Serbia, Bulgaria and Romania.

The story of St Nino, for all its fabulous embellishments, is built on a solid foundation of fact. Our basic knowledge of the saint's life and work is contained in a chapter of the *Church History* composed by Tyrannius Rufinus as early as AD 403 − only two generations after the saint's mission. Although Rufinus does not give the actual name of the apostle of Georgia whom we know as St Nino, his account includes such central episodes of the later Georgian national legend as the miraculous cure of Queen Nana, the eclipse of the sun which envelops the Georgian King, Mirian, and the supernatural erection of the central pillar of the Saint's church at the Georgian capital at Mtskheta.

The Georgian medieval legends of St Nino add several interesting elements, such as a detailed description of the pagan idols, later miraculously destroyed by giant hailstones. There is also a valuable account of the Jewish communities in Georgia, which have long played a significant role in the country's cultural and economic life.

Two centuries after St Nino, a group of missionaries known as the Syrian Fathers introduced the ascetic life into Georgia, and founded several monasteries. Their biographies, partly legendary, were collected and revised by Catholicos Arsenius II of Georgia between 955 and 980, but they go back to a much earlier period.

Pious hermits though they were, these Syrian Fathers were practical social workers and excellent organizers. St Iese of Dsilkani helped his parishioners by diverting the River Ksani to flow through their town and thus improved their water supply. The Fathers − like St Francis of Assisi − were fond of animals. Ioane Zedazneli lived on top of a mountain and made friends with local bears. St Shio employed a tame wolf to guide donkeys bringing supplies to his grotto. St David of Gareja lived in a cave with a dragon in the basement. The dragon killed and ate the saint's tame deer, so God sent down a thunderbolt which burned the dragon to a cinder.

During the Romantic period, in the nineteenth century, the theme of the holy man subjected to irresistible temptation became popular in European literature. There is more than one Caucasian version of this story and the legend was recreated in 1883 by a Georgian poet, Prince Ilia Chavchavadze (1837−1907), in his poem *Gandegili* (The Hermit).[2] The poem tells of a holy ascetic living high up on Mount Kazbek, and how temptation came to him in the shape of a shepherd girl, who seemed to his fevered mind as if endowed with supernatural powers of seduction:

He heard the melody of silver strings;
    As on a lyre, love on his heart did play.

What meant this sweetness hitherto unknown?
　He could not tell this tender feeling's name;
If it was sinful, why was it so like
　Immortal life, his soul's incessant aim?

And so the hermit bends down to embrace the sleeping maiden, when suddenly there is heard an outburst of fiendish mockery as the demon host celebrates the triumph of earthly temptation. The hermit rushes demented from his refuge to wander on the crags. When at last he makes his peace with God, it is to die, and the poem continues:

And there where saints once sang their grateful hymns,
　And glorified God's wondrous works and ways,
There where they offered daily sacrifice
　Of lamentation, love, and prayer, and praise,
There, midst the landslips and the broken stones,
　Only the wind moves to and fro, and sighs.
While, fearful of the mighty thunder-clap,
　Within its lonesome lair the wild beast cries.

DAVID OF SASSOUN

A legend which also ranks as a national epic is that of David of Sassoun, a popular hero of a mountain region in south-western Armenia, now part of Turkey. It is difficult to classify the David of Sassoun stories as ancient, medieval or modern. The action takes place about 1000 years ago, during the period of Saracen domination of Armenia. However, the tales were collected and put into shape by Armenian folklore specialists only towards the end of the nineteenth century. These scholars had to piece the stories together and compose a connected narrative out of dozens of isolated episodes and fragments, handed down orally by village story-tellers.

The ancestor of the mighty heroes of Sassoun is the Lady Dzovinar, who agrees to marry the ninety-year-old Caliph of Baghdad to save her people from annihilation. Dzovinar bears the Caliph twin sons, Sanasar and Balthasar. Sanasar in his turn marries Princess Golden-Braids of the Copper City, and they have three sons. The eldest of them is called Mher or Meherr, which is the Armenian form of the name of the Persian god Mithra. Superhuman powers are attributed to the Great Meherr, recalling those of Mithra himself; Meherr also plants a splendid garden at Dzovasar and founds a hospice for the sick and wounded.

Meherr's legitimate son is David of Sassoun. However, Meherr also goes to Egypt and has a passionate affair with the Egyptian queen − a sultry lady in the tradition of the famous Cleopatra − and they have a son, called Misra Melik, which means 'King of Egypt'. The bitter strife between the two half-brothers is a central feature of the Sassoun saga. Eventually David beats his rival and chops him in half with his sword.

David of Sassoun is generally a benevolent hero, who kills robber demons and punishes greedy tax-gatherers. He helps the ploughmen by ploughing up vast tracts of land single-handed. He is also a great womanizer and makes ardent love to the seductive Chimishkik Sultana, Princess of Akhlat, and to the beautiful Khandut Khanum, Princess of Tabriz.

The last of the Sassoun heroes is Little Meherr, a tragic and mysterious figure. Little Meherr labours under a paternal malediction; he is sterile and cannot produce an heir, and wanders sorrowfully from place to place. Eventually Little Meherr finds refuge inside a crag near Van known as Raven's Rock, or as Mher Kapisi.

With Little Meherr is his magic steed, which had found the soil of the old world too soft and crumbling to support its mighty hooves. Twice a year, the crag splits open and Little Meherr rides forth to see whether the sinful, imperfect world has changed, and can support him and his charger. But soon the horse begins to sink into the yielding surface and Little Meherr hurries back into the safety of his cavern — he can never remain outside for more than two hours at a time. This is an interesting variant of the 'Fettered Titan' legend.

THE SNAKE-EATER

From mountain Georgia comes the story of Mindia the Snake-Eater, adapted into verse very effectively by Vazha-Pshavela (1861–1915). Mindia is a member of the mountain tribe of the Khevsurs. In his youth, he is taken prisoner by the demon Kajis, and held in captivity for twelve years in their grim supernatural realm. Mindia notices that the Kajis' favourite dish is a cauldron full of snake-meat, from eating which they seem to derive much of their supernatural powers. Overcoming his revulsion, Mindia one day devours a chunk of this hideous meat. To his amazement, he feels a surging stream of strange delight pulsing through his veins. All the secrets of nature are revealed to him: he can listen to a dialogue between two blades of grass, and interpret the rustling of leaves in the woods. The languages of birds and animals hold no secret for him. His demon Kaji jailers fume and burst with rage to see how their prisoner, Prometheus-like, has gained access to their jealously guarded, secret world.

Eventually Mindia makes his escape and returns to his native village in the Caucasus Mountains. The tribe elects him its leader, since he can detect the advance of enemies many leagues off, and enlist all the animal and vegetable world as allies in battle. With

Mindia at its head, the tribe considers itself invincible. But sad to say, with the passage of time, Mindia's magic powers begin to fail. He gets married and is obliged to hunt and to cut down trees to feed his wife and children and keep them warm. The plants and animals refuse to share their secrets with him any longer. Mindia feels increasing alarm for the future welfare of his country, when he is no longer able to afford leadership to it.

The crisis comes in the form of an onslaught by a barbarian tribe from North Caucasia. Mindia's comrades rush to find him and demand that he take charge of the defence. But he finds the old inspiration gone, now that he cannot rely on his plant and animal friends for news of enemy movements. Mindia chooses for the battle a site which turns out to be unsuitable. He is carried from the fray mortally wounded, and sees his village go up in flames as the invaders triumph. He expires on the grass in a stream of blood.

A GEORGIAN ROBIN HOOD

The Caucasus is a happy hunting-ground for bandits and outlaws. The Armenian revolutionary bandit Kamo (Ter Petrossian), for example, replenished the treasury of Lenin's Bolsheviks on several occasions by his daring raids on the Russian Imperial Bank. After cheating death repeatedly during his bold exploits, Kamo perished in a bicycle accident in Tiflis shortly after the triumph of Communism in Georgia in 1921.

The best example of a romantic legendary bandit is Arsena of Marabda who lived during the first half of the nineteenth century under the Tsarist regime. Arsena was a vassal of a leading Georgian noble, and eloped with one of his master's serving girls, with whom he lived as an outlaw. For years, he would swoop down from the hills and despoil prosperous merchants, handing his booty to the deserving poor. On one occasion, Arsena was betrayed and taken to Tiflis in chains. He staged a daring escape from the bath-house where he was taken under escort, disguising himself by putting on the overcoat belonging to the guard commander. Arsena eventually perished in an obscure affray. Arsena's legend is embodied in an anonymous narrative ballad, *Arsenas leksi* (The Lay of Arsena). A historical novel about Arsena was published by the Georgian Soviet writer Mikheil Javakhishvili (1880–1930); it was greatly admired by Stalin, though this did not save Javakhishvili from being murdered by Beria's henchmen during the Purges.

CHAPTER 16

ETHIOPIA

Ethiopia is an ancient and culturally diverse country, covering an area as large as that of France and Spain, and with traditions dating back several thousand years. It is rich in legends, many of which are preserved in medieval manuscripts in the old ecclesiastical language, Ge'ez, a Semitic tongue related to Hebrew and Arabic, but now virtually dead. Other tales have been handed down orally in a variety of Semitic, Cushitic and other local languages.

In terms of their origin and subject-matter, the country's legends can be divided into five broad categories:

1 Stories connected with and redounding to the glory of the Ethiopian Christian state, whose rulers claimed descent from King Solomon of biblical fame and the Queen of Sheba. For the most part written in Ge'ez, some of these are incorporated in otherwise essentially factual chronicles.

2 Stories, also in Ge'ez, concerned with Ethiopian Orthodox Christianity, which in the fourth century became the state religion of the Aksumite kingdom in the north of the country. Many tell of the establishment of churches and monasteries by holy personages, whose miracles are described in a multitude of 'lives of saints'.

3 Stories in Ge'ez which are essentially of foreign origin and are set outside the country. Many of them deal with the lives of biblical characters, notably the Virgin Mary, and others with secular figures, including Alexander the Great.

4 Stories of Muslim shaikhs and other figures of the Islamic regions, particularly to the east, south and west, sometimes written in Arabic but more often transmitted orally in vernacular languages.

5 Stories, for the most part known only orally, relating to specific ethnic groups, including the Oromo (or Galla), the most numerous non-Semitic group, who inhabit much of the centre and south areas.

The monk beheaded by Emperor Fasiladas flies up to heaven (page 148)

SOLOMON AND MAKEDA

Politically, the most important legend concerned with the Ethiopian state is the story of the visit of the supposedly Ethiopian Queen of Sheba to King Solomon. Widely known in the northern provinces of Ethiopia, it forms a central theme of the *Kebra Nagast* (Glory of Kings), which was written in the early fourteenth century by Yashaq, a priest of the northern Ethiopian city of Aksum. Though probably inspired by legends of the Queen which circulated throughout the Middle East, the work is an original Ethiopian composition in which the bare bones of the story are clothed with much detail and the enunciation of lofty precepts. The text of the *Kebra Nagast* appealed to the Ethiopian emperors, who saw in it a valuable title to biblical lineage.

The *Kebra Nagast* (of which there is an English translation)[1] relates that the Queen, whose name was Makeda, heard of Solomon's wisdom from a merchant. Desiring to learn more, she determined to travel to Jerusalem, for she declared: 'Wisdom is far better than treasure of gold and silver... a kingdom cannot stand without wisdom.' Taking with her countless presents, laden on 'seven hundred and ninety-seven camels' and 'mules and asses innumerable', she began the journey, and despite 'the delicacy of the constitution of women' and 'the burning heat of the sun', she persisted 'for her heart had confidence in God'.

On arriving at her destination, she was received by Solomon with great honour. She found him both wise and gracious, and was quickly converted to Judaism. Solomon invited her to a banquet, where he gave her 'meats which would make her thirsty'. At the end of the meal, when the courtiers and servants had departed, he asked her to remain with him for the night. She agreed, but asked him to swear not to take her by force. He consented on condition that she, for her part, swore not to take by force anything in his house. To this she laughingly agreed and they both went to bed. Makeda soon fell asleep, but after a while she awoke, her mouth dry with thirst. Thinking her host was soundly sleeping, she got up to drink from a jar of water which the wily monarch had previously placed nearby. He thereupon seized her and asked why she had broken her oath. She answered, in fear, 'Is the oath broken by my drinking water?', to which he demanded whether she knew anything 'under the heavens better than water'? Recognizing the truth of his words, she accepted that he was free from his oath, but begged him only to allow her to drink. After she had done so, 'he worked his will with her and they slept together'. The legend goes on to tell how the Queen, on returning to Ethiopia, gave birth to Solomon's son Menelik, the reputed founder of the Ethiopian royal dynasty.

THE FOUNDING OF GONDAR

Ethiopian history of later times gave rise to innumerable legends. One, once widely believed, was that Emperor Lebna Dengel (1508–40), the ruler whose realm was overrun by the Muslim conqueror Ahmad Gragn, saw an archangel — Rufa'el or Ura'el in different accounts — who prophesied that the monarch's descendants would one day live and rule in a new capital which would begin with the letter G. Belief in this prophecy is said to account for the founding in the late and early seventeenth centuries of a succession of towns so spelled: Guzara, Gorgora, Gomnage, Ganata Iyasu and finally Gondar, which was to be the capital for over two centuries.

The establishment of Gondar by Emperor Fasiladas (1632–67), and the building of its famous castles, was itself the subject of many a legend. One tells how Fasiladas, a stout supporter of the Ethiopian Orthodox faith which he had restored after his father had attempted to replace it by Roman Catholicism, one day saw a buffalo and chased it to a pool where it vanished. At that moment an old and venerable hermit, doubtless satisfied by the restoration of the age-old creed, came out of the water and, speaking with the voice of the Archangel Ura'el, told Fasiladas that God had guided him to the place designated for the new capital of Gondar.

Fasiladas, deeply moved, duly established himself in that place and began building a castle. Not long afterwards there arrived an embassy from Europe with a Princess Zeliha, who had been despatched as a bride for the Emperor's father. The latter was by then dead, and to return her seemed insulting, so it was proposed that she should be married to the new Emperor, though the Church declared that having been betrothed to the father she could not be wed to the son. She was beautiful, however, and Fasiladas chose to defy the clergy. This aroused the anger of the Almighty, who sent down on Gondar a terrible epidemic. The Emperor wept, but the hermit reappeared and told him not to despair, but to build a church in honour of St Michael. This was done and the disease disappeared, soon after which the hermit died.

Some time later, Zeliha's sister Meliha arrived in Gondar. Younger and even more beautiful than the Queen, she attracted the interest of her royal brother-in-law, who took her also as his wife. The clergy began to murmur and a monk from a distant monastery came and excommunicated the imperial sinner. Fasiladas had the monk beheaded in the public square, whereupon many people declared that they had seen the victim's head with wings flying to heaven in the company of angels. On hearing this wondrous news many more monks flocked to Gondar to excommunicate the monarch. They too were beheaded, and duly went to heaven. In this manner no less than 9099 monks are said to have perished.

At last the Almighty touched the heart of the Emperor, who wished to repent but found no one willing to absolve him of his sins. Eventually he learned that in the high mountains of Samen there was an old nun who might help him. He went to her in penitence, but she refused to pardon him, referring him instead to an old slave-woman in the capital. To this woman he proceeded. She was, as might be imagined, much confused when her royal master prostrated himself before her, but she comforted him, saying: 'Why, O Emperor, do you thus humiliate yourself before me? Only the Almighty condemns and absolves, but if you please, listen to my advice: there where the road across the river is dangerous, build a bridge, and issue a decree that everyone crossing it should not neglect to say, "May God save the soul of Fasiladas!" The Almighty will certainly grant this prayer repeated ceaselessly by an entire people!'

The Emperor is said to have followed this advice and constructed seven bridges. Whatever the truth of the legend, the fact is that three centuries later caravaneers and others were still wont to cry out, 'God save the soul of Fasiladas!'

The founding of other Ethiopian capitals is also the subject of legends. The site for the town of Dabre Tabor, for example, was selected in the early nineteenth century by a local chief, Ras Gugsa Mersa. It is said that he planned to establish his capital elsewhere, but was deterred by a monk who declared: 'Your town must not be built here, choose another place; you will find as a guide a female leopard who has just lain down; you must kill this beast, and clear the forest; there you must build your town.'

PANTALEWON AND YARED

Some of the earliest and culturally most significant of the Ethiopian ecclesiastical legends occur in the lives of the so-called Nine Saints, who came from 'Rom' (Byzantium) in the sixth century and were of Syrian origin. They are remembered for establishing a number of monasteries in the country around Aksum. One of the most famous of these holy men was Pantalewon, who is said to have made a tiny cell for himself on a mountain top, where he stood for no less than forty-five years without sitting or lying down. One of his colleagues, Yeshaq, wrought so many miracles that Pantalewon exclaimed, 'You have terrified me', and the man and his monastery were thereafter called Garama, literally 'he terrified'.

Another early churchman whose life is the centre of legend was Yared, who lived at about the same time as the Nine Saints. In his youth he fled from a harsh master and found refuge in the wilderness, where he saw a worm trying to climb a tree. The creature kept on falling down, but persevered until it succeeded. This sight gave Yared courage. He returned to his master, and was subsequently ordained as a deacon. Later he had a vision which carried him to heaven, where he is said to have learned plain-chant and the rules for writing hymns. The story is told that one day when he was singing before Emperor Gabr Masqal, they both became so entranced that the Emperor dropped his spear, the point of which pierced Yared's foot without him knowing it.

THE CHURCHES OF LALIBALA

Other legends, of a later period, centre around Emperor Lalibala (1172–1212) who, though reputedly a monarch of a usurping dynasty, was later canonized. When he was born a cloud of bees is said to have swarmed around him, which caused his mother to cry out, 'The bees know that this child is king.' She therefore called him Lalibala, which means 'the bee recognizes his sovereignty'. Subsequently a jealous sister attempted to kill him by sending him poisoned beer. At the time he was in the company of a deacon, to whom he politely offered the first drink. The man fell down dead, and a dog that licked a few drops of the potion also died immediately. Lalibala realized that the poison had been intended for him and was full of remorse. He took up the bowl and drank it, but it proved a blessing in disguise, for he had been suffering from tape-worm, which the drug expelled, after which he enjoyed perfect health. Not long afterwards angels transported him to the first, second and third heavens, and God commanded him to build ten monolithic churches at his capital – which was afterwards called after him. In this task the workmen were assisted by angels, who toiled with them by day and in the night did twice as much work as the men had done in the day. The rock-hewn churches of Lalibala remain to this day, some of the finest building in the land, and are much admired by tourists.

TAKLA HAYMANOT

Another legend which was in its time of considerable political importance tells of the abdication of Lalibala's grandson Na'akueto La'ab in favour of Yakuno Amlak, a Prince who claimed descent from Solomon and the Queen of Sheba. The transfer of power, for which there is in fact no documentary evidence, is said to have been effected by Takla Haymanot, an Ethiopian monk who had been ordained Abuna, or Metropolitan, and had founded the famous monastery of Dabra Libanos. Legend has it that he was a man of such sanctity and devotion to his country that he persuaded Na'akueto La'ab to resign his crown in favour of Yakuno Amlak. A treaty was then concluded between the two monarchs which is supposed to have had major importance for the Church, for it specified that one-third of the kingdom should be ceded to the Abuna for his own maintenance and the support of the clergy, convents and churches in the kingdom.

Other ecclesiastical legends, which contain many a kernel of historical truth, tell of the efforts of Takla Haymanot and other holy men to convert the non-Christian peoples of the south. Such legends abound in stories of the overturning of idols and the slaughter of snakes previously regarded as divine. In a typical incident, the people are said to have worshipped a certain tree. The saint approached it and commanded it in the name of the Lord Jesus Christ to rise up. It immediately 'uprooted itself with a great noise like that of thunder during the rainy season' and killed twenty-four people in the process. Takla Haymanot, however, caused the dew of heaven to fall upon them and they all came to life again, after which he baptized the entire population of the area. He taught them the Christian religion and his words 'entered into their hearts like oil into the bones'.

CLAN HEROES

There are other legends of the history of the extensive populations of the south later incorporated into modern Ethiopia. According to one of them, when the Oromo people came to the Jimma area of the south-west, they were composed of nine groups united under the leadership of a Sorcerer-Queen called Makahore. She had in her possession a *boku,* or sceptre, which if placed on the ground caused it to shake and men to fear. On reaching the borders of Jimma she put down her *boku* and the ground began to tremble. The neighbouring Kaffa people thereupon fled beyond the Gojeb River, which thus became the frontier between the two peoples, as it is to this day.

Many folk heroes in Ethiopia are the subject of poems which, like genealogical trees, are handed down from generation to generation. For example, a characteristic Chaha poem from the Gurage area tells of the heroes of the Ameya district and of the emergence of the powerful clan lineage of Manto, and exclaims:

Brave men were born in the hills of Ameya.
Yes! In the hills of Ameya they were all brave...
They were feared and people trembled.
Since the time when the Mantos were born no one dared to look
them in the Face.[2]

Legends of this kind sometimes played an important role in perpetuating the memory of clan fathers, whose lineage provided a basis for semi-communal land-ownership, especially in the north.

THE WEST

Arthur and the Sword in the Stone, of Legendary Britain (page 239)

CHAPTER 17

CLASSICAL GREECE AND ROME

Greek legends have been the stock in trade of European literature
down to the present century – as in Joyce, Eliot, O'Neill, Sartre,
Cocteau, Kazantzakis and Seferis, to name but a few. They are stories
of adventure and war, courage and treachery, love and pride, murder
and revenge. They are all fascinating, they all have numerous
different versions and they have been explained in many different
ways. There is no agreed approach to their interpretation, but the
Greeks themselves valued them not only as entertaining stories but,
on one level at least, as examples of the heights and the depths which
human nature is capable of reaching. Only a fraction of them can be
summarized here, and each is presented in the form which for one
reason or another is the most familiar.

LEGENDS OF CRETE

Europa, daughter of the King of Tyre, was abducted by the god Zeus
in the form of a bull. He carried her across the sea to Crete, where she
bore a son, Minos, who grew up to be King of Crete, lord of
a formidable sea-power, a notable law-giver and a just judge. His wife
Pasiphae was moved to passion for a bull. The Athenian inventor
Daedalus formed a model cow in which she could lie and enjoy her
unnatural love. The child of this union was the Minotaur, half-man,
half-bull. He was hidden away in another of Daedalus' inventions, the
labyrinth or maze.

Minos invaded the Greek mainland and exacted a tribute of
human lives from Athens, seven young men and seven girls to be sent
to Crete every year as victims of the Minotaur. The monster was

Bellerophon and the Chimaera (page 162)

eventually killed by the Athenian prince Theseus. Minos imprisoned Daedalus in his own maze with his son Icarus. Daedalus invented wings for them both and they escaped, but Icarus flew too near the sun, the wax fastening his wings melted and he was drowned in the sea. Daedalus went to Sicily. Minos pursued him there and was killed by treachery, to become judge of the dead.

Folk memories lie behind these stories, of Crete as a great sea-power with wide interests in the Mediterranean, of its legal codes, of the cult of bulls and rites of bull-leaping which can be seen in Cretan frescoes and ivories, of the labyrinthine corridors of the palace at Cnossus and the symbol of the *labrys* or double-axe (labyrinth means 'place of the double-axe'). Minos may have been the name or title borne by all the Kings of Crete and the Minotaur appears on Cretan seals, perhaps as a symbol of the bull-cult. Some modern writers have seen in the figure of Daedalus the dual potential of science and technology, to bring great benefits but to cause disaster by reaching too far, beyond the human grasp.

THE TROJAN WAR

Priam was King of Troy. His son Paris was a herdsman in the hills when he was asked to judge three goddesses in a divine beauty competition. The competitors offered bribes, Hera power, Athene military glory, Aphrodite the most beautiful woman in the world. In the romanticism of youth Paris gave the prize to Aphrodite.

The most beautiful woman in the world — Helen — was already married. Helen was the daughter of Zeus by Leda, whom he seduced in the form of a swan. She and her sister Clytemnestra were married to two brothers, Menelaus of Sparta and Agamemnon of Mycenae.

Paris visited Sparta on a diplomatic mission. Menelaus went away on business, and returned to find the love-birds flown to Troy. The Greeks were up in arms for revenge. Agamemnon as commander-in-chief mustered a great fleet at Aulis. Among the Greek chieftains were Nestor, lord of Pylos, filled with the wisdom of age, the cunning Odysseus, King of Ithaca, and Achilles, the greatest fighter of them all. Achilles was the child of Peleus and the sea-goddess Thetis, whose son was destined to be greater than his father. He was, in a late version, proof against wounds except for his 'Achilles heel', where his mother held him when she plunged him in the charmed waters of Styx, the underworld river. According to one story, it was fated that Achilles would either live a life of glory and die young, or lead a long, quiet life in obscurity. His parents tried to keep him safe by dressing him as a girl, but Odysseus discovered him among the women and so he sailed to Troy.

At Aulis the fleet was held up by contrary winds. Agamemnon had killed a sacred deer of the goddess Artemis, and she demanded his daughter in return. He duly sacrificed his daughter Iphigeneia, the wind changed and the fleet sailed.

For ten years the Greeks besieged Troy. Achilles killed Hector, the Trojans' heroic defender, and was in turn killed by Paris. Eventually the Greeks pretended to retreat, leaving behind a huge wooden horse in which armed men were concealed. The Trojans should have feared the Greeks even when they brought gifts. The priest Laocoön warned them but was overwhelmed by sea-serpents, and his warning was disregarded. So were the warnings given by Cassandra, who was doomed — for withholding her promised favours from the god Apollo — to prophesy truth and be disbelieved. The Trojans pulled the horse within the walls. The Greeks returned in the night, the men inside the horse opened the gates and the city was sacked.

The Trojan War was a major theme of early epic. Homer in his *Iliad* (really 'The Wrath of Achilles') recounts one episode of the war with a wealth of traditional material and a genius for story-telling. In the end it is the tale of how the brutal Achilles learned to pity. Our picture of the sack of Troy is influenced by the Roman poet Vergil. Euripides, writing his plays under the shadow of war, used the Trojan War as a theme. In the *Trojan Women* he shows the sufferings of the conquered: 'not glory at all, but shame and blindness and a world swallowed up in night'. In *Helen* he makes play with a legend that the real Helen was spirited away to Egypt and the war fought over a wraith; he intends it as a commentary on all war.

When the great mound of Hissarlik near the Dardanelles was excavated by Heinrich Schliemann in 1873, not one city of Troy was found but nine or ten. Troy VIIa was destroyed in about 1250 BC, the traditional date of the Trojan War. The city commanded the anchorage for ships waiting to pass through the Dardanelles, which gave it a stranglehold on the Black Sea trade. The Greeks may well have wished to destroy it, and it would not be the first time that the abduction of a princess has been a pretext for war.

THE STORY OF MYCENAE

Pelops, a Prince from Asia Minor, went to Greece and fell in love with Hippodameia, Princess of Pisa. To win her he had to beat her father in a chariot-race, and if he failed he would be put to death. He succeeded by bribing her father's charioteer to unfasten the lynchpins. For his treachery his whole house was placed under a curse. Pelops prospered for the moment, and the Peloponnese bears his name. Among his sons were Atreus and Thyestes.

Atreus and Thyestes quarrelled over power and a woman. Atreus killed the sons of Thyestes (except for Aegisthus) and served them up to him as food. (In Seneca's play *Thyestes* he produces their heads, saying, 'Do you recognize your sons?', to receive the grim reply, 'I recognize my brother.') Atreus had two sons, Agamemnon, King of Mycenae or Argos, and Menelaus, King of Sparta, who married, respectively, Clytemnestra and Helen.

While Agamemnon was away at Troy, Clytemnestra took his cousin Aegisthus as her lover. Agamemnon returned. He had killed Clytemnestra's daughter Iphigeneia, and he added to his offences by having as his concubine the priestess Cassandra, vowed to be Apollo's or no one's. Clytemnestra persuaded him into a bath, entangled him in a robe, and killed him. Their son Orestes was away at the time. His sister Electra remained and meditated revenge. Eight years later Orestes returned, and the two killed their mother and her usurping lover. Early versions show no guilt about this, but a more sophisticated age brooded on the conflict of loyalties in which justified revenge necessitated the offence of matricide, and showed Orestes pursued by the Furies or Spirits of Vengeance.

This dark tale of a curse haunting and polluting a family for successive generations was dramatized by the three great Greek tragedians and has gripped generations of audiences. To Aeschylus the murder of Clytemnestra by her children presents a moral problem, to Sophocles an exciting drama, to Euripides a shameful crime. Strauss's great opera *Elektra* owes something to the last two. The story also lies behind O'Neill's *Mourning Becomes Electra* and Eliot's *The Family Reunion*. Mycenae was a historic citadel, whose days of glory were 1400–1150 BC. It is not impossible that there is a historical basis to the story of Agamemnon, Clytemnestra, Orestes and Electra. Electra has become the prey of psychoanalysts as the type for father-fixation.

THE ODYSSEY OF ODYSSEUS

Odysseus also, in time, returned from Troy. In the early traditions Odysseus is brave and wise; later his cunning turns to deceitfulness and his courage to cowardice. The *Odyssey* (attributed to Homer but surely not from the same hand as the *Iliad*) tells the story of his return. He has fairy-tale adventures, encountering and blinding Polyphemus, the monstrous one-eyed Cyclops, to whom he gives his name as Noman, so that the monster cries out, 'No man is hurting me.' The sorceress Circe turns his men into beasts. He goes to the land of the dead. To pass the Sirens, who attract sailors to death on the rocks by the charm of their song, Odysseus blocks his crew's ears and has himself tied to the mast. He sails safely between Scylla and Charybdis, a monster and a whirlpool (usually placed in the Straits of Messina). The nymph Calypso tries to stay him with love, and he visits the idealized land of Phaeacia with its charming princess, Nausicaa. Eventually he reaches his homeland. Odysseus is assumed dead and his wife Penelope is beset by suitors. She will not give them an answer until she has woven a shroud for her father-in-law, Laertes, which she secretly unravels every night. In the end she agrees to yield to the man who can bend Odysseus' bow. Odysseus enters the palace disguised as a beggar, and in a touching scene his old dog Argus recognizes him and dies of joy at his master's return. Odysseus bends the bow, kills the suitors and regains his Kingdom.

The *Odyssey* is an outstanding example of the myth of the quest, in this case the quest for a homeland. Many of the episodes belong to the world of fairy-tales, some to a myth of the seasons, death and resurrection. The Romans called the hero Ulysses, and James Joyce structured his novel of that name around the *Odyssey*.

THE THEBAN CYCLE

Cadmus was the son of Agenor, King of Tyre in Phoenicia. When his sister Europa was abducted by Zeus, Cadmus and his brothers were sent in search of her. Cadmus came to Delphi, where he was told by the oracle to follow a cow and settle where she led him. He did so, and founded the city of Thebes. In fetching water from a sacred spring, he killed a holy snake. On the advice of Athene he took out its teeth and sowed them in a furrow. A harvest of armed soldiers emerged and Cadmus set them to fight one another. Five survived to become the progenitors of the Theban nobility; they were called the Spartoi or Sown Men.

Besides accounting for the origin of the Theban aristocracy, the legend also explains that one of the benefits of Cadmus' rule was the introduction of alphabetic script (which did indeed derive from Phoenicia). Though he and his wife, Harmonia, were happy, their family failed to prosper. One grandson, Actaeon, accidentally saw Artemis bathing naked and was hunted down by his own hounds. Another, Pentheus, opposed the god Dionysus and was torn to pieces by the god's ecstatic followers, including his own mother.

Laius, the great-grandson of Cadmus, kidnapped and raped Chrysippus, the son of Pelops. For this Pelops cursed his line. Laius duly became King of Thebes and married Jocasta. An oracle had said that his son would kill him, and so the baby boy, Oedipus, was exposed to die in the hills. Rescued by a shepherd, he was brought up in Corinth. He learned from an oracle that he was destined to murder his father and marry his mother. He therefore turned away from Corinth and those he believed to be his parents, went to Thebes and so met, quarrelled with and killed Laius. He now saved Thebes from the monstrous Sphinx by answering her riddle: 'What has four legs and two legs and three legs and when it has most then is it weakest?' The answer was 'Man', who crawls, then walks upright and in old age leans on a stick. For this he was rewarded with the Kingdom and the hand of the Queen, his mother Jocasta. They had four children. But the truth came out, and in one version Jocasta committed suicide and Oedipus blinded himself, fulfilling the riddle with his weak youth, proud manhood and blind man's stick.

The sons, Eteocles and Polynices, quarrelled over the Kingdom. Polynices raised an army with six allies (the 'Seven against Thebes') The attack failed but both brothers died. The Thebans decreed that Polynices should remain unburied. His sister Antigone buried him, and was herself condemned to death.

The Theban tales were a favourite theme of drama. Surviving plays include the *Seven Against Thebes* of Aeschylus; the *King Oedipus, Oedipus at Colonus* and *Antigone* of Sophocles; the *Phoenician Women* and *Bacchae* of Euripides; and there were many others. The story of Oedipus, the prisoner and victim of a relentless chain of events outside his control, who rises to become rich, powerful and successful but is brought down in horror and defeat, has been a happy hunting-ground for theorists. For Freud it expressed a suppressed part of all males, the desire to kill the father and possess the mother. For Jung it showed the archetypes of the Terrible Mother, the Hero, the Old Wise man, the Shadow and the Anima. For Lévi-Strauss it held together two dichotomies, one the overrating and underrating of blood-kinship, the other the assertion and denial that man is autochthonous (sprung from the soil). One thing it is not − a myth to explain cult-practice.

JASON AND THE ARGONAUTS

King Athamas of Boeotia had two children, Phrixus and Helle. They escaped the jealousy of their step-mother Ino, the daughter of Cadmus, on the back of a fabulous ram with a fleece of gold and powers of flight and speech. Helle fell off and drowned in the water which bears her name, the Hellespont. Phrixus reached Colchis on the east coast of the Black Sea, and sacrificed the ram to Zeus. The fleece was preserved, guarded by a snake.

At Iolcus in Thessaly, Pelias had usurped the throne of his brother Aeson. His nephew Jason, 'the man with one sandal', came to claim the throne. Pelias agreed on condition that Jason first secured the Golden Fleece. With divine help, Jason built the ship Argo and manned it with adventurers including the semi-divine Heracles (whom the Romans called Hercules), Orpheus the great minstrel, and other heroes. After an eventful voyage they reached Colchis, where the King's daughter, Medea, a sorceress, fell in love with Jason and helped him to steal the Fleece. They fled together, and Medea murdered her brother and scattered his limbs to delay her father's pursuit. Their return journey took them deviously, perhaps by the Danube, the Elbe, the Baltic, the North Sea and the Straits of

Gibraltar. Finally Jason returned to claim his throne. But Medea, promising to rejuvenate Pelias, tricked his daughters into boiling him to death in a cauldron, and she and Jason had to go into exile in Corinth.

There Jason tired of his dangerous, barbaric consort and arranged to marry the local princess. Medea killed the bride by sorcery and murdered her own two sons by Jason to punish him. She escaped to sanctuary in Athens, and eventually returned to Colchis. Jason was killed by a rotting spar falling from his old ship.

The voyage was a theme of early bardic poetry, and there is reason to think that it took firm shape in the trading city of Miletus. Euripides has a fine play about Medea's revenge on Jason, and in the fourth century BC Apollonius of Rhodes wrote an epic account of the Argonauts. The Golden Fleece itself seems to reflect an early practice of using a sheepskin to pan for gold, and the Colchis region was rich in gold, silver, iron and copper. The story as a whole is a typical accumulation of folkloric stories round the two themes of the hero's quest and the stranger's tasks, in which he receives supernatural help. It has been suggested that the return journey gives information about the amber route from the Baltic.[1]

THESEUS AND THE MINOTAUR

Theseus had a mortal mother, Aethra, who was loved by a man, Aegeus, King of Athens, and a god, Poseidon. His human father had placed his sword and sandals under a weighty slab of rock. When Theseus was strong enough to recover them he set out for Athens. On the way he dealt with a number of brigands, including the notorious Procrustes, who shortened or lengthened his victims to fit his bed. At Athens he escaped poisoning by Medea, sustained his father's authority and subdued and captured the great wild bull of Marathon.

Theseus volunteered to go to Crete as one of the Minotaur's victims. The ship had black sails, and he told his father that if he killed the Minotaur he would change them for white. In Crete the Princess Ariadne fell in love with him and helped him to find his way in the labyrinth, where the Minotaur lived, with a skein of thread. Theseus killed the monster and escaped from Crete with Ariadne and her sister Phaedra. Tiring of Ariadne, he abandoned her on the island of Naxos, where the god Dionysus found her and made her his bride. But Theseus forgot to change his sails. Aegeus committed suicide on seeing the black sails and Theseus became King of Athens.

Theseus was regarded in Athenian tradition as the ideal wise king, who welded together the villages of Attica into a single state. He appears as the model of hospitality, the faithful friend, the just ruler. The principal legends about him have to do with women. Like

Heracles before him, he led an expedition against the Amazons, the women warriors and huntresses of Greek legend, who were supposed to live somewhere on the borders of the known world. They would have nothing to do with men, except occasionally for breeding purposes, and they kept only their girl children, killing (or disabling) the boys. Theseus abducted their leader, Hippolyte, who bore him a son, the virginal, nature-loving Hippolytus. With his friend Pirithous he abducted Helen, and he then helped Pirithous in an attempt on Persephone, the Queen of the Dead, which failed. Theseus was rescued by Heracles, but Pirithous had to be left behind in the underworld. Theseus married Ariadne's sister Phaedra, who fell in love with her step-son Hippolytus. He repulsed her and in shame and fear of exposure she committed suicide, leaving a note charging him with attempted rape. Theseus was deceived and cursed his son, who was killed by a sea-monster. He discovered the truth too late.

Theseus appears in a number of Athenian tragedies and his story is told by Plutarch. His story has become blurred with that of Heracles and it is hard to know whether there was a historical person behind the legends, though to the classical Athenians there certainly was.

LEGENDS OF ARGOS

Inachus, the river-god of Argos, had a daughter named Io. She was loved by Zeus, who gave her the shape of a heifer to protect her from his jealous consort, Hera. But Hera found her out and sent a gadfly to drive her from land to land, until in Egypt she gave birth to Epaphus. His great-grandsons Aegyptus and Danaus quarrelled, and Danaus returned with his fifty daughters to Argos. Their cousins, the sons of Aegyptus, came after them to marry them. Danaus persuaded his daughters to kill their husbands on the wedding night. For this, in one version, they were purified and married to the winners of a race; in another, they were punished in Hades by having to fill leaking pots. One of them, Hypermnestra, disobeyed her father and became the ancestress of the Kings of Argos and of Perseus, one of the most famous of all Greek heroes. Perseus was brave, lucky, favoured by the gods and, equipped with supernatural weapons, a notable slayer of monsters.

Acrisius, King of Argos, was told that his daughter Danae would bear a son who would kill him. He immured her in a bronze tower, but Zeus visited her in the form of a shower of gold and she bore a son, Perseus. Acrisius pushed mother and baby out to sea in a box, but they were washed up on the island of Seriphos. When Perseus grew to manhood, the King of Seriphos, who feared him and hoped to be rid of him, set him to secure the head of the Gorgon Medusa, which turned all who saw it to stone. Perseus consulted the aged Graeae, who had but one tooth and one eye between them, and by taking that tooth and eye persuaded them to tell him where the Gorgons lived. He also stole shoes of swiftness and a helmet of darkness. The Gorgons had snakes for hair and tusks for teeth. Invisible in his helmet, Perseus watched Medusa's reflection in his shield and struck off her head. From her blood sprang the winged horse Pegasus, on which he made his escape. Subsequently he rescued the Princess Andromeda from a sea-monster to which she was offered as a sacrifice, turned his mother's persecutors to stone with the Gorgon's head, and returned to Argos. There he accidentally killed his grandfather, Acrisius, while throwing a discus, so that in the end the prophecy came true.

LEGENDS OF CORINTH

Sisyphus, the legendary founder of Corinth, stands with Odysseus as the supreme Greek example of the trickster of folklore, 'most crafty of men'. In one story he trapped and imprisoned Death. In another, doomed to death, he told his wife to pay him no funeral honours. Then, in Hades, he asked to be allowed to rise from the dead to punish his wife's negligence and, once out, refused to return. In the end he was condemned to push uphill a boulder which everlastingly rolled back down again.

His grandson Bellerophon resisted the advances of Stheneboea, Queen of Tiryns, who charged him with attempted seduction. He was sent to Lycia with a sealed message asking for his execution, and the King set him to fight the monstrous Chimaera and the Amazons. With the help of the goddess Athene and the winged horse Pegasus he succeeded in these tasks. The Lycian King in admiration gave him his daughter as wife, but in his overweening pride Bellerophon tried to storm Olympus on his horse. He was thrown down by Zeus and spent the rest of his life as a lame outcast, 'hated by the gods'.

LEGENDS OF AETOLIA

Althaea was mother of Meleager, who at his birth was promised a great destiny but death as soon as a brand in the fire burned out. Althaea seized the brand and hid it, and Meleager grew up to prosperity. When Aetolia was ravaged by a boar, he called the heroes of Greece to help him hunt it down. One who came was Atalanta. She had been abandoned at birth in the mountains, suckled by a bear, and brought up to the tough life of a huntress. She gave the boar the decisive wound and was awarded the trophy. When Meleager's uncles tried to deprive her of the prize Meleager killed them. Althaea, maddened by the death of her brothers, threw the brand back into the fire, thus killing her son.

Atalanta would marry only a man who could beat her in running, and the penalty for failure was death. She was outwitted by a certain Milanion, who tempted her by dropping golden apples in her path. She could not resist stopping to pick them up, and so lost the race.

THE SAGES

The great Greek sages are historical figures, though history is overlaid with legend. Epimenides of Crete (about 600 BC), for example, is said to have lived for 154 or 299 years, to have slept for over fifty years in a cave, to have been able to leave his body, to have consorted with nymphs, to have heard divine voices and issued divine oracles, and to have done without food. He was probably a shamanistic figure, ascetic, mystical, subject to trances.

Anecdotes also gathered round Thales of Miletus (early sixth century BC), who is traditionally acknowledged as the father of philosophy. Sometimes he is the impractical dreamer, falling down a well while looking at the stars. Sometimes he is the practical genius, diverting the river Halys for King Croesus' army, predicting a good olive-crop and cornering the presses, measuring the height of a pyramid by its shadow or the distance of a ship at sea. In one excellent story he receives an award as the wisest of men, disowns it and passes it on. It goes all round the legendary Seven Sages and returns to him: he gives it to Delphi. (The other Sages, according to the usual list, were Bias, Chilon, Cleobulus, Periander, Pittacus and the Athenian statesman Solon.)

The greatest accumulation of legend is round Pythagoras (later sixth century BC), a mathematical and mystical genius who emigrated from Samos to southern Italy. His travels to Babylon and Egypt may be authentic or may be part of the legend. The most striking legendary story told of his golden thigh, showing him to be a reincarnation of Midas (who was, disastrously, given the gift that all he touched should turn to gold). Other tales have him hearing supernatural voices and charming animals. One story illustrates his belief in the transmigration of souls: he stopped a man beating a dog because in its howls he recognized the voice of a dead friend.

THE ALEXANDER LEGEND

It is not surprising that legend clung to Alexander the Great, who was recognized as a god in his own lifetime. He crossed the Hellespont in 334 BC, swept through Asia Minor, down to Egypt, north across Mesopotamia and Persia to the Caspian Gates, through the Hindu Kush to Samarkand and Tashkent, over the mountains through Kashmir and across the Indus into India. He then went back to

Karachi and along the coast, experiencing formidable privations, to
Babylon, fighting all the way. He smashed the power of Persia and
created a vast empire of his own, which no one afterwards could hold
together. He was not yet thirty-three when he died, in 323 BC.

About AD 300 some unknown but ingenious author in Alexandria
put together bits of propaganda, legend, tradition, history and
moralizing, attributed the whole to Alexander's historian Callis-
thenes, and so launched the *Romance of Alexander*. From Alexandria
it spread in different languages and various versions. Alexander's real
father was Philip II of Macedon, but in the Romance he is the son of
an Egyptian King, Nectanebus, who went to Macedon and told.
Olympias, Philip's Queen, that the god Ammon would father a child
on her. Which Nectanebus himself, masquerading as the god, duly
did.

Alexander insists that he is mortal, because divine honours
endanger the soul, but he prays to be received among the gods, like
Heracles. He travels widely, sometimes in disguise, and visits historic
sites such as Delphi and legendary places such as the land of Darkness
and the Well of Life. He builds cities. He conquers Rome and
Carthage, and sails out into the Atlantic. He talks with the wise men
of India. It is a fantastic farrago, incorporating solid historical
material, and it was the joy of the Middle Ages (see ALEXANDER THE
GREAT – IN WESTERN EUROPE).

THE FOUNDATION OF ROME

From the time of their contact with Greek civilization the Romans
aspired to claim a Greek foundation. Dionysius of Halicarnassus
(first century BC) has a curious story that the Aborigines, themselves
of Greek origin and ultimately from Arcadia, joined with immigrant
Pelasgians from Thessaly in the first settlement. He adds three more
Greek settlements for good measure, by Evander and the Arcadians
around the Palatine hill, by Hercules and the Peloponnesians round
the hill of Saturn, and finally by the Trojans, who counted as
Greeks.

Evander is a semi-divine figure, born of the god Hermes and
a prophetess named Themis or Nicostrate (whom the Romans called
Carmenta, from *carmen,* a chant or a spell). He was said to have led
a colonizing expedition in two ships from Pallanteum in Arcadia after
a political set-back at home. The colonists occupied a hill which they
called Pallanteum or Palatine (an impossible derivation) with a shrine
to Pan. The Romans had a country god named Faunus, whom they
identified with the Greek Pan, and sometimes with Evander. It is
doubtful if Evander would have caught their imagination had Vergil
not memorably portrayed the warmth of his hospitality.

To Vergil we owe the greater familiarity of the story of Aeneas, a heroic Prince of Troy in the *Iliad.* Vergil inherited from Greek sources the account of his escape from the sack of Troy with his aged father and small son, and of his subsequent wanderings, which in one source included a landing in Latium, the area round Rome. Aeneas was another semi-divine figure, for his mother was the goddess Aphrodite, known to the Romans as Venus. It was probably when Rome was at war with Greece that the attraction grew of a founder who was a political enemy of the Greeks but could be considered a product of Greek culture.

Vergil inherited a colourless figure and a colourless legend, and out of it created one of the world's great epics, the *Aeneid.* He tells the story of the fall of Troy and the subsequent wanderings of Aeneas (based on the *Odyssey*). He shows the hero wrecked on the shores of Carthage and falling in love with Dido, Queen of Carthage (who sums up the later threats to Rome by Hannibal of Carthage and Cleopatra, a queen from Africa). Recalled from love to duty, Aeneas abandons Dido to suicide, lands in Italy, consults the Sibyl or prophetess at Cumae, and descends to the underworld where he is afforded a vision of the future greatness of Rome. At last he comes to the Tiber and is welcomed and entertained by Evander on the future site of Rome. He battles with the local prince, Turnus, for the hand of Lavinia, daughter of King Latinus the eponymous ancestor of the Latins. Aeneas kills Turnus in single combat.

At this point the *Aeneid* breaks off, left unfinished at Vergil's death. According to other authors, Aeneas married Lavinia, built the town of Lavinium in her honour, succeeded Latinus as King and was eventually killed in battle against the Etruscans.

Although Aeneas was the forefather of Rome's greatness and the legendary ancestor of the Caesars, in the generally accepted tradition he did not found the city of Rome itself. He built Lavinium, near Rome, at the place where he saw the portent of a white sow with thirty young. This foundation was mentioned by Timaeus (third century BC), who claimed to have seen Trojan relics there, and the burial place of Aeneas was a tourist attraction. His son Ascanius or Iulus was said to have founded Alba Longa, historically a far more important centre. But Alba was still not Rome, and the putative foundation-dates were three centuries apart. The intervening period was filled with a barren list of names.

Various dates were given for Rome's foundation, from 814 to 729, the preferred date being 753. The founder is sometimes called Rhomus or Rhome, from a Greek root meaning 'strength', a false derivation of an Etruscan name. He ends up as Romulus, with a twin brother, Remus. According to the legend, the Princess Rhea Silvia, a Vestal Virgin, was raped by the god Mars and gave birth to twins. By order of their uncle Amulius, the usurping king of Alba Longa, they were exposed to die, but they were suckled by a she-wolf and rescued by a herdsman named Faustulus. The twins grew up, living as romantically righteous adventurers. They killed Amulius and restored the throne to the rightful King, their grandfather Numitor. They determined to build a new city. Romulus chose the Palatine hill, Remus the Aventine. Was the city to be named Rome or Remora? Romulus had an omen of twelve vultures in his favour. The brothers quarrelled. In one version, Remus jumped over the half-built walls − an evil omen since enemies might do likewise. Romulus struck him dead, with the words, 'So perish all who cross these walls.' To people his city Romulus proclaimed it an asylum for fugitives and criminals, but they were short of women. He announced a festival, and when the neighbouring Sabines came to it the young Romans abducted the Sabine girls. The Sabines countered with war, but the women intervened between their husbands and fathers, and made peace. Romulus became the ideal king, and was given divine honours, being identified with the god Quirinus. According to tradition, he disappeared mysteriously during an eclipse of the sun, and was said to have been taken up into heaven.

Archaeology has done much to sort out the actual history. From about 1600 BC immigrants from central Europe were settling in the Po Valley, in Tuscany and indeed in Rome. About 1200 BC further immigrants, with a knowledge of iron, settled around Monte Cavo and Alba Longa. Gradually they came down from the mountains to the seven hills by the river Tiber, probably about 900 BC. From the seventh century BC the villages on the separate hills began to form a single community.

THE KINGS OF ROME

Tradition identified seven Kings of Rome: Romulus, Numa Pompilius, Tullus Hostilius, Ancus Marcius, Tarquinius Priscus, Servius Tullius, Tarquinius Superbus. The number is suspiciously magical, and seven kings seem few for 240 years, but there may be historical tradition behind the names.

Numa was said to have been born on the day that Romulus laid the foundations of Rome and to have been invited by the Romans to succeed Romulus because of his piety. Not a martial figure like Romulus, he appears as the founder of Roman religious practice. His mistress, the water-nymph Egeria, gave divine sanction to his innovations. With a mixture of wine and honey he trapped two other divine figures, Faunus and Picus, who revealed to him prophecies and charms. In some traditions he was even made a follower of Pythagoras.

With Tarquinius Priscus (the Old) the legends record a period of Etruscan rule. By tradition his dates were 616−579 BC and this is in fact the period when Etruscan influence was first effective in Rome.

Later tradition was equivocal about this period of growth under alien rule. Livy portrays Tarquin's wife Tanaquil as a dominating, domineering, intriguing woman; in its way it is one of the great semi-historical portraits. The most famous of Tarquin's legends told how an old woman brought him nine sacred books for which she asked an exorbitant price. When he refused she destroyed three and asked the same price for the remaining six. Again he refused, again she destroyed three, and this time he paid the full price for the last three. These were the Sibylline Books, consulted in time of crisis by order of the Senate.

Servius Tullius in general was well thought of by the later Romans. In one tradition he was born a slave (*servus* means slave). Others gave him a royal mother and a divine father, or said that he was sired by a miraculous phallus rising from the fire. Like Numa, he was given a divine consort with prophetic gifts, Nortia or Fortuna. As Numa gave Rome her religious institutions, so Servius, it was said, gave the city her political institutions.

The last King, traditionally, was Tarquinius Superbus (the Proud), who appears as a typical autocrat, spurred on by the ambitions of Servius' daughter Tullia, whom he married and who resembles Lady Macbeth. At her instigation he murdered her father and seized the throne. In one story he secured the town of Gabii and his son Sextus asked what he should do with the leading citizens. Tarquin said nothing, but swished off the tallest poppy-heads near him. Stories of this kind were told to explain and justify the overthrow of the monarchy and its replacement by a republic.

Tarquin's sons, accompanied by their cousin Brutus, went to Delphi to ask the oracle who would succeed him. The oracle said that it would be the first to kiss his mother. Brutus saw a double meaning, fell to the ground and kissed Mother Earth. Sextus raped Lucretia, the lovely and virtuous wife of Collatinus. She told her family and called them to vengeance, and then committed suicide. Collatinus and Brutus now roused the people and they liberated Rome from the autocracy. The single permanent monarch was replaced by two consuls, chosen annually. Later family pride put at least five names into this first consular year, but whoever else was there Brutus had pride of place. So was the oracle fulfilled. The name of Brutus as liberator was important for the later Brutus who killed Julius Caesar.

THE EARLY REPUBLIC

Traditionally the Republic was established about 509 BC. The State was still in danger. The Tarquins roused the Etruscans under Lars Porsena to fight for their interest. Brutus' own sons tried to betray the city, and Brutus had them executed. Horatius Cocles (the One-Eyed) guarded the approach to the city while the single wooden bridge over the Tiber was destroyed and then swam the river to safety. When Porsena made peace, Tarquin roused the Latins. They faced the Romans and were defeated at the battle of Lake Regillus, where the divine twins Castor and Pollux were said to have aided the Romans.

So the legends proliferated. Many appeared in the historical records of the early historians Fabius Pictor (third century BC) and Valerius Antias (first century BC), and have come down to us in the pages of Livy. One, familiar from Shakespeare, tells how Cnaeus Marcius won the sobriquet Coriolanus by capturing Corioli from the Volsci. Charged with tyrannical behaviour and indifference to the fate of the common people, he was banished, went over to the Volsci and all but conquered Rome in their name, but was dissuaded by his mother, who thus gained a victory for Rome but destroyed her own son.

Another group of legends centres on Camillus, conqueror of the powerful city of Veii after a ten-year siege (which recalls, and is meant to recall, the siege of Troy). Veii would not fall until the Alban Lake was drained, so Camillus drained it. He tunnelled into the city under the temple of Juno, heard the priest over his head declare that whoever offered sacrifice would win the war, burst out and offered sacrifice. He showed impiety by having four white horses to celebrate his triumph, and was exiled. The next danger was from an invasion of Gauls from the north. They sacked the city. The priests and elders sat silently in the forum or in their houses awaiting the Gauls. A Gaul touched the beard of one, who struck him with his staff, at which the Gauls massacred them all. Only the Capitol held out. The Gauls made a surprise night attack, but Juno's sacred geese gave the alarm and Rome survived, to be rescued by the exiled Camillus.

Even in the third century, when the historical ground is firmer, an accretion of legend continues. Stories accumulate round such figures as Scipio, the conqueror of Carthage: a snake crawled over his cradle and left him unharmed; the dogs in the Capitol never barked at him; he had divine inspiration in dreams; he must have been of divine parentage.

Behind some of these legends there is a kernel of historical truth. Others are invented to glorify descendants or other later figures. Some explain a later survival or practice. Some are typical folklore or belong to the pattern which accrues to great men: Alexander, Scipio and Augustus have common stories about them.

JULIUS CAESAR AND AUGUSTUS

Julius Caesar, a subtle propagandist, began to create his own legends. Such authentic sayings as 'Came, saw, won' or 'Caesar's wife must be above suspicion' were spoken with an eye to posterity. Within a century or so, through the literary power of Lucan and Plutarch, the legend had taken shape. Caesar standing before Alexander's statue and lamenting that he had accomplished nothing at the age at which Alexander had conquered the world; his restless energy, 'counting nothing done if anything remained to do'; the dark days before he took the decisive step of crossing the Rubicon, the boundary of his legal province, to attack Rome; the horrors and portents which accompanied the Ides of March, and the comet which appeared at his death.

Miraculous stories were told of the birth of his heir, the future Augustus. His mother dreamed that she had intercourse with Apollo in the semblance of a snake. While pregnant, she dreamed that her inner organs spread over the sky, and her husband saw the sun rising from her womb. As a child Augustus disappeared from his cradle and was found on a high tower with his face to the sun. As a boy he told the frogs to stop their noise and the place was free from the sound of frogs thereafter. An eagle snatched a loaf of bread from his hand and returned it to him. When Augustus was an adolescent, Cicero dreamed that he had been lowered from heaven by a golden chain and given Jupiter's whip. Another senator dreamed that Jupiter set an image of Rome in the boy's lap. When he was pulling on the *toga virilis* as a sign that he was grown-up, his robe split and fell to the ground. It was a bad omen, but the lad quickly said, 'I shall have the whole senatorial power beneath my feet.' His adoptive father Julius found a palm tree which he took as an omen of victory for himself; shortly after it put out a shoot which towered over the parent tree. So, after the event, the legend grows.

CHAPTER 18

GERMANIC LEGENDS

Widsith spoke, unlocked his word-hoard, he who of men had fared through most races and peoples over the earth; often he had received in hall precious treasure... 'I have heard of many men ruling over the people; every prince must live fittingly... Thus the minstrels of men go wandering, as fate directs, through many lands; they utter their need, speak the word of thanks; south or north, they always meet one wise in measures, liberal in gifts, who wishes to exalt his glory before the warriors, to perform valorous deeds, until light and life fall in ruin together: he gains praise, he has lofty glory under the heavens.'

Widsith, from which this extract comes, is probably the oldest poem in the English language. Perhaps composed in seventh-century Mercia, it shows Germanic legend of the heroic age in its life-setting, in tales told in the halls of the mighty by a wandering narrator to men in quest of fame and glory. The tales begin with historical persons and events, but they are not intended merely as chronicles of past time. They are meant to exalt the memory of notable men and women of the past, and to place before their hearers types of conduct worthy of emulation.

We are dealing here with tribes and nations in Northern Europe, mainly in the period before the fourteenth century, who spoke related languages which are the ancestors of German, English and the Scandinavian languages. Hard and fast lines are difficult to draw, however, and much that is true of the Germanic peoples and their traditional heroic stories also applies to other Indo-European peoples, including the Celts.

Beowulf and the dragon (page 173)

COURAGE AND DUTY

Germanic legend as a whole is anonymous, aristocratic and exemplary. It has definite literary conventions, and has been passed down to us not by way of oral tradition but in written form. The written form, however, is only the final deposit of a long oral treatment, in which have been gathered up actual memories of past events on the one hand, and popular folk-tales on the other. In the chieftain's hall warriors would sit over their beer and their stories, to be entertained and prepared for their next battle by hearing tales of past heroes. They would not expect, nor did they hear, little stories about little people. Only when the story-telling tradition passes over to democratic Iceland does a certain shift of emphasis take place, from the spectacular exploits of kings to the everyday acts of hard-headed farmers – though even a farmer could, and did, exhibit truly heroic virtues. There were still battles to be fought, insults and injuries to be avenged, the honour of families to be protected. The Germanic character is still affirmed, with its emphasis on strength, rescourcefulness and courage in face of the onslaughts of enemies and of fate. But in the early days these were pre-eminently the virtues of kings and their henchmen.

Germanic legend is seldom simple. Stories are interlocked and interwoven with one another, sometimes on no better basis than that they have gathered around a particular name or a particular family. To bring together all the stories told of the hero Sigurd (or Siegfried), for instance, would be a self-defeating exercise: between those in the Icleandic *Edda* and those in the German *Nibelungenlied* there is a great gulf of time and place. From the other end of the Indo-European spectrum, the incredible complexities of the Indian *Mahabharata* illustrate the way in which 'family legend' may develop, given a fertile soil.

The characters of Germanic legend, however, unlike those of India, are entirely human beings. The legends contain no half-human incarnations of gods. The hero's virtues and vices may be spectacular, but they are human virtues and vices, and over all the heroes there looms an inexorable fate, to which even the greatest of them must finally submit. In the legends men and women summon up all their resources to carry out what they conceive to be their duty. Beowulf sets sail to rid a far land of monsters, Amleth feigns madness to avenge his father, King Olav uses fair means and foul to convert his people to Christianity. Small wonder that the hero of Germanic legend is so strongly reminiscent of the Vikings, of those who, as the rune-stone has it, 'voyaged boldly to far lands seeking gold, and eastward they fed the eagles'. The only immortality they sought was that expressed in the Eddic poem *Havamal*:

Flocks die, friends die,
you yourself die likewise;
but if one has won an honoured name,
then that can never die.

How far specific Germanic legends rest on a foundation of solid historical fact is a vexed question, upon which it is unsafe to generalize. The most celebrated of German legend-cycles, the *Nibelungenlied,* we are nowadays assured, is independent of history. But in other cases − notably the Icelandic Sagas − the genuinely historical element is self-evident, though certainly embellished at many points by the addition of imaginative detail. In general, folk memory is a tenacious instrument (often when it has no particular need to be) and even when legends tell us little about historical events, they provide invaluable insights into the values and conditions of the age in which the tales were first told.

BEOWULF, GRENDEL AND THE DRAGON

The only Germanic legend or cycle which has genuinely pre-Christian roots is the Old English story of *Beowulf,* 'the oldest epic in any non-classical European tongue', usually dated to the eighth century. Certainly the form in which we now have it exhibits clear Christian influence but, even so, its Christianity is Germanic Christianity, a dualistic battle of light and darkness, life and death, in which the Christian god has gained the upper hand. Otherwise its material could hardly be more Germanic.

The first part of *Beowulf* is set in a great hall called Heorot, built by the Danish king, Hrothgar. The hall was the scene of nightly merry-making, the sound of which came to the ears of 'a mighty fiend from hell', a water-monster called Grendel. Lurching out of the slimy depths of his lair in the marshes, he broke in while everyone was asleep and killed thirty men. His repeated attacks so terrorized Hrothgar's men that they refused to set foot in the hall after dark. They prayed to their heathen gods, but this was useless: 'Hell was in their hearts; they knew nothing of a Creator, the true God, judge of all acts; nor did they know how to worship the glorious King of heaven.'

A party of Geats (Swedes) under Beowulf came to rid the land of the mischief. Beowulf was already a renowned warrior and giant-killer, the strength of his grip was said to equal that of thirty men. To enhance his reputation, he proposed to fight Grendel to the death with his bare hands, without sword or shield. He said that fate must decide the issue, but the Christian interpreter puts the outcome in the hands not of fate, but of God. 'God in his wisdom must allot the victory as he thinks fit.' And so he did. Grendel, 'fast in the clutch of the strongest man alive', was torn literally limb from limb, and stumbled off to die in the slime.

This was not the end. Even monsters must have their revenge, and Grendel's mother was Beowulf's next opponent, though this time the battle was fought out in the monster's own element, water, deep in the lake where she lived. Again, Beowulf won with God's help, and the hero 'rejoiced in his work'.

The third struggle in *Beowulf* highlights the inevitable outcome of all purely mortal striving. Previously fate (or God, for Christian hearers) has been on Beowulf's side, but this time he has to overcome a dragon guarding a treasure-hoard, to exert his strength 'without Fate allotting him fame in battle'. His sword fails him, and even when his kinsman Wiglaf comes to his help, Beowulf receives a mortal wound; though with the last vestiges of his strength he deals a death-blow to the dragon. 'That was the last victory for the prince by his own deeds, the end of his work in the world.' But still he can rejoice that he has fought a good fight: 'I have lived the appointed span in my land, guarded well my portion, contrived no crafty attacks, nor sworn many oaths unjustly. Stricken with mortal wounds, I can rejoice in all this.' Finally he dedicates the dragon's treasure to the good of his people and declares: 'Fate has swept all my kinsmen away to their destiny, earls in their might; I must needs follow them.'

This is the main story of *Beowulf,* but within it there are smaller episodes, reminiscences of other events, one of which throws light on the Germanic conventions of family loyalty and blood vengeance. The Germanic peoples saw the life of the individual as anchored in the family of which he was part, within which the blood relationship was sacred. (Alliances by marriage, on the other hand, could not be fully trusted.) When blood had been shed, even by accident, the onus was on the father and the brothers to exact compensation. But how to act when the crime has been committed *within* the family, by one member against another? Hrethel, king of the Geats, had two sons, Haethcyn and Herebeald; accidentally, Haethcyn killed Herebeald. Now what was the father to do? He could not avenge one son by killing the other, for if he did, he would violate the family of which he was head and protector. The poet speaks of this dilemma as 'the doom which was to attend the old hero, probe the resources of his soul, and tear the life from his body', and comments: 'This was an inexpiable accident, and a heart-rending crime; for whatever happened, Herebeald must die unavenged.' Where no vengeance may be exacted, the balance of things has been disturbed, and must remain so.

HAMLET'S REVENGE

The theme of vengeance occurs constantly in Germanic legend. An intriguing example is provided by Saxo Grammaticus in his *Danish*

History, written in about AD 1200. This is the story of Amlath (Hamlet), which in a later version provided Shakespeare with one of his most celebrated plots.

In Saxo's version, Amleth is a Prince whose father has been killed by a jealous uncle, Feng, and whose mother, Gertrude, then marries the murderer. Although Feng claims that the deed was done for Gertrude's good, Amleth plans an elaborate revenge. Saxo says that Amleth 'chose to feign dulness, and pretend an utter lack of wits. This cunning course not only concealed his intelligence but ensured his safety', for who would pay attention to the ravings of a madman? Amleth himself is made to say that 'it is better to choose the garb of dulness rather than that of sense… Yet the passion to avenge my father still burns in my heart; but I am watching the chances, I await the fitting hour.'

The fitting hour arrives. Amleth kills a defenceless Feng, whose sword he has fixed in his scabbard, and snares and burns alive all Feng's company — apparently an insane act of wholesale slaughter. It is, then, odd to find the Christian Saxo commending Amleth for his courage and astuteness. 'O valiant Amleth, and worthy of immortal fame, who being shrewdly armed with a feint of folly, covered a wisdom too high for human wit under a marvellous disguise of silliness! and not only found in his subtlety means to protect his own safety, but also by its guidance found opportunity to avenge his father. By this skilful defence of himself, and strenuous revenge for his parent, he has left it doubtful whether we are to think more of his wit or his bravery.'

GRETTIR THE STRONG AND HRAFNKEL

The story of Amleth leaves no doubt of what virtues the Germanic mind considered worthy of emulation. Similar themes occur again and again in the Icelandic Sagas, though there the values they represent are brought down to the level of ordinary men and women. The late thirteenth-century saga of Grettir the Strong *(Grettissaga)* describes the exploits of a man who was to become something of a national hero, Grettir Asmundsson of Bjarg. Even as a youth Grettir was able to overcome bigger and older men, but his spectacular exploits begin when he encounters and defeats a giant, Karr the Old. He also defeats a company of berserkers (warriors of the god Odin: the word *berserk* means 'dressed in the skin of a bear') by plying them with drink and trapping them. He kills a giant bear and in terms reminiscent of *Beowulf,* he meets Glam, a huge Swede. Grettir kills Glam, as Beowulf kills Grendel, but the troubles begin all over again when Glam's ghost returns and haunts the district. There is another struggle, in the course of which Glam places a curse on Grettir, that his strength and his 'luck' will wane. Although Glam's ghost is disposed of, the curse bites, and Grettir is wrongly accused of arson, and outlawed. The feats of daring continue for a time, but fate has turned against him. Accidentally, he breaks a witch's leg, and she brings runic magic to work against him. She carves runes of ill-luck on a log and throws it into the sea in such a way that the waves drive it to shore close to Grettir's home. Grettir finds the log and, not noticing the runes, tries to cleave it with an axe, which glances off and cuts his leg to the bone. At this point Grettir's enemies overtake him. Unable to defend himself, he is killed by his enemies, and once more the fates have been vindicated.

Grettir was a man of great strength, which finally deserted him. Another saga theme is that of the sacred vow, which can be illustrated from *Hrafnkel's Saga.* Hrafnkel was a landowner who possessed a great horse, Freyfaxi, which he had dedicated to the god Frey and which was therefore sacred. He swore a solemn oath to kill anyone who rode the stallion without his permission. A young man called Einar found the horse and could not resist the temptation, riding Freyfaxi from dawn to mid-evening. Hrafnkel found out, and had to avenge the breaking of the vow by killing Einar. The inevitable machinery of vengeance was set in motion. Hrafnkel was outlawed, Freyfaxi was thrown over a cliff, and what remained of Hrafnkel's possessions was destroyed by fire. But in this case Hrafnkel's enemies overreached themselves in taking the law into their own hands and going beyond what the court had decided. In the end Hrafnkel dies in his bed and his enemies have been unable to complete their intended revenge. Hrafnkel, though a violent man and free with his axe, had only done what he was compelled to do. He had paid the penalty and was finally vindicated.

SIGURD AND BRYNHILD

The importance of human relations as a recurring theme in Germanic legend is clear. In the greater cycles of legend, however, many separate motives are interwoven, either within one longer plot or as independent stories told of a particular hero. An admirable illustration is provided by the complex of legends associated with the name and family of Sigurd (in Norse) or Siegfried (in German).

Sigurd is mentioned in some twenty of the poems in the Icelandic *Poetic Edda* (a collection of thirty poems by unknown authors). Gaps in the story are filled in by the prose *Volsunga Saga,* and some stories are retold by Snorri Sturluson, an Icelandic historian of the early thirteenth century. *Thidrek's Saga* gives a version from Lower Saxony, while the High German tradition is represented most fully in the *Nibelungenlied,* from which source − not least thanks to the operas of Richard Wagner − it has passed into the cultural mind of modern Europe.

In the *Poetic Edda* Sigurd is at the court of King Gjuke. Gjuke has a son, Gunnar, and a daughter, Gudrun, who becomes Sigurd's wife. Together they go to pay court on Gunnar's behalf to a Princess called Brynhild. 'He (Sigurd) should have had her, but she was not for him.' Angry Norns (Fates) stood between them. Brynhild loves Sigurd, and would prefer to see him dead than in another woman's embrace, but she belongs now to Gunnar, and laments that 'My lasting longing is the work of a malicious Norn.' She then determines that Sigurd must die. She instructs her new husband, Gunnar, to carry out the murder, but he refuses (another case of a conflict of loyalties). Brynhild stabs herself, living only long enough to prophesy what will happen to the other actors in the drama, and to give instructions about her funeral.

A totally different element in the early Sigurd legend is also found in the *Poetic Edda,* in the 'Prophecy of Gripe'. Gripe is an old and wise King, and in a series of questions and answers he tells Sigurd what will happen to him. Sigurd will become a great hero, generous to a fault, beautiful, wise and courageous. He will avenge his father and do battle with a great dragon; and only then will he meet the family of Gjuke, an encounter which will lead to his final downfall. When his future has been told, Sigurd can only say: 'Farewell! Against fate no one can emerge victorious.'

The episode of Sigurd and the dragon is famous in its own right. A dragon named Fafnir guards a hoard of gold. Sigurd conceals himself in a pit and with an upward thrust of his sword, Gram, kills Fafnir as he slithers past. He then cuts out the dragon's heart and roasts it, burning his finger in the process. He puts his finger to his mouth and swallows a drop of the dragon's blood, which enables him to understand the conversation of two birds hard by, who are discussing how the dragon's brother, Regin, plans to kill him. The information helps him to forestall the plot and ride away with the treasure.

THE DEATH OF SIEGFRIED

The Sigurd—Siegfried legend reaches its highest degree of articulation in the German *Nibelungenlied,* written by an unknown author in Austria, in about 1200, and essentially a story of vengeance. Here Siegfried is the son of Sigmund and Sieglind, the King and Queen of the Netherlands. Before the tale begins he has killed the Nibelung Princes, taken their treasure and the great sword Balmung, and acquired a magic cloak of invisibility. He has also slain a dragon and bathed in its blood, which has made his skin so tough and horny that no sword can bite it — except at one vulnerable spot between his shoulder-blades, where a leaf stuck to him while he was bathing.

Siegfried goes to Burgundy, where he encounters the Princess

Kriemhild, her three royal brothers, Gunther, Gernot and Giselher, and their 'grim retainer', Hagen. Siegfried obtains the hand of the Amazonian Queen Brunhild of Iceland for Gunther. Brunhild is surpassingly beautiful and immensely strong. Whoever hopes to win her must outdo her in throwing the javelin, hurling the weight and the long-jump. If he fails in any of these contests against her, he stands to lose his head. Using his cloak of invisibility and his own unrivalled physical strength, Siegfied first enables Gunther to defeat Brunhild in the contests and then, after they are married, enables Gunther to take the resisting Brunhild by force. In return, he is given Kriemhild in marriage, but Gunther is now afraid of Siegfried. Hagen tricks Kriemhild into revealing the secret of Siegfried's vulnerable spot and treacherously kills him out hunting, with Gunther's connivance.

The death of Siegfried occurs before the story is halfway through. When Kriemhild finds her husband's body on her doorstep, she becomes the centre of a course of tragic events. 'From the moment she learned of Siegfried's death she was the sworn enemy of her own happiness.' She sees his unmarked shield and concludes that he has been murdered without a chance to defend himself. 'If I knew who had done this, I should never cease to plot his death.' The murderer is identified by the dead man himself, for as Hagen approaches the bier the corpse's wounds begin to bleed afresh.

In the meantime, the Nibelung treasure, now the property of Kriemhild, is brought to the Burgundian capital of Worms on the Rhine — 'as much as a dozen wagons fully loaded could carry away from the mountain in four days and nights coming and going thrice a day.' But Hagen gains control of the treasure and sinks it in the Rhine, hoping some day to retrieve it for his own use.

The *Nibelungenlied* now introduces the notorious figure of Attila the Hun, under the name of Etzel. He is a pagan and the widowed Kriemhild a Christian, but he hopes that she may become his Queen and sends to Burgundy for her. She returns with Etzel's messengers to Hungary and becomes his wife. Interestingly enough, the Etzel of this story is not the vicious barbarian of popular fame, but a grand and sympathetic ruler of his people. Kriemhild has not forgotten Hagen, and she sends for her brothers to visit her. Hagen warns them that they may well lose their honour and their lives, 'for in matters of revenge King Etzel's Queen has a long memory'. Giselher accuses Hagen of cowardice in face of the inevitable encounter, and finally Hagen consents to go, though he warns the brothers to travel heavily armed. So they journey to Hungary.

DIETRICH AND HILDEBRAND

Here two fresh characters are introduced, Dietrich and his henchman Hildebrand, both of whom preside over whole legend-cycles of their

own. The most important of these is the *Lay of Hildebrand
(Hildebrandslied),* which tells how Hildebrand had once followed his
lord, Dietrich, into exile, but has now returned with an army. Being
confronted by a rival army, and asking the name of its leader, he finds
that he is face to face with his own son, Hadubrant. Hadubrant does
not believe that Hildebrand can possibly be his father. Insults are
exchanged and a duel is fought, which appears (for the text is
incomplete) to end with the death of the son and the suicide of the
father. The familiar elements of war, exile, revenge and moral
dilemma are all there.

Dietrich of Bern (Verona in Italy) is the legendary alias of
Theodoric the Great, the Gothic King of Italy from 493 to 526. In
legend a slayer of giants and monsters, his exploits are told in various
German poems and in the thirteenth-century *Thidrak's Saga.* He was
driven out of his Kingdom by an enemy, Ermanaric, and took refuge
at Attila's court. In the end, after years in exile, he returned to Italy
and defeated Ermanaric in battle at Ravenna.

THE FINAL VENGEANCE

In the *Nibelungenlied,* however, Kriemhild is still the central
character, and Hagen the focus of her hatred. Things are made worse
when Hagen produces Siegfried's sword. 'The sight of it revived her
sorrow and she began to weep; and this, I fancy, was why Hagen did
it.' Then Hagen confesses to Kriemhild that he was her husband's
murderer. From this point, events move to an inexorable climax.
Inevitably the Burgundians and the Huns fight. Kriemhild burns
down the hall in which the Burgundians are sheltering, but enough
survive to continue the struggle. Dietrich has pledged not to attack
the Burgundians but, fearing that harm has come to Etzel, his
warriors move in, and finally Gunther and Hagen confront Dietrich
and Hildebrand as virtually the sole survivors. In the end, Dietrich
fights and binds Hagen and Gunther, and delivers them to Kriemhild.
She gives Hagen one last chance to tell her where he has hidden her
treasure. He refuses, and both prisoners are killed, Gunther by the
Queen's men, Hagen by Kriemhild herself with Siegfried's own
sword. She is then killed by Hildebrand. All the complexities have
resolved themselves in a final scene of death, and the story ends with
the laconic observation: 'The King's high festival had ended in
sorrow, as joy must ever turn to sorrow in the end.'

VALDEMAR AND TAABE

Examples of other common legendary themes can be cited from
lesser-known tales deriving from Denmark. There is the story of King
Dan, who insisted that he was not to be cremated but buried on his

horse, surrounded by his men. 'Tell your King,' he instructed his attendants on his death-bed, 'that he shall think of me when he is in trouble. Then I will come with all my men and drive away the enemy and help him to rule all the world.' This type of story, somewhere between a legend and a folk-tale, is also told of King Arthur and Sir Francis Drake. The hero, victorious in his lifetime, promises to return from the grave to deliver his people in time of danger.

Other Danish legends have to do with the building of a castle, fort or earthwork. The celebrated Gurre Castle was actually built by King Valdemar Atterdag, but legend ascribes it to the earlier Valdemar the Great. He was bewitched by his mistress, Taabe, to such effect that on her death he refused to be parted from her corpse. Eventually a servant discovered the source of the mischief, an amulet which the corpse was still wearing. The servant stole it, and with it the King's love. In horror, the servant threw the amulet away, and on the spot the King built his castle, out of love for the place where the amulet had fallen.

The theme of deceit occurs in the tale of Queen Thyre, wife of Gorm, who owes a vast sum in taxes to a German emperor. She pretends to love him and persuades him to postpone the collection of his taxes for three years, during which time her people protect themselves by building a defensive wall (the *Danevirke*). When the wall is complete, she announces to the angry German that she is faithful to her husband after all, and so secures peace for her country.

INEVITABLE FATE

By far the most important single theme of the legends is that of fate – the belief that the lives of men and women, high and low, individually and collectively, are finally under the control of a destiny which, try as they may, they can do nothing to avert. This dominant idea runs all through the Germanic story-telling tradition. An Anglo-Saxon poet, gazing in wonder at the remains of a Roman city (probably Bath), writes: 'Bright were the castle-dwellings, many the bath-houses, lofty the host of pinnacles, great the tumult of men, many a mead-hall full of the joys of men, till Fate the mighty overturned that.' Here fate is perhaps little more than an image of Time, but elsewhere it is abundantly clear that the legends are meant to warn that no one, however strong or resourceful, can escape his allotted fate.

The 'heroic' view of destiny is a vision of inflexible law and inescapable predetermination. In Germanic belief, each man had a certain span of life, a certain measured time to live, and not only the time but the place and circumstances of his death were determined from the moment of his birth, by the Norns, or Fates – three female figures, whom the Norsemen called Urd, Verdandi and Skuld. (The three occur in Shakespeare as the three 'weird sisters' of *Macbeth*, who are not witches but the fates: 'weird' *(wyrd)* is the Anglo-Saxon word for 'fate', and one of the Norns is called Urd, which is a form of the same word.)

In his *Danish History*, the tenth-century author Saxo Grammaticus tells how Friedleif wanted to look into the future destiny of his son Olaf. He went into a temple, where he saw three seated figures, the Norns. One gave the son beauty; the second gave him generosity; but the third, 'a woman of more mischievous temper and malignant disposition', spoiled his character. 'Thus the benefits of the others were spoilt by the poison of a lamentable doom.' Also from Saxo comes this fragment of a conversation between two Kings. Hildiger says to Halfdan: 'Time is left for our purpose; our two destinies have a different lot; one is surely doomed to die by a fatal weird, while triumph and glory and all the good of living await the other in better years. Thus our omens differ, and our portions are distinguished.'

Fate is not always distinguished from luck, since a 'lucky' man is one on whom the fates have smiled. Fate and luck are, in a measure, contagious. The Icelandic *Flateyarbok* tells the story of an 'unlucky' merchant called Hroi, who entered into an alliance with the Danish King Sveinn Fork-beard. The question then was whether the King's good luck was stronger than the merchant's bad luck. The outcome is unimportant; what matters is that a man's fate can topple others beside himself, and bring suffering on many who might otherwise have escaped.

Even after the conversion of the Germanic peoples to Christianity, which took place during the third to the eighth centuries, and the theoretical replacement of the idea of fate by that of divine providence, the Germanic priorities continue to be observed. Although the anonymous author of *The Fates of Men* can write piously, 'Thus wondrously the God of hosts throughout the world has fashioned and bestowed the arts of man and ruled the destiny of everyone of mankind on earth', another anonymous Anglo-Saxon writer expressed more of the popular mind when he wrote tersely: 'The glories of Christ are great. Fate is strongest.' And several centuries later, we still find a Norwegian king standing by the jetty watching the departure of a ship carrying his friend and ally Kjartan (hero of the *Laxdaela Saga, c.* 1245) and saying: 'Great is the worth of Kjartan and his kindred, but to cope with their fate is not an easy matter.'

CHRISTIAN HEROES

The conversion of the Germanic peoples to Christianity by no means brought the legend-making process to an end. Rather, the old-established Germanic ideals came to be embodied in the lives of Christian heroes. There were many of these, but particularly appropriate examples are provided by the two Olavs, Kings of Norway: Olav Tryggveson and Olav Haraldsson the Saint.

Olav Tryggveson was King for only five years, from 995 to his death in battle in 1000. The tale of his adventures begins even before his birth, with the story of the persecution and flight of his mother, Astrid. At the age of three, the infant Olav was made a slave in Estonia. Six years later he encountered in a market-place the Viking who had sold him into slavery, and killed him with an axe. The boy was then brought up in the court of Queen Allogia of Novgorod, eventually becoming a renowned Viking chieftain. On one of his expeditions to the Scilly Isles, it is said, he was converted to the Christian faith and baptized by a hermit. At all events, it was as a Christian that he returned to Norway. At this point legend again makes its presence felt. According to the chronicler Adam of Bremen, Olav was a necromancer who finally became an apostate and committed suicide. The Sages tell precisely the opposite story, that the magicians were those whom Olav attempted to exterminate. It is clear, however, that Olav did not entrust the proclamation of the Christian mesage entirely to priests, but acted on his own behalf.

In the process he aroused much opposition, not all of it doubt and stubbornness. The story is told that one night he was visited by a mysterious old man, one-eyed and wearing a large hat which hid much of his face. The stranger kept the King fascinated with his conversation far into the night, until one of Olav's bishops intervened. The food in the kitchen was found to be polluted, at which point the King identified the mysterious visitor as none other than the god Odin himself, come to try to draw him back to the faith of his fathers. The stratagem failed and Olav's Viking virtues were placed at the service of the White Christ, but his exploits were still those of the Germanic hero, a man of courage, strength and resourcefulness. After his death, stories were told of his reappearances, as a pilgrim to Rome, as a merchant in the Mediterranean, and even as the abbot of a monastery near Jerusalem (though a more unlikely abbot it would be hard to imagine).

Olav Haraldsson was in many ways a similar figure, another former Viking (he took part in the sack of Canterbury in 1011), who penetrated as far as the Mediterranean before becoming a Christian. According to legend, it was at Gibraltar that a 'tall, striking and terrible' man came to him and said: 'Return thou to thine estate for thou shalt become Norway's King to all eternity.' And return he did, to complete the processes of unification and Christianization which the earlier Olav had begun — a transition which was not easily accomplished, as the following episode suggests.

In Gudbrandsdalen, Olav was told scornfully by the locals that he and his followers were worshipping a god whom they had never seen.

'But we have a god we can see every day. Today he is not here, for the weather is too wet, but you will see him in good time; he is big and terrifying and I think you will be full of fear when he comes to the *Thing*.' On the following morning, sure enough, the local farmers came to the *Thing* (assembly), dragging after them a huge image of the god (apparently Thor). 'Now our god has come,' they shouted, 'he who rules over all and he is looking at you with his keen eyes.' Just then the sun rose, and Olav's moment had come. 'Look up,' he cried, 'look towards the east, where comes our God surrounded by light.' As the men of Gudbrandsdalen looked eastward, Olav's henchman raised his club and broke their god's image apart – and out of it there came tumbling mice, rats, snakes and other impurities. 'So that is your god,' the men were told, and the message struck home.

The old gods, giants, trolls, monsters, berserkers – all are grist to the mill of Germanic legend. It matters little whether the hero is a half-mythical figure whose origins are inaccessible to us, a well-attested historical king or an Icelandic land-owner. In every case stories were told not merely because they were good, or fanciful, or horrific. They were told to those who wished for nothing better than to become heroes in their own right, remembered for the courage, cunning and resourcefulness with which they had gained the upper hand over their enemies. If in the end even the heroes had to submit to fate, or to God, then this too was what every man expected.

CELTIC LEGENDS

CHAPTER 19
IRELAND

A large volume of information has been collected from Irish folk tradition about figures of Irish history, ranging from Brian Boru and Strongbow to Owen Roe O'Neill, Cromwell, Bonnie Prince Charlie, Dean Swift, Daniel O'Connell and Eamonn de Valera, to mention but a few. Stories about saints and poets abound, as do stories about 'wise' men or women, notable misers and musicians, 'poor scholars', prodigious athletes and gifted craftsmen, outlaws and informers. Echoes of important events in Irish history flood the folk memory, which has a proclivity for telescoping events and transferring traditions from individual to individual, from one generation to the next. The Vikings and the descendants of the Cromwellian settlers are both credited with the practice of *ius primae noctis* (the right of the first night with a bride), and the birthmark in the form of a cross is transplanted from the back of Daniel O'Connell to that of Eamonn de Valera.

CU CHULAINN

However unhistorical they may be, the early Irish stories known as the Ulster Cycle were told as historical. Passed on by word of mouth long before they were written down, most of them are about the warriors of Conchobar of Ulster, said to have ruled at the beginning of the Christian era. Conchobar's greatest champion was his nephew, Cu Chulainn. Brave, intelligent, generous, loyal, beautiful to look at and loved by many women, Cu Chulainn as a boy deliberately chose a short life, an early death and undying fame rather than a long safe life and obscurity. He did battle with human enemies, supernatural beings and monsters, armed with his special weapon, the *gae bolga*,

Cu Chulainn of Ulster

a barbed spear, and aided by his great horse, the Grey of Macha. When the rage of combat was on him, his whole body became terrifyingly distorted, 'the hero's light' shone from his forehead and a column of dark blood rose up from his head. On one occasion when he was in his battle-fury three vats of cold water were needed to cool him down.

According to one tradition, Cu Chulainn's father was the god Lug. He was already a formidable warrior as a small boy and he got his name, which means Hound of Culann, at the age of twelve (or five, some said), when he killed the huge watch-dog of Culann the smith, picking it up by the legs and dashing it to pieces against a stone. He carried off the beautiful Emer as his wife and her father, Forgall, had plotted his death; the hero stormed Forgall's fortress and pursued him to his death off the ramparts. He had earlier overcome a warrior-woman, Aife, who bore him a son, Conlai.

Cu Chulainn eventually killed his son, in a tragic conflict of loyalties. Conlai, who was brought up in his mother's country, swore never to reveal his identity to any one man and never to decline a fight. When he came to Ulster and was challenged to identify himself, he defeated two of Conchobar's best warriors, and Cu Chulainn had to defend the honour of Ulster against him. Though he knew his opponent was his only son, Cu Chulainn fought and killed him. Then he took up the boy's body and threw it before Conchobar and the warriors, saying: 'Here is my son for you, men of Ulster!'

There is another tragic conflict of loyalties in the *Tain Bo Cuailnge* (The Cattle-Raid of Cooley). Queen Medb of Connaught led an army against Ulster to seize a great bull which she coveted. Cu Chulainn kept her army at bay alone, fighting single combat after single combat while Conchobar's other fighting men were sick of a mysterious disease. Then the enemy sent against him his dear friend and foster-brother, Fer Diad. Cu Chulainn again put his duty to Conchobar above his affections, and after three days of combat he killed Fer Diad.

Cu Chulainn came to his own death in battle. On his way to the fight he passed by a fire where three old hags were cooking a dog. The flesh of the dog, his namesake, was taboo to Cu Chulainn, but it was also taboo to him to pass a cooking-fire without eating some of the food. He hesitated, and then ate a joint of the meat, using his left hand, which lost its strength. In the final battle, surrounded by his enemies, he tied himself to a standing stone so he would die on his feet. They did not know he was dead until a raven came to take his eyes.

THE SLEEPING HERO

The other great fighting hero of early Irish tradition was Finn Mac Cool, the central character of the Fenian Cycle. Most of these stories are set in the south of Ireland where Finn was the leader of the army of Cormac Mac Airt, said to have been High King of Ireland in the third century AD. Finn was born after his father had been killed in a fight, and he was brought up secretly in the forest. He was a great poet, he had the gift of second sight and he owned a magic hood, by wearing which he could turn himself into a dog or a deer. He was the Father of Oisin (or Ossian), to whom many of the tales in the Fenian Cycle are attributed.

Finn is one of the figures to whom the 'sleeping hero' legend is attached in Ireland. It may have come to Ireland with the Normans and is told mainly about Gearoid Iarla ('Earl Gerald', possibly the 11th Earl of Kildare who died in 1586). Others to fill the title role, as it were, include Balldearg O'Donnell, Hugh O'Neill and Robert Bruce. Among the basic motifs which occur in the legend are the location of an enchanted sleeping army or hero in a lake or cave, the fated hour of delivery from enchantment and near-awakening as the result of some act of a visitor. Here is a version of this legend as recorded by a nineteenth-century Irish writer, William Carleton:

Then there was *Beal-derg* (Balldearg), and several others of the fierce old Milesian chiefs, who along with their armies lay in an enchanted sleep, all ready to awake and take a part in the delivery of their country. 'Sure such a man' and they would name him, was once going to a fair to sell a horse – well and good; the time was the dawn of the morning, a little before daylight: he met a man who undertook to purchase his horse; they agreed upon a price, and the seller followed the buyer into a Rath [fort], where he found a range of horses, each with an armed soldier asleep by his side, ready to spring upon him if he awoke. The purchaser cautioned the owner of the horse, as they were about to enter the subterraneous dwelling, against touching either horse or man; but the countryman happened to stumble, inadvertently laid his hand upon a sleeping soldier, who immediately leaped up, drew his sword, and asked, *'wuil anam inh?'* Is the time in it? Is the time arrived? To which the horse-dealer of the Rath replied, *'Ha niel. Go dhee collhow areesht.'* No; go to sleep again. Upon this, the soldier immediately sank down in his former position, and unbroken sleep reigned throughout the cave.

FROM CROMWELL TO O'CONNELL

The curse of Cromwell is counted one of the most terrible of Irish curses. The Irish do not remember him fondly, the English scarcely remember him at all, in folk tradition at least. There used to be an old abbey by the River Blackwater, which flows through Fermoy in

County Cork, before there was any bridge and the people knelt on the opposite river bank while Mass was being celebrated in the abbey. One morning Cromwell's men attacked the abbey and drove the monks into the river where they drowned. Ever since the Blackwater claims three victims annually.

The theme of violent death seems to dominate stories about Oliver Cromwell in Ireland. While the circumstances of Cromwell's own death (in England in 1658) are not remembered, tradition records that Irish soil refused to accept his body which is said to lie buried in layers of lead at the bottom of the Irish Sea, where it makes the sea rough. Tradition tells us that until coffin and body melt away, Ireland will never be free.

Irish tradition does not even give Cromwell unqualified credit for his remarkably successful campaign in Ireland, for at least some of his success was believed to be due to the venality of the Irish and their incorrigible disloyalty to one another. Cromwell, it seems, proved this very point by paying a sneak visit to Ireland before his campaign began. He attended an Irish wake and before the night was out, succeeded in persuading a grieving widow to part with her husband's remains for a small consideration. On his return, he told his army that they could take Ireland with 'roasted apples' for, said he, 'when we can buy the dead, we can surely buy the living'.

Of Bonnie Prince Charlie — the Young Pretender (Charles Edward Stuart, 1720—88, grandson of James II, King of England, Scotland and Ireland), there is only one trace in Irish tradition and that is found in a legend that describes his visit as a fugitive to County Donegal. He is said to have baffled his pursuers with the help of a friendly smith who shod his horse with the shoes in backwards. This legend slots snugly into the background of an Irish-speaking Ireland where the English- speaking stranger (Bonnie Prince Charlie) creates embarrassing difficulties for his hosts. For lack of English, they are unable to tell him it is bed-time and when, eventually, he does fall asleep, someone is heard to remark that there isn't as much English in the place as will wake him in the morning.

Daniel O'Connell (1775—1847), famous as a national leader, lawyer and parliamentarian, is undoubtedly one of the most outstanding figures in Irish legendry. There are dozens of stories attaching to his name and many of them still enjoy a lively popularity in modern-day Irish oral tradition. Numerous legends commemorate his skill and cunning as a lawyer, especially cases which he won by the use of clever ruses. On one occasion, he is said to have been approached by a client who had been bamboozled into selling six cattle for the price of two to a greedy shopkeeper. 'Dan' (as he is popularly remembered) resolved to beat the shopkeeper at his own game by having his client submit to having the tops of his ears cut off and dispatched to England in a matchbox. Then Dan (in disguise) and his client visited the greedy shopkeeper and, acting under Dan's instructions, the client ordered and paid for as much tobacco as would reach from the tops of his toes to the tops of his ears. The two yards or so of tobacco handed over by the shopkeeper proved totally insufficient, of course, the tops of the client's ears being at the time a great deal further distant than two yards from the tops of his toes. Thus, the shopkeeper was forced to make a handsome settlement with Dan's client.

DANISH HEATHER BEER

The Norse raids and settlements have left their mark on the Irish landscape in the shape of a scattering of Scandinavian place-names around the Irish coast. More significantly, perhaps, the memory of *Na Lochlannaigh* — the Danes as they are invariably called in Ireland — still survives on the lips of Irish people to the present day. The custom of *ius primae noctis* is attributed to them in County Donegal in the context of the Sweeney clan. Nine young girls of the name were to be married and the Danes claimed their right to this custom of sharing a bed with them on their wedding night. The Sweeneys dressed up nine of their young men as women and armed each of them with a dagger. In the morning there were nine dead Danes which put an end to *ius primae noctis* in Donegal — at least among Sweeneys, who were known ever after as Clan Sweeney of the Daggers.

By far the commonest legend about the Vikings, however, is that known as 'Danish Heather Beer'. The Danes, it seems, knew and cherished the secret of how to make beer from heather which they guarded well from the Irish even to the very day when, after the Battle of Clontarf, there were only two Danes left in Ireland, father and son. The Irish were at first intent on killing them, but wiser counsels prevailed and the Danes were closely questioned about the brewing process which their people had long held secret from the Irish. Eventually, the father agreed to tell the secret, but on one condition: namely, that his son should be killed immediately, for he said he could not bear the shame of having his son hear him divulge this information. In reality, he was afraid that his son might tell the secret if he, the father, happened to be killed first. The son was promptly dispatched by the Irish whereupon the father cried triumphantly that they might as well kill him too for he had no intention of ever giving them the secret recipe. So, the Irish never found out the secret of how to make heather beer.

LEGENDS OF PLACES

Rivers, rocks, cliffs and caves, mountains and lakes — their origin and the explanation of the meaning of their names, is a subject which has occupied Irish imagination from the earliest times and, indeed, forms a significant part of early Irish literature. The names of gods and goddesses of the dim past are discernible in certain place-names, such as *Cnoc Aine* (Aine) and *Tigh Dhoinn* (Donn), while *Sui Fhinn* (commonly anglicized as Seefinn) commemorates Finn Mac Cool. One of Finn's war-band is remembered in the name 'Dermot and Grania's Bed', as it is called on the Ordnance Survey maps. There is hardly a county in Ireland which does not boast at least one of these 'beds', which are otherwise known to archaeologists as dolmens. The affair of Dermot (Diarmaid) and Grania (Grainne) is well documented and celebrated in Irish literature and folklore. Grania, daughter of Cormac Mac Airt, the High King, was to marry Finn Mac Cool. She determined to elope with Dermot, one of Finn's men, and having administered a sleeping draught to the assembled company at her betrothal feast, persuaded Dermot to carry her off. Many marvellous adventures and escapes followed with Finn and his men in hot pursuit of the fleeing couple and Dermot and Grania seeking refuge in many different parts of Ireland, avoiding capture by all kinds of magic means and stratagems. The various places where they made their bed are still pointed out and their story remembered. Finn and Dermot made peace in the end, but later Dermot was killed by a magic pig which he was hunting and Finn, though he had the gift of healing, nevertheless allowed him to die.

The Melusine legend, called after the heroine of a legend associated with the house of Lusignan of France, also embodies elements of tragedy and romance. In Ireland, it is specially, though not exclusively, connected with Lough Inchiquin in County Clare. A supernatural woman, who is supposed to have resided in this lake, married a local man by the name of Quin on condition that none of the local O'Briens who had held her prisoner for a spell would ever be invited to their house. Quin broke his promise to the lady of the lake and she went back into the lake taking her children with her. Quin followed after and they were never seen again.

Irish tradition is full of stories about houses, towns, islands and even countries which are covered by water but which become visible to human kind from time to time. Animals are seen grazing, clothes bleaching and crops growing on these mainly submarine territories which are given names like Hy Brasil, Tir na hOige, Mainistir Leitreach and Beag-Arainn. The existence of one such island is explained by the action of Finn Mac Cool in combatting certain sea pirates. As in the case of the creation of Lough Neagh and the Isle of Man, Finn seized a handful of land and threw it to the west towards the mouth of Galway Bay. The hole which was left behind became Lough Corrib and the piece of land which Finn threw to the west broke into four pieces, three of which fell close to the mouth of the bay and became the Aran Islands, while the fourth landed much farther away and disappeared out of sight. The next time the robbers returned, the sunken island rose up from the sea by magic and then sank again, taking the robbers and their ships to the bottom.

Among the legends of Tara, in County Meath, the old capital of Ireland, is the story of the Lia Fail, the Stone of Destiny, on which the High Kings were crowned. It was said that King Conn of the Hundred Battles discovered it at Tara, for he trod on it and it shrieked many times, the number of shrieks showing how many rightful kings would be descended from him. According to one tradition, it was taken to Scotland in the sixth century for the crowning of an Irish king there, and as the Stone of Scone it became the coronation stone of the Scots kings. Edward I of England bore it off to London and it was enclosed in the coronation chair in Westminster Abbey. However, many people denied that the Lia Fail ever left Ireland, and many that the stone King Edward carried off was the true Stone of Scone.

Places formerly inhabited by the fairies − 'gentle' places as they are called − are still pointed out and they, like lone (fairy) bushes, are often accorded more than a modicum of respect; any interference with them is considered likely to lead to disaster. A recent case in point concerns the removal of a lone bush from in front of the premises of a large Dutch industrial firm in Limerick. Dutch labour had to be called in to do the job since none of the local employees was prepared to touch it. A short time later, the factory closed with the loss of 1400 jobs.

The list of fairy legends common in Ireland runs to many hundreds. There is also a mass of stories about changelings, mermaids and the Devil.

ST BRENDAN AND ST PATRICK

Saints' names, apart from being regularly associated with churches, graveyards, holy wells and the like, are also connected with miracles and cures, prophecies and sayings, blessings and curses, prayers, charms and conversions, and also pilgrimages and local devotions. A handful of stories about Ireland's premier saints must suffice to illustrate the richness of these traditions.

The famous story of St Brendan's voyage to the west in search of 'the land promised to the saints' has its background in Irish seafaring and reflects genuine knowledge of the Atlantic mingled with fantasy. There had been many earlier pagan and Christian tales of adventurous voyages. St Brendan (*c.* 486-*c.* 575) and his companions encountered numerous marvels, monsters and wonderful islands, including an island of sheep, an island of birds, a towering column of crystal rising from the sea, and an island shrouded in fire and fumes where giant smiths were at work (possibly Iceland). They also celebrated Easter on the back of a friendly whale. When they reached the paradisal promised land they were told that God would one day reveal it to all Christians, but for the time being it must remain concealed. St Brendan's Isle was shown on medieval maps in various positions in the Atlantic and the story that the Irish saint had found an unknown country far to the west influenced Columbus.

One of the most widely known legends about St Patrick (*c.* 390-*c.* 461) is the story of his meeting with Oisin (Ossian), last of Finn's men and recently returned from Tir na nOg, the Land of Youth, where he had spent some 300 years. Patrick, intent on converting Oisin to Christianity, as he had done the rest of the Irish, grants him an opportunity to have a peep into hell, where, he contends, the rest of the Fianna – Oisin's long-dead companions – are sojourning. Oisin sees one of them, Goll, herding all the devils in hell into a corner and thrashing them with a flail whose thong snaps at a crucial moment, thus frustrating all his efforts. Patrick, thinking of Oisin's baptism, asks him if having seen hell there is anything he would wish for. Oisin replies that all he would wish for would be for Goll to have a thong in his flail which would never break.

In the end Oisin succumbed to Patrick's blandishments and became a Christian. At his baptism, however, Patrick accidentally pierced Oisin's foot with his crozier, which fact he did not discover until the ceremony was concluded. Oisin endured the pain without a murmur and when questioned as to why he did not object maintained that he thought it was all part of the baptism.

Other stories associated with St Patrick explain why dogs resemble human beings in nature and lick one's hand so affectionately, why the plaice has a crooked mouth, why salmon leap and why green ribbons and shamrock are worn on St Patrick's Day (17 March), Ireland's national holiday, while the achievement of Patrick's servant boy in diverting his master's curse on Ireland explains why the tops of the rushes are black, as are the tips of cows' horns, and why the froth and foam of the river is worthless.

Patrick, it seems, lay down to take a nap one day, but before dropping off to sleep he warned his servant boy to pay careful attention to any utterance he might make. No sooner had Patrick dozed off than the boy heard him cry 'My curse on Ireland', to which the boy quickly added 'Let it be on the tops of the rushes', and these have remained black ever since. 'My curse on Ireland', cried Patrick again. 'Let it be on the tips of the horns of the cows', said the boy, and these as everyone knows are black even to the present day. Finally, Patrick cursed Ireland for the third time. 'Let it be on the froth of the river', said the servant boy and so it is that the froth of the river is of no value to anyone.

ST BRIGID AND ST COLMCILLE

St Brigid is closely associated with fertility — with agriculture, cows and milk and the weather. On her feast day, 1 February, traditionally the first day of spring in Ireland, a ritual sod was turned to symbolize the beginning of the new agricultural year. Brigid was, indeed, still is, a popular figure not least in the religious sense to judge by the many prayers and invocations containing her name. A common Brigidine legend relates how she came into possession of the whole of the Curragh of Kildare, an area specially associated with her name. She is said to have removed horse's ears from a famous king, who showed his gratitude by granting her as much land as she would ask for. She said she only needed as much land as her cloak would cover, but when she laid her cloak on the ground, it spread and spread until it covered all of the Curragh of Kildare. Another legend tells of how she helped to spare the blushes of the pregnant Virgin Mary by diverting the attention of a crowd of people to herself and thus permitting the Virgin to pass unnoticed. Brigid seized a harrow and having replaced its teeth with lighted candles drew the harrow through the crowd whose gaze was thus averted from Mary. So it is that by Mary's grateful ordinance the feast of St Brigid (1 February) takes precedence over Candlemas — 2 February.

'To every cow its calf and to every book its copy' sums up one of the best-known stories about St Colmcille or Columba (sixth century). He it was who brought Irish Christianity to Scotland and founded the famous monastery of Iona. As a young monk in Ireland, energetic and ambitious, he had completed the painstaking task of stealthily copying a valuable 'book' or manuscript. He was discovered and his right to retain the copy he had made was disputed, with the result that his copy was confiscated after the judgment quoted above had been pronounced. Colmcille was a member of an important and powerful clan and civil strife ensued which finally led to his repentance and exile to Iona.

Colmcille is famous in folk tradition for his prophecies and also as a protector of seamen. He is said to have laid a curse on certain Irish rivers as a result of having slipped on a salmon while attempting a crossing, thus explaining the absence of salmon in these rivers to the present day. Popular tradition seems to indicate that he was vindictive and miserly in character.

Stories about Our Lord, the Blessed Virgin and the Holy Family are found in abundance in Irish tradition. These include the popular Cherry Tree Carol which tells of a fruit tree bending down its branches so that Mary might take some fruit, and also the explanation for the emergence of avarice within the Church, due to an ill-considered act of St Peter. Christ and St Peter, the story goes, while out on their travels came across an emaciated beggar lying in filthy rags by the roadside. The beggar asked for alms and Christ gave him a penny. Later, they came upon a jolly beggar in the prime of condition and Christ gave him a shilling. Peter asked for an explanation of Christ's actions and Christ ordered him to retrace his steps, saying that he would find the jolly beggar in the nearest tavern spending his shilling and entertaining his friends; the wretch by the roadside, on the other hand, he would find dead and concealed in his rags would be a fortune of money, all of which was to be thrown by Peter into a nearby river. Peter did as he was told and found everything as Christ had said he would. He gathered up the miserly beggar's money and threw it all into the river ... except for one coin which he kept. This resulted in the entry of avarice into the church and explains the greed of the clergy ever since.

CELTIC LEGENDS

CHAPTER 20
WALES

A characteristic of Welsh legends is the role played by place-names and features of landscape. Stories, even those of mythological origin, tend to have a precise and real geography. From early times, prehistoric remains and other signs of antiquity have acquired legendary lore. Cromlechs, for example, are often identified as the quoits of heroes, especially Arthur. The tale of 'Math' in the *Maginogion,* a medieval collection of Welsh stories, describes the vengance wrought by the hero Lleu Llaw Gyffes on his wife's lover, Gronwy Befr. Gronwy held up a stone slab to protect himself, but Lleu hurled his spear with such force that it pierced both the stone and Gronwy, killing him. The stone with the hole through it is still there, says the story-teller, on the bank of the River Cynfael (where it was rediscovered in the 1930s).

Some legends are designed to provide historical explanations of present circumstances, and may be regarded as traditional history, while others are simply popular stories told of historical characters. Much of the traditional history of early Britain centred around the various invaders of the island. The Roman conquest naturally loomed large in it, and the memory of having been part of the Roman Empire appears to have been of great significance in the medieval Welsh consciousness. An example of the Roman connection is the legend of 'the Dream of Maxen' in the *Mabinogion.* Maxen was a wise and handsome Emperor of Rome, who dreamed that he travelled to a faraway fortress where he saw a beautiful girl, seated in a chair of red gold, and fell in love with her. Haunted by the dream, he sent envoys to search for her and they eventually found her at Caernarfon (Caernarvon). Her name was Elen Luyddawg, Elen of the Hosts.

Gwion Bach and the witch Ceridwen (page 200)

Maxen went to Britain and married her. He ruled in Britain for seven years, but was recalled to Rome to oust a usurper.

Maxen is a conflation of two historical figures, the early fourth-century Emperor Maxentius and Magnus Maximus, a general who was proclaimed Emperor by his troops in Britain in AD 383 and led his army to the Continent to win the purple. He was regarded as responsible for the abandonment of Britain by Rome, which left the island open to the Saxons. Many of the main dynastic families of medieval Wales traced their descent from 'Maxim Guletic', and the departure of his troops was the basis of a legend about the colonization of Brittany. According to 'the Dream', when Maxen left Britain a British war-band led by Elen's brothers went with him and recaptured Rome for him. Later some of them settled in Brittany and married local women but, lest the language of their offspring should become impure, the mothers' tongues were cut out: hence the Welsh name for Brittany, Llydaw, here fancifully derived from *lled-taw,* 'semi-silent', because the men could speak but the women could not.

VORTIGERN AND THE SAXONS

The other notable invaders of historical tradition are the Saxons. The British author Gildas, writing in the sixth century, says that they came in three long-boats and were kindly received by the British King, but later turned against their hosts and ravaged the island. According to the *History of the Britons,* traditionally attributed to the ninth-century Welsh writer Nennius, these first settlers were led by two brothers, Horsa and Hengist. They were welcomed by the British ruler Vortigern (Gwrtheyrn in Welsh) as mercenaries and were granted the Isle of Thanet. Vortigern became infatuated with Hengist's daughter Rowena (Rhonwen), which enabled the Saxons to demand Kent as the marriage fee. The strained relations between Britons and Saxons appeared to be resolved when Hengist invited his hosts to parley at a feast. The unsuspecting Britons sat down to eat, but at a pre-arranged signal each of the Saxons set upon his neighbour and knifed him. This Betrayal of the Long Knives marked the end of tolerable relations.

Vortigern, fool or quisling, became the archetypal villain of the historical tradition, blamed for letting the Saxons loose on Britain. He fled from place to place, pursued by the wrath of heaven and by his enemies, Welsh and Saxon, until finally he was burned to death in his castle, Craig Gwrtheyrn on the Teifi, by fire from heaven.

In another story told by Nennius, Vortigern attempts to build a fortress at Dinas Emrys in Gwynedd, but the foundations laid by day keep disappearing during the night. A wondrous boy named Emrys explains that two dragons, one red and the other white, sleep in a pool beneath the foundations. The dragons awake and fight, and are revealed as prophetic symbols of the British-Saxon conflict. The role of Emrys in the story was later transferred to Merlin. Modern excavations at Dinas Emrys unearthed the pool and a stone pavement, but the dragons had flown.

ARTHUR AND HIS MEN

As has been mentioned, topographical features are among the earliest elements in the Welsh Arthurian legend. Arthur may well have been a historical character, but whatever his origins, by the time substantive references to him appear he is already developing into a legendary figure linked with topographical phenomena. In one part of Nennius' *History of the Britons* Arthur is portrayed in a historical context as a leader of British armies fighting the Saxons, but in the section of the work termed *Mirabilia* (Marvels) the more popular view of him is clearly seen. Here he slays his own son Amr and from the grave springs the fountain Llygad Amr (Amr's Eye, Gamber Head, Herefordshire). Another marvel is Carn Cafall (now Corn Gafallt near Rhayader, Powys) where Arthur's hound Cafall left his footprint on a stone while hunting the boar Troit. At a later period rocks, cairns, hills and caves bearing Arthur's name are legion and are found all over Wales.

More interesting, however, is the suggestion of a particular tale associated with the second of these marvels. The hunting of the boar Troit, or Twrch Trwyth, forms a major episode in the earliest extant Arthurian story, 'Culhwch and Olwen' in the *Mabinogion.* The hero, Culhwch, is fated to marry only Olwen, the giant's daughter. Before he may do so, he must perform certain tasks and win specified objects, among them the comb and shears lying between the ears of the fearsome boar Troit, a prince who has been transformed into a beast for his sins. Culhwch enlists the help of Arthur and his men. The boar is in Ireland, but crosses to Dyfed with his progeny and is hunted across South Wales, leaving a trail of place-names containing elements meaning pig, boar or swine. The boar swims the estuary of the River Severn hotly pursued by Arthur's men, who succeed in snatching the comb and shears from his head before driving him off the cliffs of Land's End. The reference in Nennius shows that this story was well established as an Arthurian tale as early as the ninth century.

Arthur is often a hunter of fierce and monstrous beasts. In other stories he and his men free the land of dragons, of a monstrous cat, and of 'dog-heads'. A difficult poem in the *Book of Taliesin,* 'The Spoils of Annwn' (ninth or tenth century), seems to recount Arthur's expedition to the otherworld (Annwn) to win a magical cauldron, one of whose properties was that it would not boil the food of a coward, though it was unstinting in its provision for heroes.

Arthur appears as the leader of a group who fought giants, slew monsters, overcame oppressions and performed heroic deeds. As such his legend probably had some stable episodes and invariable features, together with a number of 'floating' ones which could be associated with him as with any hero, which makes it difficult to describe a Welsh Arthurian cycle. The accounts of the hero's birth and boyhood are first found in Geoffrey of Monmouth and in Continental romance (see ARTHUR AND LEGENDARY BRITAIN), though a Welsh tradition claims that he was brought up at Caer-gai in Gwynedd. Consistent features in his legend are the names of his possessions (his sword Caledfwlch, for example, and his ship Prydwen), his wife Gwenhwyfar (later Guinevere), and his closest associates — Cei (Kay), Bedwyr (Bedevere) and Gwalchmei (Gawain).

The abduction of Arthur's wife is apparently a basic feature, which first appears in the twelfth-century *Life of Gildas* by Caradoc of Llancarfan. Here Guennuvar (Guinevere) is carried off to Glastonbury by Melwas, the King of the Summer Country (Somerset). Arthur beseiges Glastonbury, but peace is restored by the good offices of Gildas. The abduction of Arthur's Queen is a fundamental element in the Arthurian legend in all its forms and periods.

ARTHUR'S DEATH AND RETURN

Another early feature is the story of Arthur's death. The *Welsh Annals* note the Battle of Camlan, in 537, in which Arthur and Medraut perished. The location of Camlan is not clear and suggested sites range from Birdoswald (Roman Camboglanna) on Hadrian's Wall to the River Camel in Cornwall, but the tradition of this final battle in a civil war which devastated Arthur's realm is a secure one. Medieval Welsh allusions refer cryptically to the plotting which preceded the battle, to the treachery of Arthur's nephew Medrawd (Medraut or Mordred) and to the mortal wounding of Arthur.

As in the case of other successful leaders whose death was catastrophic, Arthur developed messianic features. He did not die, but was carried away to the Isle of Avalon (of Afallach in Welsh) to be healed of his wounds by queens or maidens. One day, when the need arose, he would return to aid his people. The vitality of this belief, shared by Welsh, Cornish and Bretons, as a political factor to be taken seriously is stressed by fourteenth-century chroniclers, and probably explains Henry II's earlier determination to exhume Arthur's body at Glastonbury to scotch the idea once and for all. The return from Avalon, however, is not well attested in early Welsh sources, though there can be little doubt of the popularity of the belief.

More common in modern Welsh folklore is the legend of the hero sleeping in a cave, surrounded by his men. Many localities claim Arthur's cave, but the familiar form of the legend relates how a Welshman crossing London Bridge (or at Bala fair) was accosted by a stranger who asked him where he had cut the hazel stick which he carried. Together they returned to the spot in Wales and dug at the base of the hazel tree until they found an underground cavern. Venturing in, they saw a company of warriors asleep, their chief in the centre and vast treasures around. The Welshman took as much of the treasure as he could carry and was warned by his companion not to touch the bell in his path, which would arouse the sleepers to save Britain. If it rang and a sleeper asked, 'Is it day?', he was to answer, 'No, sleep on'. After the first expedition, the Welshman returned for more treasure, rang the bell and forgot the correct answer, whereupon he was beaten and ejected, and was never again able to find the entrance to the cavern.

The same story is also told of Owain Lawgoch, a Welsh nobleman of the fourteenth century who aspired to win the principality of Wales. It probably reflects a conflation of the theme of the sleeping messianic hero with that of buried treasure. Another legend of Arthur's death has him killed at Bwlch y Seathau (Pass of Arrows) in Snowdonia and buried at Carnedd (Cairn) Arthur, while his army sleeps in Ogof Llanciau Eryri (the Cave of the Young Men of Snowdonia).

OWEN GLENDOWER

Legendary accretions seem to be almost contemporary with some historical figures. Certainly stories began to circulate about Owain Glyndwr (Owen Glendower) soon after his death (*c.* 1416). He led a rebellion against the English and for a short period at the beginning of the fifteenth century was the virtual ruler of Wales. His military success, and perhaps his guerrilla tactics, gave rise to stories of near escapes, and to a role as a magician in touch with supernatural forces (as portrayed by Shakespeare in *Henry IV,* Part One). It is difficult to know how old the stories of the portents marking his birth are, but the tradition that on the storm-wracked night that he was born his father's horses were discovered standing in pools of blood was well established by the sixteenth century. By this time, too, a belief in his disappearance rather than death seems to have been common. A chronicle of the rebellion ends at 1415: 'Owen went into hiding and thereafter his hiding-place was unknown. Very many say that he died, the seers maintain he did not.' Roughly contemporary is the story told by Ellis Gruffydd, the sixteenth-century chronicler, that the Abbot of Valle Crucis met Glyndwr out walking early one morning. Owain teased him about his early rising. 'No,' replied the abbot, 'it is you have risen too early, a hundred years before your time'. There is, in fact, no record of his death, and legend has it that he wandered alone in the hills, finally finding refuge with his daughters in Herefordshire, at Monnington or at Kentchurch Court. The most obviously popular characteristics of his legend are the tales relating to his periods of flight and hiding: the caves at the River Dysenni where he was concealed, the sticks which he dressed as soldiers at Dol Penni to trick the English, and the almost vertical gully in Moel Hebog, Snowdonia, which he climbed to avoid certain capture when the house where he had sought refuge was surrounded.

LEGENDARY ROBBERS

The traditional patterning of Glyndwr's career is clear, even to the extent of topographical features being claimed for him as for Arthur. A more modern example of the metamorphosis of a historical person into a popular hero is Thomas Jones, a sixteenth-century landowner, antiquary and poet of Tregaron, Dyfed. Manuscript sources show him to have been a gentleman of substance and learning, but these features have been wholly superseded by his folklore persona as highwayman, trickster and master of disguise, traits associated with his popular name, Twm Sion Cati.

Also well known are Gwylliaid Cochion Mawddwy (the Red-Haired Bandits of Mawddwy in Gwynedd), a band of robbers who are the object of ambivalent attitudes in modern Welsh folklore. These bandits, said to be soldiers without a cause after the conclusion of the Wars of the Roses in the fifteenth century, terrorized the inhabitants of the mountainous regions of Meirionydd and Montgomery until the authorities, represented by Sir John Wyn of Gwydir and 'Baron' Lewis Owen, caught and hung some hundred of them one Christmas-tide. The pleas of two brothers for pardon were rejected and their mother swore that Owen's enemies would wash their hands in his blood. On their way from the Montgomery Assizes in 1555 Owen and his son-in-law were ambushed and left for dead, but some of the bandits later returned to fulfil the curse to the letter.

PRINCE MADOG

One of the better-known, though least historical, legends is that of Madog, son of Owen Gwynedd, the twelfth-century Prince of Gwynedd. The genealogies list the sons of Owen, but know nothing of Madog. Traditionally, however, he was a sailor who, weary of the feuding between his brothers, sailed to the west in his ship Gwennan Gorn. He returned after some time, fitted out twelve more ships, sailed away and was never seen again. During the seventeenth century reports began to circulate of explorers in North America encountering 'white' Indians, the Mandans, whose language bore a resemblance to Welsh. It was claimed that they were descended from Madog and his company, said to have landed in Mobile Bay, Alabama, in 1170. The belief still has adherents, some of whom in 1953 set up a tablet at Mobile commemorating Madog.

THE SAINTS

Saints and poets, not surprisingly in view of the supernatural powers claimed for both groups, also attract legends to themselves. By Welsh saints are meant the monastic missionaries and hermits who established the Church in Celtic lands in the sixth and seventh centuries. In many respects they came to play the role of sacred heroes, having a similar biographical pattern and fulfilling similar functions to those of their secular counterparts with whom in legend they frequently come into conflict. Secular authority is typically represented by Arthur or Maelgwn Gwynedd, a sixth-century ruler of Gwynedd, usually portrayed in the saints' lives as pagan buffoons or penitent tyrants. Maelgwn attempted to steal St Brychan's milch-cow, but was thwarted and obliged to give handsome grants and privileges to the saint. When he and his men tried to steal provisions from saints such as Curig, Padarn or Mechyll, they were blinded and the stolen food turned into moss or leaves.

Arthur's role is similar. When he attempts to steal the jacket of St Padarn he is swallowed up to his chin by the earth, and his appropriation of the altar of St Carantoc (fl. sixth or seventh century) as a table leads to further discomfort as food and dishes placed upon it are tossed off. He fails to slay a serpent causing terror in Devon, which Carantoc tames merely by his prayers. Envious to the end, Arthur claims white, red-eared cattle from Cadog, but as they swim across the river towards him they revert to the bundles of ferns from which the saint had fashioned them. These anecdotes were designed to extol the saints as objects of admiration, as against popular secular heroes.

Few of the legends of the saints have survived in modern Welsh folklore. The patron saint of Wales is Dewi — David (fl. sixth century) whose best-known legend is that when a vast crowd at Llandewi Brefi, Dyfed, was unable to hear him preach, a handkerchief was laid out on the ground which rose to be a small hill, from the summit of which the saint preached and was entirely audible. Dewi is also said to be the founder of Bath, where he blessed and made wholesome the previously poisonous waters.

Saints frequently have supernatural mastery over nature. When St Tydecho's milkmaid tipped her pail into the stream above the village of Llanymawddwy, Powys, he turned the brook into a stream of milk for the villagers. No Englishman might pass under the curving bough of St Beuno's tree at Llanfueno, though Welshmen might go unscathed. Stags ploughed for Tydecho and for Dainiol, while a wolf harrowed for Tydecho. Dyfrig, like Kentigern, Cadog and Brynach, founded a monastery at a spot to which he was led by a white sow. Gulls feed the infant St Cennydd (*c.* sixth century), who was cast into the sea off the coast of Gower in a wicker cradle. For Beuno a curlew recovers a book dropped into a river and miraculously kept dry and unspoiled (as was a book of Dewi's in a shower of rain).

TALIESIN AND MERLIN

The old Welsh poet was primarily a eulogist, a praise-poet at the King's court, but in origin he was a priest and lawgiver who could call on shamanistic powers in his craft. This, coupled with the respect and fear due to books and learning, has made of Welsh poets of all times figures very akin to wizards. Legend gathered around Taliesin, who was court poet to Urien, a sixth-century King of Rheged (in modern lowland Scotland and Cumbria). We may speak of two Taliesins (though one in origin), the author of genuine praise-poems to Urien and other kings, and a central character in a cycle of stories found in fragmentary form in poems in the *Book of Taliesin* and in a fuller prose narrative, *Hanes Taliesin* (the Story of Taliesin), first found in a sixteenth-century version. Here a boy named Gwion Bach is set to watch the cauldron in which the witch Ceridwen is boiling up the brew of knowledge, and inadvertently swallows the three drops of liquid containing all the power of the concoction. Ceridwen pursues him through successive transformations, hare and hound, fish and otter, bird and hawk, and finally grain of corn and hen, in which form she swallows him. He is reborn from her as Taliesin and she casts him away to the mercies of the sea in a bag of skin. The vessel is found at a fishing weir on the River Dyfi by Elffin, son of Gwyddno Garanhir. The remainder of the tale portrays the boy's early skills as a versifier and recounts his bardic contest with Maelgwn Gwynedd's poets, his storm-raising to release his patron Elffin from prison, and a horse-race in which Maelgwn is again beaten and which leads to the discovery of hidden treasure.

Taliesin was also claimed as a prophetic poet, but better-known in this role is Myrddin. He was regarded as a genuine poet in the medieval literary tradition, and though there are no indubitable examples of his poetry, there are poems, mostly of a prophetic nature, in which he is the speaker. According to his legend, he was a member of the court of Gwenddoleu, another North British King, and became insane at the Battle of Arfderydd, in 573, in which his lord was slain. Terrified of the victor, King Rhydderch, he became a wild man in the woods of Celyddon, where he conversed with Gwenddydd (his sister or mistress) and acquired the gift of prophetic song. He is the supreme prophet of Welsh tradition even to modern times, and in this role is linked with Arthur by Geoffrey of Monmouth, who appears to be responsible for the name Merlin and who introduced him into the tale of the conception of Arthur. He was originally unconnected with Arthur, but there seems to have been a number of developments in Welsh tradition. He suffered a threefold death, by drowning, transfixion and stoning, in Geoffrey's *Life of Merlin,* a fate possibly reflected in numerous poetic references to Myrddin 'on a pole' and in a weir. Other Welsh sources claim that he had a house of glass, on the Isle of Bardsey according to one text, and that he took to it the Thirteen Treasures of the Island of Britain. (See ARTHUR AND LEGENDARY BRITAIN; LEGENDARY MAGICIANS.)

DROWNED CITIES

A well-known story about Llyn Syfaddon (Llangors Lake, Talgarth, Powys) is that beneath it lies a city, submerged because of the sinful life of its people. Beneath the waters of Bala Lake, too, is the city of a wicked prince who scorned a voice which was heard repeating, 'Vengeance will come'. Tales of such inundations, the result of unjust or sinful living, are common. The best-known of them is the legend of Cantre'r Gwaelod, an extensive and once fruitful kingdom said to lie beneath Cardigan Bay. Its ruler was Gwyddno Garanhir, who entrusted the care of the dykes protecting his low-lying kingdom to Seithennin. The latter neglected his duties following one of the periodic orgies to which the court was addicted and a sudden onrush of the sea drowned the land and most of its inhabitants. On clear days the remains of its walls may be seen in Cardigan Bay and the sound of its bells heard. The earliest, fragmentary version of this story occurs in a tenth-century poem in the *Black Book of Carmarthen,* where it seems that a maid was responsible for letting in the water, perhaps by omitting to replace a covering over a well.

This is a motif in other inundation tales and is used to explain the origin of Bala Lake and Llyn Llech Owen (Lake of Owen's Slab) near Gorsalas, Dyfed. This Owen forgot to replace the slab on the well after watering his horse, and looking back saw to his amazement that the well was overflowing. He rode to encircle the waters, bounded them and so formed the lake. In another version he slept at the well and awoke to find himself on an island in the middle of the lake. In stories of this kind, again, legends are linked to topographical features.

CELTIC LEGENDS

CHAPTER 21

SCOTLAND

Scotland shares much legendary material with her neighbours, England and Gaelic Ireland. The popularity of Arthur and Robin Hood can be seen from ballads and from place-names like Arthur's Seat, in Edinburgh, and surnames like Littlejohn. The Merlin of early Welsh tradition ran wild in the 'Caledonian Forest'. His grave is shown by the Tweed, near Drummelzier, and his prophecies were long popular, including one that Scotland and England would have the same king when the river flooded his grave, which is said to have come true in 1603. Many of the early Irish legends, notably the Fenian Cycle, have lived on longer in the oral tradition of the Gaelic-speaking Highlands than in Ireland itself, and are intertwined with Scottish places and people. The Campbells claim descent from the Fenian hero Diarmaid and also from King Arthur.

The early saints of the kingdom included both Irishmen and Angles – Columba or Colmcille (sixth century), and Cuthbert (seventh century), Britons of Strathclyde (Kentigern and Ninian (fifth century), and even Picts. Their legends were mostly composed much later and draw on a common Christian stock of miracles to fill out shadowy lives. Kentigern was born of a reputed virgin who survived being thrown off a hill and set adrift in an oarless coracle. There are tales in his life which, it has been claimed, were later used in early Irish sagas. But the only figure who really comes to life is St Columba, whose biography was written in his abbey of Iona only about a century after his death in 597. One apocryphal story from modern times has sinister overtones. Columba's brother, St Oran, volunteered to be buried alive, standing upright in a pit, as a foundation sacrifice for the church on Iona. After twenty days

The Clan Chief's familiar spirit as a frog (page 205)

his head was uncovered and he immediately told Columba that the latter's ideas of heaven and of eternal damnation were wrong, at which his brother hastily had him covered in again!

WALLACE AND BRUCE

Scotland's nationhood and her national legend really date from the Wars of Independence against Edward I of England around 1300. William Wallace, Guardian of Scotland for less than a year, later betrayed and cruelly executed, was the common man's hero. His legend, as given in the long poem written nearly two centuries later by 'Blind Harry', turns a rather ordinary knight, notable mainly for his devotion to his country, into a great guerrilla leader, immensely strong, driven into the forests as an outlaw after he avenged the murder of his sweetheart by an English governor. Blind Harry probably invented or borrowed from similar legends, such as that of Robin Hood, more than he found in oral tradition.

The much earlier poem by John Barbour on the eventual victor against the English, King Robert the Bruce, probably has less invention in it, but also makes much of the hero's period as a homeless wanderer, pursued by bloodhounds and brigands, before his first victories in 1307. It is here, rather than in the many stirring and ingenious tales of battles and captured castles, that recent tradition has added details — Bruce turning his horse's shoes back to front to mislead his pursuers, or the episode of the spider. The latter should be set in a bedroom where Bruce lay sick before his decisive victory at Inverurie. The spider failing six times to swing on the end of its thread from one roof-beam to the next recalled the King's six defeats, but its success the seventh time gave him heart. Later versions setting the scene in a cave, where a spider's web across the entrance made Bruce's enemies think it not worth entering, are distortions of the original story.

Nearly all Scottish legends, however, are local rather than national. Otterburn or Chevy Chase, the only Border battle to inspire a great ballad, was essentially a clash between two men, Henry Percy ('Hotspur') and James, Earl of Douglas, who challenged Percy to come and take back his captured lance-pennon. Douglas died before his side won, so that Percy was told to yield to the bracken bush where the Earl's body lay hidden from his men. Throughout the fifteenth and sixteenth centuries, and continuing into the seventeenth, most parts of Scotland were seldom troubled by the royal government. The heads of local clans and families in the Highlands, the Borders and elsewhere were free to carry on their blood-feuds and cattle-raids. Local bards were ready to celebrate every little victory, and the result was a true 'heroic age' of the sort which gives birth to legends. In the Lowlands many such legends may still have been current in Sir Walter

Scott's time, but only a few prose tales which he wrote down and some
fine ballads of burning castles, empty saddles and wonderful escapes
from prison have survived. In the Highlands hundreds of clan legends
are still told which have been largely ignored elsewhere because they
are in Gaelic, but they are local tales. National affairs such as the
escape of Bonnie Prince Charlie are mentioned only if he actually
passed through the neighbourhood, and Montrose's brilliant Highland campaign in support of Charles I appears mainly as a backdrop
for the exploits of his Gaelic lieutenant, Alasdair, son of Coll
MacDonald, who in fact was too taken up with his family feud with
the Campbells to give much help to his commander.

SIR LACHLAN MACLEAN

A typical clan hero is Sir Lachlan MacLean of Duart, a sixteenth-
century chief from Mull, whom the MacLean historians credit with
a whole string of imaginary or grossly exaggerated victories in battle.
One highly romantic tale makes the Tobermory galleon − a survivor
of the Spanish Armada which was blown up in Mull's main harbour
− the ship of a Spanish princess who had fallen in love with Sir
Lachlan in a dream and vowed to search the world until she found
him. But Lady MacLean heard of the affair and had the galleon's
powder magazine fired, killing the princess, who lies buried across the
Sound of Mull in Morvern. When the news reached Spain, a galleon
under Captain Forrest was sent to wreak vengeance on the women of
Mull, but the Mull Witch *(An Doideag Mhuileach)* raised a storm
and brought witches from all over the Highlands to settle on the ship's
rigging in the form of crows. The captain had magic of his own
sufficient to combat nine witches, but when eighteen roosted on his
ship she went down. Apart from this sequel, the story of the princess is
typical of many late, sentimental legends, more often dealing with
Norse princesses and probably inspired by James Macpherson's
re-working of the Fenian legend in his popular *Ossian* (1763).

Sir Lachlan's heroic status is best shown by the story of his death at
the Battle of Gruinart in Islay in 1598. Though his opponents, the
MacDonalds of Islay, won the battle and the story is now told only in
Islay, he is definitely the main character, and like Cu Chulainn and
other ancient Gaelic heroes his death follows inevitably from the
breaking of a series of personal taboos. An almost contemporary
account already mentions that before setting out he was warned by
a witch not to do three things. The lists vary, but in one version he was
not to sail his galley widdershins (anticlockwise) around a certain
island; not to land in Islay on a Thursday; and not to drink from
a certain well. He deliberately defied the first taboo, and was driven
to land in Islay by a storm on Thursday. Before the battle a small,
perhaps supernatural archer called Dubh-Sith (possibly 'Black

Fairy') offered his services to Sir Lachlan and was refused, but was gladly enlisted by Sir Lachlan's opponent, Sir James MacDonald. In the heat of the fight Sir Lachlan bent down to drink from a well, not knowing that it was the one mentioned in the prophecy. He exposed a chink in his armour, through which he was shot with an arrow and killed by Dubh-Sith, hidden in a tree. Sir Lachlan's foster-mother came to bury him, and when her own son mocked the body flopping about on a horse-drawn hurdle, she killed him on the spot to avenge the insult. A fallen hero is still a hero.

CLAN CHIEFS

The same stories turn up in different parts of the Highlands attached to different heroes. The chief is killed by an arrow through his eye. A birth is delayed by witchcraft until the witch is told that the baby has been born and revokes the spell, so that the child is born with all his teeth. A son is born after a usurper has killed his father, and returns from overseas to reclaim his heritage. In one case this is told of an heir who in fact was probably over forty years old when his father died, but the story has still been assimilated to the familiar pattern. Not all of the tales are complimentary to the chiefs, especially since the Highland clearances soured the attitude of Highlanders to absentee chiefs who drove crofters from their land to make sheep-runs. There are stories of ridiculous extravagance, like shoeing the chief's horse with loosely fastened golden shoes which fell off and were left to lie in the streets of Edinburgh, and of cruel punishments, like castrating a man who let a deer escape in the hunt, or killing a ploughman who nibbled a weed from the furrow because it might imply to the chief's guest that his servants were poorly fed. There are stories about chiefs who practised witchcraft, with a familiar spirit in the form of a monstrous frog hopping from wave to wave in the wake of the chief's ship, and a gigantic figure whistling him out of his deathbed, so that only the strongest man in the clan could prevent the dying man running out to join his master the Devil. All these stories were told of the chiefs of the Clanranald MacDonalds of South Uist. In Shetland, where mainland Scottish lairds managed to acquire much land from the native proprietors, many unpleasant tricks are ascribed to them, like offering to seat a man in the laird's own chair and let him eat off the laird's own table for the rest of his life if he made over his land, and then paying him off with an old chair and table.

Often, as in the Arthurian legends, the chief's followers outshine their master. Many famous archers, for instance, are said to have pinned the leader of a band of sea-raiders to the mast of his galley with a well-aimed arrow and then picked off the rest of the crew. South Uist even has its own William Tell, who shot an egg off his son's head, but was ready to shoot the chief, who made him do it on the pretext of a wager, if he had failed. Hereditary lines of poets, physicians and pipers are credited with magical powers or, like the MacCrimmons, the most noted pipers of the Highlands, are said to have learned their art from the fairies. Thousands of legends tell of contacts with the fairies and other supernatural beings, of witchcraft and the Evil Eye, of second sight and prophecy. Outlaws and robbers are not usually heroes of legend, for a man outlawed by one clan could seek the protection of another, and cattle-raiding was done by the clan, not by unlicensed individuals. Resistance to the government and its laws in more recent times is another matter, and there are plenty of minor local legends of people getting away with smuggling, illicit distilling or poaching, and escaping the press-gang.

MICHAEL SCOT AND THOMAS THE RHYMER

Two gifted characters, who lived before the Wars of Independence, are famed in both Highland and Lowland legends. One is Michael Scot, a learned Scotsman who became physician and astrologer to the Holy Roman Emperor Frederick II in the thirteenth century. Having studied with the Arabs in Spain and being associated with the greatest enemy of the Pope, he became known as a magician in both Italian and Scottish tradition. His feats include getting the Devil to split the Eildon Hills into three, and in the form of a flying horse to carry him to Rome (or Paris). The Devil kept trying to make him mention the name of God and so break the spell, but Michael was not caught. He repented on his deathbed when a traveller whom, some say, he himself had sent to hell reported on the special bed of pain prepared for him there. His body was laid out on a hill and three ravens swooped towards it, but they flew so fast that they overshot and before they could return three white doves had arrived, which was the sign that Michael's soul was saved.

Thomas the Rhymer was also a historical figure who owned land at Earlston in Berwickshire. He was known as a prophet in the fourteenth century, soon after his death. A modern ballad and a medieval poem both tell the story of how the Queen of Elfland came to fetch him, showed him the wonders of the otherworld and as a reward for seven years' service in silence with her gave him 'the tongue that can never lie'. Gaelic legends make him the son of a dead woman, conceived after her death in fulfilment of a vow she made when alive, and say that he still lives inside the fairy hill at Tomnahurich, in the town of Inverness. He is guardian of the Fenians and other heroes who sleep there until the day of Scotland's greatest need. From time to time he has been seen at markets, buying horses for them to ride.

CHRISTIAN WESTERN EUROPE

CHAPTER 22

NEW TESTAMENT FIGURES AND SAINTS

Apocryphal stories about Jesus, his mother Mary and other characters in the New Testament sprang up early in the history of Christianity. The four gospels of Mark, Matthew, Luke and John deal principally with the public career of Jesus, from his emergence as a teacher in Galilee at about the age of thirty to his execution on the cross two to three years later. They say very little about his childhood, his home life and his parents. Christians naturally wanted to know more and the gaps and bare patches in the gospel stories were soon filled with the wild flowers and weeds of legend. These tales were not accepted as canonical in the West, but they were extremely popular in the Middle Ages and were frequently illustrated in art. In the seventeenth century the Roman Catholic and Protestant authorities decisively rejected them and they began to fade out of popular culture, though some of them have left their traces to this day.

The most influential of the apocryphal books in the Middle Ages was a 'gospel' attributed to Matthew. Now known as Pseudo-Matthew, it probably dates from the eighth or ninth century, but it brings together considerably older stories. Its two main sources dated from the second century, if not before. One was the Book of James or Protevangelium, a spurious account of the early life of the Virgin Mary, ostensibly written by James, the brother of Jesus, who

The Legend of the Cross (page 212)

was a leader of the Christians in Jerusalem after Jesus' death. The other was the Gospel of Thomas, dealing with Jesus' childhood and attributed to the apostle Thomas or 'Thomas, the Israelite philosopher'.

THE LIFE OF MARY

In view of her importance in Christianity, there is remarkably little information in the New Testament about Jesus' mother. The apocryphal tradition set out not merely to remedy this deficiency but to glorify Mary and to emphasize her stainless purity and lifelong virginity. Her parents were said to be a rich and pious Jewish couple living in Jerusalem, Joachim and Anna (neither of whom appears in the canonical gospels). For twenty years, to their bitter disappointment, Joachim and Anna failed to produce a child. Eventually, in despair, Joachim went out into the wilderness to fast and pray. At home, Anna was sitting sadly under a laurel tree in her garden when she saw a nest of young sparrows in the branches. She burst into a lament, contrasting her barren state with the fecundity of the birds, and suddenly an angel appeared to her and told her that she would bear a child whose fame the whole world would acknowledge. Then messengers arrived, saying that Joachim was returning, for he too had been told of the promised child by an angel. Anna went out to meet him and threw her arms round his neck, rejoicing. In due time the child was born and they named her Mary. (The church of St Anne in Jerusalem traditionally stands on the site of Mary's birthplace.)

When Mary was three, Joachim and Anna took her to the Temple where, as they had vowed, she was to be brought up in holiness. The little girl ran up the great stairway and danced for joy on the steps of the altar. She remained in the Temple until she reached puberty, when the High Priest, Zacharias, was divinely inspired to find her a husband and guardian. He summoned a number of widowers, to each of whom he gave a wooden rod. The last of them was an elderly carpenter named Joseph. When he was given his rod a dove flew up from it and perched on his head, as the sign that he was to marry Mary. Joseph protested in vain that he was too old and already had children by his first wife, now dead. The High Priest insisted and the couple were married. Joseph took Mary to his own home, but the marriage was not consummated, then or later.

According to this story, Mary's birth and life were pre-ordained by God. The tale echoes the Old Testament account of the birth and upbringing of the great prophet and king-maker Samuel, though the idea of a girl being reared in the Temple is entirely unhistorical. One difficulty about the belief in Mary's lifelong virginity was that Jesus had brothers and sisters, who are mentioned in the New Testament. The story explains this by making Joseph a widower and its picture of Joseph as much older than Mary still survives in Christian tradition.

In the popular eye, Joseph tended to become a comic and inadequate character, the aging husband yoked to a young wife.

THE BIRTH OF JESUS

The apocryphal story of Jesus' birth follows the canonical gospels of Luke and Matthew, with additional details. The details in the New Testament itself are now regarded as legendary by many Christian commentators and where exactly the line between fact and poetic fiction falls it is impossible to say.

Mary was sixteen when the angel came to tell her that she was to be the mother of Jesus. Joseph's anger and dismay at her pregnancy, and his bafflement when an angel explained the truth to him, were exploited for their humorous effect in medieval plays.

Joseph and Mary set out from Nazareth to Bethlehem to be taxed, Mary riding an ass and Joseph leading an ox which he hoped to sell to pay the tax. Mary's time came on her and she gave birth to Jesus in a cave. She was attended by a midwife and another woman named Salome, who refused to believe that Mary could have borne a child and still be a virgin. Salome insisted on examining Mary. Her hand withered and she screamed with pain, but she was healed the moment she touched the baby. On the third day Mary moved the child to a stable and put him in a manger, where the faithful ox and ass worshipped him. (The cave or stable is now the crypt of the Church of the Nativity in Bethlehem.)

This story is the source of some of the familiar details of Christmas cribs in churches. The canonical gospels say nothing of the midwife and Salome, or the ox and the ass, and they do not specifically mention a stable. Luke tells of the shepherds coming to see the Christ-child, and in Matthew 'wise men from the East' follow the star and bring him gold, frankincense and myrrh.

Matthew does not say how many wise men there were, but three gifts suggested three givers and in legend the wise men soon became the Three Kings. They were said to be the rulers of Persia, Saba and Sheba, and were given the names Gaspar, Melchior and Balthasar. They came to stand for the three parts of the known world – Europe, Asia and Africa – doing homage to Jesus, and the link with Africa eventually gave the third King a black skin. They went away to India and were buried there, so the story ran, but their bones were afterwards brought back to the West and came in time to Cologne, known in consequence as the City of the Three Kings. Encased in a magnificent reliquary, they rest in Cologne Cathedral to this day.

JESUS AS A CHILD

Legendary details were also added to the brief story in Matthew of the flight into Egypt. It was said that the wicked King Herod himself scoured Bethlehem to find and kill the young Jesus. When he discovered that Joseph and Mary had fled with the child he pursued them with a force of cavalry. Riding ahead of his troops, he had almost caught the Holy Family when, by divine intervention, his horse threw him. Herod was stunned and the fugitives escaped.

On the way across the desert to Egypt, lions and leopards frisked about the Holy Family, bowing their heads reverently and wagging their tails in worship of Jesus. They frightened Mary at first, but Jesus assured her they were harmless. When the family rested beneath a tall palm tree and Mary longed for the dates, which were too high for Joseph to reach, Jesus commanded the palm to bow down. It bent down to Mary's feet, they picked the dates, and the tree remained bowing submissively until Jesus ordered it to stand up again.

Later in the journey came an encounter with two robbers. One of them wanted to plunder the family, but the other bought him off with thirty pieces of silver and was blessed by Mary. These two were afterwards the bad and the good thieves who were crucified with Christ at Calvary, and the same thirty pieces of silver which had protected Jesus were afterwards paid to Judas Iscariot for betraying him. Eventually the family came safely to the Egyptian city of Sotinen, in the district of Hermopolis, where 365 idols stood in the temple. When Mary and Jesus went into the temple the idols fell to the ground and were smashed to pieces.

The Gospel of Thomas and other 'infancy gospels' told of many miracles worked by Jesus as a boy, in Egypt and after the family returned to Nazareth. One sabbath day when Jesus was five, he made twelve clay sparrows. Reproved for playing on the sabbath, he clapped his hands and the sparrows came to life and flew away, chirping. He restored a dead child to life and healed his step-brother James, who had been bitten by a viper. Joseph was not the most competent of carpenters and once, making a bed to order for a rich customer, he cut one of the beams too short. Jesus grasped the beam and stretched it to the correct length.

There were also stories of cruel and vicious miracles. A child who accidentally bumped into the young Jesus was promptly felled dead and when the parents and neighbours complained to Joseph they were struck blind. Joseph twisted his son's ear hard for this, but more incidents of the kind were in store. Jesus walked on water, encouraging his playmates to do the same, and they were drowned. Similarly he walked up a sunbeam and his friends, who followed him, fell down and were hurt. The neighbours became so frightened that one day, seeing Jesus coming, they hid their children in the village oven. When Jesus asked what was in the oven, knowing perfectly well, they said only sucking pigs. As soon as Jesus had gone, they opened the oven and found their children transformed into pigs: all cooked and ready to eat, according to some versions of the tale.

These stories testify to the popular demand for a god to wield massive and arbitrary supernatural power, for good and evil alike and as immune from moral considerations as a huge charge of electricity. There is also a strong anti-Semitic strain in many of the apocryphal narratives, and the victims of Jesus' childish spite are Jews. The legendary accounts of the young Jesus have parallels in stories of heroes and holy men all over the world: the supernatural conception (though the virgin birth itself is not in fact a common theme outside Christianity); the birth in unusual circumstances, accompanied by signs and portents, like the Star of Bethlehem and the worshipping ox and ass; the bringing of gifts by mysterious personages; the upbringing in obscurity; and the youthful wonder-working which displays the hero's supernormal powers. These legends of Jesus were not only popular in Christendom but, through translations into Arabic, entered the Muslim world as well.

THE THREE MARYS

A confusing number of Marys occur in the New Testament. According to John's gospel, the Virgin Mary and Mary Magdalene were present at the Crucifixion and Jesus entrusted his mother to the care of St John. A legend grew up that John took the Virgin and Mary Magdalene to Ephesus in Asia Minor, where both women died, and there was a later tradition that Mary Magdalene had been betrothed to John before Jesus called him to be a disciple. It was more often believed, however, that the Virgin Mary died at Jerusalem. All the apostles witnessed her passing, but when her tomb was afterwards opened it was empty. This story supported the old popular belief that she had been taken up body and soul into heaven, which was finally given official sanction by Pope Pius XII in 1950.

One line of tradition about Mary Magdalene identified her with the unnamed sinful woman who repentantly anointed Christ's feet (Luke 8:37). This is the source of the popular picture of her as a reformed whore, which still survives but which has no warrant in the New Testament. She was also identified with Mary of Bethany, the sister of Martha and Lazarus, whom Jesus raised from the dead. She was associated with two other Marys, who were thought to have been present at the Crucifixion and were believed to be the Virgin Mary's half-sisters. They were daughters of Anna by two husbands she married before (or after) Joachim. There was a story that the Three Marys — the two half-sisters and Mary Magdalene — with Martha and Lazarus were set adrift in a rudderless boat with no sails. Miraculously preserved from harm, they crossed the sea to the South of France and brought Christianity to Provence. Martha encountered a dragon at Tarascon, subdued it by sprinkling holy water on it and, using her sash like a dog's lead, conducted the obedient monster to Arles, where it was put to death. Mary Magdalene herself spent the last years of her life as a hermit.

The legend is still very much alive and every year in May the images of the Three Marys are carried in procession through the Camargue village of Les-Saintes-Maries-de-la-Mer on the coast, where they landed with their black servant, Sara. In gypsy tradition this Sara (a gypsy) foresaw their coming and helped them to land.

PONTIUS PILATE

Another New Testament figure about whom people wanted to know more was Pontius Pilate, whose story could be used for both Christian and anti-Christian propaganda. Pilate's forged memoirs, intended to discredit Christianity, were issued by the pagan authorities in 311, but have not survived. On the Christian side, some legends pictured Pilate as a believer at heart, forced by the wicked Jews to order the execution of Jesus. There was a story that the Emperor Tiberius became convinced of the divinity of Christ and condemned Pilate to death for his part in the Crucifixion. Praying to Jesus, Pilate heard the voice of the Saviour from heaven, saying that future generations would bless him for his role in bringing about the death through which mankind was redeemed. Then Pilate's head was cut off and an angel of the Lord received it. His virtuous wife Procla, who had urged him not to crucify Jesus, saw the angel, was filled with joy and died on the spot. The tendency of this type of legend was to turn Pilate into a Christian saint, as he became in the Coptic Church in Egypt, but in the West he was generally viewed in a vengeful spirit. The Emperor Tiberius fell deathly ill, it was said, and hoped to be healed by Jesus until he heard that the great miracle-worker was dead. Pilate protected himself from the Emperor's fury for a time by wearing Christ's seamless robe, in which he could not be harmed, but in the end he was compelled to commit suicide. His body was thrown into the Tiber, but it attracted such a horde of evil spirits that it was recovered from the river and dropped into a lake in the French Alps, near Mount Pilat (named after Pilate).

Tiberius was finally healed, in this story, by the wonder-working cloth of St Veronica. She was the woman who, according to legend, compassionately wiped Christ's face with her veil or handkerchief when he laboured under the weight of the cross on his way to Calvary. The cloth, which bore the imprint of Christ's face, is a famous relic, long preserved in St Peter's, Rome.

THE LEGEND OF THE CROSS

Poetic and beautiful legends developed about the cross on which Christ was executed. One widely accepted story was that when Adam lay dying he sent his son Seth to Eden. The angel who guarded the gate of the paradise garden gave Seth three seeds of the forbidden fruit from the tree of knowledge. Seth placed the seeds on Adam's tongue and Adam died happy in the knowledge that mankind would be saved from the consequences of his sin in Eden. The three seeds grew into a great tree, from which the cross was fashioned. Christ was crucified on it at the centre of the world, at the place where Adam had been created and where he lay buried. And Christ's blood falling on Adam's skull saved him, too, at the last.

Adam's skull is sometimes shown beneath the cross.in paintings of the Crucifixion, and the story is another example of a legend supporting and emphasizing a particular Christian doctrine. Christ was the Second Adam who came to repair the catastrophe which the first Adam had caused. By eating the fruit of the forbidden tree Adam had condemned all humanity to death, but from that same fruit sprang the tree on which Christ died to bring mankind eternal life. The cross itself was believed to have been discovered in Jerusalem in 326 by the Empress Helena, mother of Constantine the Great.

SAINTS AND MARTYRS

The apostles and saints, as the heroes of Christianity's early expansion, naturally attracted legends. Spurious 'acts' of the apostles were written, including those of Peter, Andrew, Philip, Thomas and Paul, in the second century. The Acts of Thomas recounts the missionary labours of the doubting apostle in India and, along with much fiction, the tradition that Christianity was carried to India at an early date may be correct. Similarly, the largely fictitious Acts of Paul contains an account of that redoubtable Christian which may be accurate. This describes St Paul as a short man, balding and bandy-legged, with a hooked nose and eyebrows joining in the centre.

Many legends of the saints elaborate on genuine history to make a more dramatic story out of a real event. The tale of the Theban Legion and its commander, St Maurice, is probably based on the execution of a group of Christian soldiers at Agaunum (St Maurice en Valais, Switzerland) late in the third century. In legend they swelled into an entire Roman legion, of more than 6000 troops from Egypt, massacred for refusing to sacrifice to pagan gods.

Besides exaggeration of numbers, there was a tendency to make the deaths of martyrs more elaborate and gruesome than they probably were in real life. St Sebastian, riddled with arrows and beaten to death with clubs in the late third century, is a case in point. St Laurence, who was executed at Rome in 258, was said to have been roasted on a gridiron. After a time he sardonically told his tormentors to turn him over as he was cooked enough on one side (and he became the patron saint of cooks).

The lives as well as the deaths of saints were elaborated and dramatized in legend. There is certainly no need to write off all the miracles associated with the saints as spurious, but some are pious fictions. St Catherine of Alexandria was said to have been a beautiful and aristocratic maiden of the fourth century who denounced the pagan gods and refuted the arguments of fifty pagan philosophers who engaged her in debate. The Emperor Maxentius wanted to marry her, but she refused because she was the bride of Christ. She was imprisoned and a dove fed her in her cell. When she was sentenced to be broken on the wheel, it smashed to pieces at her touch. She was beheaded and milk instead of blood flowed from the wound. Angels bore her body to Mount Sinai, where the monastery dedicated to her has stood for centuries. She was a popular saint in the East and in Europe, but her connection with reality is tenuous and her feast day (25 November) was abolished, amongst others, by the Vatican in 1969.

Though most of the early saints celebrated in legend were no doubt real people originally, some almost certainly were not. The story of St Christopher seems to derive entirely from his name, which in Greek and Latin means 'Christ-Bearer'. He was a pagan of gigantic size and strength, who hoped to serve the most powerful king in the world. He lived by a river, across which he charitably carried travellers. During a fierce storm one night, he set out to take a small child over on his shoulders. As he waded through the turbulent waters, the child grew heavier and heavier, but Christopher struggled bravely on and at last gained the far bank. 'If I had borne the whole world on my back,' he complained to the child, 'it could have been no heavier than you.' The child said, 'You have borne on your back the whole world and him who created it, for I am Jesus Christ, the King'. Christopher had achieved his ambition and was converted.

A much odder saint who probably never lived is St Wilgefortis, the bearded lady, also known as Uncumber or Liberata. She was supposedly a Portuguese princess who became a Christian and swore a vow of virginity. When her father pressed her to marry a pagan king, she prayed to be made ugly and God gave her an abundant beard and moustache. Her infuriated father had her crucified. In the sixteenth century in England women sometimes offered oats to her statue, calling her St Uncumber in the hope that she would 'uncumber' them of their husbands. Her legend seems to be based on a misunderstanding of an early type of crucifix, with a figure of Christ bearded and fully clothed, which was later mistakenly assumed to be a crucified woman.

Some Christian legends took over pagan figures and motifs. St Hippolytus was dragged to death by horses, as was his namesake, the son of the Greek hero Theseus. St Brigid or Bride of Ireland, it seems, was originally a pagan goddess. St Barlaam and St Joasaph appear in a Christian story adapted probably in the ninth century from an Indian legend of the Buddha. St Jerome (d. 420), like Androcles in the classical fable, made friends with a lion from whose paw he removed a painful thorn. The best-known example of a Christianized pagan legend is the story of St George and the dragon.

The real St George was apparently a Christian soldier who was martyred at Lydda in Palestine in about 300, but his fame rests on the popular medieval tale of him rescuing a princess from a dragon. The dragon, which was terrorizing the countryside, had demanded a human victim and the king's daughter was to be offered to the monster, dressed as a bride, when the brave knight St George intervened. Piercing the dragon with his lance, he led it captive with the princess's girdle. When the king and his people promised to become Christians, St George killed the dragon. The tale is strikingly similar to the Greek legend of Perseus and Andromeda, which was traditionally set near Lydda and which was presumably adapted into Christianity because St George could stand for the valiant Christian who fights the monstrous power of evil (the dragon), which threatens to devour and despoil the Church (the princess).

CHRISTIAN HEROES AND HEROINES

The legends which grew up about Jesus, Mary and the saints were not told merely for entertainment. Some of them are exciting and attractive stories in their own right, certainly, but they were intended to convey lessons in holy living, faith and courage. They were regarded as true stories, recording events which had actually happened and showing how, ideally, life ought to be lived. They gave the Church its own heroes and heroines to set beside, or rather above, the gods and goddesses of pagan cults and great figures of the Old Testament.

The same tendencies to invent, dramatize, elaborate and edify observable in the development of pagan legends operated in the Christian milieu as well. St Patrick, in the fifth century, expelling all the snakes from Ireland, shows a heroic Christian dominating the forces of evil. St Francis of Assisi, in the thirteenth century, preaching to the birds and singing duets with a nightingale, teaches a lesson in sympathy and rapport with the animal kingdom.

The legends, of course, are Christian propaganda. They were meant to convince people of the truth of Christianity, but to view them solely in this light is to overlook the fact that they arose naturally from their Christian environment as expressions of faith. They express what those who told them believed. Some of these stories have become part of the psychological inheritance of the West. When cold water is thrown on them in the interests of historical accuracy it brings a sense of loss which is not confined to practising Christians.

CHRISTIAN WESTERN EUROPE

CHAPTER 23
CHARLEMAGNE LEGENDS

Charlemagne (Carolus Magnus, Charles the Great) was one of the greatest rulers of all time. King of the Franks from AD 768 to his death in 814, he united most of western Europe into one vast Christian state, with the exception of the British Isles and parts of Italy and Spain, and was anointed Emperor by the Pope in Rome in 800. As with all such dominating figures, there was no one of his stature to succeed him; after his death western Europe crumbled once more into separate warring kingdoms, not to be brought together again for a thousand years, first in Napolen's short-lived empire in the early nineteenth century, and again in the twentieth century – possibly a more lasting solution, not being dependent on the necessarily ephemeral genius of one man.

Although to modern eyes he was the great pioneer of political unity in western Europe, to medieval eyes Charlemagne was the great pioneer of religious unity, the implacable enemy of the Arabs and Islam. His influence in that sphere, however, was not the equal of his grandfather's – Charles Martel. The latter's victory over the Arabs at Poitiers in 732 had ensured that they would never be the force in France that they had become in Spain. It is not inconceivable that the legend that accrued to Charlemagne's name owed something to Charles Martel, legend being ever more faithful to the spirit of an era than to precise historical facts. Charlemagne fought many more battles against the pagan Saxons in Germany than against the Arabs, and when he advanced into Spain in 778 he was in league with one

Charlemagne with his nephew Roland, and Oliver (page 217)

Arab faction against another. On receiving news that the Saxons were again troubling his eastern frontiers, he withdrew prematurely across the Pyrenees and the rearguard of his army was attacked and annihilated by the Christian Basques.

ROLAND AT RENCESVALS

In legend this disaster was quite transformed. Charlemagne was presented invading Spain as the champion of Christianity against the Arabs, with his rearguard fighting a courageous action against vastly superior Arab forces. This transformation, which provided the subject for the finest epic poem ever composed in French, *La Chanson de Roland,* is easily understood when the period in which it occurred is considered. The eleventh century saw the beginning of the crusading era, when religious fervour against Islam was at its height. The First Crusade of 1095 was in fact preceded by a number of expeditions against the Arabs in Spain.

The *Chanson de Roland,* however, far transcends mere religious propaganda. The earliest and most outstanding of the *chansons de geste* ('songs of deeds' — *geste* from Latin *gesta,* in the sense of achievements in war), it is a work that can be read on many different levels, a series of Chinese boxes in which you never penetrate through to the final one. The work of an unknown author, it comprises 4000 lines in the Anglo-Norman dialect, quite possibly composed in England, at least as regards the best extant version (the sole manuscript of which is still on the English side of the Channel, in the Bodleian Library at Oxford).

When the story opens, Charlemagne has subdued all Spain after seven years of campaigning, with the exception of Saragossa (Zaragoza) and its Saracen king, Marsile. Hard-pressed, Marsile assembles his 'dukes and counts' and seeks counsel. Only one, Blancandrin, speaks up: Marsile should promise to follow Charlemagne to his capital, Aix-la-Chapelle, and there become a Christian. This promise, which he will have no need to keep, will induce Charlemagne to leave Spain. Blancandrin accordingly leads a deputation to Charlemagne.

The Emperor is relaxing in an orchard with his nephew Roland, Oliver and other leaders of his army. Roland is the first to speak in the long debate which follows, maintaining that the Arabs are treacherous and not to be trusted. Roland's stepfather Ganelon, however, argues for accepting the Arab offer and carries the day. But who is to be Charlemagne's emissary to Marsile? Roland volunteers at once, but his friend Oliver objects that he is too impetuous. Oliver offers to go himself, but Charlemagne will not permit any of his twelve peers, the élite of his army, to undertake so dangerous a mission. Roland puts Ganelon's name forward, so underlining his inferiority to the twelve peers. Ganelon has no grounds on which to refuse. He is furiously angry and declares that if he returns he will take his revenge. Roland enrages him all the more by tauntingly offering to take his place. In his agitation Ganelon drops the glove, the symbol of his office as Charlemagne's emissary, and the French interpret this as a bad omen.

Riding to the Saracen camp with Blancandrin, Ganelon plots Roland's death. The Arabs are to attack the rearguard, which will be commanded by Roland and Oliver, and with Roland dead Charlemagne will lose all desire to wage war. In the Saracen camp the plot is sealed.

Ganelon returns to Charlemagne and the French prepare to go home. The Arabs take up position to ambush the rearguard. Charlemagne dreams of impending disaster. The next day, when he asks his barons to appoint commanders for the rearguard, Ganelon at once proposes Roland's name – and Roland can only accept. The Emperor, uneasily suspecting treachery, offers Roland half the army, but Roland haughtily declines.

The French army begins its homeward march through the passes of the Pyrenees and now only the rearguard is left in Spain. The Saracens prepare to attack. Oliver sees them approaching, and three times urges Roland to recall the main army while there is still time:

'Companion Roland, pray sound your horn!
Charles will hear it and turn back the army.'
Roland replies: 'I should be acting like a madman,
In sweet France I should lose my reputation...'

'Companion Roland, pray sound the oliphant [horn],
Charles will hear it, and turn back the army.
The king will come to our assistance with his barons.'
Roland replies: 'May God forbid
That my relatives should be blamed on my account
Or sweet France disgraced...'

'Companion Roland, sound your oliphant,
Charles will hear it as he goes through the passes.
I promise you, the Franks will at once turn back.'
'God forbid,' replies Roland,
'That it be said by any man
That I blew my horn because of a pagan!
Never shall my relatives suffer this reproach...'

Archbishop Turpin absolves the men of their sins and the Battle of Rencesvals (Roncevaux and Roncesvalles are alternative forms) begins, with Roland striking the first blow. Gradually the enemy's superior numbers tell. A fearsome storm hangs over France and darkness falls at noon, portending Roland's death.

The rearguard is worn down until only sixty men are left, and Roland decides to recall Charlemagne. Oliver objects that it is now too late and tauntingly repeats Roland's earlier remark about disgracing his relatives. Blowing the horn with all his might, Roland bursts a blood-vessel in his temples, which is the eventual cause of his death. The blast of the horn is audible for miles. Charlemagne, hearing it, at once decides to return, but it is indeed too late. Oliver is killed, and at last only Turpin and Roland remain alive. Turpin attempts to find water for Roland, but collapses, dead. Roland, after trying in vain to shatter his great sword, Durendal, on the rocks, places it and the horn beneath him, his face turned toward the Saracen army which, aware that the French are returning, has decided to withdraw. Roland dies, and angels from heaven bear his soul aloft.

CHARLEMAGNE'S REVENGE

Arriving at the scene of the massacre. Charlemagne and his men mourn the loss of the rearguard. Pursuit is quickly undertaken and as Charlemagne races towards Saragossa, God holds the setting sun still in the sky. Many Arabs are killed by the sword and others are drowned in the swiftly flowing Ebro. Charlemagne gives thanks to God, and when he rises to his feet, the sun has set.

Massive Saracen forces under the Emir Baligant come to Marsile's aid, and battle is joined. Charlemagne and Baligant fight hand-to-hand and the Emperor, with the exhortations of the angel Gabriel ringing in his ears, is the victor. Having lost their leader, the Arabs take flight and Charlemagne occupies Saragossa. The French are now free to return home, where Alde, Oliver's sister and Roland's betrothed, falls dead at the Emperor's feet on hearing of Roland's death.

The trial of Ganelon begins. He defends himself vigorously, but is put to death. On hearing from the angel Gabriel that his troubles are far from over, Charlemagne laments. With this glance ahead to an uncertain future, the *Chanson de Roland* ends.

LEVELS OF MEANING

At one level, the epic is about the clash between Christianity and Islam. The latter is misrepresented as 'paganism', but the Arab foe is redoubtable and far from subdued even at the poem's end. At another level, it is a demonstration of the feudal system in the service of Christianity; at another, of the might of the invincible but always very human Charlemagne, with whom the work begins and ends. At one level of human relationships, a quarrel between step-father and step-son leads to treachery and disaster; at another, an intimate friendship between two companions, despite their disagreement at the start of the action, inspires the rearguard in its time of trial. Arising from this same friendship, the poem poses the question of what true courage is: is it heedless of danger, impetuous, as in Roland's case, or is it thoughtful, preferring to put all the chances on its side, as in Oliver's? The poet makes a simple distinction between them, while making it clear that neither lacked the qualities of a good vassal: 'Roland is bold and Oliver is wise, both have amazing courage.' Carried further, this can be seen as a contrast between idealism and realism. Roland is entirely in the grip of ideals which allow of no compromise, Oliver is ever conscious of the realities of the situation: there is a time to summon help, there is a time to fight and die.

At yet another level, this most complex of epics shows the testing of human nature when placed in extreme situations. The characters are not simple stereotypes or allegories. There is much to admire in Ganelon, but he cannot control his hatred of Roland which, we are made to feel, existed long before the action of the poem began. Charlemagne is the indomitable leader, towering over the entire work, yet strangely hesitant when decisions have to be taken. Roland is the brash, haughty, boastful warrior, whose flaw is what his contemporaries called *desmesure* (literally, 'lack of measure'), the overweening self-confidence which the ancient Greeks called *hubris*. The text exposes a duality in all men, for we all have battles to fight in our minds more tormenting even than those in the field. This was possibly a message for the new heroes of the crusading era when the poem was composed. No man is a simple embodiment of a single virtue, no man is all hero or all traitor, no man is all courage or all wisdom. We can only decide on the course of action which conscience and temperament, rightly or wrongly, dictate, and carry it out as best we may. We blunder, and find what remedies we can. God alone is greater than all this.

The poem also poses the question of what constitutes victory and defeat. Roland is dead, the rearguard annihilated, and yet they died unconquered, to the end faithful to the proud spirit of the Church Militant, convinced as Roland said that 'the pagans are wrong and the Christians are right'. Charlemagne's revenge on the Arabs does not replace defeat with victory. It confirms that earlier and finer victory, which is why scholars call the work, which has no title in the manuscript, *La Chanson de Roland* rather than *La Chanson de Charlemagne*.

The poem is written with great artistry, related to the oral presentation for which it was designed. Crucial moments are given a three-fold repetition, as in Oliver's urging of Roland to recall

Charlemagne while there is yet time. The repetition gains its full effect when read aloud, as intended, slowing down the time sequence, focussing attention on the crucial moment, building up a dramatic climax. As almost half the work is in direct speech, it is a kind of drama performed by a solitary individual, the medieval minstrel.

The poem's antecedents and authorship are mysterious. Whether Roland ever existed is an open question, but a few surviving fragments of Latin texts show that the legend was known in the second half of the eleventh century, and several cases are recorded from this period of families having one son called Roland and another called Oliver. The story that William the Conqueror's army went into action at Hastings in 1066 led by a minstrel singing the exploits of Charlemagne, Roland and Oliver at Rencesvals may not be mere fancy. It is generally accepted now that the *Chanson de Roland,* as it has come down to us in the Oxford manuscript, was the work of a single author of genius. The last line seems to offer a clue to his identity: *Ci falt la geste que Turoldus declinet.* Several translations have been suggested. 'Here ends the story which Turoldus narrates' is just one possibility. Is Turoldus the author's name, or merely that of a reviser, or of a scribe who copied out the manuscript? The truth may never be known.

CHARLEMAGNE, PÉPIN AND BERTHA

Many stories grew up about Charlemagne, of the kind which tend to cling round great figures of the past. He was the son of King Pépin of the Franks and Queen Bertha, and one story was that two traitors succeeded in tricking Pépin into accepting another woman, an impostor, as his Queen instead of the real Bertha, who is here made a Hungarian Princess. The unfortunate Bertha spent years in poverty in the forest until the imposture was revealed, when she gained her rightful place at Pépin's side and became the mother of Charlemagne. In another story, the same traitors, Rainfroi and Heldri, poison Pépin and Bertha, and for his own safety the young Charlemagne has to be sent away to a Saracen court, where he is brought up. Another tale was that Charlemagne committed incest with his sister and that Roland was the child of this union. There were also stories of heroes supposed to be vassals of the great Emperor, including Ogier the Dane, who is mentioned in the *Chanson de Roland,* Doon de Mayence and Huon de Bordeaux.

The legends enjoyed immense success throughout western Europe. The Latin *Historia Karoli Magni et Rotholandi,* of about 1140, was supposed to be an account of Charlemagne's wars in Spain written by Archbishop Turpin himself, here said to have survived the disaster. A Latin work of the same period, the *Poema de Almeria,* alluding to Roland and Oliver, was translated into Spanish. In

Germany, a cleric called Konrad produced the *Roulandes Lied* in about 1170. In Norway, a vast compilation of Charlemagne legends was assembled during the thirteenth century under the title *Karlamagnussaga,* and in the following century further versions appeared in Welsh, English and Dutch. There were also Italian epics centred on Charlemagne and Roland, and Roland is the central character of Ariosto's *Orlando Furioso* of 1516, one of the masterpieces of the Italian Renaissance. In 1485 Caxton printed the *Lyf of the Noble and Crysten Prynce, Charles the Grete,* translation of a late French prose romance, *Fierabras.* Fierabras was a Saracen giant who was defeated by Oliver and converted to the Christian faith. He also appears in an English verse romance, slightly disguised as *Sir Ferumbras,* but the main characters are Charlemagne and that staunch pair, the headstrong Roland and the cautious Oliver. Many other works were produced, largely on the lines of 'further adventures of...', the fame of their heroes guaranteeing a certain easy success, but the action growing ever more fanciful and far-fetched. The old epic elements are greatly diluted, and none of the later essays in the genre can be set beside the *Chanson de Roland* which is arguably the most outstanding work of French literature before the Renaissance.

CHRISTIAN WESTERN EUROPE

CHAPTER 24
MEDIEVAL TROY LEGENDS

Prominent amongst the most famous and frequently treated of all legends are those relating to Troy, and in particular to the siege of Troy by the Greeks. The most famous versions are the earliest: the *Iliad* and the *Odyssey,* both of which are usually attributed to Homer, who is believed to have lived in the eighth century BC. These two works cover only a small part of the entire legend, and probably represent a fusing together of several shorter works which may already have had a long existence in oral tradition, for the legend is based on historical events of the twelfth century BC or earlier (see CLASSICAL GREECE AND ROME). It is safe to state, therefore, that the legend is at least 3000 years old. In the course of its long life, episodes from it have occupied the attention of authors from antiquity through the Middle Ages and the Renaissance to the present day: including Homer, Sophocles, Euripides, Vergil, Dante, Boccaccio, Chaucer, Shakespeare, Milton, Racine, Schiller, Goethe, Tennyson, Giraudoux, Joyce and Eliot.

The Middle Ages, which engendered so many legends of its own, in this instance inherited an epic from the heroic age of Greece, but the stories of Troy only achieved fame in the medieval period when its own heroic age, dating roughly from the eighth to the eleventh centuries, was over. They rose to a new celebrity in the later twelfth century, not as an accretion from oral material, as had happened long before in Greece, but through a deliberate literary revival for a society no longer satisfied with tales of incredible adventures and

Jason, Medea and the Golden Fleece (page 224)

amazing exploits in battle, and in an age with little interest or belief in the Greek gods, whose quarrels and jealousies decided the issue in the original stories.

THE 'ROMAN DE TROIE'

There would have been little knowledge of these Greek tales in the Middle Ages without the *Roman de Troie,* a massive poem of over 30 000 lines, written about 1165 by Benoît de Sainte-Maure. Benoît, a Frenchman from a small town to the south of Tours, was a poet at the court of King Henry II of England, where he replaced the Anglo-Norman chronicler Wace as a more up-to-date, elegant and erudite writer. He dedicated his *Roman de Troie* to Henry's Queen, Eleanor of Aquitaine, who had a considerable influence on the literature of the second half of the twelfth century.

In his prologue Benoît explains that Homer got his facts wrong because he lived long after the siege of Troy, whereas he himself is following the account by Dares, a native of Troy who lived through the siege and kept a diary of it, a far more authentic account than Homer's. It had long been lost, but had turned up in Athens, where it was translated from Greek into Latin. The Latin version probably dates from the sixth century AD. Its pretensions to being an eyewitness account are not to be taken seriously. For the last third or so of his romance Benoît made use of another pretended eyewitness account, supposedly by one of the attacking Greeks, Dictys of Crete. It is amazing that he made as much as he did from this unpromising material, but he also drew on his extensive reading, on his views of human nature and, like most medieval writers, on his imagination. Like Dares, he begins with the story of Jason and the Golden Fleece (see CLASSICAL GREECE AND ROME).

THE GOLDEN FLEECE

Jason and his crew, accompanied by Hercules, sail to Colchis, bent on the seemingly impossible task of bringing back the Golden Fleece. Jason's handsome appearance is described at length and Medea, daughter of the King of Colchis, falls in love with him the moment she sets eyes on him. She agrees to reveal the secrets which will enable him to seize the Fleece, provided he will marry her and take her back with him to his country, a proposal which he willingly accepts. This love-story is dwelt on at length and, in a manner which was to become extremely fashionable in courtly romances, Medea attempts to analyse her conflicting feelings in a long monologue, well aware of her own folly, yet powerless to control it. At last, when Jason's retinue have at last retired for the night and all is silent, she sends her servant to bring Jason to her bed, and they sleep together until early morning. She bestows various magic gifts on him to make him invincible. Jason takes advantage of all this, but has no intention of keeping his promises. He betrays Medea and after his triumph over all the perils that lie in wait for him − a triumph owed entirely to Medea's help − he returns victorious to Greece.

The story now moves on to the first destruction of Troy by the Greeks, King Laomedon of Troy having offended Jason and Hercules by ordering them off his territories during their quest for the Golden Fleece. Greeks and Trojans wearing the armour and wielding the weapons of doughty medieval knights engage in battle on horseback depicted, as in the *chansons de geste* (songs of deeds), mainly as a series of single combats. Finally Hercules, hacking a path through the fray ('he made two halves of one knight'), encounters Laomedon and sends his head flying with one blow of his sword. The Trojans, demoralized by the loss of their King, give way. Troy is sacked and destroyed, and the Greeks depart.

PARIS AND HELEN

The *Roman de Troie* now plunges into the story of how Priam, Laomedon's son, set about rebuilding Troy. The splendour and luxury of the rebuilt defences, in which marble was extensively used, are described at length. The very least of the fortresses would have had no fear of all the might of the King of France. Greatest of all was the citadel, Ilion, described in great detail for the richness of its workmanship. The twelfth century, an age of castle-building, was keenly interested in such matters, and Benoît was determined to dazzle his audience with unheard-of splendours.

After the failure of their mission to try to make peace with the Greeks, the Trojans debate at length among themselves. Paris, second son of Priam (Hector being the eldest) presents as a dream the story of how he was asked to judge between three goddesses and award a golden apple to the fairest. He awarded it to the goddess of love, Venus (Aphrodite in Greek), in return for her promise to give him the most beautiful woman in Greece. Since he is assured of Venus' help, he offers to lead an expedition against the Greeks. After much deliberation this is agreed, despite Cassandra's warning that if Paris takes a Greek woman for wife Troy will be destroyed.

Paris' abduction of Helen is portrayed as revenge for the Greeks' capture of Priam's sister Hesione. Paris addresses Helen as a true medieval courtly lover: 'All my life I shall be your loyal lover, your loyal husband. Of this you may be sure and certain. Everybody shall obey you, everybody shall serve you.' Helen, already in love with him, only pretends to feel sorrow at having been carried off to Troy.

Priam now feels sure that he has the means of freeing his sister from the Greeks, yet he raises no objection when Paris marries Helen! Only Cassandra condemns Paris, forecasting imminent disaster, and Priam quickly has her shut away in an isolated room. In the first clash between Greeks and Trojans after the abduction of Helen, the briefly described action is followed by a long speech by Agamemnon, the Greek commander-in-chief, devoted to a painstakingly moralizing analysis of the rights and wrongs of the whole affair, the type of weighing-up of pros and cons favoured in the courts of northern France in the twelfth century.

Much space is taken up with parleys between the two sides, the Greeks demanding the return of Helen, the Trojans of Hesione. Action when the Greek fleet at last reaches Troy is vigorously portrayed: 'flour that is being sifted does not fall as thickly, or rain or hail in the wind, as the barbed arrows, the darts and quarrels.' A long series of seven battles is punctuated by the deaths of several heroes and a truce to bury the dead. One can only admire the ingenuity of a writer able to introduce an infinite number of variations into this basic material of swordplay and violent clashes of arms, inherited more from the *chansons de geste* of the eleventh and early twelfth centuries than from earlier Latin sources, with precise technical details of the effects of weapon-blows on chain armour (there is no evidence that the Greeks and Trojans used chain mail) that can only have been of interest to the knightly and militaristic society of the feudal era.

TROILUS AND BRISEIDA

A romance is now introduced, between Troilus, Priam's youngest son, who has distinguished himself in battle, and Briseida. She is the daughter of the Trojan soothsayer Calchas, who had defected to the Greeks on the orders of the god Apollo and who now requests the Trojans to send his daughter to him. (This romantic interlude may be Benoît's own invention.) Briseida takes leave of her lover after a tearful night spent together, but Benoît, clearly something of a misogynist, declares that her sorrow will not last long. 'Woman's grief is short-lived, she weeps with one eye and laughs with the other. They quickly change their minds. Even the wisest woman is very foolish. Whatever a woman has loved in seven years, she has forgotten in three days.'

No sooner has Briseida arrived in the Greek camp than Diomedes, King of Argos, declares his love, and Briseida gives him a reply that leaves him grounds for hope. In the next battle her Greek lover unhorses her Trojan lover and sends her his horse as a present. She sends him an ambiguously worded reply, telling Diomedes that she feels no hatred for him. Troilus later succeeds in wounding Diomedes and Briseida is so moved with pity for Diomedes that she at last grants him her love, deserting Troilus while realizing her own wickedness: 'No good song will ever be sung about me' (an excellent prophecy in the light of the portrayal of her character by Chaucer and Shakespeare). Troilus, shortly before his death at the hands of Achilles, reflects bitterly on the treachery of woman.

ACHILLES AND POLYXENA

Yet another love-story is woven into the narrative. Achilles, who has earlier killed Hector, falls in love with Hector's sister Polyxena. It is a fatal love for Achilles, who 'will be in the grip of Love and Death'. There is no love scene between the two, but Achilles' armour avails him nothing against Love. This mighty hero of so many bloody encounters blushes, then grows pale, feels cold, then hot, and all his thoughts centre on Polyxena. He meditates at length on this hopeless love, and sends a message to Hecuba, Polyxena's mother, declaring that if Polyxena will marry him, he and his men will withdraw from the war. The reply comes from Hecuba's husband, Priam: first dismiss your army, then you can marry Polyxena. Achilles tries to persuade the Greeks to give up the siege, but in vain, and can only forbid his own followers to continue the struggle. He now plays chess while the war rages. Eventually he allows his men to fight again, and himself returns to the fray when they are greatly reduced in numbers. After killing Troilus, he goes unarmed to a meeting with Hecuba and is ambushed and killed by Paris, who is bent on avenging the deaths of his brothers. Paris himself is killed soon after by another Greek warrior, Ajax, and Achilles' son Pyrrhus sacrifices Polyxena on his father's tomb.

THE WOODEN HORSE

Apart from the love-stories and the various parleys, there are two other major interruptions to the battle sequences. The first is a description of the Alabaster Room in Priam's palace, the carvings encrusted with every type of jewel and precious stone, the pillars of gold, the richly painted, ornate walls and ceiling. Such luxuries were all the more fascinating to Benoît's northern French audience because the Crusades, in southern Spain as well as in the East, had recently brought northerners into contact with them. The other, with a similar motivation, is a long description of that ever-mysterious and fascinating Orient, which allows Benoît once more to display his erudition. The excuse this time is that it was from the East that Panthesila, Queen of the Amazons, came to help Priam.

Panthesila accomplishes great feats of arms, but is eventually killed in battle. After long discussions, two Trojan nobles, Aeneas and Antenor, begin peace parleys very much against Priam's wishes.

Meantime, Calchas and another priest of Apollo, Chryses, devise the idea of the wooden horse, and the story follows the traditional pattern. The soldiers hidden in the horse successfully prepare the way for the Greek army and the subsequent sack of Troy is described at length. The fate of various Greek leaders is then dealt with. Agamemnon is killed by his wife Clytemnestra, aided by her lover, and is avenged by his son Orestes. The narrative ends with the adventures of Ulysses (Odysseus) after his departure from ruined Troy, telling how he was eventually killed by his son Telegonus (Telemachus), who did not recognize him though, in one of those ironies of fate beloved of the ancient legends, he was actually searching for his missing father at the time.

LITERARY DEVELOPMENTS

How was this immense work presented in court? Almost certainly, it was not read by individuals in private, but recited aloud in sessions occurring over several days, having this much in common, at least, with Homer's epics. The fame of the *Roman de Troie* soon spread beyond France, with German and Dutch versions appearing in the thirteenth century. A Sicilian author, Guido delle Colonne, produced a Latin abridgement which became tremendously influential in its turn. Not acknowledging Benoît for source, it has been described as one of the most successful cases of literary robbery ever known. Benoît's story of Troilus and Briseida, whose name became Cressida through confusion with Chryseis, the daughter of Chryses, was to enjoy immense success – in Boccaccio's *Il Filostrato,* in Chaucer's 'sorrowful tale' of *Troilus and Criseyde,* and in Shakespeare's *Troilus and Cressida.*

In the *Roman de Troie* the epic spirit, with its emphasis on bloody battles and fine feats of arms, is giving way to other interests, in particular to stories of love and passion, which were to become a vital element in European literature from the late twelfth century onwards. Henceforth the hero must know how to behave in the boudoir as well as on the battlefield. In this respect the medieval Troy legends, for all their debt to the remote past, pointed the way ahead for generations to come.

THE TROY LEGENDS: PRINCIPAL MEDIEVAL VERSIONS

Benoît de Sainte-Maure's *Roman de Troie,* in French verse (*c.* 1165), was the key work in the medieval development of the legends. It was based on the following sources:

De Excidio Troiae Historia (History of the Fall of Troy), attributed to

Dares the Phrygian, translated from Greek in a Latin version, probably of the sixth century AD.

Ephemeris Belli Trojani (Diary of the Trojan War), attributed to Dictys of Crete, the Latin version dating possibly from the fourth century AD.

Various other sources, including Servius' *Commentary on Vergil,* a fourth-century text tesigned for use in schools. Benoît apparently did not use the *Ilias Latina,* the first known translation of the *Iliad* into Latin, which dates from the first century AD.

Benoît's *Roman de Troie* soon inspired versions in other European languages, including the works listed below:

Herbort von Fritzlar *Liet von Troye,* in German, early thirteenth century, an abbreviated version of Benoît.

Konrad von Würzburg   *Trojanerkrieg* (Trojan War), in German, thirteenth century, mainly based on Benoît.

Segher Dieregotgaf   *Trojaensche Oorlag* (Siege of Troy), in Dutch, thirteenth century.

Jacob van Maerlant   *Istory van Troyen,* in Dutch, thirteenth century.

Guido delle Colonne   *Historia Destructionis Trojae,* in Latin prose, late thirteenth century, a highly influential abridgement of Benoît.

Unknown   *Cronica Troyana,* a Spanish version, fourteenth century.

Unknown   *Siege and Battle of Troy,* in English, fourteenth century, based on a variety of sources.

Unknown   *'Gest Hystoriale' of the Destruction of Troy,* in English, fourteenth century, based principally on Guido delle Colonne.

CHRISTIAN WESTERN EUROPE

CHAPTER 25
ALEXANDER THE GREAT

Alexander the Great (356–323 BC) was one of the most successful conquerors the world has known, and in his short lifetime became the centre of a legend which was to go on growing for centuries after his death. Although historical accounts of his career existed, of varying reliability, the European Middle Ages preferred a version now known as Pseudo-Callisthenes, in which legend predominated over fact (see CLASSICAL GREECE AND ROME). The Middle Ages usually drew no clear line of distinction between fact and fiction, and favoured the most colourful and richly anecdotal stories of the heroes of the past, partly for their intrinsic attraction, and partly for the moral conclusions which could be drawn from even the most extravagant of them.

Though immensely successful, Pseudo-Callisthenes was a hotch-potch of indifferent literary quality, assembled from various sources and combining historical and legendary material. For example, it has the hero fathered by the magician Nectanebus, the last independent King of Egypt, who was dethroned by a Persian invasion, sought refuge in Macedon and paid his attentions to Alexander's mother-to-be, Queen Olympias, in the form of a dragon.

Pseudo-Callisthenes had a most complex and tangled history, inspiring manifold translations and fanciful biographies of Alexander. In no European country did the legend of Alexander flourish quite as much as in France, and the most substantial of all the medieval Alexander poems is the *Roman d'Alexandre,* put together from earlier materials by Alexandre de Paris, about 1185. There were

Alexander the Great

also versions of the hero's exploits in German and other European languages.

LEGENDARY CONQUESTS

What the various versions of the hero's career all have in common is the concept of Alexander as conqueror, but the conquests of the legendary figure extend beyond the realm of men to that of the elements. One extremely popular story was the tale of him flying through the sky in a chariot drawn by gryphons, which were enticed into the air by a joint of meat dangled in front of them. Another was the story of him journeying to the bottom of the sea in a glass submarine, which allowed him to explore the marvels of the seabed. Both adventures are found in Pseudo-Callisthenes and became widely known.

The celestial journey was above all a fantasy designed to entertain, but in addition it certainly had a symbolic significance, which is hard to determine. In Germany, where theological condemnation of Alexander's pride was common, the hero decides not to climb too high when a voice warns him that only those may rise to heaven who deserve to do so, by their good deeds. The enterprise appears too risky to him, and down he comes, so far from his starting point that it is months later when he finally regains his army, his clothes worn to rags.

The submarine adventure is even more fanciful. Alexander and his men kill a giant crab and find six large pearls inside it. Alexander decides to look for more on the seabed, and has a large glass vessel constructed, protected by a cage of iron. It is attached to a chain and lowered to the bottom. A giant fish seizes it and eventually deposits it on the shore. Later versions embroider on this one in a variety of ways. For instance, Alexander is accompanied by a dog, a cat and a cock. The dog is an automatic rescue device, for Alexander would kill it in order to be washed up on shore, a characteristic of the sea being that it rejects blood. The cat is an air purifier, for it would inhale Alexander's breath and return it cleansed of impurities, and the cock is a clock, for its crowing would tell Alexander the time. A later German version takes medieval fantasy much closer to modern science by conjuring up the notion of a long neck of glass protruding out of the water, a thirteenth-century style schnorkel. Alexander thus becomes the hero of a sort of medieval science fiction, the immensely fertile imagination of those times anticipating centuries beforehand inventions now taken for granted. Such early fantasies are those of an age when man depended far more than he does today on animals, and it was to the animal kingdom, itself partly mythical, that his imagination turned in the first instance, rather than towards the invention of machinery.

MORAL TALES

A rich fund of anecdotal material was drawn from the romances by
preachers and moralists, with Alexander as the central figure.
A favourite tale with moralists was the story of Alexander's journey
to the Earthly Paradise (first known in the West in a twelfth-century
Latin prose version, which in the following century was incorporated
into the *Roman d'Alexandre*). Journeying up the Ganges, Alexander
comes to a city protected by a great wall. He is unable to enter, but an
old man presents him with a stone which has a special meaning.
Alexander returns home and for long the mystery remains unsolved,
until at last an old Jew discovers the secret. The stone will outweigh
any amount of gold, but if dust is scattered over it, the lightest feather
will outweigh it. This is God's warning to Alexander to restrain his
greed and to remember that death will reduce even him to nothing.
The idea that even the mightiest of men are helpless in the face of
death was one of which medieval moralists never tired.

Another favourite story told how Diogenes, the Cynic philosopher
who lived in a barrel, was asked by Alexander what he could do for
him, and replied: 'Get out of my sunlight.' What mattered to
Diogenes was the one thing which Alexander, for all his might and
liberality, was powerless to bestow. There was also the tale of
Alexander giving an old soldier an entire city, and when the soldier
protested that he was not worthy of so fine a gift he was told that it was
not a question of what he was worthy to receive, but of what was
worthy of being a gift bestowed by Alexander. Classical writers such
as Seneca and Cicero had condemned Alexander for a misplaced and
inconsiderate liberality which was merely part of his vanity. The
Middle Ages, however, were ever ready to admire generosity in the
powerful, not only as a Christian virtue, important though that was,
but for a more mercenary motive, because the medieval man-of-let-
ters depended on the nobleman's patronage.

Alexander's name became practically synonymous with liberality.
François Villon, the fifteenth-century French poet, relates in his
Testament the tale of Alexander's generous treatment of the pirate
Diomedes (Dionides in other versions), brought before him to be
sentenced. Alexander asks why he is a pirate, to which Diomedes
replies: 'Why do you call me a pirate? Because you see me roving the
sea in a tiny craft? If I could arm myself like you, I should be
Emperor.' He explains that fortune has never deigned to smile on
him. Alexander not only pardons him but changes his lot for the
better, and Diomedes lives happily ever after. Villon uses the
anecdote to emphasize his own lucklessness and destitution.

In the main, the Middle Ages admired Alexander, although in
Germany he was subjected to much theological condemnation
because of his pride, which made him the very embodiment of the

Devil. In France the courtly tradition held such negative attitudes at bay until the end of the Middle Ages.

THE MYSTERY OF THE ORIENT

The tales of Alexander brought to the West the image of a wise, beneficent and all-powerful ruler. They also, and more characteristically, brought with them all the magic and mystery of the Orient, further bedecked by the amazingly fertile, if naive, medieval imagination, feeding on the easily aroused superstitions of the time. Alexander was a conqueror whose adventures could the more readily be adorned with exotic features because his enemies, unlike those of Charlemagne, were not pagan forces which threatened to crush Christianity in the West. The powerful crusading motive was absent here, and there is none of the religious propaganda that inspires so much of the Charlemagne epics. Mighty conqueror though he was, Alexander was also the adventurer who routed a herd of wild elephants by making some pigs squeal, who consulted the prophetic trees of the Moon and the Sun, defeated giants armed with clubs, encountered fire-breathing birds and fire-breathing Cynocephali (men with dogs' heads and gryphons' claws), headless men some 4 metres tall and 2 metres wide (12 and 7 feet) whose eyes and mouths were set in their chests, bird-headed men, water nymphs whose embrace was fatal to their lovers, and giant women with hooves for feet or with the tusks of boars and the tails of oxen.

The whole highly coloured and extravagant dream faded with the dying Middle Ages. The Renaissance, partly influenced by certain Greek texts not available to medieval western Europe, was more interested in the historical Alexander, scornfully dismissing the medieval flights of fancy and, parsimonious even of admiration for the real figure, echoing the strictures of classical writers. One is reminded of Alexander landing from his aerial adventures and turning up months later amongst his soldiers, once more a mortal among men.

THE ALEXANDER ROMANCES: LITERARY HISTORY

The literary history of the legend is extremely complicated, and can only be outlined here. The most important derivative of Pseudo-Callisthenes, for western Europe at least, was the fourth-century Latin version by Julius Valerius, *Res Gestae Alexandri Macedonis* (Achievements of Alexander of Macedon). A summary of this, made some five centuries later and known as the *Epitome,* was extremely influential. The most important vernacular derivative of the *Epitome,* in turn, was the Old French *Roman d'Alexandre,* whose own history was again singularly convoluted.

The earliest version survives only in an early twelfth-century fragment of verse, written in Franco-Provençal by Alberic de Pisançon. There is a more complete version, based on Alberic, in Middle High German by Pfaffe Lamprecht, known as the *Alexander-lied* and dating from about 1150. Lamprecht also made use of a tenth-century Latin transcript of one of the Pseudo-Callisthenes manuscripts, usually referred to as the *Historia de Preliis* (History of Battles), which became a source of many vernacular versions, not only in Germany.

In France, a Poitevin poet revised Alberic's poem between 1165 and 1175, and soon after three other Alexander poems were composed in the twelve-syllabled lines which became known as alexandrines and played an important role in French literature. The first of these, *La Fuerre de Gadres* (The Foraging of Gaza) by a certain Eustache, deals with Alexander's siege of Gaza and the capture of Tyre. The second, by Lambert le Tort, is known nowadays as *Alexandre en Orient*. Based mainly on the *Epitome,* it tells of the defeat and death of King Darius of Persia, of the two defeats of King Porus of India, and of Alexander's encounters with the marvels of the East. The third poem, *La Mort Alexandre* (The Death of Alexander), tells the apocryphal story of Alexander's murder by poison and burial.

It was these four versions, beginning with the Poitevin poem, which Alexandre de Paris assembled to form the *Roman d'Alexandre,* about 1185. Various sequels were added because, to suit the medieval outlook, Alexander's death had to be avenged. These sequels are entirely fictitious, earlier works having at least a basis in history. Equally fictional are a number of romances, such as the early fourteenth-century *Voeux du Paon* (The Peacock's Vows) by Jacques de Longuyon. The whole emphasis has changed by this time: less campaigning and more social life, with the ladies playing an important role and Alexander not only the all-conquering hero but also the gallant gentleman.

German versions include Rudolf von Ems's *Alexander* of about 1250, und Ulrich von Etzenbach's *Alexander,* slightly later. Both were influenced by the *Historia de Preliis* and by a Latin epic, Gautier de Châtillon's *Alexandreis,* written between 1178 and 1182, a school textbook considered at the time to be comparable to Vergil's *Aeneid.* It is characteristic of the complex interrelationships of the Alexander romances that this Latin work by a Frenchman, based on one of the more reliable historical accoounts of Alexander (by Quintus Curtius in the first century AD) should have inspired versions in German, Spanish, Dutch, Icelandic and Czech, but nothing in French. French writers definitely preferred the more highly coloured legendary accounts of Alexander's life. Other medieval treatments of the legend have survived from Italy, England, Scotland and Ireland, including the fourteenth-century English *Kyng Alisaunder.*

CHRISTIAN WESTERN EUROPE

CHAPTER 26

ARTHUR AND LEGENDARY BRITAIN

The last words of one of the most famous and enjoyable books in the English language — 'The whole book of King Arthur and of his noble knights of the Round Table' — were written by Sir Thomas Malory, in 1469 or 1470, as a prisoner in Newgate jail in London. In 1485 Malory's book was printed by William Caxton, who edited it and gave it the title by which it has been known ever since, *Le Morte Darthur* (The Death of Arthur). For close to 500 years the heroic saga of the Round Table has attracted readers in multitudes and has inspired poets, novelists and painters, who include Tennyson, the Pre-

KING ARTHUR'S FAMILY TREE
(According to Sir Thomas Malory)

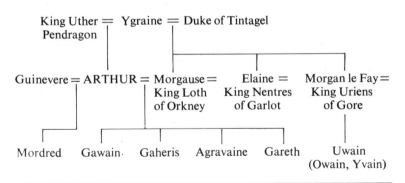

Sir Gawain and the Green Knight (page 242)

Raphaelites, Swinburne, Hardy, William Morris, Charles Williams, T. H. White, John Steinbeck and Mary Stewart.

The *Morte Darthur* is the standard version of the Arthurian cycle in English, but the tales of Arthur and his knights had delighted story-tellers and audiences all over Europe for centuries before Malory's time. If all the stories were collected together, in their different versions and languages, they would run to millions of words. They appealed to the Middle Ages, as they still do today, as exciting adventure-stories in a pattern which is now familiar, and which they did much to establish: heroes and villains larger than life, beautiful heroines and seductive enchantresses, battle and derring-do, love, sex and treachery, perilous encounters and hairbreadth escapes, the thwarting of evil designs and the triumph of courage and honour. Behind all this, however, is a much deeper attraction. For medieval audiences, Arthur and his knights were not made-up characters but real people. They had lived at some uncertain period in the past, but in medieval surroundings. The tales of their adventures were true stories which showed how men and women could best live their lives in an imperfect world. Though the legends are now recognized as fiction, they have never lost their appeal to idealism. Tennyson, dedicating his *Idylls of the King* to Queen Victoria, summed up what is perhaps the central theme which gives the Arthurian legends their compelling power: 'Ideal manhood closed in real man.'

The Arthur of legend is a great king of Britain, noble, brave, just, generous and warm-hearted. His realm is called Logres (from the Welsh word for England) and he rules in glittering splendour from his capital city, many-towered Camelot. Beautiful women and the gallant knights of the Order of the Round Table adorn his court. His adviser is Merlin, the master magician. His wife is Guinevere, the loveliest woman in Britain. His dearest friend and champion is Lancelot of the Lake, the best knight in the world. But Arthur's brilliant career is doomed to a tragic end. Guinevere and Lancelot fall passionately in love. For a long time they keep their relationship secret, but in the end the truth comes out. Arthur's happiness is shattered, his Kingdom is plunged into civil war, and the fellowship of the Round Table is destroyed. Struggling to salvage what he can from the wreck, the King is betrayed by his bastard son, Mordred. Fatally wounded by Mordred in his last battle, Arthur is carried away to Avalon, the mysterious paradise in the west, from which he will return to lead his countrymen at the time when they most have need of him.

ALBION AND THE TROJANS

Though Arthur is the greatest of British legendary heroes, the legends are largely the product of medieval French culture, with its outpost in England where the aristocracy spoke French. The major creative period in their history runs from about 1150 to 1250, and it was principally from French stories of this vintage that Malory produced his version of the legends. Behind the French tales are the older Celtic stories of Arthur and his men, transmitted into medieval France and England by Welsh and Breton minstrels. Far in the past behind the Celtic tales is the obscure figure of a real man, the Arthur of history (see WELSH LEGENDS). He was apparently a British war-leader of about AD 500, who defeated and for a time held back the encroaching Saxons who had moved into the power-vacuum in Britain after the collapse of Roman authority early in the fifth century.

The first full and connected account of Arthur that has survived, and probably the first ever written, came out in England in the 1130s. *The History of the Kings of Britain* was written by Geoffrey of Monmouth, thought to be of Welsh or Breton descent. Based partly on earlier writers and on oral tradition and partly on its author's own vivid imagination, it provided a legendary history of Britain from the earliest times, which was accepted as authentic for 400 years by all except a few crabbed scholars.

According to the *History,* the British came of Trojan stock and their kings were descended from no less a figure than Aeneas, Prince of Troy, the hero of Vergil's *Aeneid,* and the legendary forefather of the Caesars. After the fall of Troy, Aeneas escaped from the city and made himself King of Italy. He had a grandson named Brutus. Before Brutus was born, it was prophesied that he would cause the deaths of his father and mother, that he would go into exile and would eventually rise to the highest honour. All this came true, for his mother died in giving birth to him and when he was fifteen he killed his father in a hunting accident. Sent into exile in Greece, he gathered a following among the descendants of other Trojan expatriates. The goddess Diana appeared to him in a dream and told him to take his people to an island beyond the setting sun, where he would found a second Troy.

Brutus obeyed and led his followers to a rich and delightful island in the northern seas, called Albion and inhabited only by giants. The Trojans landed at Totnes in Devon, where they were attacked by a war-party of giants, led by Gogmagog, who stood 3−4 metres (12 feet) tall. They killed the giants, took possession of the island, which they named Britain for King Brutus, and built the city of New Troy, afterwards London. When Brutus died, his three sons divided the island between them. They were Locrinus, who gave his name to Loegria (England), Kamber of Kambria (Wales) and Albanactus of Albany (Scotland).

This was essentially an old story and the bones of it are found in a Welsh writer, Nennius (about 800), and in earlier Irish annals. It

gave the Britons an illustrious ancestry and put the British ruling
house on a level with other European dynasties, which also claimed
a Trojan lineage. Albion was a genuine early name for Britain. The
names Gog and Magog come from the Old Testament and the Book
of Revelation, where they are evil powers.

The *History* continues on through a long line of legendary British
kings, some of whose names are familiar from Shakespeare and other
later writers. King Lear had three daughters, the wicked Goneril and
Regan, who dispossessed him, and the loyal Cordelia, who helped
him regain his throne. King Gorboduc and Queen Judon had two
sons, Ferrex and Porrex, who quarrelled over the succession. Porrex
killed Ferrex in battle and was vengefully hacked to pieces in his sleep
by Judon and her maidservants. King Cymbeline was an old man
when the Roman Emperor Claudius invaded Britain (AD 43.) King
Coel, who may be the original of Old King Cole, was the grandfather
of the Emperor Constantine the Great (fourth century AD), whose
mother was Coel's daughter Helena.

Eventually the Romans withdrew from Britain. The country was
promptly invaded by the barbarous Saxons, in alliance with a Welsh
nobleman named Vortigern, who usurped the British throne (see
WALES).

ARTHUR AND MERLIN

At this point the *History* introduces a character whose fame was to
rival Arthur's own. The Saxons turned against Vortigern, and he fled
to Wales. There he encountered a mysterious boy from Carmarthen.
(Dyfed) whose father was a demon and mother a princess. His name was
Merlin and he had magic powers and the ability to see into the future
(see LEGENDARY MAGICIANS). He told Vortigern that the conflict
between the Britons and the Saxons would go on until the coming of
the Boar of Cornwall, who would trample the Saxons under his feet.
The Boar of Cornwall is Arthur, and the great hero is here a figure of
destiny, whose coming is foretold by a prophet.

The rightful heir to the kingdom, Aurelius Ambrosius, now
gathered an army and burned Vortigern alive in his own stronghold.
He regained the throne, but the many Saxons in England remained
a permanent threat. Aurelius was poisoned by a treacherous Saxon
and was succeeded by his younger brother, Uther Pendragon.

Uther fell passionately in love with the beautiful Ygerna (later
Ygraine), who was married to the Duke of Cornwall, one of Uther's
most powerful supporters. The Duke retired with his wife to
Cornwall, where Uther attacked him. Ygerna was immured in the
impregnable fortress of Tintagel, while the Duke stayed with his
army. Merlin used magic drugs to transform Uther into the likeness of
the Duke, and Uther went to Tintagel and to Ygerna's bed. That night

Arthur was conceived, and that same night Ygerna's real husband, the Duke, led a sally against Uther's troops and was killed. Changed back into his normal form, Uther seized Ygerna and apparently married her without delay.

This story of Arthur's conception at Tintagel remained unchanged in all essentials throughout the entire subsequent history of the legends. It gave Arthur's birth an air of magic and mystery in symmetry with the mystery which would also surround his death, and it has parallels in legends of other heroes, including Alexander the Great. The hero is sired by someone other than his mother's husband and in a way which is against nature and contrary to accepted morality – by a god or a mysterious stranger, by incest, rape, trickery or magic. The underlying implication may be that the abnormality of the act and the overwhelming passion which inspires it create or liberate a powerful magic force with which the hero is imbued and which drives him to transcend normal human limitations.

THE SWORD IN THE STONE

According to the *History,* Arthur succeeded to the throne when he was fifteen years old, on Uther's death. He decisively defeated the Saxons and in later years he conquered Scotland, Ireland, Iceland, Norway, Denmark and France under his standard of the Golden Dragon. He also fought and killed the evil giant of Mont-Saint-Michel, and his fame spread to the ends of the earth. Arthur is here a great conqueror, a British Charlemagne.

French writers, however, followed by Malory, added other tales to the *History's* account of Arthur's early life. As soon as he was born, it was said, Merlin claimed him and took him away to be brought up secretly in the country, unaware of who he really was. Uther Pendragon died, and after a long interregnum Merlin summoned all the nobles to London, where he had provided a great square stone in which was an anvil. In the anvil a naked sword was held fast, and in Malory's words, 'letters there were written in gold about the sword that said thus: WHOSO PULLETH OUT THIS SWORD OF THIS STONE AND ANVIL IS RIGHTWISE KING BORN OF ALL ENGLAND.'

Many lords and knights tugged at the sword, but could not move it. At last the young Arthur, now almost fifteen, came by when no one else was about and casually pulled out the sword. When this was discovered, his true identity was revealed to him and he was crowned King. This story, again, has parallels in other legends, where the hero is brought up in obscurity and comes to his adult sphere of action from the outside, as a stranger.

Merlin was the young King's counsellor and helper. It was Merlin who took him to a lake to obtain the great sword Excalibur, which was held up by a hand rising from the water. It was a gift from the Lady of the Lake, a powerful fay (fairy) who lived in an enchanted palace in the depths of the water. (In an earlier form of this story Excalibur was the sword which Arthur drew from the stone.)

Merlin, however, could not protect Arthur from the machinations of his half-sister Morgan le Fay, the great enchantress, who tried to encompass his death. The King was saved by the counter-magic of the Lady of the Lake. Nor could Merlin prevent him from sleeping with another of his half-sisters, Morgause, in ignorance of their relationship. The child of this incestuous union was Mordred and Merlin correctly predicted that Mordred would destroy Arthur and his knights.

THE ROUND TABLE

From this point on, in the French tales, the emphasis shifts away from Arthur himself. The focus is now on the adventures of his knights. There were two main stories about the founding of the Round Table. According to the simpler one, Arthur enlisted so many knights of renown in his household and the rivalry between them was so keen that he had the Round Table constructed to avoid disputes over who should sit higher in his hall.

The other story links the Round Table directly with the Holy Grail, the great relic of Christ's Passion which was guarded in secret in a mysterious castle by a succession of Grail Keepers. The Grail was the cup of the Last Supper, from which Jesus gave his disciples to drink of the wine that was his blood. In it Joseph of Arimathea collected some of the blood that flowed from the Saviour's wounds on the cross. Joseph of Arimathea set up a Grail table in commemoration of the Last Supper. One place at it was left empty, to represent the seat of Judas Iscariot, who hurried out into the night to betray Jesus. The Grail table in turn was the model for the Round Table, which was made for Uther Pendragon on Merlin's advice. Again, one place was always left empty. This was the Siege Perilous, or dangerous seat, which only the supreme hero who was to win the Grail could safely occupy. Here the Round Table is no longer a mere piece of furniture, a device to avoid quarrels over precedence. It is a symbol of the fellowship of Jesus and his disciples at the Last Supper, and an image on earth of the ideal society of heaven.

The champions of the Round Table are knights errant, wandering knights, who ride out from Arthur's court in quest of adventure. The theme of the quest, the search, is central to these tales. The typical knight errant, like the heroes of innumerable modern adventure-stories and thrillers, is a solitary figure. He goes out into the world to battle alone against evil. He hopes to win undying fame, high reputation among his fellow knights and the love of a fair lady. In his adventures he kills giants, dragons and wicked tyrants, foils wizards and enchantresses, rescues damsels in distress, saves lives, rights wrongs, helps the unfortunate and makes the world a better place. Ultimately, perhaps, the true object of his quest is to find something in himself, a perfect integrity of character. Through all the perils that confront him he seeks to do his duty. He is the man who repeatedly risks his life for his ideal of what he ought to be.

THE FAIR UNKNOWN

The adventures are set in an enchanted landscape, full of magic. The King and his knights move from the natural to the supernatural plane and back again, without any sense of strain or incongruity being expressed, either by the story-teller or by the characters themselves. It does not in the least surprise a hero of the Round Table to encounter an enchanted castle, or a ship that sails by itself or a hideous hag who turns into a beautiful girl.

A good example is the story of *Le Bel Inconnu* (The Fair Unknown) by Renaud de Beaujeu. The hero is a young knight named Guinglain, who goes to Arthur's court. Brought up by his mother alone, he does not know his name, and because he is strikingly handsome Arthur calls him the Fair Unknown. He is sent to rescue the Queen of Wales, Blonde Esmerée, who has been turned into a dragon by two evil sorcerers. She can only be released from the enchantment by a kiss.

Guinglain sets out and, after overcoming numerous dangers, reaches the Golden Island, where there is a magnificent palace with crystal walls and a garden in which flowers bloom and birds sing all the year round. The lady of the island, La Pucelle aux Blanches Mains (the Maiden of the White Hands) is a fay of surpassing loveliness who falls in love with Guinglain. He is powerfully attracted to her, but he remembers his mission, steals away from the island and goes to the Waste City of Senaudon (Snowdon), where the unfortunate Blonde Esmerée is held captive.

Guinglain comes to the Waste City in the evening. The city is in ruins and apparently abandoned. He rides through the fallen gate and along deserted streets to a great palace of marble, where he is attacked by a huge knight on a fire-breathing horse. After a fierce struggle Guinglain kills the knight, whose body turns into a mass of mouldering corruption before his eyes. Then an eerie glow of light spreads through the dark hall. It comes from the jewelled eyes of a hideous dragon, which glides towards Guinglain and kisses him on the mouth. The spell is broken, the dragon is restored to human form as the beautiful Blonde Esmerée, and a mysterious voice tells Guinglain his name. He eventually marries Blonde Esmerée and they are crowned King and Queen with tumultuous rejoicing in the city, which is now restored to life and full of people.

In this story the hero, by courage and resolute devotion to his duty, achieves his quest, wins a beautiful wife and becomes a King. He also discovers his own identity, vanquishes the power of evil and gives life back to the Waste City which evil had made desolate and dead. The motif of the bewitching enchantress, La Pucelle, who loves him and tries to keep him with her in her magic island, away from the world of action, occurs frequently in the Arthurian stories. The hero is tempted to escape from reality into a dreamland of romantic love, a place where no changes occur, no decisions are made, no battles are fought. But if he is to be true to himself and his duty, he must resist the temptation, however compelling, and return to the real world of decision and action.

LANCELOT AND GAWAIN

'No knight was ever born of man and woman,' says a character in Chrétien de Troyes' *Lancelot,* 'and no knight ever sat in a saddle, who was the equal of this man.' For many story-tellers and their audiences Lancelot of the Lake was quite simply the best knight in the world. Unrivalled in combat, towering in size and strength, handsome and sensitive, he was the matchless exponent of the Arthurian virtues of honour, courage, loyalty and generosity. These are the supreme values of chivalry, the code of the medieval knight, which the modern world inherited as the code of the gentleman, and the supreme values of 'heroic' warrior-aristocracies in general.

Lancelot was the son of the King of Benoic, a territory somewhere in western France. He was descended from King David, and so came of the same kin as Christ. His father was killed in battle when he was a baby and he was snatched away from his mother by the Lady of the Lake. She brought him up in her enchanted palace, ignorant of his true parentage, and when he was eighteen sent him to Arthur's court. He became the King's greatest supporter and friend, and time and again when Arthur was in trouble or danger, Lancelot came to his rescue. His tragedy was his consuming passion for Guinevere. He attributed all his success and renown to the inspiring power of her love, but he was caught in an intolerable conflict between his loyalty to Arthur and his love for Arthur's wife. His affair with the Queen robbed him of the supreme honour of winning the Grail and in the end pitted him against the leader he loved.

Another famous knight of the Round Table, Gawain, was Arthur's nephew and one of his heroic comrades in the old Welsh tales. In the French legends his character was altered for the worse, to make a contrast with Lancelot, and he became cruel, vengeful and a relentless womanizer. In England, however, he remained an admired hero, as he is in a splendid fourteenth-century poem, *Sir Gawain and the Green Knight.*

At Camelot on New Year's Day there rode into Arthur's hall a gigantic green warrior on a towering horse, holding a holly branch in one hand and an immense battle-axe in the other. His skin was green, his hair was green, and even his horse was green. He had come to play what he called a game. Any champion who dared could strike him one blow with the axe, on condition that a year later the champion submit to a return blow from the green knight. Gawain took up the challenge and struck the green knight a blow that cut his head clean off his shoulders and sent it rolling on the floor. The green knight calmly picked up his head by the hair and turned the face towards Gawain. The eyelids opened and the mouth spoke, telling Gawain to meet him for the return blow a year later at the Green Chapel.

The year passed all too quickly, and Arthur's court was plunged in grief for Gawain, sure that he was going to his death. Gawain set out, however, on his famous warhorse, Gringolet, saying that a man must face his fate, whatever it might be. After a long journey he came to a noble castle, where he was welcomed by the jovial Sir Bercilak and his lovely young wife. He stayed there until New Year's Day, royally entertained by Bercilak and, though sorely tempted, resisting the persistent attempts of Bercilak's wife to seduce him.

When New Year's Day came, Gawain went to the Green Chapel, hard by. The green knight appeared and Gawain bravely bared his neck for the stroke of the axe. The green knight raised the axe high, but struck Gawain only a glancing blow, which nicked his skin. He then explained that he was Sir Bercilak, transformed into the green knight by the magic of Morgan le Fay, who had planned the whole adventure in the hope of discrediting the Round Table. Gawain had been spared because he had honourably refrained from making love to Bercilak's wife and had shown himself to be the most faultless knight in the world.

TRISTAN AND YSEULT

Heroes who were originally independent of Arthur were drawn into his orbit and made knights of the Round Table by story-tellers. One of these was Tristan, in legend the nephew of King Mark of Cornwall. Tristan was an orphan, brought up in his father's country by a loyal servant. He grew up to be a redoubtable warrior, went to Cornwall and became a favourite of his uncle, King Mark. A huge Irish champion named Morholt came to Cornwall, demanding a tribute of young men and girls as slaves for the King of Ireland. Tristan defied Morholt and killed him. Later, Mark sent Tristan to Ireland to find him a wife. Tristan killed a ferocious dragon which was ravaging the country, and his wounds were tended by the beautiful Princess Yseult the Fair. She discovered, however, that he had killed her uncle, Morholt, and hated him in consequence. It was agreed that Tristan should escort Yseult to Cornwall, where she was to marry Mark. They set off by sea, and by accident drank a love potion, made by Yseult's mother and intended for Yseult and Mark on their wedding night. Instantly they fell irresistibly and passionately in love.

In Cornwall, Yseult and Mark were married. The lovers succeeded in deceiving Mark but the unfortunate King became increasingly suspicious and was finally convinced that his wife and his nephew were cuckolding him. Tristan went into exile in Brittany, where he married a Breton Princess, Yseult of the White Hands. He chose her because she had the same name as his own Yseult the Fair, but he could not consummate the marriage. His wife, who loved him, became fiercely jealous of her namesake.

Tristan was severely wounded in battle and sent a ship to Cornwall, asking Yseult the Fair to come and heal him. It was arranged that if the ship returned with her on board it would hoist white sails, and if not, black sails. The Cornish Queen came willingly, but the jealous Yseult of the White Hands, keeping watch, told Tristan that its sails were black. At this he gave up his hold on life, and Yseult the Fair died of grief beside his corpse. Their bodies were buried at Tintagel. Two trees grew from their graves and the branches intertwined and joined above them.

The story is about love as an overwhelming force which sweeps human beings away on a tide they cannot resist, against their better nature and despite their obligations to others. It carries them to the heights of rapture, but in its grip they break every tie of loyalty and trust. Mark and Yseult of the White Hands are as much the victims of the tragedy as Tristan and Yseult themselves.

The legend was originally Celtic. When it was brought into the Arthurian cycle, the tragic love story was watered down, presumably because the conflict between Tristan's loyalty to Mark and his passion for Mark's wife too closely resembled the story of Lancelot and Guinevere. Mark now became a cowardly and treacherous villain, and Tristan a knight of the Round Table, whose loyalty was owed not to Mark but to Arthur.

THE QUEST OF THE GRAIL

The search for the Grail was the noblest adventure which the paladins of the Round Table undertook, and it foreshadowed the end of Arthur's Kingdom, for, once the Grail hero occupied the Siege Perilous the magic circle of the Round Table was complete. Different Arthurian stories frequently contradict each other, and the stories of the Grail are no exception. Generally, however, Gawain fails ignominiously in the Grail quest and Lancelot fails because of his adultery with Guinevere. In some stories the Grail hero is Perceval, whose legend seems to be based on that of an earlier Welsh hero,

Pryderi. Perceval is brought up in seclusion in the forest in Wales by his mother, his father having died soon after his birth. Comically naive and bumptious, he goes to Arthur's court and gradually learns civilized behaviour and the knightly code. After many adventures he finds the Grail castle, heals the ailing Grail Keeper, who is his grandfather or his uncle, and becomes Keeper in his stead.

In the 'Vulgate Cycle', which Malory followed, the Grail hero is Galahad, a brand-new character invented to be the best knight in the world and achieve the Grail. He is the bastard son of Lancelot and the grandson of King Pelles, lord of the Grail castle of Corbenic. Like Perceval before him, he has a hereditary claim to be Grail Keeper, but as he is allowed no human failings he is an unconvincing, cardboard character. Brought up in a nunnery, he goes to Arthur's court, sits in the Siege Perilous and sets out in search of the Grail. Finally Perceval and Bors, Lancelot's cousin, accompany him to Corbenic, see the Grail in all its majesty and wonder, and take it away from Logres to Jerusalem. Galahad is borne up into heaven soon after, and so is the Grail. Perceval dies, and Bors alone returns to Camelot.

GLASTONBURY

Though the Grail is taken away from the world in this story, a popular belief grew up that it was hidden at Glastonbury in Somerset, which has the richest accumulation of legends of any locality in Britain. According to tradition, it was the place where the earliest Christian missionaries to Britain settled and the site of the first church ever built in the British Isles. This was the famous Old Church, a small building of wattle and daub which was burned down in a disastrous fire in 1184. Glastonbury was also identified as the Isle of Avalon, to which Arthur was taken after his last battle, and in the 1190s the monks of Glastonbury Abbey claimed to have discovered the bodies of Arthur and Guinevere, buried in the abbey grounds. The monks also believed that the Old Church had been built by Joseph of Arimathea and his disciples, who arrived in Britain in AD 63, but they laid no claim to the Grail itself.

In its final form, however, the popular legend says that Joseph of Arimathea landed in Britain with a small band of missionaries. With them they brought the Grail. When they reached the foot of Glastonbury Tor, Joseph thrust his staff into the ground, and it immediately took root and put out buds. It was the ancestor of the famous Glastonbury Thorn, which flowers every year at Christmas. They built the Old Church, and to preserve the Grail from profane hands Joseph buried it somewhere at the foot of the Tor. According to a variant of the story, Joseph and his companions found the Old Church already standing when they came to Glastonbury. It had been built by Jesus himself, who was brought up to the carpenter's trade

and had visited Somerset some years before. Hence the opening lines
of Blake's *Jerusalem:*

And did those feet in ancient time
Walk upon England's mountains green?

THE PASSING OF ARTHUR

In the last part of the story Arthur himself is once more at the centre
of the stage. When Lancelot came back unsuccessful from the Grail
quest, he returned to Guinevere's bed. Mordred and Agravain,
Gawain's brother, caught the lovers together and Arthur could no
longer close his eyes to the liaison. The consequence was civil war and
the knights of the Round Table split into two factions, one supporting
Arthur and the other Lancelot. The war moved to Lancelot's own
country in France and Gawain was severely wounded in combat
against Lancelot. Then word came that Mordred, left behind to
govern England and guard Guinevere, had treacherously seized the
throne and intended to make Guinevere his Queen. The final
catastrophe is approaching. The fellowship of the Round Table is
splintered and destroyed. Lancelot is estranged, Galahad and
Perceval are dead, Gawain is dying. Merlin has long since vanished
from the scene (see LEGENDARY MAGICIANS). The wheel of Fortune
has carried Arthur up to the summit of power and glory, but now,
inexorably, it is taking him down into the depths.

Arthur returned to England at once. In a great battle against
Mordred on Salisbury Plain the knights still loyal to Arthur were slain
and the King was left with one companion, Sir Bedivere. Determined
to revenge himself on his treacherous son, Arthur killed Mordred
with a spear-thrust, but the dying Mordred gave Arthur a mortal
wound. On Arthur's orders, Bedivere took the great sword Excalibur
back to the lake from which it came. He hurled it out into the lake and
an arm rose from the water, caught the sword and brandished it, and
drew it down beneath the surface. Arthur himself was taken away to
Avalon by water in a barge, by many fair ladies. Among them were
Morgan le Fay and the Lady of the Lake.

In Malory, Avalon is Glastonbury and Arthur is buried there, but
an element of doubt remains as to whether he really died at all. 'Yet
some men say in many parts of England that King Arthur is not dead,
but had by the will of our Lord Jesu into another place; and men say
that he shall come again...And many men say that there is written
upon the tomb this: HIC IACET ARTHURUS REX QUONDAM REXQUE
FUTURUS' (Here lies Arthur, King once and King to be). The old
Celtic tradition that Arthur would return to the world had survived
into Malory's time and lingered on long after.

At Cadbury Castle in Somerset − which may have been the

headquarters of the real Arthur – popular belief had it that Arthur and his knights were sleeping in a cavern beneath the hill awaiting their time to return, and similar beliefs are known elsewhere in Britain. Arthur represented something too noble and glorious to be relegated to the past with no hope of recovery. In his hold on human hearts he remains 'the once and future king'.

MEDIEVAL ARTHURIAN LITERATURE

The following works are the main landmarks, but many other Arthurian stories appeared in French, English, Latin, German, Norse, Dutch, Spanish, Portuguese and Italian, usually based on the principal tales in French.

Geoffrey of Monmouth *Historia Regum Britanniae* (History of the Kings of Britain), in Latin, 1136 – the first full and connected account of Arthur that has survived; *Vita Merlini* (Life of Merlin), in Latin verse (*c.* 1148).

Robert Wace *Roman de Brut* (Story of Brutus), in French verse, 1155 – an expanded version of Geoffrey of Monmouth's *History* (above).

Chrétien de Troyes French poet, writing about 1170–90, leading architect of the literary genre of Arthurian romance; his Arthurian tales were *Erec et Enide; Cliges; Lancelot* – the first story of Lancelot and Guinevere's love affair that has survived; *Yvain,* and *Perceval* or *Le Conte du Graal* (Story of the Grail) – the earliest surviving story about the Grail, left unfinished at the author's death; four different Continuations or sequels to it appeared later.

Eilhart von Oberge *Tristan,* in German verse (*c.* 1180).

Renaud de Beaujeu *Le Bel Inconnu* (The Fair Unknown), in French verse (*c.* 1190) – adventures of Guinglain.

Layamon *Brut,* in English verse (*c.* 1190) – an expanded version of Wace's *Roman de Brut* (above).

Béroul *Tristan,* in French verse (*c.* 1190–1200).

Hartman von Aue *Erek* and *Iwein,* in German verse (*c.* 1190–1200) – based on Chrétien's *Erec* and *Yvain* (above).

Robert de Boron *Joseph d'Arimathie* and *Merlin,* in French verse (*c.* 1200) – the earliest surviving account of the early history of the Grail.

Ulrich von Zatzikhoven *Lanzelet,* in German verse (*c.* 1200).

Wolfram von Eschenbach *Parzival,* in German verse (*c.* 1210) – Perceval is the Grail hero.

Gottfried von Strassburg *Tristan und Isolt,* in German verse (*c.* 1210)
— generally considered the finest medieval treatment of the story.

Unknown *Didot Perceval,* in French (*c.* 1210) — Perceval wins the
Grail.

Unknown *Le Haut Livre du Graal: Perlesvaus* (The High Book of
the Grail: Perlesvaus), in French (perhaps *c.* 1210) — Perceval is the
Grail hero.

Unknown 'The Vulgate Cycle', in French (*c.* 1215−30), the modern
name for the first attempt to put together a complete account of
Arthur and the Round Table; it has the following 'branches' or
sections:
Estoire del Saint Graal (History of the Holy Grail), the early history of
the Grail.
Estoire de Merlin (History of Merlin), dealing with Merlin, and
Arthur's early career.
Lancelot del Lac (Lancelot of the Lake).
Queste del Saint Graal (Quest of the Holy Grail), how Galahad won
the Grail.
Le Mort le Roi Artu (The Death of King Arthur), the final tragedy.

Unknown *Suite du Merlin* (Sequel of Merlin), in French (*c.* 1230),
a continuation of the 'Vulgate Merlin' — part of another attempt at
a complete account of Arthur, now known as the 'Post-Vulgate
Romance'.

Unknown *Le Roman de Tristan de Leonois* (Story of Tristan of
Lyonesse), now known as the 'Prose Tristan', in French (*c.* 1230)
— here Tristan is made a knight of the Round Table.

Unknown *Sir Gawain and the Green Knight,* in English verse, late
fourteenth century.

Sir Thomas Malory *Le Morte Darthur* (The Death of Arthur), in
English, completed 1469−70, printed in 1485 by Caxton, who gave it
this title (Caxton's edition was the only one known until an earlier
copy was discovered at Winchester College in 1934) — the standard
version of the cycle in English, based principally on the 'Vulgate
Cycle', the *Suite du Merlin* and the 'Prose Tristan'.

CHRISTIAN WESTERN EUROPE

CHAPTER 27
EL CID

Rodrigo Diaz, better-known as El Cid Campeador, is the most famous hero in the history of Spain, and over the centuries many legends have developed about him. He is generally depicted as the great national hero who, when things seemed blackest for Spain, led his forces against the occupying Moors and spectacularly defeated them. In a historical perspective, El Cid's career is seen as the turning point in the long struggle to reconquer Spain from the Moors, and the most famous part of his legend today concerns his final victory over them. After his death, his corpse was strapped on his horse and then, apparently immune to the arrows of the terrified enemy troops, he led his men for the last time, to fight the Moors in death as in life.

El Cid was born in 1043, at a crucial time in the history of Spain. The Moors, or Arabs, who had conquered the whole of Spain in 711, still held most of the centre and south (which they called El Andalus) and although the Christian kingdoms in the north had slowly recovered much territory, the continuing progress of the Christian reconquest was dramatically challenged in the eleventh century. In 1086 the Moorish Kingdoms of El Andalus were themselves invaded from North Africa by a fanatical Muslim sect called the Almoravids, who took up the fight against Christian Spain as a holy war for Islam.

Like the Moors, the Christians in the north were divided into separate and rival Kingdoms — Leon, Navarre, Aragon, Galicia and Castile — which fought each other as much as they fought Moors.

El Cid, the scourge of the Moors in Spain

Rodrigo (or Ruy) Diaz, El Cid, came from the town of Burgos in Castile and was, in real life as well as in legend, a superb military commander. He became commander-in-chief of the Castilian army, but was discredited and exiled when, in a power struggle between Castile and Leon, the throne of Castile fell to the Leonese King, Alfonso. Exile in those troubled times was not unusual. A good warrior could sell his services to another king and be welcomed as a mercenary. Nor was it considered dishonourable for an exiled Christian knight to serve a Moorish King, which is exactly what El Cid did. He became commander of the armies of the Emir of Zaragoza and led them in successful campaigns against both Moorish and Christian forces. However, he was careful never to engage the Castilian troops of his own King, Alfonso, as there was always the possibility that the ban of exile might one day be lifted and he could return to Castile. (In fact it was not permanently lifted until much later, by which time El Cid had become so powerful in his own right that he did not need to return.)

It was probably at this time that he was first called El Cid, from the title Sayyidi. He himself always used his other, Spanish, title of Campeador (Victorious Warleader). It seems ironic that as his legend developed only his victories against the Moors were remembered, yet it is by the Arabic title of El Cid that he is still popularly known.

El Cid built up a large army of mercenaries and although he continued to help the Emir, he was also strong enough to conquer territory in his own right. His greatest triumph was the conquest of Valencia from the Moors in 1094, which he ruled over, as rich and powerful as any king, until his death in 1099. After his death, his men were unable to hold Valencia against Almoravid attack and were forced to abandon it in 1102. El Cid had married Jimena Diaz, a Leonese noblewoman. They had two daughters, and a son who died young in the service of Alfonso.

A LEGEND IN HIS LIFETIME

El Cid was considered a great hero in his own lifetime. A contemporary Latin poem, *Carmen Campidoctoris* (Song of the Warleader), sings his praises as greater than any of the legendary warriors of Greece and Troy. 'What use now are the brave deeds of those pagan heroes, they have faded into the past. Let us sing instead of the battles waged by our great warleader, Rodrigo.' In the poem the hero becomes so powerful that he is exiled because the king fears he will usurp the throne. In exile his victories are even greater, against Christian as well as Muslim enemies, so that in the end his name is feared in every kingdom in Spain, and all the kings pay him tribute. He is a soldier's hero, the military commander who has never lost a battle.

In the 200 years after El Cid's death, the Kingdom of Castile became the most powerful force in the Christian north, and pushed its way south until, by the mid-thirteenth century, only the southern tip of Spain was still in Muslim hands. For the Castilian people, El Cid had become the symbol of their position as the dominant power in Spain, and they saw in their hero's career a justification for Castilian supremacy in the fight against the Moors.

The greatest extant version of the legend of El Cid dates from the early thirteenth century: *El Poema de mio Cid* (the Epic Poem of My Cid). The hero starts off as a penniless exile, quite unjustly banished from Castile by a weak Leonese King. But in exile he wins enormous wealth, for himself and his faithful men, through his superior military skill. He becomes ruler of Valencia, always setting an honourable and exemplary fashion, even towards his enemies. As a result the King and all the court are convinced of his true worth and accept him back into Castilian society with great honour.

El Cid is then involved in a marriage scandal over his daughters, who are rejected by their noble Leonese bridegrooms as not sufficiently high-born. Whereupon the hero in a thrilling court scene and trial by combat, turns the tables on his opponents, discredits them and marries off his daughters instead to the Crown Princes of Aragon and Navarre. By the end of the epic, the anonymous thirteenth-century writer proclaims El Cid as the true ancestor of all the kings of Spain, and the fount of honour for all Spanish people.

THE HERO AS A SAINT

El Cid's body is generally accepted to have been brought back to the Castilian monastery of Cardeña for reburial after the fall of Valencia. By the end of the thirteenth century his tomb had become a shrine, surrounded by the tombs of all his followers (both real and legendary), his wife and even his horse. It was a popular place of pilgrimage and no doubt a rich source of income and prestige for the monks of Cardeña.

In the monastic development of the legend we have the first mention of the dead hero's body being placed on his horse to lead his men against the Moors, which would soon become the most popular motif in the whole Cid legend. However, in their version the monks also brought in St James, the patron saint of Spain, and a heavenly host of warriors, to fight the Moors on El Cid's behalf and make certain of victory. There are many legends in Spain of St James appearing in battle at the crucial moment — he is sometimes known as Santiago Matamoros, or St James the Moor-Killer, and his relics are still venerated at Santiago de Compostela in Galicia. It would appear that here we have a merging of the two legends.

The Cardeña legend of El Cid said that his body had first been embalmed before being placed on his horse, and had afterwards been displayed in the monastery church for many years before being buried in the tomb. A 'history' of El Cid in an early fourteenth-century chronicle describes a miracle performed by the embalmed body of the hero, when it was on display in this way. An inquisitive Jew went to pull the beard of the dead Cid (in Spain this was the most deadly of all insults) and the corpse's hand came down and drew his sword out of its sheath to defend himself. Needless to say, the Jew was converted to Christianity on the spot! As a result of this and other stories, a movement was started to have El Cid canonized as a saint. The process was begun in the sixteenth century by King Philip II of Spain, but was never completed in Rome.

THE HERO AS A GREAT LOVER

So far, the legends have been concerned with a view of El Cid as a battle commander and politician, whose actions are always governed by the highest and most honourable intentions, even to the extreme of saintliness. But there is another view of the hero, portrayed in short romantic ballads of the fifteenth and sixteenth centuries which remain popular right up to the present day.

In the ballads El Cid, although still a superb and successful fighter, is a headstrong young man and something of a Don Juan figure. In one of the most popular ballads he kills a count who has insulted his father, and the count's daughter, Jimena, asks the king first for vengeance and then, since she has no one to support her, asks for El Cid's hand in marriage instead. In other ballads the hero is reproached by the king's daughter, Urraca, saying they were childhood sweethearts and he has broken his promise to her. His behaviour in all these ballads is brash and rude, especially towards his enemies and social superiors, and although he still comes out on top in any situation, he gets his way by threats and violence.

Perhaps this change in the hero's image should be seen in the context of the changing social conditions in Spain once the reconquest was completed in 1492. Spain now had to adjust to conditions of peace. Society no longer relied on a large military class to defend it, and so the status of the fighting man became less important and prestigious than it had been. El Cid still remained the national hero, with his victories in the past being used to explain Spain's position in the present as the centre of an expanding empire. But unlike the earlier versions of the legend which reflected the values of the dominant military class, in the ballads El Cid becomes a hero of the ordinary people. He reflects their view of the world and he behaves according to their standards of the day.

THE LEGEND IN MODERN TIMES

El Cid is still the national hero of Spain, although the stress is once again on his merits as a great military leader, who led the Spanish people to greatness. During the Civil War of 1936—39 both sides expressed the view that they were fighting in the tradition of El Cid. The Republican soldiers called themselves 'the sons of El Cid' because they were fighting for a free Spain and driving out foreign invaders (Franco's Moorish troops and the Germans and Italians); whereas the Nationalists felt they were fighting a crusade to keep Spain Catholic and drive out the 'infidels' (the Communists). Indeed, Franco himself was often directly compared to El Cid by his followers, as an army leader who, at a time of cristis, had come from exile to lead Spain to victory against her enemies.

Under Franco's regime, El Cid was given an imposing new tomb in Burgos Cathedral, and in 1943 there were national celebrations in honour of both the ninth centenary of El Cid's birth and the millenary of Castilian independence. These events, coming so soon after the traumas of civil war, possibly helped in some way to reassert the unity of the Spanish people within the commonly accepted legend of El Cid, the national hero.

CHRISTIAN WESTERN EUROPE

CHAPTER 28
NEW WORLD LEGENDS

It is commonly thought today that before the discovery of America everyone believed that the world was flat and that a ship which sailed too far to the west would drop off the edge. In fact this is not true. It was accepted in the fifteenth century, at least by educated people, that the earth was round. Columbus was certainly not the first to believe that sailing far enough to the west would eventually bring one to the countries which lay to the east of Europe.

At this time the eastern countries were still shrouded in mystery for the West and people often referred to them vaguely as the Indias. Few Europeans had penetrated far into Asia. One of the few was Marco Polo, in the late thirteenth century, and his stories about the empire of the Great Khan became famous. Cathay was the name he gave to what we now call China, where he lived for several years, and his description of the country's high standard of civilization and its wealth of spices, silks and gold fired the imagination of Europeans. Marco Polo was also the first to tell the western world of an even richer country, which he had not visited but had heard about in Cathay. This was Cipangu (Japan), which he described as being so rich that the King lived in a palace made of solid gold encrusted with jewels.

Europeans in the late fifteenth century still thought that Cathay and Cipangu would be exactly as Marco Polo had described them, and that the first European country to establish a direct trading link with the Great Khan would reap rich rewards. Columbus became obsessed with reaching Cathay and Cipangu. Indeed, the lure of the gold of

The Amazon warriors of the New World (page 255)

Cipangu was used as bait to encourage sailors to join his expedition and on his first voyage he took with him a letter from the rulers of Spain to the Great Khan. Columbus made landfall on the islands now called the Bahamas, but he was convinced that he had found the Indies, and called the natives there Indians. He was disappointed at not finding the high level of civilization and wealth he had expected, but he still believed that Cathay and Cipangu were just a few kilometres or miles away.

Throughout his life Columbus was reluctant to give up his claim to having found a western route to Cathay and Cipangu, and tried to stifle any evidence to the contrary, but as more explorers followed in his wake, the extent and nature of the American continent became apparent. The eastern seaboard of Central America held little in the way of gold or spices, and exploration became concerned with finding a way through the newly discovered land to the rich countries of the Indies which, it was still believed, must lie beyond.

THE AMAZONS

From the very first weeks of the discovery of America explorers saw, or were told about, tribes which consisted solely of warlike women, who fought more bravely than most men. At certain times of the year, it was said, men from the surrounding tribes were forcibly brought into this female enclave for stud purposes. Those male unfortunates whose performance in this respect was considered unsatisfactory were summarily killed. The rest were sent back to their own tribes once all the young women had been made pregnant. If the child of such a mating was a girl, she remained with her Amazon mother, but if a boy was born he was either returned to his father's tribe or left in the jungle to die. (However, other versions of the legend said that the women conceived from the wind.)

In appearance these Amazon warriors were fair-skinned and tall, with their hair plaited and twisted around their heads. They wore very little clothing and fought with bows and arrows. Some accounts said that their right breasts had been amputated, to make it easier to draw the bow.

As the discovery of the great continent continued, a more elaborate description of the Amazon society developed. They were now reputed to be very rich in gold, and were ruled by a powerful queen or priestess, who reigned in great splendour. They lived in towns with stone houses and had temples dedicated to the sun-god, filled with gold and silver ornaments and rich paintings. Everyone ate off gold plates and wore robes of the finest alpaca wool.

The legend of the Amazons was not born in America, but goes back to classical times (see CLASSICAL GREECE AND ROME), although it was given a new lease of life by the discovery of the New World.

Greek authors located the Amazons on the Black Sea or in Africa, and mentioned the detail that the right breast was removed in infancy to allow the women to shoot better with the bow. Possibly this detail is a rationalization of the word Amazon in Greek: *a* (without) and *mazos* (breast). Descriptions of such topsy-turvy societies where all the social roles are reversed are a feature of many widely differing cultures all over the world. The legends arise out of the strangeness and remoteness of other societies (real or imaginary), which are conceived of as so different that they must be totally opposite to one's own.

In medieval Europe the classical legends of the Amazons were believed to be true and it was accepted that such a society, consisting solely of women, did exist on an island in some faraway corner of the world, somewhere off the coast of Asia. The island was marked on some maps, as the Feminine Isle. It was also believed to be situated near a corresponding Masculine Isle, for men only. In 1492, for example, the Feminine and Masculine Isles were shown in Martin Behaim's globe of the world, not far from Cipangu and the coast of Cathay.

When Columbus on his first voyage found two islands he could identify as the Feminine and Masculine Isles, it was for him, and for many others, 'proof' that he had indeed discovered a route to the Indies. They were, respectively, the islands of Martinino (probably Martinique) and Carib (Dominica). He did not visit the islands to verify the facts for himself, but was told about them by an Indian informant. Since communication between the Spaniards and the Indians was at that time by means of sign-language only, it is obvious that what Columbus understood owed far more to his own pre-existing ideas of what he expected to find, than to the reality.

Nor was Columbus the only explorer or conquistador to rely on hearsay evidence and classical legends for the existence of Amazon tribes in the New World. As the exploration of the continent continued, from all over America came accounts of the existence of such tribes of women: Hernán Cortés heard of them on the coasts of Panama; Jerónimo Dortal near the mouth of the Orinoco; the Germans Georg Hohermuth and Philip von Hutten heard that Amazons lived not far from the valley of Bogotá, in Columbia.

HOW THE LEGEND DEVELOPED

Perhaps the most famous account of an Amazon tribe in the New World came from Father Carvajal, a Dominican friar, who accompanied Captain Francisco de Orellana in 1542 on his journey of exploration down what was then called the Marañón River. Carvajal described how the expedition passed through the lands of Indians who were subject tribes of the Amazons, and how the Spaniards fought against Indian bands led by these Amazon warriors. 'You must know that they (the river Indians) are tribute-paying subjects of the Amazons, and when they heard we were coming they went and asked (the Amazons) for help. About ten or twelve came to their aid, and we saw them ourselves fighting in front of the Indian captains. And they fought so bravely that the Indians did not dare turn tail and run, and any that did were clubbed to death in front of our eyes, which is why the Indians defended themselves so well.'

According to Carvajal, Captain Orellana was an accomplished linguist and had picked up the language of these Indian tribes. Thus he obtained from informants further details of these Amazon warriors — that they exacted great tribute from all their subject tribes, and were rich in gold and silver, precious jewels and fine clothes. They lived in a land seven days' journey from the river, comprising at least seventy towns of stone-built houses (unlike the straw huts of other Indians in the region). They would kidnap a man in order to get pregnant, keeping the girl children and killing the boys.

This account by Carvajal is the foundation for all the later stories of Amazons in the New World. His description of the Amazons on this river became so well known that they gave their name to it, and it remains to this day the Amazon River — an enduring legacy of one legend from Ancient Greece which found a new home in the Americas.

THE TRUTH BEHIND THE LEGEND

If we accept that tribes consisting solely of women, not to mention having all the other characteristics of the Amazons, did not exist in fifteenth-century America, indeed have never existed anywhere, why should there have been so many separate accounts of them in the New World? One explanation already suggested is that the conquistadors went out with preconceived ideas of what they would find, and tended to interpret the facts in the light of their pre-existing notions. They may well have been encouraged in this by an anxiety on the part of their Indian informants to supply only the kind of information the conquistadors expected to hear. This was not entirely due to Indian ideas of the correct behaviour due to strangers (although this was certainly a factor), but probably owed more to the conquistadors' practice of cruelly torturing Indians until they gave the 'right' answers.

Another theory is that the later stories of the Amazons, as told to Carvajal, were due to the simple riverine Indians' misunderstanding of what went on in the far-off and much more complicated social organization of the Incas. The so-called Amazons were really the Inca Virgins of the Sun, who served in the temples and were kept in seclusion in richly decorated convents, with working parties of men being brought in as forced labour to do their agricultural tasks.

On the other hand, some conquistadors not only heard about Amazons from informants, but actually saw them with their own eyes and fought against them. In all their accounts, however, the women are fighting side by side with men, contrary to the standard legend when the armies consist solely of women. Now from present-day evidence of Amazonian tribes it would appear that warfare is an activity engaged in only by men, and although in times of extreme danger women may stand with their menfolk, there are no recorded instances of women fighting with bows and arrows, which are exclusively male weapons. But there is an independent eighteenth-century description of the Jurimagua tribe on the Amazon, where the Indians said the women had once fought with bows and arrows as valiantly as the men, and it has been suggested that these were the original Amazons. On the other hand, many Indian myths involve role-reversals of this kind.

Yet other modern commentators have suggested that the Spaniards mistook long-haired or 'feminine-looking' Indians (for instance, the Tupinambá) for women, although all contemporary accounts which mention the women's appearance say that they were near naked with only the private parts covered. One way in which the contemporary eyewitness accounts all diverge from the classical legend is that there is no mention of the women having had one breast removed. By contrast, almost all the second-hand reports of Amazons stress this detail. There was a tendency for more fabulous aspects of the classical legend to be read into eyewitness stories.

As time went on the legend was kept alive, retaining its essential core but incorporating new ideas as attitudes and values changed. As late as the eighteenth century the French explorer of the Amazon, La Condamine, decided that 'in this continent did exist a republic of women, who lived entirely separate from the man'. He suggested that the women who formed it had 'thrown off the yoke of their tyrants (husbands)', with whom they had lived in a 'vilifying condition of slavery', and he likened the feminine republic to settlements of escaped slaves in North America.

The fact that later American legends of the Amazons endow them with progressively more and more wealth can be better understood if you consider the two great events which had occurred in the sixteenth century to change men's expectations of what the New World could offer in the way of material riches. In 1520 Hernán Cortés marched into the Aztec capital, Tenochtitlán (modern Mexico City), and discovered gold in greater quantities than could be conceived of back in Europe. Then, in 1532–33 Francisco Pizarro conquered the Inca Empire, in what is now Peru, which produced gold and treasures in still greater quantities. From then on the aim of the conquistadors was not so much to find a route through America to the lands beyond, but to find riches in the New World itself. If two gold-rich civilizations had been found in what had previously been thought a poor continent, then it was now believed others must exist also. And attention was soon focused on finding the *source* of all the gold.

THE LEGEND OF EL DORADO

After the conquest of the Incas, stories circulated in Peru about El Indio Dorado (the Golden Indian), who was rumoured to be the chief of an as yet undiscovered tribe nearby. This chief would wear no other garments except a covering of fine gold-dust from head to toe, which was put on him each morning, using a special resin to make it stick, and washed off each night. In later versions of the legend, the chief, who now belonged to the Muisca Indians, used to cover himself in gold-dust only at certain times, in order to perform a special ritual which involved going out on a raft on a lake and sacrificing golden objects and jewels by throwing them into it.

By the seventeenth century this lake was identified as Lake Guatavita, 50 kilometres (31 miles) north-east of Bogotá, and the reason for the ritual ceremony was to placate the spirit of a previous chief's wife who, when accused of adultery, threw herself into the lake with her child and turned into a monster which still lives in the depths. Yet later versions, in the seventeenth century, said that this ceremony only took place at the investiture of a new chief. By the eighteenth century the venue for the ritual had switched from the high Andes to the plains of the Orinoco River. There El Indio Dorado was a young man, sacrificed each year to the gods, when his body would be slit open and powdered with gold-dust.

All the versions of the legend just mentioned are agreed on one thing — that El Dorado referred to a *person*. But other documents of the sixteenth and seventeenth centuries use the name El Dorado in the sense of a *place*. The conquistador Gonzalo Pizarro wrote in 1542 that he had been looking for 'the Lake of El Dorado', and this is perhaps how the switch may have arisen. The conquistadors were interested in finding all the gold objects supposed to have been thrown into the lake, so for them the name El Dorado became attached to the place where the gold was, rather than to the person who had put it there. In the same way, chroniclers of the mid-sixteenth century spoke of the Province of El Dorado, and the Valley of El Dorado, when they were referring to lands which the conquistadors believed to be very rich in gold.

A SPUR TO EXPLORATION

At first the legend of El Dorado, whether the name was that of a person or a place, was believed to refer to the Muisca (sometimes called the Chibcha) Indians who lived in the Andean valley of Bogotá, in Columbia. But it gradually became obvious that the gold resources of the Muisca had always been very limited. Although it was true that they had occasionally thrown gold offerings into the lakes around Bogotá, these are so deep that little was ever recovered by the conquistadors, certainly not enough to justify the legend of a people so rich in gold that they could afford to throw it away.

However, there were still vast areas of the New World which were unexplored territory, so various expeditions were launched, spurred on by the hope of finding that elusive El Dorado and all the gold it must contain. In the 1590s Antonio de Berrío felt sure he would find the province of El Dorado in Guiana, which he said would contain twenty times as much gold as Peru. He believed it was the land the Incas had originally come from. The region of Guiana, between the Orinoco and Amazon rivers, was covered with tropical jungle and inhabited by Indian tribes of comparatively simple technology. Not surprisingly, Berrío found very little gold, but he refused to be disheartened by this, as he argued that the Indians had been warned to hide it before the Spaniards came.

Although the conquistadors had changed both the venue of the legend and its main referent, the idea that El Dorado was linked to a lake remained constant. Berrío sited his El Dorado around a great lake called Manoa, and even though the lake was never discovered, it became established on the maps of the day.

RALEIGH: PURSUIT OF A DREAM

Not all the searchers for El Dorado were Spanish. One of the greatest of all, if one of the last, was Sir Walter Raleigh. He had almost certainly obtained a copy of Berrío's account, and this inspired Raleigh to head a short exploration down the Orinoco and Caroni Rivers, to claim El Dorado for the British Crown. In 1596 he published a book which became an instant best-seller in England and the rest of Europe − *Discoverie of the large, rich and beautifull Empire of Guiana, with a relation of the great and golden citie of Manoa (which the Spaniards call El Dorado)*. In Raleigh's book not just one, but all the Indians of El Dorado covered themselves in gold-dust, and he claimed to have been shown exactly where their gold mines lay.

It was probably due to Raleigh that the legend of El Dorado became popular all over Europe. For him, however, his book was his last great success. He was imprisoned for political reasons, and only released in 1616 in order to find the gold mines of El Dorado and annex them to the English Crown. His second expedition was a total disaster − the mines proved not to exist, no gold was found, nor was El Dorado. Raleigh returned to England to face the block in 1618.

After Raleigh, the expectations of finding El Dorado declined. But the legend itself remained, as a relic of something which had turned into the never-never world of dreams. El Dorado, from being a gold man, had then become a city, a country, a lake, even a mountain of gold. It now became a chimera, a promised land of plenty which is always receding into the distance. The explorer and naturalist Baron Alexander von Humboldt in 1852 called El Dorado 'that will-o'-the-wisp which ever flees the Spaniards and ever calls them after it'.

CHRISTIAN WESTERN EUROPE

CHAPTER 29
ATLANTIS

The idea of a lost paradise and a golden age, of a time when our distant ancestors lived in a happiness and security that the world has lost, makes a powerful appeal to the imagination. In the Bible, the first human beings lived in the idyllic Garden of Eden, from which they were driven out. In Greek mythology the first race of men on earth, the golden race, enjoyed a contented, carefree existence denied to their successors. Atlantis belongs to this same pattern of ideas. The legend may well be founded on fact, but its romantic attraction lies in nostalgia for the lost paradise, where the human race spent its happy, innocent and protected childhood.

FAMILY TREE OF ATLAS

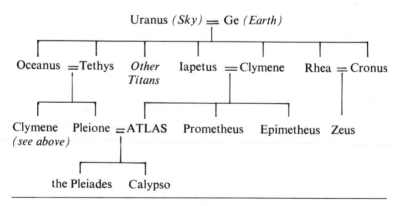

Zeus destroying Atlantis (page 263)

The legendary Atlantis was a large island in the Atlantic, possessed of a high civilization, which was suddenly overwhelmed by an immense cataclysm and sank beneath the sea. The story comes from Plato in the fourth century BC, in two of his dialogues, the *Timaeus* and the unfinished *Critias*.

According to Plato, the famous Athenian statesman Solon visited Egypt and went to the city of Sais in the Nile Delta. There he was told by the Egyptian priests that, 9000 years before, the island of Atlantis opposite the Pillars of Hercules (the Straits of Gibraltar) ruled a formidable maritime empire. Its sway extended to the western shores of the Mediterranean and to other islands in the Atlantic, beyond which lay a continent. Atlantis was rich in minerals, timber, crops and animals, including elephants. The Atlanteans were skilled metal-workers and great architects and engineers, builders of magnificent temples, palaces, harbours and docks, canals, bridges and tunnels. Their chief god was Poseidon, lord of the sea, of earthquakes and of bulls, and they conducted a ritual bull-game in his honour. For many generations they were a virtuous people, gentle, wise and law-abiding, but in time they grew obsessed with power and wealth. They attacked Athens and Egypt, and Zeus determined to destroy them. There were violent earthquakes and floods, and in a single day and night Atlantis disappeared under the sea. The same catastrophe swallowed up the Athenian army.

ATLANTIS AND CRETE

Solon lived in the sixth century BC and, taking the date in the *Timaeus,* Atlantis must have been destroyed about 9600 BC. This is considerably earlier than any such advanced civilization existed, so far as we yet know. It is possible that Plato simply made the story up, as Aristotle, his pupil, thought he did. If so, he may have had in mind earlier Greek traditions about mysterious islands and catastrophic floods.

The names Atlantis and Atlantic mean 'belonging to Atlas', who was one of the Titans, the old gods who ruled the world before Zeus. A magic island connected with Atlas is mentioned at the beginning of Homer's *Odyssey.* It is far away in the middle of the sea and is ruled by a daughter of Atlas, who knows the ocean's depths and has charge of the great columns that hold up the sky to prevent it from falling on the earth. Other writers imagined Atlas as a giant holding up the sky on his shoulders, in the form of Mount Atlas in Morocco, and the Pillars of Hercules which Plato mentions were, in mythology, the columns that separated sky and earth.

Phoenician seamen and traders probably brought back news of real islands in the Atlantic from very early on. Certainly there were many Greek stories of marvellous islands in the west, including the

Fortunate Isles or Isles of the Blest, where the deserving dead went to live a happy life. There were also tales of land sinking beneath the sea and the Straits of Gibraltar were believed to have been opened up by an earthquake. If Plato did invent the story of Atlantis, there was no shortage of material for his imagination to work on.

Recently, however, a new theory has been gaining ground. Much of Plato's description of Atlantis, including the bull-game, recalls the civilization of Minoan Crete in the Bronze Age. Crete was then a great maritime power, dominating the Aegean world until its sudden mysterious decline in the fifteenth century BC. It is now known that at that time a colossal volcanic explosion blew a hole in the middle of the island of Thera (or Santorini), to the north of Crete. The eruption was on an even more gigantic scale than the celebrated explosion of Krakatoa in the East Indies in 1883. The centre of the island disappeared under water and Crete itself must have suffered crippling damage by earthquakes, tidal waves and a fall-out of volcanic ash. It looks as if this catastrophe accounts for the otherwise unexplained decline of Crete, and it may be that the Egyptians preserved a memory of it which lies behind Plato's story. Crete is not in the Atlantic but it was, from an Egyptian viewpoint, a powerful island kingdom in the west. If Plato's figure of 9000 years was a mistake for 900 years, the destruction of Atlantis would fall in the fifteenth century BC, which is the right date for the Thera explosion and the collapse of Cretan power.

ISLANDS IN THE WEST

Medieval writers accepted Plato's story as it stood. They knew of another vanished paradise, the Garden of Eden, also lost through human wickedness and divine punishment, though Eden was widely believed still to exist somewhere on the earth, just beyond the bounds of known geography. They also knew of other mysterious and magic islands in the Atlantic. Besides the Fortunate Isles, sometimes identified with the Azores, there were the Celtic otherworld islands in the west, whose inhabitants remained forever young and led an idyllic life of pleasure and ease. There was St Brendan's Isle, somewhere in the Atlantic. There was the Isle of Brazil, supposed to lie to the west of Ireland and reported in the seventeenth century to be inhabited by huge black rabbits and a wicked magician. There was Antillia where, according to Portuguese tradition, seven Christian bishops ruled the fortunate inhabitants of seven Utopian cities. The West Indian islands discovered by Columbus were named the Antilles for Antillia.

Western Europe had also heard of other lost lands and cities overtaken by the sea: Lyonesse, the vanished land between Cornwall and the Scillies; the submerged Breton city of Ys; or the lost Green

Isle, known in popular tales from Spain and Portugal to Scotland. Legends of this kind were probably based on distant memories of real incursions of the sea, and they made it easier to accept Plato's Atlantis.

THE QUEST FOR ATLANTIS

The discovery of the Americas, and so of Plato's continent beyond the Atlantic, gave a fresh impetus to speculation about Atlantis which has continued ever since. In 1882 Mr Gladstone, as Prime Minister, tried to persuade the British Cabinet to finance an Atlantis exploration vessel. Eminent authorities from Sir Francis Bacon in the seventeenth century to the German naturalist Alexander von Humboldt in the nineteenth identified Atlantis with the American continent itself. It was thought that Plato must have heard some rumour of the Americas, which had perhaps been discovered by Phoenician sailors. Bacon's Atlantean empire stretched from Mexico to Peru, but other locations in North America, South America and the West Indies have been suggested.

Innumerable other places have been identified as the site of the lost Atlantis in one theory or another. It has been located, for example, in Portugal, Spain, France, the Netherlands, Ireland, England, Germany and Sweden; in the Atlas Mountains, under the sands of the Sahara, in Ethiopia, Nigeria and South Africa; in Corsica, Malta, Palestine, Arabia, Iran and Sri Lanka; beneath the Caspian Sea, in the Crimea and the Caucasus; in the Arctic, Greenland and Siberia. In 1953 it was announced that the ruins of the citadel of Atlantis had been seen by divers in the North Sea, off Heligoland. The Basques have been claimed as the surviving remnant of the Atlanteans and their language as a survival of the Atlantean tongue. Alternatively, the white-skinned, fair-haired, blue-eyed Berbers of North Africa have been identified as the direct descendants of the Atlanteans.

Most Atlantis theorists, however, have put Atlantis where Plato said it was, in the Atlantic. In 1979 Russian oceanographers reported that they had photographed the remains of massive wells and stairways deep in the Atlantic, midway between Portugal and Madeira. They suggested that these were the ruins of Atlantis, and were promptly denounced by adherents of the Cretan theory.

If the Atlantic were drained, a long mountainous ridge, studded with volcanoes, would be visible, running north-south from Iceland to the Antarctic. This ridge is often claimed to be the backbone of the sunken Atlantis, overtaken by the melting of the glaciers at the end of the last Ice Age, some 12 000 years ago. Geologists will have none of this theory, but enthusiasts for an Atlantis in the Atlantic maintain that the lost island or continent accounts for the fact that many of the same species of animals and plants exist on both sides of the Atlantic Ocean. It is also supposed to explain similarities between ancient Egyptian and Mayan architecture, and between the Egyptian and Peruvian calendars, the use of the cross as a symbol in both the Old World and the New, and the flow of the Gulf Stream, which originally had to make a detour around the north of Atlantis. The suicidal behaviour of lemmings and the migration of eels to the Sargasso Sea have also been traced back to Atlantis.

DONNELLY AND AFTER

The classic exposition of this line of theory is Ignatius Donnelly's *Atlantis, or the Antediluvian World,* published in 1882 and frequently reprinted. Donnelly was an American lawyer and Congressman who regarded Atlantis as the birthplace of civilization (he also believed, incidentally, that Bacon wrote Shakespeare). The Aryan and Semitic races, Donnelly maintained, both sprang from Atlantis. The cultures of ancient Egypt, the Maya, the Aztecs and the Incas stemmed from Atlantis, whose people also colonized the Mississippi River, the Mediterranean, the western coasts of Europe and Africa, and the shores of the Baltic, the Black Sea and the Caspian. A distorted memory of the cataclysm in which Atlantis was engulfed survived in the world's many myths of a Great Flood. The memory of Atlantis as an ideal haven of peace and happiness inspired the story of the Garden of Eden. Its kings and queens became the gods and goddesses of the Greeks, the Hindus and the Scandinavians. Olympus and Asgard, the homes of the Greek and the Norse gods, were both, in origin, Atlantis. Egyptian and Inca mythology derived directly from the Atlantean religion, the worship of the sun.

Many other writers have followed in Donnelly's footsteps and it was largely his influence which turned Atlantis into something of a cult. The theory requires an extreme diffusionist view of history, that all civilization springs from a single original cradle, as opposed to the evolutionist view of widely separated cultures developing independently, on roughly parallel liness as a response to similar conditions. It has appealed strongly to occultists, reacting against the theory of evolution and the materialism associated with it. They believe in a golden age of wisdom and high spiritual achievement in the distant past, which they contrast with the leaden age of the present. They have made much of the theme, which is only sketched in by Plato, of the Atlanteans as a wise and virtuous people corrupted by greed and power-hunger that destroyed them.

The idea of an Atlantean master-race appealed to Nazi writers in Germany, who turned Atlantis into the cradle of the Aryans. Alfred Rosenberg, the leading Nazi theoretician, expounded this nation in *The Myth of the Twentieth Century* (1930), placing Atlantis in the far north. Karl Georg Zschaetsch, in 1922, maintained that the Atlanteans were fair-haired teetotallers and vegetarians, and that the only survivors of the destruction of Atlantis were Wotan, his daughter and his pregnant sister, from whom the Aryan race was descended.

Some writers have credited the Atlanteans with technological achievements far beyond anything in Plato, including the use of explosives, flying machines and.electricity. Inevitably, Atlantis has been tied in with the belief that civilization was first brought to earth from outer space by cultural missionaries in flying saucers: they brought it to Atlantis. It has also been suggested recently that the Atlanteans controlled immensely powerful lasers. Now sunk deep in the Atlantic, these account for the disappearances of ships and aircraft in the notorious Bermuda Triangle.

The Atlantis of much modern imagining combines two opposite conditions — advanced technology on the one hand, and wisdom, security and contented happiness on the other. This is precisely the combination which eludes twentieth-century man and which gives the lost paradise of Atlantis its romantic allure.

CHRISTIAN WESTERN EUROPE

CHAPTER 30

LEGENDARY MAGICIANS

Legends of magicians have a long history in the West. One which is particularly persistent and popular is the story of the man who sells his soul to the Devil. In return for Satan's favours, he makes a formal agreement pledging his body and soul to the Evil One, either at death or after a stated number of years. He signs the contract in his own blood, which symbolically conveys his life into the Devil's hands. The Devil readily accepts the bargain, for he hungers for human souls. They are his spoils in the war he has waged against God and man ever since he rebelled against the Almighty, long ago, and was hurled from his high seat in heaven.

The most famous legend of this kind is the story of Faust. Growing up round an obscure charlatan in sixteenth-century Germany, it has inspired Marlowe, Goethe, Heine, Paul Valéry, Thomas Mann, Berlioz, Gounod and many other writers and composers. In Marlowe's version (1601), Faust is a scholar who thirsts for sovereign knowledge and power, but has failed to find it in the orthodox branches of knowledge. He turns to magic, declaring that 'a sound magician is a mighty god', and when even magic proves hollow he signs his soul away to the Devil. He is provided with a demonic helper and adviser, the sardonic Mephistopheles, who summons Helen of Troy back from the dead to be Faust's mistress.

> Was this the face that launched a thousand ships,
> And burnt the topless towers of Ilium?
> Sweet Helen, make me immortal with a kiss!

Faust and the Devil

The agreement with Satan does not bring Faust the supreme knowledge he seeks, and as time runs out the terror of damnation closes round him. He repents his folly and bitterly bewails himself, but it is too late. The contract falls due and he is dragged away to the agonies of hell.

An early element of the tradition, responsible for drawing serious writers to it, is that Faust's quest was not for mere money and pleasure, but for knowledge and power. He wanted to fathom the ultimate secrets of the universe and so wield authority over all creation. In other words, like his master the Devil before him, he tried to make himself God. This is the core of the romantic attraction of Faust as a heroic figure, standing for man's defiant determination to master all he surveys.

THE REAL FAUST

Very little is known about the real man round whom the legend gathered but, judging from the comments of his contemporaries, he was a boastful mountebank. Accompanied by a performing horse and dog, he swaggered about Germany, bragging of his prowess as a magician, alchemist and astrologer to the awe of gullible audiences in alehouses. He was said to have been born at Knittlingen in Germany and to have studied magic at Cracow in Poland. He apparently died unlamented in about 1540.

The rise of this dubious personage to legendary fame began soon after his death, when various Protestant clergymen proclaimed that Faust had possessed genuine supernatural powers, given him by the Devil, to whom he had bartered away his soul. The intention was to hold Faust up as a dreadful example of intellectual rebellion against God but, all publicity being good publicity, the effect was to propel him to popular fame. Stories about earlier celebrated magicians were now transferred to Faust. His performing horse and dog were identified as demons in disguise. Gruesome tales circulated about his death, when the Prince of Darkness came for him. Faust was found strangled, with his face twisted round to the back, or his room was discovered swimming in blood, his eyeballs stuck to one wall.

An anonymous biography of Faust was published at Frankfurt in 1587. It rapidly sold out, and many more versions of his legend appeared in German and other European languages. Magical textbooks were published, supposedly written by Faust. Travelling players performed dramas and puppet plays about him.

THE PACT WITH THE DEVIL

The idea of the formal contract with Satan is much older than Faust. It was an offshoot of the Christian belief that magic could only be

performed successfully with the aid of evil spirits. The main impetus
to belief in it came from St Augustine, at the turn of the fourth and
fifth centuries, who spoke of 'a pact of faithless and dishonourable
friendship' between man and demons. Stories soon began to go the
rounds about people who had made a pact with the Evil One.

One such legend clung to Gerbert of Aurillac, who became pope in
999 as Sylvester II. His awe-inspiring reputation for intellectual
brilliance created the belief that only black magic could account for
his gifts, and he was rumoured to have signed over his soul to the
Devil in order to be made pope. He was said to have made a head of
brass which could speak and supplied answers to all questions. His
tomb in Rome was believed to weep at the approaching death of each
pope after him.

Roger Bacon, the reputed inventor of gunpowder and spectacles
in the thirteenth century, was certainly interested in magic and
alchemy, and his penchant for scientific experiments helped to give
him a reputation as sorcerer in league with the Devil. He too was
believed to own an oracular brazen head, but he cheated Satan in the
end by promising the Evil One his soul unless he died neither in the
Church nor out of it, and then he craftily constructed a cell in the wall
of a church, neither inside nor outside it, and took care to die there.

This is one of many stories in which the Devil keeps his share of the
bargain but is swindled by his human prey, who escapes either by
superior cunning or through a successful appeal to God at the last
moment. In some of the later versions of the Faust story, including
Goethe's *Faust,* the magician is saved from damnation at the end.

SOLOMON AND SIMON MAGUS

It was for eating the fruit of the tree of knowledge that Adam and Eve
were expelled from paradise, and a deep-rooted sense of the
dangerousness of intellectual enquiry underlies the legends of many
magicians, including Gerbert, Roger Bacon and Faust. Magic is evil in
the Christian tradition, not only because it involves collaboration
with evil spirits, but because in his pursuit of omniscience and power
the magician raises himself too high and challenges the prerogatives
of God.

The Bible's description of King Solomon's superhuman wisdom,
wealth and grandeur laid the foundation of his fame as a master
magician in medieval Europe. The story that the Queen of Sheba
asked him perplexing riddles, all of which he solved with ease, added
to his reputation for unnatural sagacity, and his taste for foreign
women and strange gods gave his character an intriguingly unholy
cast. In legend, he owned a magic ring, with which he subdued the
demons and forced them to build the Temple at Jerusalem. He
understood the languages of animals and birds, he flew on the wind or

on a magic carpet, and he explored the depths of the sea and the heights of the sky. The most famous western textbook of magic, *The Key of Solomon,*[1] is attributed to him.

Another famous magician was Simon Magus, whose story again contains the theme of the man who is intellectually and fatally driven to put himself in the place of God. A Samaritan of the first century AD, Simon joined the Christian Church, but was swiftly expelled from it and early Christian writers denounced him as the founder of all heresy. He claimed to be God and he took about with him a prostitute from Tyre, explaining that she was a reincarnation of Helen of Troy and the bodily vessel of his own divine Thought, through which he had created the world. (It was perhaps from this source that Helen of Troy later entered the story of Faust.)

According to legend, Simon went to Rome in the time of the Emperor Claudius and impressed everyone with marvels which were stage-managed for him by the Devil. He cured diseases and raised the dead, made himself invisible, brought statues to life, conjured up spirits and manufactured a human being out of thin air. He could also turn himself into an animal or into any shape he liked, but he was challenged by St Peter, who exposed his miracles as shams. The infuriated Simon announced that he would prove his godhead by ascending bodily into heaven from the top of a tower. He soared up into the sky, but St Peter prayed earnestly to God and the magician crashed to the ground and was killed.

THE MAN OF POWER

The miraculous abilities of legendary magicians include power over spirits, control of the weather, rapport with the animal kingdom, the capacity to change shape, to fly, to know what is happening far away, to see into the future, to heal the sick and raise the dead. The same powers are attributed to holy men, and the legendary magician is a holy man gone wrong or seen through hostile eyes. The whole tradition probably goes back to the shamans, or professional magicians and healers, of prehistoric tribes in Europe and Asia. Some shamans may well have possessed unusual psychic gifts which gave the tradition, however exaggerated, a foundation in fact: gifts of clairvoyance, telepathy, precognition and faith-healing, and the ability to produce eerily impressive effects in trance. Later, the priests, kings, prophets and oracles of the ancient world inherited the functions of tribal magicians and were credited with supernatural abilities.

The idea of 'the man of power', who can suspend the laws of nature, descended to the classical world. The Magi, the priests of Iran, were famed for their esoteric wisdom and magical powers, and they gave their name to 'magic' itself in Greek, Latin and the European languages. The priests of Egypt and Babylonia, the Brahmins of India and the Druids of Britain enjoyed the same reputation. The shaman's mantle clung to Zoroaster and Moses, Orpheus and Pythagoras, as great sages and magicians. A similar figure was Apollonius of Tyana, a Pythagorean philosopher and reputed wonder-worker of the first century AD, who was later promoted as a pagan rival to Christ.

Christ's own miracles enabled some pagans to maintain that he was a magician. Remarkable healings and other marvels of the kind attributed to magicians were recorded of Christian saints, but the Church ascribed their miracles not to any magic of their own but to God. The Church condemned magic, or all magic which was not part of its own practices. Unlike the shaman, who had enjoyed an accepted and valued place in his own community, the magician was now a deeply suspect outsider: a pagan, a Jew or a renegade Christian in league with the Devil.

VERGIL AND MERLIN

One famous pagan who strangely acquired notoriety as a magician was the Roman poet Vergil. He had a reputation for profound learning, his poems were used to foretell the future by picking a passage at random (as was the Bible), and he was believed to have prophesied the coming of Christ in his *Fourth Eclogue,* in which he predicted the birth of a wonderful child who would inaugurate a new golden age. By the twelfth century legends were circulating about him and he was regarded as a supernatural protector of Naples, where he had been buried in 19 BC. He was said to have learned magic from a book written by Solomon. Like other magicians he owned a speaking brazen head, and he also made a marble statue which bit off the hands of unfaithul wives. He fell in love with a woman named Phoebilla, who tricked him and suspended him in a basket beneath her bedroom window, where he was mocked by the whole city. In revenge, he magically deprived the city of fire, which for three days the citizens could obtain only from between Phoebilla's legs, to the embarrassment of all concerned. He also fell in love with the Sultan of Babylon's daughter and brought her to Naples across a bridge of air. The tales about him were collected together in French, in the sixteenth century, in *Les Faicts Merveilleux de Virgille* (Vergil's Marvellous Feats).

Far the most attractive of legendary magicians is the great enchanter and prophet Merlin, King Arthur's counsellor (see WELSH LEGENDS; ARTHUR AND LEGENDARY BRITAIN). In the background is the shadowy figure of a Welsh bard of the sixth century named Myrddin, and memories of the Druids may have gone to his making. In medieval legend he was the son of a demon and a virgin, the product of a plot by the lords of hell to bring about the birth of an evil counterpart of Christ. Merlin's mother, however, drank holy water and took a vow of lifelong chastity. As a result, Merlin had superhuman powers but did not inherit his demonic father's evil will and hatred of mankind. He could speak as soon as he was born and he grew up able to change shape, to create all sorts of illusions and to see into both the past and the future. The prophecies attributed to him, published by Geoffrey of Monmouth in the 1130s, were studied and interpreted for centuries.

Merlin first made his mark as a boy. Vortigern, King of Britain, was trying unsuccessfully to build a tower in the mountains of Snowdonia for defence against the Saxons. Merlin divined that the tower would not stand because there was a pool deep in the ground beneath it, a fact which Vortigern's court magicians had been too incompetent to discern. He went on to predict the coming of Arthur.

Later, Merlin transported Stonehenge from Ireland to England by magic art. He brought about the birth of Arthur also by magic and watched over Arthur's early career. It was Merlin who persuaded Arthur's father, Uther Pendragon, to have the Round Table constructed and Merlin who first revealed the existence of the Holy Grail, that supreme Christian relic, the search for which was the greatest adventure of Arthur's knights. It was not the Christian Church but the half-demonic enchanter who guided and inspired Arthurian knighthood. In these stories he seems to represent a profound wisdom from the pagan past, not in opposition to Christianity but in anticipation of it.

There were various accounts of what happened to Merlin in the end. In some he was carried off to hell by the demons who had sent him into the world, but more often he mysteriously disappeared – a story also told of Moses, Pythagoras, Apollonius and Vergil. The best-known tale is one in which he fell hopelessly in love with the beautiful Vivien (or Niviane or Niniane, sometimes identified with the Lady of the Lake). Playing on his desire for her, she wormed the secrets of his magic from him and finally turned his own enchantments against him and shut him up in a cave or a tomb or a castle of air, where he remained a helpless prisoner ever after.

With the development of modern science and technology, the great magician has become a less credible figure. Even so, the modern West has not been without its reputed wonder-workers – Cagliostro in eighteenth-century France, or Rasputin at the court of the Tsars before the Russian Revolution. The legendary magician represents one aspect of the old persistent longing to transcend human limitations. Especially in the figure of Merlin, the 'man of power' still casts a spell.

CHAPTER 31

MISCELLANEOUS LEGENDARY FIGURES

Besides the great heroes of European legend — Arthur or Alexander the Great or El Cid — there are numerous other figures whose names are well-known but who are not of such towering stature. They include kings, outlaws and guerrilla fighters. Most of them actually existed, but one or two probably did not. Some of them, like Robin Hood, come complete with a whole legendary career, while others, like William Tell and Lady Godiva, are remembered mainly for a single episode which has caught the popular fancy.

PRESTER JOHN

The name Prester John still retains something of its old magic. Prester is a shortening of presbyter, meaning priest or elder, and the name may have come originally from John the presbyter, the author of the epistles of John in the New Testament. There was a mystery about him, who he was and if he were the author of the gospel of John.

Prester John, however, is a creation of the Crusading era, when Christian armies fought to win back the Holy Land from the Muslims. Europe was cut off from the Far East by a barrier of intervening Muslim states and news of a potential ally against the infidels from the mysterious lands on the far side of the barrier aroused considerable excitement. The news was provided by a Syrian bishop, who in 1145 reported to the papal court that beyond Persia there ruled a powerful priest-king named John, a descendant of the three Magi who brought

Lady Godiva riding through Coventry (page 278)

gifts to the infant Jesus. He was a member of the Nestorian Church, one of the eastern branches of Christianity, and he had recently scored a signal victory over the Muslims in Persia. This report may have referred to the battle of Qatwan in Persia, in 1141, when a Turkish army was defeated by a Mongol war-lord known as the Gur-Khan or Kor-Khan. Some of his followers were Nestorians and his title may have been rendered into Hebrew or Syriac as Yohanan or Yuhanan, and so into Latin as Johannes, or in English John.

In 1165 someone forged a letter from Prester John to the Byzantine Emperor, Manuel I Comnenus, and to the German Emperor, Frederick Barbarossa, announcing the priest-king's intention of marching to the relief of the Holy Land. In it Prester John described himself as a devout Christian and the most powerful ruler on earth. His Empire extended from Babylon to India and no less than seventy-two lesser kings paid him tribute. So rich was his land that poverty was unknown in it and there was no stealing, lying, quarrelling or crime of any kind. To guard against any possible danger to his throne, however, Prester John owned a magic mirror in which he could see everything that happened in his country, and so could nip any conspiracy in the bud. Other marvels were later reported of his Empire, including magic jewels which controlled the temperature and a glass church which expanded or shrank to fit any congregation.

Pope Alexander III sent Prester John a letter in 1177, but what became of it no one knows. In the 1220s a rumour spread that a Christian conqueror had arisen in the East and was sweeping the hated Muslims before him. His name was reported as David and some people identified him as the son or grandson of Prester John. The rumour was true, except that the conqueror was not a Christian. He was the great Mongol war-leader Genghis Khan.

Various travellers from Europe, including Marco Polo, searched for Prester John's country, but failed to find it. Its location was consequently shifted to Ethiopia, a mysterious land isolated in its mountain fastnesses, but known to be Christian. In the first book on Ethiopia, written by Francisco Alvarez in 1540, Prester John or the Preste is given as the title of the Ethiopian King.

No legend in the sense of a story is attached to Prester John. Like King Arthur, he represents the attraction of power allied to virtue, of a ruler who unites might and right, and his realm is a never-never land of happiness, peace and plenty, which lies enticingly somewhere on the edge of the known world.

ROBIN HOOD

Another idyllic never-never land of legend is the forest which shelters Robin Hood and his men. The real life of a medieval outlaw must have been hard, especially in winter, and real bands of outlaws are generally quarrelsome and ill-disciplined, but in the earliest tales of Robin Hood which have survived the time is always summer and the outlaws live a merry life in the forest as a happy band of brothers. Though free of the shackles and constraints of conventional society, they are well disciplined and well provided for. Supporting themselves by robbing the rich and poaching the king's deer, they are smartly dressed in Lincoln green and scarlet, and they feast on venison and wine, good white bread and ale.

Robin Hood ranks second only to Arthur in legendary fame in England and, though one is a king and the other a criminal, both are upholders of true justice. Like the heroes of many Arthurian stories, and of many modern thrillers, Robin Hood takes the law into his own hands to right wrong. In the early stories he does so with a ruthless ferocity missing from the softer modern versions of his career. Although he is the common man's hero, who takes from the rich and gives to the poor, his enemies are not the wealthy and powerful as a class, but those of them who misuse their position to oppress honest men. His special foes are grasping prelates of the Church and the wicked sheriff of Nottingham, but he is a pious Christian and loyal to king and country. The modern picture of him as the champion of the English peasantry against a Norman aristocracy is foreign to the early tales.

Whether Robin Hood was a historical person or whether he is an idealization of the outlaw-figure is a disputed question, but legends more often grow up about real people than about types. Modern writers tend to date him somewhere in the period from about 1265 to 1325, but in the sixteenth century he was generally believed to have lived from about 1160 to 1247, which put him in his prime in the reigns of King Richard I and King John. He was said to come from a place called Locksley in Yorkshire or Nottinghamshire and to have been outlawed for debt. He was also said to be of noble birth and the rightful Earl of Huntingdon, but in the earlier stories he is not an aristocrat but a yeoman, somewhat lower down the social ladder.

The earliest reference to the outlaw dates from 1377, in *Piers Plowman,* where he is mentioned only in passing but in a way which shows that stories featuring him were already popular. A few ballads about him have survived from the fifteenth century or perhaps earlier. In these he is 'the best archer that was in merry England', the proud and chivalrous commander of a hundred men or more. Quick-witted, daring, resourceful, generous, humorous and sometimes cruel, he loves to make fools of the pompous and overbearing. His base is 'under the greenwood tree', in the forest of Barnesdale in Yorkshire, north of Nottingham, rather than in Sherwood Forest which is now so closely linked with him. His right-hand man is the giant Little John and his other lieutenants include Will Scathelock (Will Scarlett) and Much the Miller's son.

Maid Marian was not added to the legend until later. In a play of 1601 Maid Marian is an aristocratic young lady who is persecuted by King John and escapes to join her lover Robin in Sherwood. An early tale has Robin meeting a brawny friar of Fountains Abbey by the River Skell and forcing the friar to carry him across. The friar drops Robin in mid-stream and tells him to sink or swim. The two of them fight from ten in the morning until four in the afternoon, equally matched, until the friar agrees to join Robin's band. The friar is not named here, but he was later called Friar Tuck.

In the longest of the early ballads, the *Little Geste (Exploit) of Robin Hood and His Mesnie,* Robin and his men help a knight of ancient lineage against predatory churchmen who seek to deprive him of his land. Then Little John takes service with the sheriff of Nottingham under a false name, robs him of much silver and leads him into a trap in the forest. With sardonic courtesy Robin treats the sheriff to a feast of stolen venison, and then makes him sleep the night on the ground. The sheriff, his bones aching, swears never to harm Robin and is allowed to go free. Later, the sheriff holds an archery contest for a prize of a silver arrow with a golden head and feathers. Robin and his men compete and Robin wins the prize, but the treacherous sheriff springs the ambush he has prepared and the outlaws have to fight their way out. Little John is badly wounded and tells Robin to kill him and make good his escape, but Robin refuses and manages to carry Little John to safety on his back. Then he and his men ambush the sheriff in turn, kill him and cut off his head.

King Edward (we are not told which one, unfortunately) comes to Nottingham to punish Robin, but cannot catch him. The King and a few of his knights disguise themselves as monks and go into the forest, where Robin seizes them and demands money. Eventually Robin recognizes the King and kneels to him. The King, greatly impressed by Robin and the good discipline he keeps, pardons the outlaws and takes Robin with him to live at court, but court life does not suit the outlaw. Before long he returns to the greenwood, where he lives for twenty-two more years until he is callously murdered.

According to the early ballad about his death, Robin fell sick and went to his kinswoman, the Prioress of Kirklees, to be let blood. She treacherously left him to bleed to death, but her motive is not explained. Robin had just enough strength to sound three feeble blasts on his horn, which summoned the faithful Little John, who wanted to burn down the nunnery in revenge. Robin would not allow it, for he had never harmed a woman in his life. With the last of his strength he shot an arrow from his bow and asked to be buried where the arrow fell. The site of his grave has long been shown at Kirklees Hall. 'Christ have mercy on his soul,' the *Little Geste* ends, 'for he was a good outlaw and did poor men much good.'

HEREWARD AND WILLIAM TELL

There were several stories of Robin Hood disguising himself and going into Nottingham to spy out the sheriff's plans. The same stories had been told of earlier heroes, including Hereward the Wake, whose historical reality is not in doubt, the English resistance leader against William the Conqueror. According to legend, Hereward returned from abroad to his home at Bourne in the Lincolnshire fen country two years after the battle of Hastings, to find that his younger brother had just been killed by a party of marauding Normans. Waiting until the Normans were drunk, Hereward killed them all and set their severed heads grinning over the doorway of his house. He then joined other English rebels in Ely, where the Conqueror besieged them. Hereward spied out the enemy camp disguised as a potter, and dressed as a peasant he helped William's workmen to make pontoons, which that night he set on fire. After the fall of Ely he was eventually reconciled to William and according to one story he ended his days peacefully at Bourne. According to another, his Norman enemies took him unawares and killed him, Hereward with his last thrust despatching the man who had struck him his death-blow.

William Tell is the national resistance hero of Switzerland and his story is part of the legendary history of how the Swiss won their independence from the Austrian emperors. In 1307, so the story goes, a tyrannical Austrian governor named Gessler set his hat on a stake in the market-place of Altdorf and ordered everyone to bow to it as a symbol of the Emperor's authority. A peasant named William Tell, who was a famous archer, refused to bow and Gessler ordered him to shoot an apple off the head of his little son with one crossbow bolt. Tell took his crossbow and two bolts, performed the feat successfully with one bolt and explained that if he had failed he would have killed Gessler with the other. The governor ordered him to prison, but Tell escaped and soon afterwards ambushed Gessler and shot him down. This exploit fired the Swiss, who rose in revolt and won their independence. Whether William Tell ever existed is in doubt and his feat with the bow has been credited to other heroes, including archers of Norse legend and William of Cloudesley, a medieval English outlaw.

LADY GODIVA AND POPE JOAN

Lady Godiva rode naked through Coventry to persuade her husband to lift a burdensome tax from the citizens. She was covered only by her long fair hair, but because she was pious and kind-hearted a miracle occurred and no one saw her. Godiva was a real person, Godgifu, wife of Earl Leofric of Mercia. She died in 1067 and her memory is cherished in Coventry to this day as almost a tutelary goddess of the city. The story of her ride was current a hundred years or so after her death and probably has some foundation in fact. Long afterwards, in the sixteenth century, it was explained that no one saw her because, out of affection and respect for their benefactress, the townspeople stayed in their houses behind closed doors and windows while she rode by. The story that Peeping Tom sneaked a look at her and was immediately struck blind was added later still.

A heroine famous for her manner of dress rather than undress is Pope Joan. Her story seems to have been a sardonic invention, but it was widely accepted as true in the Middle Ages. According to one version, she was an English girl who fell in love with a monk and dressed as a man to be with him without arousing suspicion. After his death she went to Rome, still disguised as a man, and became a priest. She rose rapidly in the Church and in 855 was elected pope as John VIII. Unfortunately, she was pregnant and died in childbirth on the steps of St Peter's.

SLEEPERS AND WANDERERS

Some heroes are national figures of such importance that legend does not allow them to be lost to the world altogether. It was popularly believed in Britain for centuries that King Arthur was not dead but hidden away, sleeping in a cave or under the ground, and would return when his countrymen had most need of him. The same story was told of Charlemagne, Owen Glendower, Robert the Bruce and many other heroes. Frederick Barbarossa lies sleeping in a cave in Mount Kyffhäuser in Thuringia, waiting his time to return. Siegfried sleeps in the hill of Geroldseck.

Sometimes people cannot believe that a popular or a hated figure has really died. Sir Francis Drake, who was credited with supernatural powers and, like Prester John, owned a magic mirror in which he could see what was happening far away, was buried at sea in 1595. Many people in Devon did not believe it and expected him to return. The much later tradition of him as the spiritual guardian of England, whose aid could be summoned in time of crisis by striking the famous drum kept at his Devonshire home, seems to have been created in the 1890s by Henry Newbolt, author of the poem *Drake's Drum*. The young King Sebastian of Portugal was killed in battle in 1578, but the belief that he was not dead and would return lasted down into the nineteenth century in Portugal and Brazil. Tsar Alexander I of Russia, idealized as a liberal ruler, was rumoured to have lived on in seclusion as a hermit for many years after his official death in 1825. When Lord Kitchener was drowned in 1916, some people could not believe that a figure so vital to the British war effort had really been killed. The last Tsar of Russia, Nicholas II, and his family were supposedly murdered in 1917, but there have been many stories that one or other of them survived, and after 1954 there were persistent rumours that Adolf Hitler was still alive in hiding.

Other legendary figures are unable to die, as a punishment. The Wandering Jew, according to the best known version of his story, was a cobbler named Ahasuerus, who saw Jesus pause to rest while carrying his cross to Calvary and cruelly told him to go on to his death. 'I will stand here and rest,' Jesus said, 'but you will go on until I return.' All through the centuries Ahasuerus has wandered wearily over the face of the earth, repentant and longing for death. The legend apparently goes back to the thirteenth century and is related to the Christian belief that the Jews lost their homeland and were scattered over the world to punish them for killing Christ. There have been several cases of people claiming to have met, or even to be, the Wandering Jew. He was seen in Salt Lake City in 1868 and early in this century in Glamorgan, in Wales. In the 1940s there was a New York stockbroker who carried visiting cards engraved T. W. Jew.

The captain of the *Flying Dutchman,* the most famous of phantom ships, is in the same plight. Crewed by dead men, the ship is encountered in heavy weather off the Cape of Good Hope. Its master, Captain Vanderdeck, is under a curse, condemned to beat vainly against the wind for ever because in a storm he rashly swore that he would round the Cape if he had to keep trying to the end of the world.

THE MURDER OF HIRAM ABIFF

The Freemasons, the largest secret society in the world, have their own legends. The origins of Freemasonry are obscure, but it seems to have begun in Britain somewhere about 1600 in groups which turned away from the actual practice of the stonemason's art to 'speculative' or symbolic and ritual Masonry. The speculative Masons took over from the medieval stonemasons the legendary history of the craft, which emphasized its immense antiquity and high dignity by tracing it back from before Noah's Flood to the building of the Tower of Babel and the construction of Solomon's Temple, from which all civilized architecture was descended. King Solomon, that great sage and master magician, was an impressive figure to enrol in Masonic history and the building of God's holy house on earth was naturally regarded as the summit of the mason's art. The speculative Masons believed that the Temple was an embodiment in stone of all true wisdom.

Of the three principal 'degrees' or ranks of Freemasonry, the highest is master mason. When a candidate is initiated as a master mason a play is acted, in which the candidate takes the part of Hiram Abiff, the great hero of Masonic legend, who is said to have been the chief architect of Solomon's Temple. No one knows where the story of Hiram Abiff comes from or how old it is, but it was certainly in existence by 1730. The Old Testament mentions a craftsman named Hiram or Huram who worked on the Temple, but describes him as a skilled worker in bronze, not as a mason or architect.

According to the legend, three of the masons employed in building the Temple plotted to force Hiram Abiff to reveal the secrets of a master mason. They confronted him and threatened to kill him if he did not tell them the secrets, but he steadfastly refused. Each of them struck him a severe blow and the third conspirator killed him with a maul, or heavy hammer. They buried him hastily and fled. His absence was soon noticed and search parties were sent to look for him. One of the searchers sat down to rest for a while and then took hold of a shrub to help himself up. To his surprise the shrub came clean out of the ground. He and the others began to dig and soon found Hiram Abiff's body. They covered it over again and marked the spot with a sprig of acacia (which is nowadays sometimes placed in the grave at the funeral of a Mason). When King Solomon heard what had happened he was bitterly grieved and had the dead master mason honourably reburied in the Temple near the innermost shrine, the Holy of Holies, the dwelling-place of God himself. The three murderers, who are sometimes given the names Jubela, Jubelo and Jubelum, were tracked down and executed.

The point of the legend, of course, is the duty of keeping the secrets of Masonry, if necessary to the death. In the initiation ritual the meaning is carried a stage further. The story is acted out and the initiate is symbolically murdered and lowered into a mock grave, from which he is raised by the Master of the Lodge. This resurrection is not part of the legend itself, but through it the initiated master mason is symbolically raised to his new way of life. Here legend has turned into myth.

CHAPTER 32

THE BALKANS AND GREECE

The rich and varied legends of the Balkans reflect a constant intermingling of different cultures since the earliest incursions of Huns, Avars and Slavs into the Balkans from the fifth century AD, and the penetration into Greece of Slavs and Albanians. Unification of the Balkans and Anatolia under the Byzantine Empire gave way to conflict after the tenth century, with the gradual emergence of the Bulgarian and Serbian kingdoms, and the invasions of the Seljuk and Ottoman Turks. After the fall of Byzantium to the Turks in 1453, most of the Balkan peninsula was divided into regional states dependent on the Ottoman Empire. The modern Balkan states were not defined until the twentieth century. Until 1923 Turks were settled along the northern coast of the Aegean, while since antiquity Greeks had inhabited coastal cities of Asia Minor and the Black Sea, as well as several pockets deep in the Anatolian hinterland.

In spite of linguistic, ethnic and religious differences, then, the cultures of the Balkans and Anatolia have much in common. The legends and myths of each people retain their distinctive character, but their historical origin and geographical diffusion cannot often be disentangled. In Greece, where both language and literary tradition can be charted without major interruption from antiquity to the present day, legends are particularly well documented, with some features dating back to pagan times. This proves neither their primacy over other Balkan legends, nor their immunity to 'foreign' influence,

The legend of the Walled-up Wife (page 288)

but it does reveal a continuous process of remodelling over a long period.

ALEXANDER THE GREAT

The fantastic adventures of the world-conquering King of Macedon captivated the imagination of the medieval world more than any other ancient legend. Alexander's career was meteoric and it is small wonder that legends grew up about his birth, exploits and death. By the seventeenth century there were eighty versions of the story in twenty-four languages. Their source was the Greek Romance of Alexander, known as Pseudo-Callisthenes, which circulated widely and was constantly remodelled (see CLASSICAL GREECE AND ROME; ALEXANDER THE GREAT). The romance opens with Olympias, wife of Philip II of Macedon. Childless and worried, she is advised during Philip's absence by Nectanebus, ex-King of Egypt and an astrologer and magician, who is 'pleasure-mad for women'. He promises her an heir through the intervention of the god Zeus Ammon and visits her by night in the form of a serpent or dragon until Alexander is conceived.

Fortunately, Alexander did not resemble Nectanebus, nor even Olympias: 'he had the hair of a lion, and one eye was blue; the right one was heavy-lidded and black; his teeth were sharp as fangs...' Like all heroes, his physical and intellectual growth was precocious. He played cruel practical jokes, pushing Nectanebus into a pit to his death; he outwitted his parents and his tutor, Aristotle, over his financial allowance; he subdued the man-eating horse Bucephalus and won spectacular victories in chariot-races and battles; after Philip's death he conquered wherever he went.

Alexander is also credited with conquering man-eating female giants and six-handed or headless monsters with their eyes and mouths on their chests, known as the Ewaipanoma. Once he discovered the water of life, but his cook, Andreas, inadvertently washed fish in it. Seeing them leap from the pan, Andreas drank some himself and gave the rest to Kale, Alexander's bastard daughter. In his fury Alexander banished them both. Andreas gave his name to the Adriatic and Kale became one of the Nereids, dangerous female creatures of seas and forests. Robbed of immortality, Alexander met his death from a poisoned drink and was buried at Memphis in Egypt.

In Greek, the legend passed from the romance into vernacular literature and oral tradition. Cheap Venetian editions of the tale, in verse and prose, were printed from the sixteenth to the twentieth centuries. In the oral legends Alexander's military exploits are forgotten and he is absorbed into the supernatural world of the Nereids. It is said that he loved one of the Nereids and grew to fame, but later he angered them and his Kingdom was destroyed. Or he found the water of life, but it was stolen by his sister Kale, who thereafter became a Nereid. Nereids still lament him, sometimes causing storms at sea and asking any passing ship, 'Does Alexander live?' They are pacified only by the reply, 'He lives and rules.' These stories are not in the printed tales, and form an independent line of transmission from medieval to modern folklore.

DIGENES AND MARKO

Digenes Akrites is a Byzantine hero who has eluded attempts at historical identification, though events place him on the eastern frontiers of the Byzantine Empire around the tenth century. Son of a Syrian emir and a noble Christian mother (Digenes means 'born of two races'), he grows up as a precocious youth among the Cappadocian nobility in Anatolia. Like his father, he abducts the beautiful daughter of an aristocratic general, and after a spectacular wedding he makes peace on the frontiers and lives in grand domestic bliss. This is marred by occasional skirmishes with raiders who try to abduct his bride, and by two lapses from Christian chastity, related repentantly but not without relish to his companions at table. The first is with the daughter of the Emir Happlorrhabdes, a damsel in distress whom he rescues only to seduce; the second with the Amazonian warrior-maiden Maximo, whom he twice defeats in single combat but whose loveliness in a gossamer singlet he does not resist. He kills her the next day in a fit of remorse. He finally settles down to build a magnificent palace and gardens on the Euphrates, but is doomed, like Jesus Christ and Alexander the Great, to die at thirty-three prematurely if unheroically. 'Came also the wondrous Borderer to his death, the occasion arising from the bath.' His wife expires in his arms rather than outlive him.

This epic-romance, which survives in five Greek versions and in Russian (possibly via Serbo-Croat), is a twelfth-century literary concoction with a tenth-century historical background, reflecting a sophisticated harking back to a past heroic age rather than a lost oral epic. The modern Akritic ballads have transported Digenes into their legendary world of magic weapons, talking birds and supernatural feats. He wrestles with Death on a marble threshing-floor for three days and nights. When defeated, he summons his companions and relates his past exploits. In some ballads he strangles his wife to prevent her marrying again. The songs bear little relation to the epic and the notion of Digenes as a Greek national hero is largely the creation of nineteenth-century romanticism.

Marko Kraljevic is the most famous of Yugoslav heroes. Son of King Vukasin of Macedonia, he became a vassal of the Turks and ruled Prilep Castle until he was killed at Rovine in 1395, fighting the

Romanians on the Turkish side. In spite of this historical record, he is celebrated as a Serbian national hero in Serbian, Romanian and Bulgarian legends. Unlike the shorter Akritic ballads, the Marko poems form a coherent cycle, relating his birth, marriage, heroic exploits and death. Sung by men, they seem to reflect a genuinely old, South Slavic epic tradition. Marko is a mighty warrior and a heavy drinker, liking 'to drink wine over three days, until the wine gets into one's face'. He can be brutal to women, but is devoted to his horse Sarac, whom he feeds on wine. Some say he was the son of a *vila* (the *vile* are supernatural females not unlike the Nereids), others that he snatched a dancing *vila* as his wife with the aid of his falcon. Once he was on an unsuccessful hunting expedition with his brother, Andrija, who went into a tavern to quench his thirst and had his head cut off by thirty Turks who were drinking inside. Marko went in, drank heavily, and killed all the Turks. Then he gouged out the barmaid's eyes, tied her to his horse's tail and drove it over the hills. Before his own death, his horse Sarac, sensing his master's end, 'lifts up his voice in lamentation' outside the tavern where Marko is drinking.

THE BATTLE OF KOSOVO

In June 1389 the Turkish Sultan Murad led a strong force against the Serbian Prince Lazar and his armies. Murad was killed, Lazar was captured and beheaded, and the Serbian Kingdom lost its independence. The cycle of Kosovo poems tells of the heroes who fall and their families. On the eve of the battle Queen Milica begs her husband, Prince Lazar, to leave just one of her nine noble brothers with her, but can persuade none — not even their servant — to break his oath of loyalty. After the battle the unnamed Girl of Kosovo searches among the bodies on the Plain of Blackbirds, with white loaves and golden pitchers of cool water and red wine, in the hope of finding her betrothed, only to learn from the wounded standard-bearer that he has fallen, with all the other voivods (nobles). The stout-hearted mother of Milica prays for the eyes of a falcon and the wings of a swan to fly over the plain in search of her nine noble sons, her spirit unbroken at finding them dead, until the next morning two black ravens bring her the severed hand of Damjan, her favourite. She laments, and 'breathes her soul away'.

The older Kosovo poems are grand and tragic, lacking the supernatural and fantastic elements of the Marko cycle. Although they are based on history, many heroes and events are unverifiable. In the poems Milos, who kills Murad, is upheld as a hero, while his half-brother Vuk Brankovic is branded a traitor; whereas Vuk actually held out against the Turks after Milos' submission. The absence of Marko Kraljevic — he had already submitted — receives no comment. Explicit national feeling is present only in the more recent ballads.

KRESNIK AND KRALJ MATAZ

Kresnik is the oldest hero of the Slovenes, known in legend as a magician and monster-killer, son of the sky-god Svarog. He owes his supernatural powers to the *vile,* with whose snake-queen Mara he lived before marrying her daughter Vesina, who is also his sister. His death, at a ripe old age, was caused by their jealousy, and he dwells to this day in Svarog's crystal mountain. He is a mythological figure, possibly originating in a deity of spring, crops and cattle, and later fused with St George, the dragon-slayer.

Kresnik's legendary successor is Kralj Mataz, the killer of many Turks. He too married his sister, Alencika, rescuing her from the Turks, or from the underworld. He is sleeping now in a mountain or cave, where ravens keep watch, but he will wake to save the Slovenes in their hour of need. One Christmas at midnight a lime tree will blossom for one hour. Then, on St George's day, Kralj Mataz will emerge from his cave to make the tree flower again in token of his people's promised salvation. He takes his name from Corvinus Mathias, King of Hungary (1443–90), who extended his territories west and east against the Turks.

Comparable Albanian legends celebrate their national hero, Skanderbeg (Gjorgj Kastroit, Prince of Kruja), famed for exploits against the Turks in the fifteenth century. His death spelled the end of Albanian independence.

THE FALL OF CONSTANTINOPLE

Byzantium fell on 29 May 1453, when the Turks entered Constantinople (Istanbul). The last dramatic moments are described in legends throughout the Balkans, especially in Greece. According to one version, the final liturgy in Hagia Sophia was attended by everyone in the city, led by the Emperor and the Patriarch. Suddenly a voice from heaven bade them take the Cross, the Gospel-book and the holy table to the West, lest they be defiled by the infidel. The weeping icon of the Virgin Mary was told to take comfort, since one day they will be recovered. Some say that when the Turks broke into Hagia Sophia, the priest escaped with the holy chalice through a door which closed miraculously behind him. He will come out to finish the liturgy when the city is recaptured from the Turks. Others say that the Emperor was frying fish when the news came. 'Only when the fish in this pan come to life,' he protested, at which they leaped from the pan into a nearby well. Another tale says that the Emperor turned to marble after being struck from his horse by Turks, and waits in a cave near the Golden Gate for an angel to return his sword so that he can drive the Turks from the city.

BANDITS

These primitive rebels against authority, driven to banditry by poverty, go back to the beginning of Ottoman rule and are celebrated in ballads throughout the Balkans. Known as Hajduks (a word of Turkic or Magyar origin) in Bulgaria, Yugoslavia and Hungary, and as Klefts (robbers) in Greece, they live in organized bands in the mountains. Their lives are hard but free, and they raid and kill the rich and the monks as well as the Turks. The Hajduks are harsh, kinless men, typified in the Bulgarian song:

> We have made many mothers weep,
> We have widowed many wives,
> Many more we have made orphans,
> For we are childless men ourselves.

The Kleft may occasionally complain of his hard lot, never eating fresh bread or enjoying a night's rest: 'With my hand for pillow, my sword for mattress, I hold my rifle like a girl in my arms.' But life has compensations: Klefts roast lambs on the spit, drink wine stolen from monasteries, dance, and take enormous pride in their physical appearance.

The heroes of the older Bulgarian and Serbo-Croat ballads are usually anonymous, whereas the Kleftic songs praise known warriors, such as Christos Milionis (1740s), who set fire to himself and his band rather than submit to the Turks. Common legendary features include prodigious feats of strength, such as leaping over seven horses at once; birds and mountains which lament the outcome of battle or console the dying hero; the girl turned Hajduk or Kleft, whose bravery makes her the leader of the band, or whose sex is discovered only when she bursts a button in throwing a lance, revealing her breasts which 'shine like the sun'. The highest values are honour, strength, bravery and endurance, while the concept of freedom is fiercely individual rather than social or national. During the wars for independence in the nineteenth century, bandit chiefs formed a vital nucleus of local armed guerrillas. The myth of the bandit was influential in the emergence of national consciousness, inspiring many heroic deeds celebrated in twentieth-century partisan ballads of the two World Wars, most notably in Albania, Yugoslavia and Bulgaria.

THE SAINTS

Lives of saints contain some of the oldest and best loved legends in the Balkans. From the beginning legendary and even pagan elements were interwoven with Christian and semi-historical tales to create edifying and exciting – even titillating – stories, which were read and recited at all levels of society. St Romanos swallowed a scroll given him by the Virgin in a dream, and woke up to sing the most beautiful hymns Byzantium was ever to know. St Kosmas and St Damian, the patrons of medicine, cured a paralytic by telling him to rape his neighbour in church. Convinced it was the voice of the Devil, the paralytic prayed and made the sign of the cross, but when the command was repeated for the third time, he did as he was told and raped a dumb woman who was next to him. Then he sprang to his feet and the dumb woman cried out, glorifying God. Unfortunately, few of the earliest Byzantine saints' lives have survived the drastic expurgation by Symeon Metaphrastes in the tenth century.

Saints cure disease, protect crops and help to drive off invaders, and are therefore especially loved in rural areas, where legend and cult survive side by side, often absorbing local features of pagan origin. At Eleusis in Greece an ancient statue of the goddess Demeter was worshipped because of the protection 'St Demetra' always afforded the crops, until it was removed by British archaeologists in 1801. Local legend continued to tell of St Demetra's long search for her beautiful daughter, who had been abducted by a Turk. When at last she recovered her daughter, she returned to bless the fields of Eleusis, which have been fertile ever since. The story is related to the old Greek myth of Demeter's search for her daughter, Kore or Persephone, who had been carried off by Hades, the lord of the dead.

THE WALLED-UP WIFE

There are many other local legends, including short tales which explain how a place got its name or how mountains and rocks were formed by giants. A striking example is the old Balkan legend of the Walled-Up Wife. Its ethnic origins are impossible to determine, but it has been adapted to local tradition in every Balkan country (and in Hungary).

In the Greek version, forty-five masons and sixty apprentices build a bridge over the River Arta (Danube/Euphrates). What they build by day falls down by night. They lament (or rejoice, if it is piece-work) and are commanded by the spirit of the river to sacrifice the wife of the master-builder. He laments (or rejoices, in the hope of finding a better wife) and sends word to his wife to come slowly the next day with his food. The message miscarries, and she comes quickly. He asks her to look for his ring, which has fallen into the foundations. As soon as she has gone down to look, they all pile in lime, rubble and boulders. She curses all passers-by, but revokes the curse when reminded that her brother may pass.

In the Romanian story, Negru the Voivod commands Manoli and

nine masons to build a monastery, threatening to immure them all unless satisfied. What they build by day falls down at night. Manoli dreams that the first wife or sister to come with food next day must be walled-up. Seeing his own wife Anna approaching, he prays God to put all manner of obstacles in her path, but she heroically overcomes them all. The others rejoice, but Manoli weeps, embraces her passionately and tells her they will wall her up as a jest. When the rubble reaches her breasts, she knows it is no jest, and laments, but they continue with the task. The Voivod arrives to find the monastery completed, then orders them to destroy it and build another elsewhere. All the masons leap from the parapets. Manoli hears Anna weep, and the spot where they fell became a magic spring, bitter with Anna's tears.

In Yugoslavia, King Vukasin and his two brothers build a fortress at Skadra. They labour for three years with 300 craftsmen, but what they build by day falls down by night. A *vila* tells them to immure whichever wife comes first next day. They swear an oath of secrecy, but it is kept only by the youngest brother, Goyko. When his wife arrives, he turns away in sorrow while his brothers wall her in, as if in jest. She asks for two holes to be left, so that she can suckle her child, and to this day a healing liquid runs from the apertures, said to cure mothers without milk.

In Bulgaria, three brothers construct a building, but what they erect by sunlight falls down by moonlight. They swear a mutual oath that whichever wife comes first next day shall be immured. Only the master-builder keeps the secret, but he tries to delay his wife Struna with difficult domestic tasks. She diligently completes them all. When she arrives, he laments the loss of his ring in the foundations. She goes down, and his two brothers wall her in. She accepts her fate, asking only that two holes be left for her to suckle her child.

In Albania, the mason Rosa tries to build a fortress, which keeps collapsing. His sister, Fa, passes by just after he has learned that a woman must be immured in the foundations. The workmen seize her and wall her up. Other Albanian versions are similar to the Bulgarian and Greek ones.

The different versions illustrate how the same legend acquires the distinctive characteristics of each culture. The story is based on the primitive custom of foundation sacrifice and the site is often associated with local fertility rites. To this day, the immuring of an animal or of a person's shadow is common practice when the foundations of a building are laid.

Russian legends, unlike those of western Europe, went for centuries largely unnoticed and unrecorded by the literate classes of society. But in a vast country of isolated communities, whose people were predominantly illiterate down to the early twentieth century, culture for most Russians meant the traditional lore of their ancestors, and this included legends. Among the astonishing wealth of folk-tales, ballads and songs garnered by nineteenth-century Russian collectors, one genre emerged pre-eminent: the superb epic verse legends known as *byliny* (singular *bylina*). Ranging between 90 and 300 lines in length, the bylina was sung, or rather chanted, by peasants famed in their localities for their artistic talents. Each narrator had his or her favourite subjects, drawn from a common stock, but was free to embroider details or develop aspects of the traditional narrative. Each rendition varied, since the bylina was performed from memory. Minor variations did not matter to the narrator's audience of avid listeners. Nor were they aware that the byliny were full of historical anachronisms. For them the legends represented an ideal heroic Russian past, a time when brave men and free defended their own honour and that of their country. Most Russian peasants were tied to the land and for them freedom could only be a dream. Though conditions have changed and the tradition of the bylina is virtually dead, every Russian knows of the heroes of the legends through children's books and literary reworkings of the exploits of the wise old Ilya of Murom, the warrior Dobrynya Nikitich and the rake Alyosha the priest's son, among many others.

Sadko and the Sea King (page 295)

On the surface the byliny appear to be historical tales, mainly set in or around the two most important cities in early Russian history, Kiev and Novgorod. Kiev, beside the River Dnieper in the south-west, became the chief city of the first Russian state as it emerged in the tenth century, reached its apogee in the eleventh and capitulated to the Tatars in the thirteenth. Novgorod was the second city of the Kievan state and a major commercial centre.

VLADIMIR THE FAIR SUN

In the Kievan bylina cycle the Prince of Kiev is always called Vladimir, a name borne by two of the most famous Kievan princes: Vladimir I, who was canonized for his conversion of the country to Christianity in the tenth century, and Vladimir Monomakh, famed for his military exploits and clever diplomacy in the twelfth. In the absence of precise detail which would identify the prince of the legends with one of the historical Vladimirs, he should perhaps simply be seen as a composite figure, representative of all Kievan princes, and his character is a creation of the legends. Unlike the noble hero-figure of Western chivalry, Vladimir, though called the Fair Sun, is weak, passive, even cowardly. Thus when the dragon Tugarin comes uninvited to Vladimir's feast, insults him and caresses his wife, it is the rake Alyosha, hiding behind the stove, who is offended and comes to Vladimir's defence.

Though termed kindly, Vladimir is frequently unjust. In *Ilya and Kalin-Isar,* when Vladimir complains that there is no one to defend Kiev, he has to be reminded that he has cast the great hero Ilya years before into a dungeon. Indeed his main failing in his relations with his bogatyrs, as the heroes of the byliny are called, is his inability to appreciate their worth. In *The Revolt of Ilya of Murom Against Vladimir,* Ilya is offered far too humble a place at a feast and is so offended that he leaves. Assembling a drunken rabble, he sets about wrecking a church and ravaging Kiev, and desists only when Vladimir begs his forgiveness and seats him in the highest place at the table. But though Vladimir's bogatyrs dislike many things about his behaviour, they evidently respect his position as head of the country and come to his aid when he really needs them.

Many details indicate that a nucleus of the legends does date back to the Kievan period. There is even a historically attested Dobrynya, Vladimir I's uncle, and it is likely that some of the earliest byliny formed round folk memory of his exploits. As time passed, other byliny evolved along similar lines and were given the setting of Kiev. The enemy, who in the earlier legends must have been the Polovtsians, are now called the Tatars, who in reality did not appear until the very end of the Kievan period. The reason for this is probably that many of the legends grew up in the terrible period of the

Tatar yoke, from the thirteenth to the fifteenth centuries. Certainly only a few are of later date.

Epic legends of such artistic merit as the byliny must have arisen on the basis of an earlier epic tradition, and there are times when this is very clear. The dragons that Alyosha and Dobrynya fight are both fantastic creatures, even though they may be given precise Kievan interpretations. The tale of Dobrynya's brave battle against the fearsome dragon Gorynchishche may reflect the real Dobrynya's forcible conversion of the Novgorodians to Christianity in the tenth century, with the dragon a symbol of paganism. Tugarin, the monster fought by Alyosha, while retaining features of the pre-Christian dragon, is clearly connected to the Polovtsian khan, Tugor-kan, who threatened Russia at the close of the eleventh century.

THE WIZARD VOLKH

The legend about Volkh Vseslavich is a particularly interesting fusion of mythology and history. Volkh's first name means 'wizard', but may be a corruption of the word *volk,* 'wolf'. In Slav countries children born with the caul over their heads were thought to be werewolves, that is to be bloodthirsty and able to change shape, and also to be lucky and crafty. In the legend no mention is made of a caul, but Volkh has a magical conception and birth. By the age of twelve he has perfected the martial arts and the occult sciences. Gathering a chosen band of 300 warriors, he sets out to conquer India (the name standing for an exotic, far-off land). He decides to reconnoitre and so:

> He turned himself into a bay aurochs with golden horns,
> Raced towards the Indian kingdom,
> With the first bound he covered a whole verst,
> With the second he was no more to be seen.
> He turned himself into a bright falcon,
> He flew to the Indian kingdom,
> And when he came to the Indian kingdom,
> He settled on the white stone palace.

(A verst is a distance of about 1 kilometre/1094 yards.)
Through his magic powers Volkh turns his army into ants, and they crawl unseen into the Indian kingdom. Here he reveals the bloodthirsty side of his nature with his command to the army to butcher the whole population of India save for 300 beautiful maidens. Volkh meanwhile smashes the Indian Tsar to smithereens, takes his wife for himself and marries his army to the maidens.

Though the action of this legend appears to have little to do with Kievan history, it is probable that an ancient werewolf myth has been applied to a real Prince, Vseslav of Polotsk, for Volkh's patronymic is

Vseslavich. Vseslav, whom we know to have been born with a caul over his head, refused to accept the authority of the Prince of Kiev over the principality of Polotsk and attacked Kiev. There is a hint in the legend of Kievan fear of Volkh, and it may be that story tells in distorted fashion of Vseslav's capture of Kiev in 1068.

ILYA OF MUROM

The most popular of the Kievan bogatyrs is Ilya, with a cycle of eight legends to his name. He is a hero great in strength and courage, who is slow to develop. He is crippled until the age of thirty-three when Christ and two apostles, disguised as wandering pilgrims, come and heal him. This legend, which stresses his peasant background, is probably of seventeenth-century provenance and is the most recent in the cycle. He is the ideal simple hero — brave, wise (the epithet 'old' applied to him means old in understanding as much as in years), just and possessing a simple dignity and directness. His most typical role is that of defender of the Russian land. In only one bylina, *Ilya and Nightingale Robber,* is the enemy not a foreigner. Ilya, on his way from his native Murom to Kiev had to pass by the town of Chernigov, which he found under siege:

> He rode up to that great host,
> When he reached the mighty host,
> He trampled them with his horse and slew them with his spear,
> He slew that whole mighty host.

Declining the invitation to take over military command of Chernigov, he rode on to encounter Nightingale, a creature half-human and half-bird:

> When Nightingale whistles like a nightingale,
> When the robber villain screams like a wild beast,
> All the lush grass becomes entangled,
> The azure flowers shed their petals,
> The dark forests bow down to the earth.

Drawing his silken bowstring, Ilya felled Nightingale with an arrow through his right eye, and took him on his horse to Kiev. At Vladimir's behest, Ilya ordered Nightingale to whistle, at half-strength, but even this was enough to kill numerous people, and in retaliation Ilya cut off his head.

A number of other legends tell of Ilya's defeat of the Tatars, whether in the form of a monster or a whole army. Many scholars believe that *Ilya and Kalin-Tsar* tells of the first disastrous encounter with the Tatars in 1224, with the defeat transmuted into a victory. Accompanied only by Vladimir, disguised as his servant, Ilya rides into the midst of the Tatar host. When Kalin-Tsar orders his men to seize Ilya, he picks up one of the Tatars by the legs and wielding him like a club clears whole roads through the ranks of soldiers. As the slaughter continues, the Tatars flee and Kiev is saved.

DOBRYNYA AND ALYOSHA

The second most popular bogatyr is Dobrynya Nikitich, whose character is more developed and rounded than that of the others. He is a brave warrior, who sets out to tackle 'the great dragon Gorynchishche, the dragon with twelve heads'. Dobrynya is not only a warrior, however, but a skilful diplomat, and he negotiates a pact with the dragon that he, Dobrynya, will not kill the baby dragons, provided the dragon avoids Kiev. But dragons are not to be trusted and, in a motif similar to the story of St George, Gorynchishche abducts Vladimir's kinswoman, Zabava. Dobrynya eventually defeats him after a fierce battle. His diplomatic skills are also put to the test in *Dobrynya the Matchmaker* or *Dunay,* in which Dobrynya and his friend Dunay go on a marriage embassy on Vladimir's behalf. This bylina may well reflect the historical Dobrynya's mission to the Prince of Polotsk in 980 to seek his daughter's hand for Vladimir I.

This last legend contains martial episodes, but on the whole belongs to those non-heroic byliny whose theme is life and love. The most famous of these about Dobrynya is *Dobrynya and Alyosha,* in which the youngest of the three sworn 'brothers', Alyosha, plays a very dubious role. As Dobrynya leaves home, he tells his wife to wait for him for six years. After this she is free to marry anyone except his sworn brother Alyosha. (Ilya, Dobrynya and Alyosha have sworn to treat each other as brothers.) She waits six years, then six more, and finally decides to marry Alyosha. Warned by his 'good steed' as he returns from Constantinople, Dobrynya races home to hear from his mother that Alyosha has falsely spread rumours of his death. Disguising himself as a minstrel, he contrives to join the wedding feast and drops his wedding ring into his wife's cup. Recognizing him, she begs and receives forgiveness. Alyosha, on the other hand, receives a thorough hiding with the butt-end of Dobrynya's riding whip.

Alyosha is also a brave warrior, who saves Kiev from Tugarin, and he frequently accompanies his two sworn brothers on their adventures, but he appears again in the role of philanderer in *Alyosha and the Sister of the Petroviches.* In this legend Alyosha contrives to destroy the belief of two brothers in their sister Elena's modesty, and finally runs off with her himself. The ambiguous treatment of Alyosha in the byliny doubtless reflects his origin as the son of a priest, for priests in Russian peasant circles were traditional comic butts.

There are several lesser heroes whose adventures have little or nothing to do with warfare. One of the most interesting is Dunay, about whom there are two legends, both concerning his relationship with Nastasya, the daughter of the Lithuanian King. In the first, Dunay and Nastasya's love affair, which has dveloped during Dunay's period of service at the Lithuanian King's court, is cut short when the relationship is discovered. In the second, *Dobrynya the Matchmaker* or *Dunay,* it is the Amazon Nastasya who pursues Dobrynya and Dunay when they abduct her sister for Vladimir. Dunay then fights and defeats the valiant Nastasya, but on discovering her identity, proposes marriage rather than death. Tragically, however, Dunay is arrogant and cannot endure his wife's superior prowess as an archer. Vindictively he kills her, and then in despair himself. The concluding motif, in which the blood of the two becomes the source of two rivers, is common in legends about place names.

VASILY AND SADKO

The Novgorodian legends are altogether more prosaic. Novgorod was a mercantile city where violent conflict between social groups was common, and the local *byliny* reflect this. Vasily Buslayevich (Vasenka), for example, the son of a wealthy citizen, is soon in trouble for his violent behaviour.

> Vasenka began to go out on the streets
> To play no mean jokes on the people.
> If he grabs your hand, it comes off,
> If he grabs your foot, it comes off,
> If he slaps you on the back,
> You'll walk for ever bent over.

He recruits a band of loyal followers from among the rougher social elements and sets about clubbing the rest of the citizens to death. The legend may tell of a real social conflict transformed through time into a tale celebrating boldness and violent action. The other bylina about Vasily tells how, with characteristic independence of mind, he refuses to heed the warning on a stone that anyone who jumps it will die. He jumps it and is killed.

The other important character of the Novgorodian legends, Sadko, represents the commercial spirit of Novgorod. Though it is possible that he is the same rich merchant Sadko who founded a church in Novgorod in 1167, the bylina about him is in many ways closer to fairy-tales than any other. Sadko, a poor minstrel, is sitting sadly playing beside Lake Ilmen when the Sea King emerges from the depths to tell him that in gratitude for his playing, he will make him rich. Sadko is to bet the rich merchants of Novgorod that the lake contains fish with golden scales. The bet accepted, Sadko catches three such fish and acquires vast riches. In his desire to become rich enough to own the whole wealth of Novgorod, he sets off on a trading voyage, the description of which accurately reflects practice in medieval Novgorod. While sailing the sea, Sadko is forced to descend to the ocean depths to pacify the Sea King, to whom he has paid no tribute. There, forced to play endlessly on his *gusli* (a stringed instrument), he is saved by St Nicholas, who tells him what he must do to escape. Sadko returns home to find his laden ships sailing up the river into Novgorod. He fulfils his bargain with St Nicholas by building a church in his honour. The legend is clearly a combination of accurate historical detail and fairy-tale.

HISTORICAL SONGS

With the rise of a powerful Russian state under Moscow in the fifteenth century, tales of epic valour which had evolved in the gloomy period of Russian subjection to the Tatars began to give way to a more prosaic type of legend, the historical song. Though the two have much in common, historical songs tell of actual historical events and lack the poetic hyperbole and dash of the byliny. Cycles of such songs are known to date to the thirteenth century, but the vast majority were composed from the sixteenth to the nineteenth. They emerged round people and events that struck the popular imagination, rulers such as Ivan the Terrible or Peter the Great, or leaders of popular rebellions like Stenka Razin or Pugachev. The events depicted are by no means the most important of the period and often depart from historical fact. What they present is a popular view of history and historical figures. Thus Peter the Great in *Peter and the Dragoon* is seen as the simple friend of the common folk. In the legend, Peter's challenge to anyone to wrestle with him is taken up by a fifteen-year-old dragoon.

> The young dragoon overturned him with his left hand,
> The young dragoon caught him up with his right hand,
> He did not let the Tsar touch the damp earth.

For his skill and his respect for his sovereign, Peter offers him a reward. True to his peasant background, the dragoon declares:

> I do not want villages or estates,
> Or a chest of pure gold.
> Permit me to drink, without charge,
> Wine in the taverns of the Crown.

This story about Peter is doubtless apocryphal, but even when known events are related, the facts are distorted. Peter's visit to the town of Riga, for instance, is transposed to Stockholm where he encounters the Queen of Sweden rather than the governor of Riga. Similarly Ivan the Terrible's accidental killing of his son Ivan in a fit of rage in 1581 becomes his execution of his son Fedor for treason. The picture of Ivan as paranoid and impulsive, however, is entirely in keeping with what is known of his character.

The image of historical personages that emerges from the songs is determined by their origin among the peasantry, and the image of heroism that emerges from the byliny is uniquely Russian because the legends were preserved by the most traditionally-minded of social groups. Though lacking the sophistication and elegance of western European legends, Russian byliny have a colour and dash all their own. It is not surprising that their portrayal of a heroic age for so long gripped their peasant audiences and still appeals to educated readers.

CHAPTER 34

THE GYPSIES

Traditional Romany culture is essentially oral. There is an extensive and varied repertoire of stories, handed down by word of mouth, which embraces all categories from international folk-tale types, through legends of all kinds, to narrative joke material. Amongst Gypsy story-tellers the differences between these categories are hardly recognized, and certainly not in the terminology used by scholars, but a number of major themes in the Gypsy legends can be isolated. These include tales about the origins of the Gypsies, about Gypsy occupations, and about the supernatural, which are found generally amongst Romany communities throughout the world. There is also a cycle of legends, current amongst English Gypsies, concerning the adventures of a particular Gypsy hero.

THE ORIGIN OF THE GYPSIES

The borderline between myth and legend in aetiological tales (which explain how things came to be as they are) is ill-defined, but these tales are generally of legend type both in form and in style. In those dealing with the origin of the Gypsies, for example, God and other divine or mythical characters are presented in mundane human terms, as in the story of how God made the first Gypsy:

> One day God decided to make a man. He took some lime, fashioned a human figure and put it in his oven to bake. Then he went for a walk and finally forgot about his task. When he came

The blacksmith who refused to forge the nails (page 300)

back the man was burnt completely black. This was the ancestor of the blacks. God began again, but this time he was so afraid of missing the right moment that he opened the oven too soon. The man was completely pale. This was the ancestor of the white men. God had a third try, which this time was successful. The last man was medium done, nicely browned and nicely tanned. This was the ancestor of the first Gypsy.[1]

If this legend is designed to reinforce pride in Gypsy origins, there are many others whose function seems to be to console the Gypsies for ill-treatment and persecution suffered at the hands of non-Gypsies, and to stir the latter to pity. In these legends Gypsies are portrayed as a cursed race, condemned to wander the world forever in the expiation of sin. One such story explains why the Gypsies were expelled from India:

A Hindu king was warned by a sorcerer that an invader would attack his kingdom and destroy his family. The invader would never be harmed unless he attacked a Gypsy. The king sent for the chief of the Gypsies and secretly gave him his only daughter, Gan, who was to be brought up in safety as if she were the chief's own child. Gan grew up in the same tent as the chief's son, Tchen. One day the old chief died. The Gypsy tribe urged Tchen, their new chief, to take a wife at once; but Tchen refused to marry any of the girls who were offered to him, and threatened to kill himself, since he loved only his own sister. Tchen's mother then told him that Gan was not really his sister; but the secret had to be kept from the tribe in case the invader should kill Gan as the king's daughter. The tribe split into two groups, those who agreed that whatever the chief did was right, and those who refused to live under a chief who married his own sister. The latter chased Tchen and his followers out of the land of Hind. A great sorcerer laid a curse on Tchen and his followers, who ever since have had to wander over the face of the earth, never sleep twice in the same place, never drink twice from the same well, and never cross the same river twice in one year.[2]

Sometimes the Gypsies are said to be wanderers because they are the descendants of Cain. In other Gypsy legends they are said to have taken part in the Massacre of the Innocents at Bethlehem; to have refused to help the Virgin Mary at the time of the Flight into Egypt; to have betrayed Christ by getting so drunk when they were his bodyguard that were incapable of defending him; and to have forged the nails for the Crucifixion when no other blacksmith would.

When the Roman jailers were going to crucify Yeshua ben
Miriam, whom the world later called Jesus, two soldiers were
sent to get four big nails. They spent half the money they had
been given drinking in a tavern, and then went to look for
a blacksmith: 'Man, we want four big nails made right away, to
crucify Yeshua ben Miriam with, who has talked ill of our
emperor. Here is money to pay for them.' But the blacksmith,
an old Jew, refused to forge the nails. The soldiers set fire to his
beard and ran their lances through him.

They told the next blacksmith, also a Jew, to make them four
big nails, and put down what was left of their money. But he said
he could only make four small nails for that price. They set his
beard on fire too. Frightened out of his wits, he started to make
the nails; but when one of the soldiers said they must be good
and strong because they were to crucify Yeshua ben Miriam, he
heard the voice of the first blacksmith forbidding him to make
the nails, for Yeshua ben Miriam was innocent. He too refused,
and the soldiers ran their lances through him.

The third blacksmith they found was a Syrian, who was just
finishing work for the day. Seeing their lances all bloody, he
blew up his furnace and started to make the nails; but he too
heard the voices of both the murdered blacksmiths, and refused
to carry on. The soldiers ran their lances through him.

Outside the gates of Jerusalem they found a Gypsy smith
and ordered him to make four stout nails. The Gypsy pocketed
the money first. As he made each nail the soldiers put it in a bag.
When he was making the fourth nail towards nightfall the voices of the three murdered blacksmiths were heard again. The
soldiers ran off in panic. The Gypsy, glad he had pocketed the
money first, finished making the fourth nail and waited for it to
grow cold. But it kept on glowing, no matter how much water he
threw over it. Terrified, he packed up his tent on his donkey and
fled into the desert; but the glowing nail followed him, no
matter how he tried to get rid of it. That nail always appears in
the tents of the descendants of that man who forged the nails for
the Crucifixion. And when the nail appears, the Gypsies run.
That is why they move from one place to another.[3]

SKILLS AND OCCUPATIONS

Other legends explain why the Gypsies are skilled in metalwork
and music (because they are descended from Tubal-Cain in the Bible,
the forger of all instruments of bronze and iron); why they are skilled
in training performing animals and horses; why they are expert
fortune-tellers; and how they came by the Letters Patent, granted by
various Christian princes to the Gypsies when they first appeared in

central and western Europe in the fifteenth century. These last stories relate that, though formerly Christians, they abandoned their faith when attacked by the Saracens; and on being liberated and reconverted they were obliged by the Pope to roam the earth for seven years by way of penance. To protect them they were given letters requiring every bishop and abbot to give them alms. These tales served to validate their origins and to authenticate the documents they produced in the course of their migrations.

Further legends sanction stealing as a Gypsy occupation:

> Christ sent St Peter to find a sheep and cook it while He was healing a sick person, who rewarded Him richly. Peter began by eating the sheep's liver and kidneys. When Christ came back He asked where the liver and kidneys were. Peter said the sheep had none. At the end of the meal Christ divided the money He had been given into three heaps, one for Peter, one for Himself, and one for the man who ate the kidneys. Peter claimed that share; and Christ gave Peter His share also, and so took His cross. So it was that God Jesus founded all the estates of men — doctors, for He healed for money, Gypsies whom He taught to beg and go barefoot, while St Peter taught them how to deceive their like.[4]

THE SUPERNATURAL

In their dealings with the non-Gypsy world, Gypsies have always relied on mystery and magic. Sometimes this is overt, as in palmistry or in fortune-telling with globes or Tarot cards. Sometimes it is more subtle. When selling, bargaining or begging, it is part of the Gypsy's stock-in-trade to build up an atmosphere of mystery, often tinged with apprehension and fear; and so it is not surprising that Gypsies have many legends about supernatural figures and events, and that they often believe in the truth of these tales themselves.

Between 1914 and the mid-1920s an English collector, T. W. Thompson, recorded a large number of such stories from Gypsies travelling in the north of England. Some of these legends apparently had a specific function in the socialization of children and young people:

> You know that old Reni [...or Boswell...or Lovell]. The Devil once came after a boy of hers. He'd been shaking his sister and pulling her about — a bit roughly perhaps, but only in fun. She told him to clear off, but he wouldn't. There was a small hole by the fire, in which the kettle prop had been stuck. A little man came out of this hole — and it was the Devil come to this boy. He was frightened to death, and ran up into the wagon, where

his mother was. He went down on his bended knees and asked her to forgive him what he had done to his sister. She told him to get up and not to be so silly: he hadn't harmed her; it was only a bit of fun. He said the Devil had come after him for it, and begged and prayed so pitifully that she said of course she would forgive him. He swore he'd never lay a finger on his sister again, not even in fun. It was a near shave for him.

According to another of Thompson's informants:

There were some Gypsies who used to be round Altrincham way mostly, and there was one girl who was very very brazen. She got so bad that the Devil came and threw her into a great thick thorn hedge. She was screaming there, and her father and mother had to go and get her out. She said it was the Devil had done it. They put her in bed in the wagon, but the Devil came to her there and took her and threw her in the hedge again. This he continued to do until she mended her ways. It cured her of her brazenness, and she was one of the brazenest girls in the country.

Another tale of the Devil recounts that a woman at Stockton was crossing a bridge one day when a fine gentleman in a black suit, complete with starched shirt, top hat and gold watch-chain, stopped her and gave her as much gold as she could carry in her apron. He said he would be there next day and would give her as much again, or more. The woman told her neighbour, whereupon all the money vanished away. 'The man wasn't there next day. It was the Devil 'ticing her on.'

The Devil also appeared to the legendary character Wry-Necked Charley Lovell, the fiddler. One day he found a tall gentleman, dressed in black broadcloth, at his tent door. The stranger asked him to play the fiddle at a dance he was giving the following evening, and paid him with two handfuls of silver coins. Charley tossed and turned all night, wondering who the stranger could be. Next morning he consulted a priest, who said Charley had made a bargain with the Devil. His only hope of salvation was to play nothing but psalm tunes. This Charley duly did, and when he refused to play more lively music for the Devil and his guests, the Devil struck Charley a smart blow on the cheek, twisting his head permanently to one side. After that, he was always known as Wry-Necked Charley.[5]

Amongst Gypsy ghost legends there is a curious tale about a ghost which haunted a Yorkshire miner who married a Gypsy:

At Mexborough George Nelson lived — him as married Ardadé Heron. He worked there as a collier. Every night when he came from work (it was in winter-time) the ghost of a young lady met him at a certain stile, and walked along with him. He tried to get into conversation with her, but never a word could he get out of her. Still every night she was there to meet him. There was a pub nearby which this footpath ran. George was in there one night, and mentioned about the ghost. The landlord said it would be Miss So-and-So; he mentioned her name; she was a Mexborough young lady who lived near the pub, and she had been murdered. Soon after they went out with a gun and shot at her. She never came to accompany George home after that.

This method of laying a ghost was certainly less conventional than that adopted by another of Thompson's informants, who helped his son Bosko to lay a ghost with Bible and candle. 'We got it up into a corner of the field ... [by] a refuse heap ... we kept on, and read away at the bible, and heard a noise like bottles breaking. At last the ghost disappeared. It turned out later that it was one of Bosko's old sweethearts — a theatrical — who had been murdered there. She was a Blackburn woman.'

Other legends involve donkeys which see the ghosts of other donkeys, ghostly dogs, and haunted houses, while the Gypsy repertoire also shares with Irish and Scottish folklore tales about encounters with fairies, fairy changelings substituted for Gypsy babies, and the hearing of fairy music, 'some very curious tunes right atween the tents ... Just like a lot of fiddles it was, a long way off, but wonderful clear and sweetsome ...'[6]

HAPPY BOSWELL

Finally, there is a cycle of tales about the legendary hero known to English Gypsies as Happy Boswell, an insouciant Romany equivalent of Paul Bunyan, with his monkey, donkey and dog:

Onest upon a time there was a Romano, and his name was Happy Boz'll, and he had a German-silver grinding-barrow, and he used to put his wife and child on the top, and he used to go that quick along the road he'd beat all the coaches. Then he thought this grinding-barrow was too heavy and clumsy to take about, and he cut it up and made tent-rods out of it. And then his dickey (donkey) got away, and he didn't know where it was gone to; and one day he was going by the tent, and he said to himself, 'Bless my soul, wherever's that dickey got to?' And there was a tree close by, and the dickey shouted out and said, 'I'm here, my Happy, getting you a bit of stick to make a fire.' Well, the donkey come down with a lot of sticks, and he had been up the tree a week, getting firewood. Well then, Happy had a dog, and he went out one day; the dog hid one side the hedge, and him the other. And then he saw two hares. The dog ran after the two; and as he was going across the field, he cut himself right through with a scythe; and then one half ran after one hare, and the other after the other. Then the two halves of the dog catched the two hares; and then the dog smacked together again; and he said, 'Well, I've got'em, my Happy'; and then the dog died. And Happy had a hole in the knee of his breeches, and he cut a piece of the dog's skin, after it was dead, and sewed it in the knee of his breeches. And that day twelve months his breeches-knee burst open, and barked at him.[7]

T. W. Thompson, who collected many legends about Happy Boswell, was told that Happy was married to a Gypsy but used always to swear that he came from a very respectable non-Gypsy family. He had been apprenticed as a knife-grinder in Sheffield before he ran away, was shipwrecked, lived at the bottom of the sea for seven days, floated to an island where he made friends with the monkeys, and brought one of the monkeys along with him on the rest of his adventures. And he would declare that 'the monkey could swear to it all'. As an epitome of Gypsy mystification in its lighter mood, you need look no further than the legends of Happy Boswell and his monkey.

AFRICA AND
THE AMERICAS

The snake-eating eagle of Middle America (page 338)

CHAPTER 35
AFRICA

More than half the land-mass of Africa, from the Sahel zone and the
Lake Rudolf plains southward to the Cape, constitutes what is known
as the Sub-Saharan African Major Cultural Region. Within this huge
area, although there are some striking contrasts of terrain, the major
region is marked by a cultural unity which sets it apart from other
areas of the world. At the same time, the culture is not absolutely
homogeneous but, in the recent past at least, was sufficiently
diversified to allow a number of cultural regions within the major
region to be recognized. One characteristic which all these regions
shared was the late arrival of writing, when compared to North Africa
and the Near East. It is true that in the Sahel zone and in the cities
along the East African coast the Arabic script has been used by
literate members of the upper classes for a thousand years, and
probably more, but even that time-span is short compared to Egypt
and Mesopotamia, and over most of the major region writing was
only introduced in the nineteenth or twentieth centuries. As a result,
most of the stories which have been collected in the area come not
from written documents but from the mouths of story-tellers, who
have themselves received the stories from other narrators.

One consequence of the recent arrival of writing is that there is
a marked lack of the chronicles of past events which people in
Europe, the Near East and the Far East tend to take for granted. For
example, if we want to know what was happening in western Europe
or in the north of China during the tenth century, then we can find
a detailed description which may be misleading but is nonetheless rich
in incident. If we ask the same question about the Congo Basin, we
are left with no answer at all, except that the people there must have
been already somewhat like the modern people of the area. The
books on African peoples are therefore usually filled with abundant

The death of Chaka (page 319)

facts about recent or contemporary practices, but they are poor in details for the periods before 1850. There are certainly some accounts of what happened before that time, which have been remembered by particular individuals who were interested in the events of the past; they include the names of kings, famous battles, famines and migrations of groups of people. But these traditions add up to a very small total of facts, or alleged facts, compared to the details in written records from some other major regions.

When looking at the written accounts and the oral traditions it is clear that much more has been forgotten, and therefore lost, in the oral versions than in those which have been written. However, the written versions of past events are not infallible. Are they even at all reliable? Writers, like narrators, can forget. They can also be ignorant, stupid, ill-informed, uncritical and partisan. A clear distinction is often drawn between two mutually exclusive categories, myth and history, but it is more realistic to regard all stories of the past as myths, from which it may be possible to extract some events which could possibly have taken place. History is a specialized branch of mythology, and the term legend can be used to mean those critical areas where extracting events from myths is especially difficult.

THE GREAT THEMES

All over the world people tell stories which contain the same basic themes, and these themes can be reduced to two pairs of opposites; a perfect original order, corrupted to the present pitiful conditions; and the contrast between success and failure in the efforts of the hero. Writers and story-tellers alike are drawn by these great themes, which are apparently innate in all of us, to fit the details of events into the mythic patterns. They moralize about good and bad, they identify heroes and build the story around them. Their narratives rapidly become stories of heroes against villains.

Events which actually occurred are most likely to be incorporated into myths when they are heroic. All over the world there are stories of younger brothers, orphans or other insignificant people who overcome all obstacles and triumph against odds, and it is often difficult or impossible to tell whether a particular hero was really under-privileged in some way, or whether he has been credited by later narrators with a childhood of the type appropriate to a hero.

Since stories about heroes are remarkably similar in all parts of the world, it is not surprising that the narratives from different areas of Africa are very like each other. A selection of examples will demonstrate some of the important elements in the stories.

One of the distinctive features of Africa south of the Sahara, at the time when European travellers came into contact with its different regions, was a mosaic of areas where kings ruled over states of varying sizes intermixed with others where there were no states and no kings, and where people lived in small autonomous communities without formal governments. Not surprisingly, the heroes of many stories in areas with traditions of kings were themselves kings, though royal heroes also occurred in kingless regions, and the other way round.

At the western end of the great northern savanna, just south of the Sahara, is a distinctive region which includes the Futa Jalon highlands, the basin of the Senegal River and the upper stretches of the River Niger. Most of the landscape is grassland, parkland or dry woodland and, like the rest of the northern savanna, the area has been exposed for centuries to invasion and migration from the Sahara. Among the results have been the introduction of Islam and of the Arabic script, as well as the stimulation of military ambition among the kings of the area. From time to time there have been particularly far-flung attempts at empire-building, as in the cases of Ghana and Mali (not to be confused with the modern states named Ghana and Mali after these famous empires of the past). Another effect of the contacts with the Sahara has been the formation of castes of blacksmiths, leatherworkers and *griots,* a French word applied to musicians and entertainers who specialized in memorizing the ancestry and exploits of kings, and in reciting heroic narratives, to a musical accompaniment. In the eyes of many of the local people, the most famous items in the *griots'* repertoire are versions of an epic about a King, or Emperor, called Sunjata, who is said to have established the major state of Mali (or Mandinga), which was flourishing in the fourteenth century.

THE SUNJATA EPIC

Sunjata, say the *griots,* was the son of a King, but he was an unprepossessing and crippled child, who suffered from the envy and hatred of his mother's co-wives and of his half-brothers. So he went into exile, and from there returned to become the King of the world, a conqueror like Alexander. Apart from the sufferings of his childhood and youth, the dramatic tension of the story centres on his struggle with the evil empire-builder Sumanguru (or a similar form of the same name), whose vast military power is based upon his knowledge of incantations and medicines. He is a mighty violator of virgins, who flogs venerable old men for the pleasure of it, and wears shoes made of human skin. He is the epitome of all evil, the Devil's lieutenant on earth and the enemy of Islam, whose champion, we can all guess, is − Sunjata. Sunjata wins, but only after his sister has volunteered to wheedle out of Sumanguru the secret of his power, an incident here described in a version from the Mandinka people of the Gambia River area:

His sister changed into a chameleon;
When you looked at her,
If you blinked she would assume another shape.
She addressed Sumanguru and he answered;
She said to him, 'The fighting has dragged on for a long time;
I was looking for a way, but I did not find a way;
I have come to you.'
Sumanguru said, 'Let no one enter my house
Except this woman.'
He sent away all his wives.
They lay down till night fell,
Then he said to her, 'What has brought you here?'
She said, 'I have come;
All the fighting that you have seen between yourself and
Manding [is because] they wanted to give me to Faa Koli
And I refused him.
I said that I wanted to marry you;
That is the cause of the hostility between you and Manding.
I have not come *fui kang* [for no purpose].
I have come to tell you the secrets of Manding,
I have come to help you with the war against Manding
And to destroy Manding so that you might marry me.'
He said, 'Very well,
You find me ready for that,
But since God created me,
I have never before seen a woman like you.'
He wanted to do some trader's business with her [a ribald
euphemism for copulation],
And was about to turn over onto her,
But she said, 'No! You must not behave like that!
Before two freeborn people form an intimate relationship with
                    each other,
They must tell each other their taboos;
You must tell me what can injure you,
You must tell me what can strengthen you;
I shall keep clear of whatever can injure you,
I will do whatever will strengthen you;
I will tell you what can damage Manding,
And I will tell you what can strengthen it.
But that I should just come like this,
Without our saying anything, without our knowing each other's
                    secrets,
That I should come and give myself to you –
That is not possible.'
Sumanguru said, 'Woman, you have spoken true,
But I, Sumanguru...'

She said, 'Yes?'
'I have a gnome
With a hundred heads.
If anyone is to shoot those hundred heads,
If he is to shoot them,
The arrow which will shoot them,
An arrow without an arrowhead –
When you have made that arrow,
You must bury it inside the town
For forty-one days,
And everyone, man and woman, child and adult,
All must pass their first water of the morning
Upon that arrow,
Upon those hundred arrows;
It will then become poisonous.[1]

This incident recalls the account of Samson and Delilah in the Bible, with the important difference that Samson is the hero and Sumanguru the villain. Both stories are examples of the devious wiles of women, a theme found all over the world.

The Sunjata epic has various forms. Somebody must have established the Empire of Mali and he may well have been called Sunjata, but we know extremely little, if anything, about him. He could well have been a Muslim, as the modern *griots* assert he was, but that must remain equally uncertain. It is clear, however, that empire-building is old on the savanna.

THE PRAYER OF MODIBBO ADAMA

Further east along the northern savanna, and astride the borders of the modern states of Nigeria and Cameroun, is the area called Adamawa. The landscape here is not unlike that of the Senegal-Niger region, with parkland and some areas of hills. Until the early nineteenth century most of the people of the area seem to have lived in autonomous villages without kings, or else in very small kingdoms, not much different from their stateless neighbours. At that time, however, the Fulbe (Fulani) pastoralists and townspeople of the area became involved in a *jihad,* or Muslim righteous war, proclaimed further west by Usmanu dan Fodio, and they proceeded to establish a Kingdom incorporating the whole area, and itself part of the greater Fulbe Empire which was coming into being.

The leader of these local Fulbe, and to whom Usmanu gave the position of King, was Modibbo Adama, who reigned from 1809 to 1848, and after whom the whole territory of the Kingdom came to be called Adamawa. In the early decades of this century stories were still being told about him in the area:

Modibbo Adama set out to fight against Mandara, he assembled his warriors, and they went forward till they reached Pette, and there encamped. He sent to the Chief of Mandara, and ordered him to submit. The Chief of Mandara replied to him in friendly terms, and sent him a female slave as a concubine, together with some presents. He left Pette, and went and encamped at Pata. He sent and commanded them to come to him, but they refused. He sent back a second time, but they would not consent to come. Then he went out to attack them. When they met the Mandara he drove them back till he reached their city and attacked it; he drove them out, and they fled and left their town. He stayed in the city of Mandara with all his people. And they, on account of the wealth which they found there, could think of nothing else. At the times of prayer they did not go to the place of worship, and Modibbo would go alone. Then he prayed, 'If it is thus my people are, may God give the owners of these houses back their homes!' Thereupon the people of Mandara came back and fell upon them in the town, and drove them out.

Then the men of Mandara pursued Modibbo through the day, and up to the time of afternoon prayer they had not given up the pursuit. When Lauwal saw that it was the time of prayer, he dismounted from his horse, drew in the girths till the rings met, put his foot in the stirrup, and mounted, telling them to tell Modibbo to dismount and pray, for it was the time of afternoon prayers. With this he turned on the Mandara, his younger brother Ba-Hamidu followed him, and they drove off the Mandara. Modibbo had dismounted, finished the afternoon prayers, mounted, and started on again, before they finally returned and joined the moving column. When Mallam Hamidu turned back upon the Mandara he forgot to take off the sheath of his spear, and fought thus with it in its cover, until it tore right through it without his noticing. It was not until he came back and joined the people that they called his attention to it. Thereupon some said it was because he was afraid; had he not been afraid it would not have happened. When he heard this he was greatly displeased. From that time he never again fought with a spear, or any weapon at all except a stick. However fierce the battle a stick was all he considered necessary.[2]

There is not much room for doubt that Adama existed, and that he was involved in an empire-building exercise which was designed to assert the authority of Islam, and of Fulbe rulers, in that part of the savanna, but there is no guarantee that the stories told about him some generations later were accurate. One feature of the Adamawa narratives about Adama and his descendants and successors is the number of times that their expeditions and campaigns are said to have failed, as in the attack on Mandara. We might expect people to forget or play down their defeats, but the Adamawa Fulbe clearly have not, perhaps because they see in them the judgments of Almighty God.

THE DEATH OF ILELE

To the south of the savanna in Central Africa lies the great mass of the Wet Forest. Most of the peoples of this region have no traditions of states or kings, but live in autonomous villages, each in its own clearing in the forest. Among these peoples are the Nkundo who, at least until recently, recited an epic about the family of Lonkundo, whom they regard as the founder of the entire Nkundo people. Lonkundo and his descendants are not necessarily kings, although the Nkundo know about kings, but their genealogical saga rather resembles the narrative of Abraham, Isaac and Jacob in the Book of Genesis. The members of the Lonkundo family, however, are not mere mortals. One of them, Ilele, is Death, who at one stage in the story is killed, although Death later reappears in the world:

> One evening Ilele told his wives: 'This night my death will come flying over the house, it will be dropped in the yard. Nobody is allowed out at any time.'
>
> They all obeyed except the pregnant Mbombe, who felt that she must have some fresh air, so she went out of her hut and walked about in the yard in the middle of the night. At moment a hornbill came flying over with a *sau*-fruit in his bill. Mbombe fell in love with the bird and called it. The hornbill dropped the *sau*, which fell on the yard. Mbombe picked it up and tasted it. It was delicious − sour-sweet − and she ate it all. From that moment she craved *sau*-fruits and refused any other food. She cried day and night until Ilele gave in and started out in search of the *sau*-tree.
>
> Ilele took his bell, raised it towards the east and towards the west. When it was pointed at the western sky the bell began to ring. Ilele started out in a westerly direction until he found the *sau*-tree. At its foot he found a beggar sitting, with scabby sores all over his body; his name was Fetefete. The beggar refused to go away unless Ilele promised to throw him a fruit. Ilele climbed the tree and threw a fruit down which hit Fetefete on his sores. Fetefete was angry and began to yell: 'Master of the Fruits, someone is stealing, Sausau, someone knocked my sores open.' Sausau, the owner of the tree, heard it, and sent his servants, who were all birds, to go and chase the thief away. They arrived near the tree in great swarms and attacked Ilele, but he

succeeded in hitting each of them with a *sau*-fruit. He jumped out of the tree with two baskets full of fruit, which he brought to his wife. He gave her one of the baskets, and she ate all the fruit at one go. Then she started crying until he gave her the other basket. When that was finished they went to bed.

The next morning she began again, crying on and on. Ilele told his wife: 'Do you realize that it I go in search of those fruits today, I shall die there and never come back?'

She retorted: 'And if I do not get more of those fruits, I will have a miscarriage!' Ilele gave in, for she had his first-born in her womb. He told her: 'When my horn that hangs on the wall there begins to bleed, I shall be dead. My snare-string will turn into a snake, the monkeys will come and cry in the yard, the elephants will come out of the forest into the open, and the sky will rain.'

The next part of the story tells how Ilele left his house knowing he would never come back. He arrived at the tree, climbed it, and threw down the fruit which the beggar demanded. Fetefete yelled when it hit his sores and began singing his magic evocation of the Master of the Fruits. Sausau called together all his birds and asked them if anyone knew a device to catch Ilele:

The humming-bird said: 'What will you give me if I tell you?' It got three rings as a present and said: 'Ask the caterpillar-bird.' The caterpillar-bird was called, received a thousand rings and said: 'If Ilele loses his magic bell he will die.'

The birds flew together to the *sau*-tree, with their nets. The pheasant climbed the tree, slowly, slowly. Suddenly it struck Ilele in the eyes with its wings. Ilele dropped his bell and fell out of the tree. The tortoise caught him in his net. All the birds beat Ilele until he died.

In his hut, blood leaked from his horn. Monkeys appeared in the trees and cried loudly. Elephants emerged from the forest and walked up to the village. Many wild animals called at the house of the dead Ilele and wailed loudly. The sky started pouring sheets of rain and it grew pitch-dark. The women understood, unbound their hair and began to lament.

Mbombe, alone of all living creatures, refused to cry, for at that moment her labour began.[3]

In this part of the epic the devastating power of women is illustrated, not through their wheedling but because of their pregnancy whims, a feature on which the Wet Forest peoples place great emphasis. (There are no humming-birds in Africa and the bird in the story must be a sunbird. Neither are there pheasants in the Wet Forest — the bird which climbs the tree is probably a coucal.)

THE BIRTH OF MWINDO

Well to the east of the Nkundo, but still in the forest, live the Nyanga. They are in the foothills which approach the East African Plateau, and they have had long and strong contacts with the peoples of that area. As a result, they used to be divided into several small states, each ruled by a king with the title *mwami*. Like the Nkundo, the Nyanga had an epic, this one about a hero who in most versions is called Mwindo, although there is a version where Mwindo is the troublesome half-brother of the hero. Mwindo suffers the usual inauspicious yet miraculous birth of heroes. His father, a *mwami*, does not want boy children, only girls. One interpretation which Nyanga gives for this choice is that he was a greedy man, who did not want to pay out goods as bride-wealth for his sons, but did want to garner the bride-wealth which came in when his daughters married. In pursuit of his ambition the king forbids his wives to give birth to sons:

> When many days had passed that his wives had remained pregnant, one day six of his wives pulled through; they gave birth merely to female children. One among them, the preferred-one, remained dragging herself along because of her pregnancy. When the preferred-one realized that her compan-ions had already given birth, and that she remained with her pregnancy, she kept on complaining: 'How terrible this is! It is only I who am persecuted by this pregnancy. What then shall I do? My companions, together with whom I carried the pregnancy at the same time, have already pulled through, and it is I who remain with it. What will come out of this pregnancy?' After she had finished making these sad reflections, reawaken-ing from her thoughts, at the door then there was already a bunch of firewood; she did not know from where it had come; lo! it was her child, the one that was inside the womb, who had just brought it. After some time had passed, looking around in the house, there was already a jar of water; she did not know whence it had come; all by itself it had brought itself into the house. After some time had passed, raw *isusa*-vegetables also arrived there at the house. When the preferred-one saw it, she was much astonished; lo! it was the child in her womb who was performing all those wonderful things.
>
> When the inhabitants of the village saw that the preferred-one continued to drag on with her pregnancy in her house, they got used to sneering at her: 'When will this one also give birth?' Where the child was dwelling in the womb of its mother, it meditated to itself in the womb, saying that it could not come out from the underpart of the body of its mother, so that they

might not make fun of it saying that it was the child of a woman; neither did it want to come out from the mouth of its mother, so that they might not make fun of it saying that it had been vomited like a bat. [Many Nyanga maintain that young bats are born from their mothers' mouths.]

When the pregnancy had already begun to be bitter, old midwives, wives of the counsellors, arrived there; they arrived there when the preferred-one was already being troubled with the pains of the pregnancy. Where the child was dwelling in the womb, it climbed up in the belly, it descended the limb, and it went and came out through the medius (the middle finger). The old midwives, seeing him wailing on the ground, were astonished, saying: 'It's terrible; is the child now replacing its mother?' When they saw him on the ground, they pointed at him asking: 'What kind of child is it?' Some among the old midwives answered: 'It's a male child.' Some of the old midwives said that they should shout in the village place that a male child was born. Some refused, saying that no one should shout that it was a boy who had just been born, because when Shemwindo [the King, the name means father of Mwindo] heard that a boy had been born, he would kill him. Where the counsellors were sitting together with Shemwindo, they shouted, asking: 'What child is born there?' The old midwives who were sitting in the house kept silent, without giving an answer. After the birth of the child, the midwives gave him the name Mwindo, because he was the first male child who followed only female children in their order of birth.[4]

Like some other heroes, Mwindo is not born by any route so mundane as a woman's reproductive tract, but the amazing birth does not impress his father, who tries persistently to kill him — unsuccessfully, of course. Mwindo then pursues his father, and eventually catches him, but instead of punishing him for his wickedness he partitions the Kingdom with him.

AMAS AND MBEGA

Above the Nyanga, on the East African Plateau itself, there is a considerable variety of landscapes and three distinct cultural regions, plus a little of another in the far north. Among the traditionally stateless peoples of the area are the Sandawe, who live in dry woodland in the centre of Tanzania. They used to live in small autonomous settlements scattered through the woodland, and, like other kingless peoples, recognized war-leaders who were successful enough to command a following. Some of these war-leaders gained a great enough reputation to gather followers from more than one settlement, and in the second half of the nineteenth century one such war-leader rose to unusual prominence. He was Amas, a member of the Alagwa clan, which already had a great reputation for the successful performance of a ritual which begged God to send rain. In the 1930s some Sandawe still remembered Amas as the hero who had built a huge barricade of thorn-branches around part of Sandawe country in order to keep out the raiding Datoga from the north, and who seized so many of their cattle that he forced the Datoga to swear three times not to raid Sandawe settlements. Amas also successfully repulsed Baraguyu raiding from the south, and expelled the traders from the coast who were capturing slaves in Sandawe country. When the German administrators established themselves in Sandawe, around the turn of the century, some of Amas' descendants persuaded them to recognize their branch of the Alagwa clan as the royal family of all the Sandawe.

There can be little doubt that Amas existed, and it is possible to see in the conditions of the nineteenth century the opportunities which made him so prominent. Coastal traders were expanding their slaving and ivory-collecting far into the interior, and the disturbances and wealth of the new age probably encouraged both Datoga and Baraguyu to raid more ambitiously than hitherto. A vigorous response to these challenges apparently established Amas' reputation, but there is again no guarantee that the details remembered in this century are correct.

While the Sandawe were suffering the raids of Amas' time, the Shambaa, living on wet highlands to the north-east, had already been united in a single kingdom. The rulers of this state claimed to be descended from a hunter and blacksmith called Mbega, who had arrived in the hills from the country of the Zigula people. Judging from the number of generations recorded in the oral tradition of the royal family in the period 1870−1900, Mbega's arrival in Shambaa country was probably in the eighteenth century, although such estimates from memorized King-lists are hazardous and it is impossible to be sure that events recounted actually occurred.

CHAKA: A ZULU FAUST

Sandawe and Shambaa alike were involved in the great increase in commerce which took place in East Africa during the nineteenth century, and also in the raiding and other disturbances associated with trade. In the south-east of Africa, too, the nineteenth century was a period of dramatic change. The increase in commerce was important in this region also, and here there was the complication of the expanding Afrikaner frontier. Possibly in response to the growing threat, in the early decades of the nineteenth century the King of a minor state among the Nguni-speaking peoples built up a large and

militarily powerful Kingdom by conquering and incorporating
a series of the existing small states. In this well-watered and wooded
country below the Drakensberg escarpment the new state, named
Zulu, was apparently a radical innovation in terms of sheer size,
because the region does not seem to have had the tradition of
empire-building familiar in other parts of Africa, for instance the
northern savanna. However, although the new 'super-king' who was
called Chaka or Shaka is as well authenticated as his contemporary,
Napoleon, the traditions about him which were current after his death
(in 1828) are probably unreliable, and certainly do not all agree with
each other.

It was on the basis of these traditions, both those recited in the new
state and those known beyond its borders, that Thomas Mofolo,
a Soto author, wrote his vivid and dramatic novel *Chaka*. The Soto
people were among the victims of the Zulu expansion, and Mofolo
had no cause to admire Zulu in general or Chaka in particular. He
presents the King as a blood-crazed monster of evil, a sort of
Southern African Hitler. Chaka has the classic hero's childhood and
youth. He is inauspiciously born, conceived out of wedlock, and
driven into exile by his step-mothers and half-brothers (remember
Sunjata), but he makes a triumphant return to become King in his
father's place. Mofolo presents this monster-hero as a Southern
African equivalent of Faust in Europe. Faust sells himself to the Devil
in return for knowledge and power; Chaka agrees with a very
powerful diviner that in return for the greatest power any king in his
part of the world has ever had, he will pay whatever price the diviner
asks. At the end of the novel the diviner, Isanusi, comes to claim his
price:

> Dingana perceived that Chaka was still in a trance and then
> Mopo signed to him by winking with his eye to approach, for
> their hour had come. He looked round at Mhlangana and he
> also approached. Dingana approached Chaka and made as
> though to admire the feathers. Then suddenly he struck him
> and the spear sank in and came out the other side. Mhlangana
> also struck him from behind and the spear came out in front:
> Mopo's spear entered his side. Their three spears met in his
> body and at that very moment Isanusi came to Chaka to
> demand his reward.
>
> When Chaka felt the spears enter his body he did not defend
> himself manfully as of old, but turned slowly round and awoke
> fom his trance and his mid-day visions. As soon as he turned, his
> pains subsided and his features regained their former state and
> Dingana and Mhlangana saw him as he had always been and
> fled in terror. And then Chaka said: 'It is your hope that by
> killing me ye will become chiefs when I am dead. But ye are

deluded; it will not be so, for Umlungu will come and it is he
who will rule, and ye will be his bondmen.'[5]

As Dingana (or Dingane) and Mhlangana (who were Chaka's
half-brothers) kill him, Chaka predicts that they will not enjoy the
Zulu Kingdom, for the Europeans − Umlungu − will come and rule
them. Mofolo writes with the wisdom of hindsight, but it is true that in
1836 the most determined of the Afrikaner frontiersmen, in order to
get out from under the jackboots of British liberalism, crossed the
Orange River in their wagons, and began one of the major legends of
Southern Africa, the Great Trek. One party of pioneers reached the
borders of the Zulu kingdom, and Dingana, now King, apparently
panicked, and ordered some of his troops to kill them. He thereby
brought down upon himself the disaster which he feared, and in
retaliation for the killings Andries Pretorius led a commando of
Afrikaners to engage the Zulu army in battle. The two forces met on
16 December 1838, and the Afrikaners shattered the Zulu, at a place
henceforth known as Blood River. Pretorius himself has joined the
ranks of the heroes. There is a city named after him, and the
anniversary of Blood River became a national holiday in South
Africa. The processes of myth which operate inside people continue
to mould the remembered versions of events.

CHAPTER 36
NORTH AMERICAN INDIAN LEGENDS

The Native Americans are famous for their legends, and almost every lake, river and mountain has its associated tale. Most ceremonies, too, have their origin legends. Unlike myths, these legends are set in the not-too-distant past and often are based upon historical people and events. Though frequently containing miraculous occurrences which do not stand up to modern scientific scrutiny they were, and still are, accepted by most of those who tell them as valid explanations of how certain things came to be. The number of North American Indian legends is myriad and only a small sample can be given here, concentrating on those which explain the origins of important cultural phenomena and those with an interesting plot development or content. A regional balance has been attempted, to give an idea of the enormous cultural variety in aboriginal North America.

THE LEAGUE OF THE IROQUOIS

One of the most remarkable political developments in North America took place among the Iroquois tribes of the Eastern Woodlands, perhaps about AD 1500. This was the formation of the League of the Iroquois, composed of five tribes who lived in what is now upstate New York and small portions of Vermont and Quebec. From east to west these tribes were the Mohawk, Oneida, Onondaga, Cayuga and Seneca. In 1722 the Tuscarora, a southeastern tribe, joined them and the League became known as the Six Nations. The League was pivotal in the English–French conflict for control of eastern North America, and had it not supported the English in the Colonial Wars it is entirely possible that French, rather than English,

Ponca scout and the buffalo (page 324)

would be the prevalent tongue in North America today. It is also said that the model of the League, an association of independent yet mutually allied tribes, was adopted by those who framed the United States constitution. The League was the brain-child, not of a member of one of the tribes which joined to form it, but of a Huron Indian, a member of a group which, though speaking an Iroquoian tongue, never joined the League and in fact remained its bitter enemy until it was finally broken and scattered by the League's military power.

According to the legend, north of the Beautiful Lake (Ontario) in the land of the Crooked Tongues (Huron or Wyandot) an unusual man was born to a virgin mother. His mother was told in a dream that her son was to be a great man, and that he should be named Dekanawideh. When he grew to manhood he was handsome and had a keen mind. Nevertheless his people did not understand him. He was always honest and told what he believed was right. He was considered peculiar, and was abused by his people because he did not consider war the greatest of all things in this life.

Dekanawideh therefore crossed the lake in a canoe and came to the territory of the Flint Nation (Mohawk). A Mohawk warrior spied him quietly smoking and meditating at the base of a tall tree, and reported his arrival in the village. The chiefs and headmen went out to question him. To this delegation Dekanawideh gave his message: 'The Creator from whom we are all descended sent me to establish the Great Peace among you. No longer shall you kill one another and nations shall cease warring. Such things are entirely evil and He, your maker, forbids it. Peace and comfort are better than war and misery for a nation's welfare.'

The Mohawk agreed with the counsel of Dekanawideh, for they were sick of war. They were willing to proceed with his plan for a league of peace, but told him that they could not do it alone. The large and powerful People of the Hill (Onondaga) must be convinced before any such league could become a reality. Furthermore, the Onondaga were dominated by a vain and powerful sorcerer-chief named Tadodaho. His body was distorted by seven crooks and his long tangled locks were adorned with writhing serpents. He customarily dined on raw flesh, including that of humans. He was a powerful wizard, who could kill men with his magic but could not be destroyed. Notwithstanding his evil character, the Onondaga obeyed him, though it cost them many lives to satisfy his insane whims.

Now, among the Onondaga there was a certain chief who had ideas similar to those of Dekanawideh. He and some of his friends had tried many times to clear the mind of Tadodaho and straighten his crooked body, but to no avail. This man's original name is now lost, but later he came to be called Hayenwatha (Hiawatha in English). Hayenwatha had seven daughters whom he loved and in whom he took great pride. Now, one by one, these daughters mysteriously died, poisoned by sorcery. The grief of Hayenwatha was terrible, and he said, 'I shall cast myself away, and become a woodland wanderer.' He left his own tribe, the Onondaga, and took up residence in the Mohawk country, living in a longhouse in the woods. Like others in that terrible time, he killed and ate his fellow men.

Nonetheless, when Dekanawideh heard of this man, and of his earlier attempts to win over Tadodaho, he considered him a possible ally, and sought out his solitary dwelling. Approaching cautiously, Dekanawideh did not enter the longhouse by the door, but instead climbed the roof and peered in through the smoke-hole. Below, Hayenwatha was cooking a soup of human flesh in a huge earthen pot, stirring it from time to time with a carved paddle. It had not yet come to a boil. Gazing at the surface of the broth, Hayenwatha saw, reflected as in a mirror, the face of Dekanawideh looking down at him. At first he thought it was his own face reflected on the surface of his inky broth. 'What a handsome face!' he exclaimed, 'Can this be the face of a cannibal?' Then he realized it was not his own visage but that of someone looking through the smoke-hole above. The realization stunned him, and somehow brought him to himself: 'Whatever grief I have suffered from evil men, I too shall follow the White Path like the stranger with the benign countenance!'

He summoned Dekanawideh to descend, saying he would come to no harm, and made him welcome. Dekanawideh, for his part, presented Hayenwatha with five beautiful strings of shells, saying, 'The grief you have suffered is terrible, but I give you these to clear your mind.' The two peace-makers now joined forces, and with the help of the Mohawk chiefs began to spread the doctrine of the Great Peace. At the end of five years they had won over the sachems (principal chiefs) of the Oneida, Cayuga and Seneca nations to their cause. The great majority of the Onondaga chiefs were also won over, but the vain and powerful Tadodaho remained unconvinced. Without his support the League could not become a reality.

Finally the two peace-makers used flattery where argument had failed. Tadodaho was informed that he would become the supreme sachem over all the League, and that his tribal town, Onondaga, would be the capital of the new confederacy. Hearing this, Tadodaho softened, and at a great council, before the assembled chiefs, Hayenwatha straightened the kinks from the powerful shaman's body and combed the rattlesnakes from his hair. His name, Hayenwatha, derives from this deed, and means 'Comber'. To this day the chief sachem of the League of the Iroquois carries the title Tadodaho, giving up his original name when he is raised to that office. Hayenwatha, too, remains as the title of one of the Mohawk sachems. Dekanawideh's name, however, is not perpetuated, for though it was he who conceived the idea of the Great Peace he was, after all, an outsider, a Huron.

THE HETHUSHKA OR WAR DANCE

The most colourful and exciting American Indian dance, and certainly the one which more than any other has captured the imagination of the Western world, is the War dance. With its spirited songs and colourful regalia, the dance has spread widely in both the United States and Canada during the past century, and is performed today by groups whose ancestors never knew it. It has even been adopted by non-Indian enthusiasts in the United States, in Britain, and on the Continent. Though performed as a secular 'show' dance since 1900, it derives from a semi-religious ceremonial performed by a Prairie—Plains warrior society called, in many tribes, the Hethushka. Debate rages as to which tribal group originated the dance, but anthropologists have narrowed its point of origin to the Prairie area, that part of North America where the Woodlands gradually give way to the largely treeless High Plains. Three Prairie tribes, Pawnee, Omaha and Ponca, all claim to have originated the dance. The following is the Ponca origin legend for the Hethushka as related by the late Joe Rush, a leading Ponca Indian singer in October 1972:

A Ponca scout was out searching for buffalo. Topping a rise, he spied a large herd. Keeping low, he observed them. One buffalo, he saw, was the chief. It was an old bull with curved horns. On its head, between its horns, was a downy eagle-plume, the symbol of high rank. This had been placed there by God. As the scout watched, a young bull approached the chief bull to challenge his leadership of the herd. He lunged at the chief bull, but the older animal neatly side-stepped. Then with his curved horns, the chief bull attacked. On his second lunge he got under the young bull and lifted him high in the air. As he fell he caught him on his horns and disembowelled him.

Although the Ponca scout thought himself unobserved, the chief bull had known he was watching the whole affair. Now the chief bull addressed the scout and informed him that his presence was known, and that he should approach. The bull spoke to the Ponca, saying: 'You have seen my power. Now I am going to give you something good to take back to your people.' He then taught him the Hethushka dance, telling him the rules which accompany its proper performance. The name of the dance, Hethuskha, means 'Curved horns' and refers to the curved horns of the chief buffalo bull. Originally there were four starting songs for the dance, all of them different from the one we use now. The chief buffalo taught these to the Ponca scout at that time. That is how we Ponca got the Hethushka dance, which has now been taken up by the Sioux, Winnebago and many other tribes.

THE PEYOTE RELIGION

Perhaps the most popular of existing Native American religions is Peyote. The peyote ceremony has attracted a great deal of attention because its ritual involves the ingestion of the hallucinogenic peyote cactus *(Lophophora williamsii),* which grows in the Rio Grande Valley and south into Old Mexico. As practised today, the peyote ceremony involves many elements borrowed from White Christianity, though basically it is a Mexican Indian complex modified by Southern Plains Indian groups such as the Comanche, Kiowa and Tonkawa. The following legend is the one which the Comanche tell explaining how they acquired the Peyote Way.

It was from the Karisu (the Carrizo, a now extinct Coahuiltecan tribe living in the northern Mexican state of Tamaulipas) that we acquired peyote in the beginning. They were enemies of our people. There was a Comanche war-leader who was so brave he went on raids by himself. On one occasion he went on a raid into Mexico with ten others. There was a fight with the Karisu and all this man's companions were killed. He struggled hard but finally they surrounded him and killed him and took all of his belongings. He was riding a pinto mule and they killed it too.

Some time after they had killed the young Comanche they held a peyote ceremony and brought everything that had been his inside the ceremonial lodge. It was all placed behind the leader on the ground and his bow was used as the sacred staff. When one is singing and shaking the gourd rattle in a peyote meeting, one often uses a bow, held in the left hand, for a staff.

While the meeting was going on, about midnight, they heard a sound outside the door, a groan. Then the young Comanche who had been killed lifted the flap. He held his hand on his forehead. One could see that he had been scalped. He groaned again and crawled into the tipi. The people near him were frightened and moved away from him towards the back of the tipi. But their leader said: 'All you people keep your seats and behave! He has come for some reason. Go back to your places!'

After the people were quieted the newcomer spoke up. 'You people do not understand peyote power. I, a Comanche, know its power. After you wore me down completely you stung me to death and took everything I had and I just came to tell you that is how it happened. Now I will tell you something more. You people smell the smoke. That is the smoke of Comanches coming to see you. They are coming to you. There are seven Comanches coming. It will be four days before they arrive here.

When these seven arrive, you are to have a peyote meeting. When you have the meeting I command you to give them my bow and this peyote. They shall take these things from you with them.'

One of the Karisu spoke up in good Comanche and answered him, 'Yes, we will do for your people what you request.' Then the young man told them he was ready to go. 'After I have taken seven steps from the door I will whoop four times. On the fourth yell I want you to sing.' With the fourth yell the leader shook his rattle and sang.

The Comanche visitors arrived in four days. A day or two later a tipi was put in order for the meeting and the Karisu and the Comanche went in together. The Karisu taught the Comanche the peyote ceremony and how to pray with cigarettes, and how to sing, and how to eat peyote. At the end of the meeting the Karisu leader said: 'Now you are to take this bow and peyote and the songs and go back home. From this time on all the tribes to the north and north-east will use this peyote.' This is the way peyote came to us.

A PUEBLO LEGEND

The Pueblo tribes of the Southwest inhabit a beautiful land of fantastic pastel-coloured buttes and great sweeping deserts. The atmosphere is usually clear and dry, permitting visibility over great distances. It is an enchanted land, but an arid and difficult one for farmers. Yet in this region developed one of the most advanced cultures north of Mexico.

Because of their adobe structures like apartment houses, grouped around central plazas, the Spanish named these desert farmers 'Pueblo' Indians. The above-ground pueblo was the characteristic domestic dwelling, but most religious ceremonies took place in semi-subterranean ceremonial chambers which the Spanish called *estufas* (ovens). The following tale of an *estufa* which miraculously sank into the earth during the height of a religious ceremony is reminiscent of European legends of sunken monasteries where, at certain magical moments, long-vanished bells toll and monks are heard chanting.

My children, long ago when I was a child like you at the Pueblo, my grandparents and even my parents used to tell me like this, that a long time ago, when at Picuris Pueblo they still used to carry on by native custom and do everything by ceremony, one spring the people were grinding flowers at Kuhppui. Even to this time you can see the place as you pass by, as it is sunken. Perhaps there may be some 250 people buried in that *estufa*.

Among those buried there are the men and women who were singing. The prettiest-looking of all were the *paiene* or 'grinders', whom they nowadays call *kwuhl'ene* or 'maidens'. But these girls ground flowers long ago in a ceremony and that is why they were so called. I suppose that all the people that were in there were dressed up nicely.

So that is the reason, my children, that the old men at the Pueblo still talk about it, that one might get rich with beads, ear-rings, and many other things that are buried there. You know that our palefaced brothers value ancient articles much. If I were to have my own way and were to be permitted at the Pueblo, I would get some of the palefaces to help me dig that place; I would gladly go to dig that *estufa*. That is all I have to say to you about that *estufa* at the Pueblo, for that is all I know. So put the impression in your head as I have told you, so that when these old people have passed away you can take their place and have this story to tell.

THE COMING OF THE WHITE MAN

Many charming legends recount the first meetings of Europeans and American Indians. Often these describe encounters which have not been recorded by White historians, but are so specific regarding details of the meetings that there is little doubt that they are based upon actual events. Through these accounts we can experience the wonder and incredulity of the first glimpse of European culture through Indian eyes. The following Chinook legend from the Pacific Northwest was recorded in 1894.

An old woman in a Clatsop village near the mouth of Big River mourned because of the death of her son. For a year she grieved. One day she ceased her wailing and took a walk along the beach where she had often gone in happier days.

As she returned to the village, she saw a strange something out in the water not far from shore. At first she thought it was a whale. When she came nearer, she saw two spruce trees standing upright on it. 'It is not a whale,' she said to herself. 'It is a monster.'

When she came near the strange thing that lay at the edge of the water, she saw that its outside was covered with copper and that ropes were tied to the spruce trees. Then a bear came out of the strange thing and stood on it. He looked like a bear, but his face was the face of a human being.

'Oh, my son is dead,' she wailed, 'and now the thing we have heard about is on our shore.' The old woman returned to her village, weeping and wailing. People hearing her called to each other, 'An old woman cries. Someone must have struck her.'

The men picked up their bows and arrows and rushed out to see what was the matter. 'Listen!' an old man said. They heard the old woman wailing, 'Oh, my son is dead, and the thing we have heard about is on our shore.' All the people ran to meet her. 'What is it? Where is it?' they asked. 'Ah, the thing we have heard about in tales is lying over there.' She pointed toward the south shore of the village. 'There are two bears on it, or maybe they are people.'

Then the Indians ran toward the thing that lay near the edge of the water. The two creatures on it held copper kettles in their hands. When the Clatsop arrived on the beach, the creatures put their hands to their mouths and asked for water. Two of the Indians ran inland, hid behind a log for a while, and then ran back to the beach. One of them climbed up on the strange thing, and entered it. He looked around inside it. He saw that it was full of boxes, and he found long strings of brass buttons.

When he went outside to call his relatives to see the inside of the thing, he found that they had already set fire to it. He jumped down and joined the two creatures and the Indians on shore. The strange thing burned just like fat. Everything burned except the iron, the copper and the brass. The Clatsop picked up all the pieces of metal. Then they took the two strange-looking men to their chief. 'I want to keep one of the men with me,' said the chief.

Soon the people north of the river heard about the strange men and the strange thing, and they came to the Clatsop village. The Willapa came from across the river, the Chehalis and the Cowlitz from farther north, and even the Quinault from up the coast. And the people from up the river came also — the Klickitat and others farther up.

The Clatsop sold the iron, brass and copper. They traded one nail for a good deerskin. For a long necklace of shells they gave several nails. One man traded a piece of brass two fingers wide for a slave. None of the Indians had ever seen iron and brass before. The Clatsop became rich selling the metals to other tribes. The two Clatsop chiefs kept the two men who came on the ship. One stayed at the village called Clatsop, and the other stayed at the village on the cape.

THE UNITED STATES OF AMERICA

Besides the legendary stories and heroes of the North American
Indians, the white population of the United States has produced its
own crop of legendary figures and, especially through films, the
names of some of them have become known far beyond the borders of
America — Davy Crockett, for example, Billy the Kid and Jesse
James. Mark Twain (1835–1910), the famous American writer, was
shopping in a small Missouri store when a friendly stranger accosted
him: 'You're Mark Twain, ain't you? Guess you and I are about the
greatest in our line.' Somewhat taken aback, the author of *Huckle-
berry Finn* asked who he was speaking to. The stranger stooped to
gather up his purchases and said proudly: 'I'm Jesse James.'

> Jesse James was one of his names
> Another it was Howard
> He robbed the rich of every stitch
> You bet he was no coward.

The classic American bandit is celebrated in ballads, stories, books,
newspapers, radio and television programmes, and films, and all
these have contributed to the growth of his legend. He operated with
his equally notorious brother Frank, but it is Jesse James, with his
melodious name, who is best remembered.

Bandits often choose their career to avenge themselves on society
for some real or imagined wrong. Their occupation flourishes during
periods of economic, political or administrative injustice, and it
sometimes becomes difficult to distinguish between a bandit and
a patriot. As legend has it, 'Jesse stole from the rich — gave to the
poor.'

Davy Crockett and the comet (page 335)

AMERICA'S ROBIN HOOD: JESSE JAMES

As a real figure, Jesse James (1847–82) was a product of the War Between the States, or Civil War, of the 1860s. Born in the border state of Missouri, he served as a guerrilla irregular in the Southern cause. After the War the James family, all Southern supporters, suffered for their allegiance. Missouri was overrun by Northern opportunists and the authorities treated ex-Confederate troops and guerrillas harshly. They were refused full amnesty, barred from professional careers, and put in prison on the slightest pretext. Young guerrillas harshly. They were refused full amnesty, barred from settle down and continued to harass the countryside. Robbery and murder were everyday occurrences. Banks — run by Northerners and suspected of bleeding the impoverished farmers — were unpopular and provided a ready target, as did the railways, which imposed punitive freight charges. A period of radical Republican rule after the Civil War inflamed the feelings of Missouri people, who had supported different sides in the conflict. Eastern contempt for the West and economic rivalry between Chicago and the cities of Missouri were other factors contributing to the legendary Jesse James.

The activities of the bandits acquired a political and locally patriotic significance. Many saw them as heroes of the Lost Cause, struggling against a tyrannical government. The journalist Major Edwards, who did so much to build up the legend, wrote of the James brothers in the Kansas City *Times*: 'Ever since the War closed and left them outlawed, they have borne themselves like men who have only to die and have determined to do it without flinching. For the last two or three years the whole country has rung with their daring and hardihood.'

Jesse James was declared an outlaw in 1866. The best-known story describes how his gang make a haul and stop at the house of a poor farmer's widow to ask for a meal. In some versions her late husband was an ex-Confederate. James discovers that she is hard-pressed by a merciless banker and gives her the money to pay off her mortgage. When the banker arrives to collect his dues, James waylays him and takes back the money he has just given away.

Tradition says he never robbed Confederates or preachers, though it has latterly been established that neither of these statements is correct. Indeed another legend describes in some detail how he stole a bishop's watch. When the prelate objected, James told him he did not need it — after all, Christ never owned one.

The legends idealize James' character. It is said that he was a good family man, never drank whiskey, taught in a Baptist singing school, and was unfailingly courteous. Scholars have found no evidence that he ever gave stolen money to the poor, but this legend has flourished, especially among poor whites and southern negroes, deprived social groups who, naturally enough, found the idea psychologically satisfying. Two events created sympathy for James. A bungled raid on the family home at midnight by some detectives resulted in an explosion which killed his young half-brother and ripped off their mother's hand. The manner of James' death — he was shot in the back by a former friend while dusting a picture — also aroused feelings of horror, for no one likes a traitor.

His mother kept her son's memory green. She opened his house to the public and charged admission. Pebbles from his grave — said by some to be from a nearby river — were sold for 25 cents. By the mid- 1930s his 2.4-metre (8-foot) marble churchyard memorial had been completely chipped away by souvenir hunters. 'A host of silly people,' observed the Richmond *Conservator* newspaper in 1882, 'preserve bloody splinters and pieces of his house at St Joseph as relics.' Treasure-seekers still hunt for his ill-gotten gains, said to be buried in the Ozark Hills.

BEANIE SHORT AND BILLY THE KID

The legend of Beanie Short (died 1865), another rebel guerrilla, shows the effect of the Civil War in southern Kentucky. Turkey Neck Bend in the river area of Monroe county, his home ground, was a stronghold of Southern loyalists. Informants who tell his story today seem proud that he killed and maimed their ancestors. Beanie Short was little better than a hoodlum, but his atrocities have been glorified as exhibiting loyalty to the Southern cause. In a typical raid, celebrated in song and story, he and his gang would ransack a house, ripping cloth from the loom, scattering the contents of a featherbed, or live coals from the fire, across the floor. One woman, who expected guests, had just baked six hot puddings when the gang arrived. Perhaps inspired by Jesse James, who made a sheriff eat a handbill advertising his arrest, they forced the woman's husband to eat the lot.

When the gang began murdering young lads, farmers took the law into their own hands. Beanie Short is said to have had premonitions of death: he heard the nails being driven into his coffin. One night he was gunned down in bed at the home of a Dr Moore. When Mrs Moore woke, she put her hand in a puddle of blood which had run down through the ceiling. The attackers were merciless: 'They beat their heads into a jelly up thar,' and his sister said: 'Poor Beanie, he sure left this world in a mighty hard shape.' Tradition says the bloodstain will not wash out: 'Why it's on that wall down thar now when it rains,' and each time it becomes brighter. There are people who search for the gold and silver that he hid after robbing trains. But there were no trains in his part of Kentucky and Tennessee during

Beanie Short's life.

Billy the Kid (1859–81), born William Bonney, was the most notorious outlaw of the American southwest, but a legendary glamour surrounds his life. He operated in Kansas, Colorado and New Mexico, where poor farmers at that time were seen as ruled by corrupt politicians. Billy is said to have committed his first murder when he was twelve, knifing a man who insulted his mother. He became a cowhand and in 1878 he fought in a cattle war in Lincoln County, New Mexico, and killed the sheriff and his deputy. Sentenced to death for murder, he escaped from jail in Lincoln, killing two guards. He was finally shot to death in a house in Fort Sumner.

Legend has it that Billy became involved when his boss, John Tunstall, was murdered and Billy vowed to avenge him. In fact Tunstall was an aggressive, ambitious man, who brought two rival groups into conflict. Billy was a paid gunman acting for one faction but, like Jesse James, his character has been idealized. Local Mexicans recall a cheerful man, who stole from whites to give to them.

THE COWBOY

The cowboy-outlaw Sam Bass robbed trains and stagecoaches with a gang of his mates. Farmers in west Texas, where he operated, supported what they saw as his fight against the railways, their enemy. Legend says he returned the money to a one-armed passenger he had inadvertently robbed and was lavish to the poor. He gave a widow 50 dollars for a night's lodging, and paid 20 dollars in gold for a dozen eggs or a few rolls. The admiration of strangers pleased him: 'What do you reckon he would have said if I'd told him I was Bass? I bet I could have broken his eyes off with a board.'

The stereotype of the cowboy was another consequence of the Civil War. Texas was not pillaged by the Northern armies and local markets could not be found for all its beef. Cities in the north offered good prices, so cattle were driven on long treks to be sold in Kansas and elsewhere. These great overland drives reached their peak in the 1870s and 1880s. The disastrous winter of 1886–87 harmed ranchers and by then the northern plains were stocking up with cattle. This brought the era to a close.

But the cowboy as a legendary figure lives on in films and television. One of his outstanding characteristics is insensitivity. A story, variously ascribed to Teddy Roosevelt and Mark Twain, describes how a man dies suddenly. A cowboy, chosen for his tact to break the news, rides up to his house. 'Are you the wife of Jack Smith?' 'Yes, I am.' 'No you aren't! You're just his widow.' In some versions he enquires: 'Are you the widow Smith?'

A parody of the cattle-drive sagas tells how a cowboy, hearing of the high price of turtle-soup, rounds up a herd of terrapins. Unfortunately they can only trek a few hundred metres (or yards) each day, so it takes fifteen years to complete the journey.

LINCOLN AND CUSTER

The Civil War made a great impact on American legend. The scar that it left on the nation is exemplified in the story of the Belled Buzzard that settled in Maryland after the fighting. Spoiled by the carnage of the battlefields, it would eat nothing but human flesh, and the ringing of its bell foretold new disasters to satisfy its appetite.

Virginia has a legend of a ghostly ship, filled with huge dancing negroes. It was seen on the Rappahannock River soon after the Civil War and before the Democratic defeat − chiefly due to the negro vote − at the polls the following day. It appeared again before Republican victories in 1880 and 1886.

Lincoln, architect and hero of the Civil War and champion of negro rights, has been described as the most legendary American President. After his death, it was said that every April, the month of his assassination, a spectral train follows the funeral route; all clocks and watches stop when it passes.

The story of General George Custer (1839−76), who served throughout the Civil War and fell with all his men at the Battle of The Little Big Horn against the Indians in 1876 is one of the most popular themes in American tradition. Legend says his chest was ripped open and the heart torn out and impaled upon a spear for the Sioux to dance round. A year after his death, James Talbot wrote that Custer had become 'one of the gods of the people'. The Associates of Little Big Horn maintain the cult, but attitudes toward American treatment of the Indians have undergone a radical change and Custer is less admired by the younger generation.

LEGENDS OF INDUSTRY

The American age of industrialism began in the 1860s. Economic interests were to the fore and cycles of legends became attached to special occupations and to master-workmen. Gib Morgen (1842−1909) told, and featured in, many legends of the oil-fields and how they struck oil, buttermilk, rum and champagne. It was said that he built a 40-storey hotel, operated on a turntable, so that each guest had a sunny outlook. A narrow-gauge railway ferried them from the lift to their rooms; whiskey and cocktails flowed from the taps. When Gib went fishing he landed a giant catfish; his line was a drilling-cable, baited with a steer on a steamboat's anchor. These stories show the wonder and the day-dreams aroused by the discovery of 'black gold'.

Coal-Oil Johnny is a generic name for anyone who squanders an oil-fortune. In the background of such stories is John Washington Steele, who inherited a fortune in 1864 and acquired a farm in Oil Creek, Pennsylvania. At the age of twenty-one he spent a million dollars in six months. Coal-Oil Johnny and his gang drove round Philadelphia in a bright red carriage, decorated with wells spouting dollar-shaped oil. He wore dollar-bills in his hat-band and button-hole. It is said that he bought the Continental Hotel because a clerk had been rude, so that he could sack him. When his money ran out, Coal-Oil Johnny became destitute and finally died in obscurity. His story is often told to show the consequences of foolish spending.

The lumber industry dates back to the colonization of America, but it did not reach its peak till after the Civil War. Its golden age was from 1870 to 1900. The end of white pine, and modernization, brought about the decline of this specialized profession. George Knox of Maine (d. 1892), alive during its peak, was credited with supernatural powers, obtained by selling his soul to the Devil for 20 dollars. He had only to speak and huge logs moved into the lumber-yard of their own accord. At his command deer ran from the woods, fish changed into steak, and whiskey fell from the trees. Naughty children were told: 'I'll send George Knox to get you.'

The best-known American lumberjack is the giant logger Paul Bunyan. Richard Dorson, the greatest living authority on American tradition, describes his legend as 'fakelore' and has shown that Paul Bunyan was invented by William Laughead, advertising agent for the Red River Lumber Company, to sell timber. The stories symbolize American love of anything big, as well as a delight in the physical mastery of nature, and the telling of tall tales. Paul Bunyan drags his spiked pole behind him and it forms the Grand Canyon. His huge Blue Ox is groomed with a garden rake. Its footprints are so large that men fall in and drown; a leak in it's water tank forms the Mississippi River. Some of the stories satirize early conditions in the lumber camps. Men feed endlessly from a lake of pea-soup, and pancakes are fried on an iron stove greased by cooks skating on hams and bear-steaks. A comparable figure is Joe Magarac, the giant Pittsburgh steel-worker, who squeezes molten iron with his bare hands to make steel rails: he is underwritten by the American Steel Corporation.

JOHNNY APPLESEED AND MOUNTAIN MARY

American agriculture has produced its own personalities. John Chapman (1774–1845) is better known as Johnny Appleseed. An eccentric New England pioneer, who settled in the Ohio River valley, he came to be regarded as unofficial patron saint of the apple orchards. A bearded, kindly hermit, bare-foot, with a tin pot on his head and a coffee sack on his back, he wandered through the countryside, planting appleseed and pruning grown trees, exchanging seedlings for the second-hand clothes and food that he needed. Settler and Indian alike respected him. He showed indifference to pain by sticking pins and needles into his flesh, and love of all living creatures by extinguishing the camp-fire lest the moths and mosquitoes singe their wings. He slept in the snow, rather than disturb bear-cubs that had settled down in his hollow log.

Richard Dorson has shown that legend has sentimentalized the life of Johnny Appleseed. He was a successful, if unorthodox, businessman who acquired a number of properties. He dressed like other people and had a predilection for the ladies. But in American folk tradition he has become a type of St Francis, or the Voice in the Wilderness, who brought news 'right fresh from heaven'. Johnny Weed, a variety of apple, is named after him.

Mountain Mary (Die Berg Maria), who grafted Good Mary apples, was a more genuinely saintly character. A Pennsylvania German hermit who died in 1819, her real name was Maria Jung and she lived in the Oley Hills. Many legends are told of her. It is said that she even loved animals usually considered harmful. When marmots infested her garden she set traps and released the animals on the neighbouring hills, telling them to go 'and trespass no more'. When she died the local preacher wrote in his journal: 'Help, Lord; the saints have decreased.'

LEGENDARY HUNTERS

Hunter and frontiersman David (Davy) Crockett (1786–1836) operated in his native Tennessee. His terrain was the canebrake, an area ravaged by hurricane and earthquake. Crockett became a member of the U.S. House of Representatives and the Whigs gladly adopted the 'Coonskin Congressman' from the recently enfranchised West. He seemed a likely vote-catcher with his picturesque turn of phrase, sense of humour and flair for telling stories. Since Crockett was a political figure, the stories told about him were often inspired by Whigs and Democrats. His adventures are described in a series of comic almanacs. Everyone dreaded the coming of Halley's Comet in 1835, but there was no cause for alarm: Crockett would climb the highest peak in the Allegheny Mountains and wrench off its fiery tail. He claimed to be so ugly that his grin would bring a racoon ('coon') down from a tree; once, so it is said, he grinned the bark off a knot that he had mistaken for a racoon. Weaned on whiskey and bear-meat, he rode up the Niagara Falls on an alligator's back, escaped a whirlwind by mounting a shaft of lightning, and drank the Gulf of Mexico dry. One winter, when the earth's axis froze, he greased it with bear-oil and brought back a piece of sunshine in his pocket.

American scholars have shown that the real Crockett was a dishonest and cowardly boaster, who deserted his wife and children. But the legend lives on and continues to delight both children and adults, as the personification of man, the fearless hunter, pitted against the wilderness. 'Thars a great rejoicing among the bears of Kaintuck, and the alligators of the Mississippi rolls up their shining ribs to the sun, and has grown so fat and lazy that they will hardly move out of the way for a steamboat. The rattlesnakes come up out of their holes and frolic within 10 foot [3 metres] of the clearings, and the foxes go to sleep in the goosepens. It is because the rifle of Crockett is silent forever, and the print of his moccasins is found no more in our woods.'

Ethan Allan (born 1739), famous in his native Vermont, was also a noted hunter. Legend says he went deer-tracking one winter and, every time he made a kill he left a piece of clothing as identification. After shooting 100 animals he was forced to run through the forest in sub-zero temperatures, dressed only in snow-shoes, bullet pouch and powder horn. When he died, the inscription on his grave read: 'A Man who tried God's Spirit to the Utmost.'

When human beings, rather than animals, become the hunter's target, there is consternation in any small rural community and legends proliferate. The story of the Bloody Miller, who killed his wife, smoked the meat and started a flourishing sausage business, occurs in different parts of the United States. There are versions in the Ozarks, a wild mountainous region, where murderers and other criminals take refuge. In Michigan's Upper Peninsula the sausage-maker was called Reutgert and local lumberjacks, enjoying a meal, say: 'Please pass Mrs Reutgert.'

Large numbers of almost surrealist modern legends circulate in urban areas, centred on aspects of modern culture. Perhaps one of the oddest is the story of alligators living in the sewers of New York City. Returning holiday-makers from Miami are said to have brought baby alligators back as pets, become alarmed as they increased in size and flushed them down the lavatory, where some flourished. Similarly people say that snakes have appeared in lavatory bowls and even wriggled out of taps. These legends may have been reinforced by the drug addict's practice of flushing dope away before a police raid.

Drugs have produced their own crop of legends. Marijuana is said to grow in the sewers of Berkeley, California, excrement acting as a fertilizer. California and Indiana have their tales of lost marijuana fields, which no one has ever found, but they fill the air with their fumes and, when the wind changes, the local population becomes addicted. Such legends are a reflection of modern drug culture.

CHAPTER 38
MIDDLE AMERICA

Legends in Middle America enshrine the least dispensable of local truths. Many of the legends current in Mexico today turn out to have their roots deep in the past before the arrival of the Spaniards, and now, as then, they serve a wide variety of needs. Stories told of the great military heroes of the remote past, for example, like the illustrious Mixtec warrior 8-Deer, reappear only slightly recast when the valour, the bearing and the approach to death of such modern counterparts as Zapata or Pancho Villa are recalled. Other stories can be fully understood only as part of old systems of belief which are more cosmological and overtly religious in nature. If these legends sometimes appear fragmentary or vaguely contoured, this has been their guarantee of survival in the face of western propaganda since the coming of Christianity to Mexico in the sixteenth century. Mesoamericans have not so much shunned this propaganda as adapted it to native needs.

This kind of assimilation (the opposite of what anthropologists call 'acculturation') has always been encouraged by the startling similarity between many American and Christian beliefs and rites. In panic and disgust the Spanish conquerors of Mexico observed tastings of consecrated flesh which corresponded with those of the Mass; and they recognized that, triumphant through self-destruction, Christ had a counterpart in the god Quetzalcoatl, who also rose again after overcoming the forces of hell. As for the Virgin Mary, there was an equivalent ready to hand in the deity known as 'the mother of our flesh', Tonantzin: hence the Aztec story of the Virgin of Guadalupe, perhaps the most powerful politically and ideologically of all these legends, not only in Mexico but much further afield in modern America.

As in other long-lived civilizations, a deeply ingrained sense of territory has found legendary expression. The foundation of the great

The Virgin of Guadalupe and Juan Diego (page 341)

city-states of the past is the subject of several of the principal works of Mesoamerican literature. Legends of this kind typically conjoin the cosmic world of gods with the daily life of their human servants, in house, street and field. By far the most famous of them is the one which concerns Tenochtitlan, now Mexico City, the capital of the Aztecs and of the modern United States of Mexico.

THE FOUNDING OF TENOCHTITLAN

The legend of the Aztecs' journey from the dim and distant land of Aztlan, somewhere in the north, to their future capital is basically a success story. At first oppressed and poor, the Aztecs end up as masters of an empire. The details of their route and their adventures on the way vary a good deal in the extant versions of the legend. The most important single constant is the leader they are said to acquire early in their travels, Huitzilopochtli, 'Humming-bird-on-the-left', who appears to them in a cave at Colhuacan and promises them great rewards in the future. 'You will be limited by nothing; nothing will escape you. They will bend to your every wish, whatever your greeds are you will be satisfied, you will take women where and when you please, nothing will escape you, you will receive gifts of everything...'

In Aztec and Toltec religion the humming-bird, like the butterfly, embodies the soul of an illustrious dead warrior; and being creatures of amazing metabolism they are themselves subject to further metamorphosis, into the major birds of prey Hawk and Eagle. This is the secret of Huitzilopochtli's announcement to the Aztecs that they will know they have reached the site of their future capital when they see an eagle, perched on a cactus growing in stony ground, and devouring a snake. The stone *(te-tl)* and the cactus *(noch-tli)* make up the syllables of the city's name, while the snake, a reminder of the burning deserts through which the Aztecs are to pass, also has symbolic meaning as food proper to a great bird of prey.

As the tribal leader of the Aztecs, Huitzilopochtli is an opaque and even contradictory figure. This is partly because, once they had achieved imperial power in Mexico, the Aztecs turned him into a solar god, a major force in their cosmology and mythology. This grandiose Huitzilopochtli accords awkwardly with the erstwhile leader of the Aztec migration, who has an indelibly secular streak. He strikes hard-headed bargains with his followers and he pitilessly harasses his sister Malinalxochitl, who is ugly. For this offence Malinalxochitl, or the moon-goddess Coyolxauhqui as she later became, is beheaded. Huitzilopochtli also does away with her son, his nephew, the hapless Copil, whose heart is buried or planted at the foot of the cactus which marks the site of Tenochtitlan, thus consecrating it.

Details from this story continue to exert a remarkable power in the modern world. The image by which the Aztecs recognized the site of their future capital — a snake-eating eagle perched on a cactus — is repeated endlessly on banknotes and other forms of currency in Mexico. Aztlan, the northern homeland from which the Aztecs set out for Mexico, has become the revered emblem of the Chicanos or Spanish-speakers who feel themselves exiles as citizens of the United States of America.

TULA: A LOST PARADISE

Other legends refer to cities so old that their existence is synonymous with the beginning of the known political world. Such a city is Tula, invoked throughout Middle America as the source of all good things, of power, writing and the finest agriculture and metallurgy, a lost earthly paradise. Tula was legendary many centuries before the Spanish conquest, and its precise role in the early history of Mesoamerica has still to be fully determined. As the garden-city from which hunger was absent and where the greatest art and refinement governed all human affairs, Tula became famous throughout North America (and may possibly be alluded to in the 'ultima Thule' of Roman writers). At first sight, Tula seems to be a never-never land, an impossible dream which could never have been real, and until quite recently it was no more credited with having ever actually existed than Troy was before Schliemann's excavations in 1873.

The wealth of Tula and of its first inhabitants, the Toltecs, was recorded by the sixteenth-century Aztecs who worked with Bernardino de Sahagún, the Franciscan missionary whose *General History of the Things of New Spain* supplies much of our knowledge of Aztec life before the conquest. Food was free in Tula, where the melons grew too fat to get your arms round and the maize ears were the size of millstones, where cotton came ready dyed in rich colours, where they had all kinds of valuable birds which talked and sang in tune, where everyone owned jade and gold, where no one was poor or had a shabby house. It is clear that the original Tula had a tropical climate and the references to cotton and gold suggest some connection with South America, where the techniques for working those materials were developed. This fits in with the sixteenth-century references to Tula in the Maya *Popol Vuh* (Book of Counsel) where the ancestors of the Quiche Maya travel east from Guatemala — that is, towards Nicaragua — to visit the city. The *Popol Vuh* tells how, being so fertile, Tula grew more and more populous until it presided over a westward migration and colonization of Middle America according to a fourfold plan. While the Quiche Maya returned to the west to occupy their Guatemalan valleys, the Mexicans went as far westwards again to assume their name as western or moon *(mezitli)* people. For

their part, the Cakchiquel Maya, neighbours of the Quiche, wrote of
the emergence of the four Tulas – in east and west, in heaven and hell
(that is, north and south, or Caribbean and Pacific) – from the
original city in the east. Both the Quiche and the Cakchiquel record
the great dividing up of the tribes at Tula in detail (a point of some
consequence for modern archaeology) and express their sense of loss
at having to leave this original Mesoamerican paradise in a lament;

> Alas, we were lost at Tula,
> we have broken ourselves up.
> We have left behind again our elder brothers,
> our younger brothers.
> Where did they see the sun then,
> where might they have been when it dawned?

The elder brothers, who travelled farthest, are the Yaqui or
Mexicans; the younger, like the Pipil (which means 'children')
remained towards Nicaragua. Towards the north or Caribbean, the
Maya of Yucatan recalled Tula in their *Community Books,* though
with some hostility, discerning in the richness of Tula the origin of
lust, sloth and corruption.

In 1948 the legendary Tula was identified as Tula in Hidalgo,
north-west of Mexico City. This Tula may in fact be seen as the
western Tula in the fourfold governmental system of the Toltecs,
a frontier town as far distant from the Maya heartland as was the
original Tula to the east.

QUETZALCOATL IN TULA

The western Tula was itself the focus of a whole cycle of legends. The
most striking of them are about the ruler of the city, Quetzalcoatl. He
arrived there as a mysterious stranger and taught the people the
'Toltec arts' of gold-casting, jewel-cutting, carving in wood and stone,
writing and feather-working. He then travelled back east to the
middle of the fourfold realm, to the place of the black (west) and the
red (east), there to burn himself to death and become the morning
star, the planet Venus.

Quetzalcoatl's departure from Tula is the culmination of a series of
defeats and humiliations brought about by his enemies in the city, led
by the sorcerer Tezcatlipoca, who distrust his claims to perfection and
resent his rejection of human sacrifice. They make him drunk on
pulque and persuade him to look at himself in a mirror. Seeing his
mortal ugliness, his swollen eyelids and bilious complexion, Quetzalcoatl allows himself to be dressed up, in order to provide the mirror
with a more prepossessing image. Then he is made drunk once more
on pulque and spiced food, and succumbs again to narcissism in an act

of incest with his sister, Quetzalpetlatl. Full of sorrow and remorse, he leaves Tula, where his subjects are left deprived and orphaned. How far the story reflects accurate history is uncertain, but disturbances in Tula towards the end of the first millennium AD did result in an exodus from the city along the route which Quetzalcoatl is said to have taken.

THE VIRGIN OF GUADALUPE

Rejected by the Spaniards and unable to return to the ordered existence of their pre-Spanish world, the Aztecs sought their own solutions. One was found in the divine apparition of the Virgin Mary on the hill of Tepeyacac in 1531. The Virgin manifested herself not to a Spaniard but to an Aztec named Quauhtlatoatzin (Eagle-that-talks), who had been baptized and changed his name to the acceptably mundane Juan Diego. The earliest account of the miraculous appearance is that of Antonio Valeriano, a nobleman of Aztec blood, said to be a friend of Juan Diego. His text is now lost, but it was translated into Spanish in 1667.

Twice a week the pious convert Juan Diego would set off from his home in Cuautitlan on a journey southward to the Catholic church at Tlatelolco, a town incorporated by the Aztecs into their capital Tenochtitlan. Praying constantly, he travelled upon the route now known as the Camino de los Indios, an old Aztec road joining Cuautitlan to the capital. On 9 December, a Saturday, however, his journey was interrupted. It was very early in the morning and Juan was just reaching the summit of the hill of Tepeyacac when he heard divine music and a voice calling him by name. The Virgin appeared to him and asked him to inform the Bishop of Mexico City (then Juan de Zumárraga) of her desire to have a church on that site.

Juan Diego was unable to convince the bishop. He returned to the hilltop that afternoon and the Virgin again appeared to him. He tried to persuade her of his inability to fulfil her mission and urged her to choose a Spaniard instead to carry out her commands. In her reply she told Juan Diego of her concern for the native population: 'As a loving mother to thee and those like thee I shall show my tender clemency and the compassion I feel for the natives and those who love and seek me.'

Inspired by this, Juan Diego again visited the Bishop, who demanded proof of the divine apparition. On Juan's way home, the Virgin appeared on the hilltop for the third time (it was by now the afternoon of 10 December) and told him to return the next day for the proof that would convince the Bishop. However, the next day Juan's uncle, Juan Bernardino, was stricken with the plague and Juan ignored the Virgin's command, remaining with his dying uncle. The following morning he decided to fetch a priest from Tlatelolco to give his uncle the last rites. Not wishing to be delayed, he tried to avoid the Virgin by going round the base of the hill. As he was passing a spring at the foot of the hill, the Virgin appeared, beneath a tree. She told him not to worry about his uncle, for she had cured him. To provide proof of her appearance, she ordered Juan Diego to pick some flowers and carry them to the Bishop in his cloak.

When Juan Diego later opened out his cloak to show the flowers to the sceptical Bishop, there miraculously appeared an image of the Virgin imprinted upon the rough cloth of the cloak.

Now convinced, the Bishop went to Juan's house in Cuautitlan to see his uncle. There Juan Bernardino recounted how, simultaneously with her fourth appearance at Tepeyacac, the Virgin had appeared to him, brought him back to health and revealed her name, which was 'Ever Holy Virgin Mary of Tecuatlazopeuch'. (Guadalupe is the Spanish version of this Aztec name.)

The image on Juan's cloak, now kept behind glass at the shrine outside Mexico City, conforms to countless European representations of the Virgin enthroned in glory, but like so many manifestations of Mexican culture the 'image' of Guadalupe was formed by a complex web of meanings and needs. Though the image is conventionally Catholic, it is imprinted upon maguey fibre, the indigenous paper or writing material of the Aztecs which is made from a hard fibre derived from the agave (maguey) plant. The 'proof' taking original form as flowers is reminiscent of the Aztec literary concept of 'flowery speech' or poetic rhetoric, and the native Mexicans often decorated their cloaks with the image of a god, such as Tlaloc, the god of rain.

The actual location of the apparition is connected with another element of native culture. Mountains generally were associated with earth goddesses and were often themselves deified. More specifically, for centuries before the coming of Christianity, Tepeyacac itself had been the site of a shrine to the Aztec mother goddess, Tonantzin. Bernardino de Sahagún bemoaned the fact that the Indians used the Aztec term in the worship of the Virgin: 'Now that the church of our Lady of Guadalupe has been built, the Indians also call her Tonantzin on the pretext that the preachers call our lady the 'Mother of God' – Tonantzin.'

This transference of allegiance, from the Aztec to the Catholic 'Mother' and protectress, served to align the alien Christian faith with a nationalist tradition, and formed the basis of the cult of Guadalupe. Mexican 'naturalization' of a basically European symbol was consciously promoted by certain writers, such as Miguel Sanchez, who in 1648 published his *Imagen de la Virgin María* in which he identified the apparition of Tepeyacac with the woman described in the Book of Revelation: 'And there appeared a great wonder in heaven; a woman clothed with the sun, and the moon under her feet, and upon her head a crown of twelve stars.' (Revelation 12).

This description could well be applied to the image on the cloak of Juan Diego, but the comparison strikes a deeper chord in Aztec religion. The woman of Revelation is with child, 'travailing in birth, and pained to be delivered'. She is attacked by a fearsome dragon, carrying in his tail 'the third part of the stars of heaven', and intending to devour the child as soon as it is born. The woman brings forth 'a man child, who was to rule all nations'. This is followed by 'war in heaven' and St Michael and his angels vanquish and cast down the dragon's forces.

There is a remarkable similarity between this vision in Revelation and the Aztec account of the solar birth of none other than Huitzilopochtli, which cannot have been lost on seventeenth-century Mexicans. The Aztec mother of the gods, Coatlicue, is miraculously impregnated by a ball of feathers. Her sons, 'the four hundred stars', turn on her and intend to kill her and her child. She is saved by the emergence of her child, Huitzilopochtli, who appears as a fully armed warrior and destroys her attackers. The associations with Aztec nationalism are all the stronger because, to escape from the dragon, the woman in Revelation is given 'two wings of a great eagle, that she might fly into the wilderness, into her place, where she is nourished ...from the face of the serpent'. The image of an eagle devouring a serpent, as we have seen, marked the site of the Aztec capital and became a symbol of Mexican cultural identity. It heightens the meaning of the Virgin of Guadalupe as the patron of Mexico City, the old Aztec capital.

The effect was to make the Virgin of Guadalupe an embodiment of the spiritual redemption of the Mexican people and a symbol of Mexican nationalism. During the War of Independence her image offered spiritual and ideological justification for the insurgents and her sacred colours of blue and white became the colours of the new Republic, established in 1823. The first president of the Republic, Guadalupe Victoria, adopted her name as a mark of patriotic fervour.

Devotion to the Virgin of Tepeyacac became synonymous with a sense of national identity and patriotism. To the Indians she was their eternal Earth Mother, a continuing link with pre-conquest religion and a sorely needed protector in a world dominated by Europeans. To the Creoles and Mestizos the 'inviolate mother' offered an alternative to their own heritage of illegitimacy, for the Virgin of Guadalupe stands in opposition to the figure of 'La Chingada', the violated woman of Mexico, raped by the Spanish conquerors and giving birth to a bastard nation. To all classes of society the Virgin of Guadalupe offered a spiritual justification of a purely 'Mexican' identity.

THE SPEAKING CROSS

Another example of Christianity being redefined in Mesoamerican legend occurs among the Maya, especially those living in the Yucatan peninsula. They have always readily agreed that words spoken like Christ's from a cross are endowed with a special authority, but the words which they revere belong to the living maize cross of their native religion. With a long literary tradition of their own, the Maya have been highly sceptical and partial in their reading of biblical doctrine and their acceptance of rites and values imported from the Old World. This legend, as a principle of national identity, has repeatedly inspired military defence of their territories.

The cross was a religious symbol in Middle America long before the arrival of Christianity. The Maya connected it with the maize plant, which was, and is, their staple crop, the foundation of their agriculture and the centre and mainstay of the whole traditional Maya way of life. It is also, in myth, the substance of which man is made. In a sanctuary dedicated to maize at Palenque, the plant is shown in human form, standing with its arms extended in the shape of a cross and worshipped by two priests. The Maya see the stages in the growth of maize as analogous to those of human development and the ripe corn is portrayed as a beautiful young man. The plant is a friend and ally, and the Tzeltal Maya still leave ears of maize to guard unattended children.

The Mayan symbol absorbed the Christian one and the old link between the cross and agriculture persisted. In Yucatan crosses are commonly painted green and placed in the fertile areas near wells to protect the fields. In Yucatan the communion wafer is made of maize flour, showing the interchangeability of the body of Christ and the 'flesh' of the sacred maize plant.

In the nineteenth century antagonism to the interference of foreigners in Maya life inspired a rebellion known as the War of the Castes. A remarkable characteristic of this insurrection was the ideological justification the rebels gained from the cult of the Speaking Cross. The followers of this cross, known as the Cruzob, maintained an independent existence for more than sixty years, governed by the mysterious voice of the Cross of Chan Santa Cruz.

The origin of this cross is disputed, but most historians regard it as the invention of a Mestizo named José María Barrera, one of the leaders of the Maya revolt. It was said to have appeared in 1850, by a well in the remote region of Quintana Roo on the east coast of Yucatan. How the cross delivered its messages was described by an English officer, Lieutenant Plumridge, who in 1861 was sent to neogotiate with the Cruzob on behalf of the government of British Honduras (Belize). 'At that moment soft music and singing that till then had pervaded the building ceased and was followed by a deafening and prolonged sound similar to thunder when heard at a distance. This too ceased and in the midst of the silence that followed was heard a rather weak voice which seemed to originate in the midst of the air and which spoke in the Maya language.'

The voice is thought to have been that of a Maya ventriloquist, Manuel Nahaut, but to the Maya its divine origin was unquestioned. The Speaking Cross proved that God and the saints were on the side of the Maya. After Nahaut's death the cross communicated more often in writing than orally, often signing missives with the name of its 'secretary', Juan de la Cruz. In one of these 'sermons of the cross' the Maya are warned not to desert the cause by mixing with the foreign enemy. 'You are talking about mixing with the enemy, although you see how the enemy exhausts me, you say that no harm will come to you through them; because I am advising you, my children, don't say that, it is what the created enemy says.'

Attempts to discredit the legend of the Speaking Gross have little effect upon the Maya and accusations of ventriloquism and fraud are brushed aside. It continues to survive as a symbol of Maya identity and salvation. More recently, maize plants have spoken to the Maya of Chiapas, warning them not to abandon their old ally, maize, for new cash crops such as coffee and sugar. The places at which these speaking plants have appeared have become sites of local pilgrimage, reminders of the Maya dependence on maize.

LA LLORONA

In searching for their heritage and their roots, modern writers in Mexico, Guatemala and Nicaragua have repeatedly turned to this whole body of legendary knowledge. One legend in particular, which has fascinated writers of the stature of Octavio Paz and Carlos Fuentes, has yet another theme and is very much alive in the oral tradition. It concerns the beautiful woman who seduces her unwary lover to walk with her, only to reveal herself as hurtful and nightmarishly perverse. A dark woman who appears out of the western sky, she has tangled hair and ash-filled eyes, and she is forever turning her head back in pain and desperation. She is sexually inverted and the man who goes with her runs the risk of becoming pregnant (with a child of faeces) unless he defends himself by thrusting a cigarette into the hole at the back of her head. This causes her to revert to the condition of a snake, who flees in fright.

Specifically as La Llorona, the woman who wails for her lost and her unattainable children, this figure is understood in modern Mexico as a response to the injustices and cruelties suffered by Mexico at the hands of the invaders. Of them, Bartolomé de Las Casas, one of the first Christian priests in the New World, said: 'There is no language, no art or humane science, that can avail to recite the abominable crimes and bloody actions committed by these enemies, not only of Commonwealths but of all humane societies.'

CHAPTER 39
THE INCAS

The Incas were originally a group of tribes which settled in the Cuzco valley of southern Peru around AD 1200. They were agriculturalists, cultivating maize in the Andean valleys and tubers on the higher ground. About the year 1438, under their ruler Pachacuti Inca, they embarked upon a concerted programme of military expansion, and by the time the Spanish conquistadors arrived less than a hundred years later, they controlled a vast empire stretching from Quito in the north to present-day Santiago in the south. The Incas did not possess the art of writing but, as the empire expanded, the deeds of each successive ruler were recorded by means of a device known as a *quipu,* a set of knotted coloured threads which served as a mnemonic of past events. Dramas, ballads and narrative poems about the exploits of dead Incas were composed by a class of specialists, the *quipu-camayoc* (quipu-readers), who diplomatically omitted the less worthy episodes and doubtless embroidered the more flattering ones. It is from this highly sophisticated source that the legendary sagas of the Inca dynasty derive. They were originally composed in the Quechua language and were turned into Spanish prose by Spanish chroniclers in the sixteenth century. Although the poetry of the original Quechua has been lost, the events described are much as they would have been related at the court of the Inca five centuries ago.

The legends of the early Inca rulers, Manco Capac and his immediate successors, follow on directly from the myths of the origin of the world and of the Inca dynasty itself, and probably bear only a tenuous relation to historical fact. From the reign of Pachacuti Inca, the narratives adhere more strictly to the historical record. Right up until the Spanish conquest, however, the accounts possess a legendary flavour which was clearly the result of a reworking of the

Yupanqui and the stranger who foretold his future (page 349)

material. The legendary histories reflect the abiding preoccupations of the Incas — wars and alliances, imperial expansion and dynastic succession.

THE EARLY RULERS

The Incas had no fixed rule of succession. The ruler chose as his successor the son who had won most honour in battle, and consequently many legends describe the precocious strength and bravery of Inca princes. The fourth ruler, Mayta Capac, is a Herculean figure in Inca legend. His father, the ageing and feeble Lloqui Yupanqui, had despaired of ever having an heir, but eventually a suitable woman was found and a son was born. Everyone considered the conception a miracle, but even more wondrous, the child was only three months in the womb and was born with teeth. When only a year old he had the strength and build of an eight-year-old, and at two was fighting and injuring much bigger boys. One day, while playing with some boys from the Alcahuisa tribe, neighbours of the Incas, he killed one of them, and on another occasion he broke the leg of the son of the Alcahuisa leader. At this, the tribe resolved to take vengeance. Ten Alcahuisa men were dispatched to the House of the Sun, where Lloqui Yupanqui and his son lived, with orders to murder them both. But the young Mayta Capac, who was in the courtyard, attacked the intruders with some balls he was playing with, killing two of them and putting the rest to flight. The Alcahuisas, fearing that when he grew up Mayta Capac would destroy them, declared war on the Incas. The old Lloqui Yupanqui was alarmed at this and reproved his son for giving cause for war, but the Inca chieftains were eager to fight and told Lloqui Yupanqui to leave the matter to his son. Mayta Capac marshalled his forces and a desperate battle was fought, from which the Incas eventually emerged victorious. The Alcahuisas again challenged Mayta Capac to battle, but as they advanced they were thrown into disarray by a hailstorm and were again defeated.

Another legend from this period, of interest for the light it sheds on Inca history, tells of the kidnapping of the Inca heir. The sixth ruler, Roca Inca, had married a woman from the Huayllacan tribe. She had previously been promised to the Ayamarcas, and the latter, angry with the Huayllacans for having broken their word, attacked them mercilessly. Eventually, in order to avoid further hostilities, the beleaguered Huayllacans agreed to the Ayamarcas' terms: that they facilitate the kidnapping of the child of Roca Inca. Accordingly the Huayllacans invited the child, aged about eight, to meet his mother's kin, saying that they would make him heir to their estates. Roca Inca consented. But once the child was in Huayllacan territory the Ayamarcas, with the treacherous connivance of his hosts, seized him and carried him off.

Tocay, the leader of the Ayamarcas, was pleased with his capture, for he considered the child's mother to be his rightful wife. But the child proclaimed boldly that he was the son of Roca Inca. Tocay was indignant and ordered that the child be killed. At this the boy began to weep tears of blood, and uttered a curse on the Ayamarcas, saying that if he was murdered their nation would be extinguished. Because of this incident, the child was nicknamed Yahuar-Huacac, 'weeper of blood'. Fearful of the curse, Tocay ordered that instead the boy should be slowly starved to death. He was taken to a remote spot in the mountains, where he remained for a year, but one of Tocay's concubines, a woman of the Anta tribe, rescued him with the help of her father and brothers. The Antas sent messengers to the Inca leader saying that his son was safe; at first he disbelieved them, but his own messengers confirmed the story. He regaled the Antas with gifts of gold, silver and cloth, but they rejected his presents, saying that their condition for returning his son was that henceforth they be regarded as Incas and be allowed to wear the Inca insignia. Roca Inca conceded their request, and Yahuar-Huacac was returned to Cuzco amidst much rejoicing. Before Roca Inca died, he made peace with Tocay, giving him his daughter in marriage, while Yuahuar-Huacac, when he succeeded as Inca, forgave the Huayllacans their treachery.

This complicated plot reveals that towards the close of the fourteenth century relations between the various tribes in the Cuzco area were unstable, with uneasy alliances forged through the intermarriage of the ruling families. The compilers of the legend recognized that at this stage the Incas did not possess military superiority over their neighbours, but they nevertheless implied the pre-eminent status of the Incas in the Antas' desire to emulate them. Yahuar Huacac's curse on the Ayamarcas presaged their subjugation by a later Inca ruler, Pachacuti, related in a subsequent episode of the cycle. This anticipatory device, used throughout the narratives, serves to weld the diverse events into a single deterministic sequence.

PACHACUTI INCA

It is Pachacuti who is accorded the most honour and praise in Inca legend, for it was he who initiated the phase of imperial expansion with his decisive victory over the Chanca tribe. The story runs as follows. The eighth ruler, Viracocha Inca, had hoped to nominate his son Yupanqui as his successor, but he was dissuaded by his advisers who insisted on his eldest son, the licentious and dissolute Urco Inca. The Chanca tribe, to the west of Cuzco, having already defeated a neighbouring tribe of the Incas known as the Quechuas (from whom the Incas derived their language), decided to seize the opportunity presented by the discord and prepared to attack Cuzco itself. Neither

Viracocha Inca nor his nominated successor Urco Inca took any action against the impending threat, and it fell to Yupanqui, then aged about twenty, to organize the Inca resistance. One day, while Yupanqui was in a mountain retreat planning his military strategy, a figure appeared to him, a man dressed like the Inca, with serpents twined around his arms and pumas between his legs and around his shoulders. This figure held up a mirror showing all the provinces that Yupanqui would subdue, and told him that he would be greater than any of his ancestors, but that he must return immediately to Cuzco, where he would conquer the Chancas.

Yupanqui obeyed. The battle was bloody and desperate. Many people, instead of participating, took to the hills to watch, for they feared the wrath of the conqueror should they be on the losing side. But many others distinguished themselves with their bravery, in particular a woman from one of the suburbs of Cuzco who fought so valiantly that the intruders were obliged to retire. The Chancas were alarmed at Yupanqui's fleetness and dexterity with his weapon, and were even more frightened when, in mid-battle, hordes of men descended from the hills, sent by the creator-god Viracocha to give succour to the Inca. Gradually the Chancas began to give way, leaving behind their prized military standards. Eventually they turned and fled, but the Incas continued in pursuit for several kilometres (or miles), killing and wounding the enemy. Then they returned to Cuzco, having won a great victory and a vast amount of plunder. They praised their leader Yupanqui for having regained their safety and freedom, honouring him with the title Pachacuti, 'overturner of the earth'.

The humble Pachacuti, however, wished to give his father the glory of the victory, and he sent one of his closest associates to Viracocha Inca with the most precious spoils of war. But when the emissary invited the old man to tread on the spoils, as was the custom, Viracocha Inca refused, saying that his son and successor Urco Inca should do so. The messenger was angry at this, and returned to Pachacuti to tell him what had happened.

Meanwhile, the Chancas were reassembling, and Pachacuti and his army again went out to meet them. A Chanca messenger demanded that the Incas capitulate, but Pachacuti sent him back with the message that the creator-god Viracocha would grant victory to whom he pleased. Once again battle was joined, and again the Incas were victorious, slaughtering the two Chanca chieftains. Once again Pachacuti sent his father the most precious booty, inviting him to tread on it; and although Viracocha Inca was still intent on the honour being offered to Urco Inca, he nevertheless acceded to Pachacuti's request. Pachacuti, together with Urco Inca, then rode in triumph to Cuzco, Viracocha Inca excusing himself on account of his great age.

Once in Cuzco, Pachacuti began to distribute the spoils of war in the manner of a ruler. He had much support amongst the people, and he consulted the image of the Sun as to who should be Inca. The oracle replied that it should be Pachacuti. Accordingly Pachacuti, seizing power from his father and brother, assumed the royal fringe and embarked on a long and glorious reign.

LATER LEGENDS

In the case of Pachacuti's succession, the oracle's verdict was unequivocal, and presaged the expansion of Inca dominion. But in the account of the succession of Huáscar, the twelfth Inca ruler, the auguries were profoundly uncertain – a portent of the denouement to come. Huáscar's father, Emperor Huayna Capac, fell ill while on a military campaign in Quito. He told his nobles that, provided the signs were auspicious, his son Ninan Cuyoche was to succeed; otherwise, it was to be his son Huáscar. When the necessary ceremonies were performed, although the signs for both sons were inauspicious, the Chief Steward of the Sun nevertheless set out to confer the fringe on Ninan Cuyochi. When he arrived, Ninan Cuyochi had already died of the same pestilence that had killed his father. Huáscar was therefore declared Emperor in his stead.

However, Huáscar's half-brother Atahualpa, who had been left in charge of the imperial army at Quito, also nursed ambitions to be Inca, and the Empire was plunged into civil war. Atahualpa's captains scored many victories over Huáscar's forces, and soon Atahualpa was declared Inca of all the land. He marched south from Quito in triumph. At Huamachuco, two of his principal lords went to consult the oracle there, which told them that Atahualpa would have an unfortunate end, because he was such a cruel tyrant and a shedder of so much human blood. On hearing this, Atahualpa was enraged. He went to the oracle and with a gold halberd cut off the head first of the priest and then of the idol, though it was made of stone. He then ordered the priest's body, the idol and its house to be burned, and the cinders to be scattered in the air. Finally he completely levelled the hill on which the shrine had stood.

Here, in an embellishment of what was, when set down by the Spanish chronicler, but recent history, is an augury of the fate that Atahualpa was to meet at the hands of the Spanish conquistadors. Although Atahualpa managed to have Huáscar murdered in 1533, he was himself garotted on the orders of the Spanish leader a few months later. His death spelled the beginning of the end for the Inca empire.

As these examples indicate, it was overwhelmingly the ruling class that featured in Inca legend. Very few legends of common folk found their way into the Spanish chronicles. The celebrated Quechua play *Ollanta,* which deals with the love between a warrior in the imperial army and the daughter of Pachacuti Inca, is now generally considered to be a creation of the seventeenth or eighteenth century. Inca legend was for the most part a state-sponsored art form which offered obeisance to the ruler and his ancestors, and which provided a rationale for imperial expansion.

CHAPTER 40

LOWLAND SOUTH AMERICA

Among the Indians of the South American jungle there exists a type of saga that is notable for the powerful dream-like charm and creativity of its narrative. As a legend of odyssey or adventure, it relates the wanderings of a lost traveller who meets in the forest, one after another, strange and terrifying beings, ogres and ogresses, a rolling head, a man with a sharpened leg or long testicles, deceitful animals, enormous birds, miraculous butterflies. From our point of view, the traveller caught in the forest amidst such a ghoulish masquerade of the weird and the absurd is as if ensnared in a painting by Hieronymus Bosch. The French scholar Claude Lévi-Strauss describes these stories (in *The Origin of Table Manners*) as 'a first attempt at fictional creativeness in its pristine freshness' and suggests that their inventiveness and flexibility might well 'illustrate a significant transition from the mythic genre to the genre of the novel'.

Despite the remarkable imagination displayed in these legends, they differ in many important details from the category of tale ordinarily classified as myth. Unlike myths, the legends are not greatly concerned with supernaturally implemented transformations and innovations, although such events may occur within their context. And whereas South American myths present a totally miraculous world, a nonsensical anti-world, the world as it is not − where identity is fragile and ephemeral, causality is perverse, and time is erased or distorted − these tales present as the stage for action the world as it is now, into which beings that have mythic characteristics enter unexpectedly to persecute the lost traveller.

Most of the South American legends are very lengthy and the versions given here are considerably shorter than the originals. The following example of a lost traveller story is from the Warao Indians of the Guianas. It is about a young man who is lost in the forest and has to slay and outwit ogres to save his life. For the South American Indian, ogres are not mythical beings, but creatures which must be

Kororomanna and the orge (page 353)

contended with today when walking in the forest and which are dangerous to men. As represented in festival masks, they are usually roughly human in form, but are very hairy, very large, or very small.

THE ADVENTURES OF KOROROMANNA

One day, an Indian called Kororomanna went out hunting and killed a quariba monkey:

> By the time he began his journey home, it was dark and he lost his way, having to spend the night in an improvised shelter in the forest. Unfortunately, he chose a bad place in which to camp, for it was right in the middle of a pathway frequented by ogres, who at night entertained themselves by noisily striking the trees. Thus it was not at all pleasant for Kororomanna, and the dead monkey's body was beginning to swell with the noxious gases inside. But at last he managed to fall asleep, only to be wakened again by the ogres knocking on the trees. He had a sudden desire to mimic them, and every time they struck a tree-branch he struck the monkey's belly with a stick, and from it came a resonant *Boom, Boom,* just like the beating of a drum.
>
> The leader of the ogres heard the curious sound and became frightened. 'What can it be? When before I knocked a tree, it never made a noise like that!' To make sure, he struck the tree hard again, and *Boom* came once more from the carcass. The ogre was really frightened now, and searched all around to find out where the extraordinary noise could come from. At last he noticed the little monkey, and saw Kororomanna roaring with laughter at hearing a dead animal break wind so noisily. The ogre leader expressed regret that he could not make such a splendid sound, for unlike ordinary mortals, ogres have no proper posteriors, but just a red spot. He begged Kororomanna to make him a posterior which would allow him to produce such a vigorous sound. So with his bow Kororomanna split the ogre's hindquarters; but so rough were his methods that the weapon transfixed the whole body and even pierced the unfortunate ogre's head. The ogre cursed Kororomanna for having killed him, and swore that his fellow ogres would avenge his death.
>
> Swarms of ogres then approached the scene of the outrage, and Kororomanna climbed a tree to hide himself. The largest of the ogres decided to climb the tree to kill him, but he climbed head downwards, and Kororomanna dispatched this ogre in the same peculiar manner as the ogre leader. He hurled the dead ogre's body down to his companions, who believed the corpse to be that of Kororomanna. As soon as it hit the ground they clubbed it to pieces, while Kororomanna slipped down and

helped them. 'Wait a bit,' he said to the ogres, 'I am just going in the bush, but will soon return.' It was not long, however, before the ogres saw that they had been tricked. They yelled with rage on finding that they had really destroyed one of themselves, and hunted high and low for their man; but with approaching daylight they were reluctantly compelled to give up the chase.

In the meantime, Kororomanna realized that he had lost his way, and during his wanderings through the forest his adventures were numerous and as strange as his first. Eventually he came across a man's skull lying on the ground and carelessly poked his arrow into its eyeball. The skull was actually on ogre, who immediately called out: 'You must not do that. But now that you have injured me you will have to carry me.' So Kororomanna attached the skull to his back by means of a bark-strip support. He not only had to carry the head, but feed it too. No matter what game he killed, he had to share it with the head, which became heavier and heavier, until one day it broke the bark-strip support. On the excuse of finding more bark, Kororomanna fled into the forest and escaped his persecutor. But he still was lost.

Next, Kororomanna met an ogre who imprisoned him in a block of wood. Eventually he was set free upon making a gift of tobacco to the ogre, who in return gave him an enormous quantity of fish put up in a tiny bundle. After this, Kororomanna finally managed to find the right path back to his mother and wife, with the help of a series of animals who showed him the way. Once home, he told the women to open the parcel and, as they did so, sure enough out came fish after fish, small and large, fish of all kinds, so many that the house speedily became filled and the occupants had to shift outside.[1]

THE ADVENTURES OF CIMIDYUE

In the following tale, from the Tucuna Indians of the Amazon Basin, the lost traveller is a woman who in the end is led back home by a butterfly. Certain butterflies, particularly those of the beautiful blue-winged *Morpho* genus, are considered by the Indians to be transformed sorcerers who have marvellous powers to do either good or evil:

Cimidyue's husband, who thoroughly disliked her, decided to lose her. He took her into the forest to hunt coatá monkeys and made an excuse to leave her with the monkeys. It was a long time before Cimidyue realized that her husband had abandoned her, and she did not know where she was or how to return home. She decided to accompany the monkeys. At sundown the monkeys assumed human form, peered down and recognized the woman. 'Why, it's Cimidyue! What are you doing here?' When she explained, they took her to a place where there was a large house. 'Here are many hammocks,' they said. 'Lie down in one and sleep.' Cimidyue obeyed, but the next morning there was no house and the monkeys again had animal form. She went on with them, wandering through the jungle.

At last they reached the dwelling of the lord of monkeys, who had human form, though he was of a race of jaguars. He invited her to help him prepare sweet manioc-beer for a festival that evening. That night the lord of the monkeys slept and snored through his nose, announcing that he would devour Cimidyue. Becoming anxious, she woke him, but this enraged him, so that he struck his nose with a large kernel of the caivarú fruit until it began to bleed. Then he fell asleep again, but soon began to snore in the same fashion. Again the woman woke him, whereupon he began to maltreat his nose furiously, catching the flowing blood in a gourd and drinking it. Then he ordered still more beer prepared, with the result that everyone was completely befuddled.

The next morning the lord of the monkeys went off hunting, but first he tied a long rope to Cimidyue's leg and kept hold of the other end. From time to time he gave the rope a tug to make sure the woman was still a prisoner. At the suggestion of a helpful tortoise, she managed to escape by removing the cord from her leg and tying it to a house-post. Running away, she passed the brother of the lord of the monkeys, who was sitting in front of the door of his house. Following the tortoise's advice, she struck him on the knee-cap with a cudgel, and the blow was extremely painful.

When he returned from the hunt, the lord of the monkeys started looking for the woman, and he asked his brother if he had seen 'a fat girl' go by. Still crazed with pain, the brother said he didn't want to hear about fat girls. Finally the lord of the monkeys gave up the search.

Cimidyue, once more lost in the forest, met with further misadventures. While running through the jungle, she heard a knocking on wood. Thinking it was some man, she followed the sound, only to find that it was merely a bird. 'If you were only human,' she said, 'you could show me the way to my father's house.' The bird answered that if she would always follow the sound of his tapping, she would arrive safely home. But he lied, and she became more hopelessly lost in the jungle.

At nightfall she encountered an inambú bird, who was preening his feathers to puff them up. Because of the bird's great size, Cimidyue thought she was seeing an old woman plaiting a basket; to her the outstretched wings looked like a house. She asked the bird for permission to sleep there, which was granted, but shortly afterwards the bird flew up into a tree and Cimidyue had to sleep alone under the tree. The next morning the bird assumed human form, and Cimidyue asked it the way to her father's house. 'Go in the direction in which I am plaiting these basket strips' replied the bird; but this was a lie.

That night Cimidyue hid beneath an enormous ants' nest hanging from a tree, but the nest was in fact a jaguar, which threatened to kill her. She fled, and that night slept among the roots of a kapok tree. A huge lizard, and then a toad, passed by, jeering at her while pretending to offer her food. Finally the lord of the tree, a blue butterfly, *Morphos menelaus,* woke up and announced that he was going to eat pineapples in a certain Indian's garden. This Indian was none other than Cimidyue's father.

Cimidyue followed the butterfly to the river. Her father's hut was on the other side, so that she had at one time crossed the river without realizing it. The butterfly uttered a magic formula which changed the woman into a red dragonfly, and the two insects flew together to the opposite bank, which Cimidyue would never have been strong enough to reach without her companion's help. To thank him, she crushed the best pineapples in her father's plantation, and the butterfly drank the juice. The father, visiting his garden, was astonished to see so many broken fruits. The next day he returned with his wife and both lay in ambush. When the butterfly and Cimidyue came again, the father recognized his fat daughter and tried to catch her, but she escaped. She was a bit crazed from her ordeal in the forest.

Then all the villagers hid in the garden, but the butterfly and Cimidyue did not return until the third day. The men managed to capture Cimidyue, while the butterfly escaped. She shrieked to the butterfly for help, but in vain. Her father took her home and gave her an emetic, so that she vomited violently and was thus restored to reason.

Some time later, Cimidyue met her former husband at a feast. He had come dressed in a mask representing a small downy lizard and had straw bound to his bead. He began singing a mocking song to his victim. She lit a piece of resin which she threw at the mask and the dry straw caught fire. The man ran off but could not rid himself of his bark costume. His belly burst with the heat.[2]

THE SAGA OF PERISUÁT

The Mundurucú Indians of Brazil have a very long legend of a young boy named Perisuát. He is taken into the forest by his uncle, who transforms himself into a tapir. The boy shoots the tapir and although the arrow does not enter the tapir's body, it feigns sleep. Thinking it dead, the boy innocently plunges his arm into the tapir's anus to remove the entrails before cutting it up. His arm becomes stuck, and no sooner has the tapir agreed to free his prisoner than it is killed by hunters. Perisuát escapes from the hunters by transforming himself into a bees' nest, but then he finds himself lost in the forest. He crosses a river on the back of a cayman which tries to gobble him up, and has unpleasant encounters with various creatures: birds, caterpillars, several male and female jaguars in human form, a tapir and his daughters, who are also in human form and want to marry him, an ogre with a pointed leg, and another ogre who catches him and from whom he is delivered by insects and a squirrel. A jaguar whose wounds he tends finally shows him the right path and when he arrives at his own village he has become so fierce that he kills his own pet birds. As a result of his long stay in the forest, his skin has become pallid and infested with vermin. His grandmother washes and nurses him, but his sickness is too far advanced and he dies.

In the South American odyssey of the lost traveller there typically exists no resolution allowing the protagonist to make a significant gain from his traumatic experiences in the forest, and the ending of the story is not a particularly happy one. Indeed, it sometimes spells disaster, as it does for Perisuát, who being ineradicably marked by his sojourn among inhuman creatures of the forest, is doomed to kill his own pet animals and die. Cimidyue, though saved from madness, does not escape from a state of wretchedness. Although she has the satisfaction of killing her treacherous husband, the act is not one that leads to everlasting happiness. Kororomanna merely makes a gift of too many fish once he arrives home, and then the story abruptly stops. In the odysseys related by the Piaroa Indians of Venezuela about lost travellers who spend long periods with the forest animals, the traveller and his kinsmen die suddenly from disease a year after his return home. The emphasis in these sagas is not on a happy ending where valour is rewarded and evil punished, for the stories do not truly finish. The return home in fact solves nothing.

Moreover, the sagas have no clear-cut heroes and heroines who have moral right on their side, nor are the lost travellers individuals of crucial historical importance. They are ordinary humans who as victims of circumstance have their ordeals thrust upon them.

This is not to say that South American epics have no highly structured form, for they clearly do — that of reduplication. The sagas are formula stories where the tale begins with an initial incident, and its form is then repeated in episode after episode. The narrative structure is a serial one, as is the unfolding of time within the epic where each episode is carefully bordered by day and night. And just as one day is equal to the next, so do the ordeals match one another in their seriousness for the traveller. There is no gradation in the series of adventures which makes one ordeal worse than the next. The narrative stress is upon sequence and seriality, and not development of plot, and it is perhaps for this reason that the story stops abruptly. The ending within such a structure simply does not matter. Each episode is a rich and elaborate whole, well worth telling in itself; and the form the first takes can be duplicated *ad infinitum* as it suits the narrator's purpose or ability.

BATTLES WITH SLAVE-RAIDERS

The same structure, based on repetition and sequence, is used for other types of legends from jungle South America, especially those dealing with past battles with enemy tribes. Throughout the Guianas there exist innumerable legends of this type, telling of the days of Carib Indian attacks, which in history were particularly intense during the eighteenth century, but which continued to some extent into the early twentieth. Europeans settled on the northern coast of South America provided the warlike Carib Indians with western arms to carry out slave-raids on other tribes. These accomplices of the white man, who paddled their great war-canoes down the rivers of the interior in search of slaves, were not only notable warriors but notorious cannibals as well; it is not surprising to find that the Carib attacks are still remembered with horror by the tribes who were their victims. In legend, however, history is made subservient to the telling of a good story; and giving these tales about 'the time the Caribs came' their own peculiar charm is the intermingling of yesterday and today, and the juxtaposition of history with the miraculous. In a Piaroa Indian version of the slave-raid battles, Perez Jiménez, the Venezuelan dictator of the 1950s, leads a Carib attack against the Piaroa. In another Piaroa story the Caribs are dressed in suits of armour of the kind worn by sixteenth-century Spanish conquistadors, and the Piaroa sorcerers, incongruously, have magical epaulettes which provide a defence against the firearms of their armoured aggressors.

Also contrary to history, in legend the victim tribe usually outwits and defeats the attackers. An Arawak and a Piaroa legend about 'How we beat the Caribs' are identical in structure. In a series of battles the Carib aggressors far outnumber their victims, but through cunning, magic and occasional violence the 'victims' win out. The numbers and plans of the Caribs are divined by sorcery; the steering paddles of the Carib canoes become hopelessly entangled in vine ropes stretched by the Arawaks across a stream; the Caribs fall to their deaths from rope ladders cunningly attached to high cliffs as a trap by Piaroa leaders. As with the legends of lost travellers, there is an initial incident, and each of the following episodes is a copy of the first in structure; but with one difference. In both the Piaroa and the Arawak stories, the numbers of warriors become greater and greater, as do the successes of the 'victims'. Fifty Caribs lead the first attack, while by the last their numbers are in tens of thousands. On the other hand, the motif of one is reduplicated in each episode of the Piaroa legend, and the motif of two in the Arawak: in the Piaroa story one Indian of the losing side in each battle is always saved, while in the Arawak tale two are always saved. In both a numerical repetition underscores the serial form of the tale.

THE HUMAN CONDITION

A quality intrinsic to all legends of the South American rain-forest, though one that is rarely mentioned, is their humour. They are always very funny tales, and considered as such by the Indians. The humour of the narrative is not subtle, but strongly slapstick in nature and, in its presentation, comparable in effect to a film cartoon in the modern West. The performance of the narrator is critical to the humour, a value that is weakened when legends are written down. Animals are imitated in sound, the reactions of the protagonists are mocked, and fear or confusion is captured through the tone of voice. Each episode provides a framework for the narrator to elaborate the absurd, and even the battle-scene in the Carib stories concludes with slapstick, as in a Piaroa version, when the Carib leader is lanced to death while in the act of making love.

In the legends of Kororomanna and Cimidyue, similarly, hilarity is provoked by the absurd. In both legends, many of the characters look peculiar and act in a disconcerting manner. In the Kororomanna story the ogre demands to be given a proper posterior for the sole purpose of being able to fart as loudly as the gaseous monkey carcass. In the tale about Cimidyue, the lord of the monkeys, when awakened for snoring, furiously maltreats his nose. As presented in the narrative, these creatures are not so much frightening as ludicrous, and although the protagonist's predicament is terrifying, the situation itself is not without comedy. For the peaceful and timid Piaroa to outwit the bellicose and cannibalistic Caribs is in itself a funny picture, just as it is ludicrous for young Kororomanna to outwit a multitude of vengeful ogres.

The heroes and heroines of the legends are rarely presented as examples to be copied; man and woman are depicted as each, in fact, are perceived to be. Through hyperbole the saga expresses a state-ment about the human condition, where the universe plays cruel jokes on mankind; and to survive people must respond in kind, though any survival achieved is but a fleeting one. To present this picture of the human situation, the narrator of the legend systematically breaks down the boundary between the serious and the risible — as we might expect it to be — and in doing so the message he relates, if not the tale, is a realistic one.

eric fraser

THE PACIFIC

The Arawa Canoe of Polynesia (page 372)

CHAPTER 41

MELANESIA

The islands of Oceania are conventionally divided into the three regions of Melanesia, Polynesia and Micronesia. There are complex interrelationships between all three areas, based on migrations, trade and intermarriage, but the greater similarities lie between Polynesia and Micronesia. Melanesia stretches from the tip of Irian Jaya in the west to the island of Fiji in the east, taking in New Guinea, New Britain, New Ireland, the Solomons and North Solomons, Vanuatu (the New Hebrides), New Caledonia and various other islands.

In the usage of western scholarship 'legend' refers to a class of stories, intermediate between 'myth' and 'history', often preserved in oral form. But Kenelm Burridge, writing on the oral traditions of the Tangu, a people of Madang province in Papua New Guinea, points out that for Tangu all their traditions are 'true', communicating different aspects of knowledge, and it is artificial to divide them into categories derived from European experience. Tangu themselves do make a distinction in principle between stories about human beings and those about *puoker* or spirits. But in practice the distinction is blurred; spirits appear as humans, humans turn into spirits. Burridge is therefore justified in using the single term 'narrative' to include all varieties of story-telling, and in analysing them as a single corpus in which the basic ideas of Tangu culture are expressed.

It is still of interest, however, to select those stories or aspects of stories which may carry historical import or most directly link a people to their past. An impressive example of how legends can be shown to preserve knowledge of ancient events is found in a recent study of the 'time of darkness' legend, which is widely known throughout the Highlands provinces in Papua New Guinea. The legend tells of a time when the sun was obscured and layers of ash fell from the sky, causing the destruction of gardens and livestock and

The snake entertains the man seeking a wife (page 366)

forcing people to stay indoors. After it, crops and gardens flourished with renewed vigour. At Tari, in the Southern Highlands, the ash is called bingi, and the people preserve in the story instructions on how to cope with falls of bingi which are seen as recurrent. Men are to build communal houses and stay indoors. Women should go to their natal places and no sexual intercourse should take place. Only youngest sons of families are to venture outdoors. If these taboos are not observed, the earth will not regenerate its crops after the ash-fall and there will be a holocaust. Obviously the story is deeply imprinted with local beliefs and social values. At the same time there is no doubt that it and the fifty or so other versions which have been collected all refer to a historical event: a volcanic ash-fall.

The anthropologist J. B. Watson, who first noted the story in the Eastern Highlands area, suggested that it dated to 1883 when the volcano Krakatoa erupted in the Sunda Straits between Java and Sumatra. The recent and comprehensive study by Russell Blong, a geologist, argues that Krakatoa is an unlikely source, because of its distance from the New Guinea Highlands and the composition of its ash-fall. Speculation is further aided here by archaeological findings. At Kuk, a site near Mount Hagen in the Western Highlands, archaeologists have found a series of volcanic deposits. The most recent layer is fixed by Carbon 14 dating methods to about 250 years ago. A possible source for this layer is Long Island, which erupted probably around AD 1700 and could have spread its ash from the north coast of New Guinea widely throughout the Highlands.

It appears, then, that these traditions of a time of darkness and ash-fall accurately recall volcanic eruptions of the past, and have been preserved for many generations. In most of the stories there is also an awareness that ash-falls have been repeated and may come again. At Tari, in fact, there were attempts to secure such a repetition by ritual sacrifices, in the hopes of renewing the fertility of the earth. Memories of occasional falls of hail, snow and frost, and of solar eclipses, have obviously accreted to the ash-fall theme also, but the main point remains, that this widespread legend contains a remarkable kernel of historical accuracy.

The story is known in the Hagen area itself, and was recorded by a missionary-anthropologist who worked there immediately after Europeans discovered the Highlands in 1933. Hageners refer to it as *ek teman,* 'a history', rather than *kang,* 'myth' or 'folk-tale', so their categories here fit with the distinction between legend and myth noted earlier. A similar distinction is made by the Daribi people, who live near Mount Karimui on the fringes of the Highlands. They speak of *po page* 'accounts of origins', and *namu po* 'tales', the former corresponding to a strict meaning of 'myth' and the latter encompassing legend and folk-tale. *Namu po* often have as their purpose the pointing of a moral through an entertaining series of events. This can be illustrated by the story of 'The Snake People', in which a major contrast is made between a wise elder cousin (or brother) and a foolish younger one.

THE SNAKE PEOPLE

In the story the elder cousin goes off to look for a wife, and resists the temptation to speak to others or take food from their gardens on the way. He enters a men's house and a little snake invites him to take some tobacco and smoke. All the other snakes then return from catching fish and coil up to sleep, but in the morning he sees they have turned into men and they give him plenty of steamed fish to eat. They also give him exact instructions on how to obtain a wife: he is to cut down two pandanus fruits at a cross-roads and then eat his present of fish. He obeys, and finds two attractive women, who address him as husband. Back at home his cousin asks him for one of them and is told to go and find his own. But the second man is greedy. When he comes to the snakes' house he helps himself to tobacco and rapes a woman, so in revenge the snakes crush him to death.

The story's main purpose is clearly to stress that modesty and patience can bring success, while greed results in disaster (the cousin who ate too much is himself eaten). It also presents snakes as superior to men. This theme reflects the widespread observation that snakes shed their skins and the belief that in doing so they rejuvenate themselves — unlike men, whose skin reveals an inevitable process of ageing.

Another Daribi snake story warns against insulting others by asking about their origins. Again, the basic motif is widespread — it is found, for example, also in New Britain and Vanuatu.

An old woman lived with her daughter. She kept a pet snake (a death adder) which copulated with her, but one day the daughter found the snake, killed it and ate it with some sago. The mother in anger took her daughter's clothes and sealed up all parts of her body with tree gum. She then walked off in the stolen clothes and found herself a husband; but he later became bored with her and killed her by a trick, searching for her daughter instead. Discovering the girl, he removed the tree gum and married her, and they had many children. One day, when the daughter — now a mother — was out fishing, the father scolded his children and told them how he had originally found their mother. When she heard about this, she was angry and ashamed. She turned into a plant and the father and children became birds.

The revelation of unusual circumstances of marriage or begetting thus leads to disaster and a final flight from human existence itself. There are several Daribi variations on this same theme. In one, a snake-man gives his daughter to an Uru man, and the daughter warns him that she must not touch water, the element from which she originally came. But his first wife taunts her with being lazy and they go to fetch water together, whereupon she jumps into the water and is never found again, though the husband dives repeatedly in desperate search for her.

It is hardly possible to argue that such stories encapsulate any particular historical events among the Daribi. Instead they put moral precepts into narrative. They do, however, reflect a feature of life in Papua New Guinea societies which it is essential to grasp, and that is the contracting of marriages with outside groups, even across language boundaries. In such marriages, it is important not to insult one's spouse or her kin, or the alliance may be broken. These fables present this point in an exaggerated − and so dramatic − way.

POWERFUL HEROES

Stories from the Highlands of Papua New Guinea tend to take this form of morality dramas, and to be concerned less with the creation of the world than with how people should behave in it. Legends from the Papuan Gulf area and from parts of the northern coast of Papua New Guinea around Madang show a much greater emphasis on the travels of culture heroes or demi-gods, who distribute skills, artefacts and customs, and even carve out striking features of the landscape as they go. It is perfectly possible − indeed likely − that such tales do in fact reflect innovations by individuals and also the incursions of people from elsewhere, bringing with them new practices.

Powerful heroes of this kind are usually presented as having magical powers and are said to have introduced new crafts or made magic for crops to grow instantaneously. Such tales of prowess have reappeared in the cargo cults, whose leaders promise salvation and the magical acquisition of western consumer goods or 'cargo', and which are most persistent where the culture hero theme is most stressed in traditional society. Mambu, a cargo 'hero' who led a brief movement in Bogia (near Madang) in 1937−38, was said to have slipped his chains when put in jail by the Administration for illegal tax-collecting, to have produced money out of thin air, and to have travelled to Australia to claim the cargo destined for him at the docks there. Mambu's story is outshone by the much larger career of Yali. Yali was involved in the war against the Japanese in New Guinea, and actually did go to Australia. He interpreted museums and zoos there as homes of the Europeans' totems, which looked after them and gave them wealth. In his own cult, which he subsequently began back in his home area, women became possessed and drew money from the air, and Yali himself was credited with the power to stimulate these events. Such powers are essentially the same as those of the first heroes who could make crops or children grow instantly out of a drop of blood or a scrap of skin.

MYTH, LEGEND AND HISTORY

Stories of miracles are, of course, one way of legitimizing leadership. Another more mundane way is simply to stress brave deeds. There is probably a great bulk of oral tradition which falls into this category. Codrington, who worked as a missionary on the Banks Islands between 1863 and 1887, reports one legend which justifies the dominance of a particular family at a place called Saa. The story is set eleven generations back in the past. There were four brothers, of whom the eldest was the chief. The chief was a quiet man but the others were hot-heads and he was tired of paying compensation on their behalf. Their enemies surrounded them, but the Saa people escaped by night. Unfortunately, they left behind a bunch of betel-nuts belonging to the chief which could be used as sorcery material by the other side. The youngest brother then joined the enemy in disguise, while they were still unaware that the escape had been made, and told them he would steal into Saa to see if the people were still asleep. Once there, he took all the nuts from the chief's tree and slipped back through the enemy ranks. So they migrated to the coast, their chief saved, and joined another village. The story validates the descent of the chiefly line, preserved also by invocation of the eleven generations of forebears on occasions of sacrifice. It also, incidentally, shows another play on the universal Melanesian theme of relations between elder and younger brother. Here, younger brother is a man of war, who brings trouble; but he also saves elder brother by his courage and wit.

Codrington's story dates from more than a century ago. In the Highlands of Papua New Guinea, where fighting is still a contemporary fact, stories of prowess and cunning are recounted regularly in speeches at festivals for peace-making, and refer usually to events within the past two generations. They are used as charters, not for chiefship, but for divisions within the group and alliances with others. Each group also has its origin story in which there is an imperceptible transition from events of a mythical nature to those which are more obviously historical. Thomas Nakinch, a young scholar from the Ulga tribe in the Mount Hagen area, has written a full-length analysis of these traditions among his own people. The major emphasis in the story is placed on the expansion and dispersion of the group. Many incidents in it may well be entirely historical, yet they also show elements which are common in other origin stories from the same cultural area.

One part of the account has to do with the beginnings of the Upuka, a group paired with Ulga proper. The primacy of Ulga is shown in the greater supernatural qualities of their founder, Mul Temb. The Upuka founder was a man, Tiltipul, a short man who lived alone with his boar pig. One day Tiltipul met another short man and his grown-up unmarried sister, who were living together at the place Munduka. Tiltipul and his new friend embraced each other, and Tiltipul married the sister. They had three sons, 'elder', 'middle', and 'youngest', who grew up very fast. Their father told them to form three sub-clans and expand the group. Later, he was buried in a landslide. The sons could not find his body, and held the funeral for him in great sadness. They discussed their situation with the mother and remembered the father's advice to found each his own group. The sons are now represented as ancestors of existing sub-clans named directly after them.

The early part of the story presents a picture of a solitary world. Tiltipul is by himself, with no wife. His delight in meeting another man is directly related to the opportunity this gives him of marriage with the man's sister, alliance, reproduction, and expansion of his descent line. One can read the story both as an expression of the fact that settlement of new areas has been a consistent feature of population movement in the Highlands and as an indication of the basic cultural values which sustain such movement. The story, then, functions as myth, legend, history, and contemporary key to action.

CHAPTER 42

POLYNESIA AND MICRONESIA

The many islands of Polynesia lie within an enormous triangle in the Pacific, with its apices at Easter Island, Hawaii and New Zealand, the sides more than 6437 kilometres (or 4000 miles) long. To the north-east of Polynesia are the island chains of Micronesia.

The cultures of these two regions have undergone a long period of separate development which is reflected in their differences. Indeed, within each region, different islands and island groups developed their own distinctive cultural styles and social organizations. The peoples of Polynesia and Micronesia, with the exception of the Maori of New Zealand, are the inhabitants of fairly small areas of land set in thousands of square kilometres or miles of ocean. In the gradual settlement of the Pacific from the west, canoe voyagers found their way to or chanced upon many of the most isolated islands. It is not entirely surprising that the ocean, canoes and voyaging feature strongly in tradition.

The islands of Yap, in Western Micronesia, are well known for their 'stone money', important items of wealth being large wheel-shaped stones, *fei,* the largest up to 3.6 metres (12 feet) across. The legend of the making of the first *fei* tells of a voyage:

There was an old man called Anagumang who had learned the seasonal movements of the stars from the female spirit-being Le-gerem. With a crew of seven men he sailed from Yap in a large canoe. Being guided by the stars of the constellation Pleiades, Anagumang brought the canoe to the Palau Islands. Passing through a reef passage in the north, they came at last to the islets of Kokial. There they found a shining stone

The battle of the Long-ears and the Short-ears (page 376)

(aragonite) and Anagumang was inspired with the idea that the stone could be made into a kind of currency. They proceeded to carve the stone into different shapes — into the shape of fish, into that of the crescent moon, and into round slabs pierced through the centre. Anagumang was especially satisfied with the last form, and, with their cargo of rock, he and his crew set off for home, a voyage which lasted five days. When they arrived in Yap, Le-gerem discarded all but the wheel-shaped stones and worked a charm which concentrated all men's desires on this form of wealth. Thereafter fighting came to Yap as the tribes competed for the new valuables.

The Palau Islands, some 402 kilometres (250 miles) south-west of Yap, were indeed the source for their 'stone money', and repeated canoe voyages were made to obtain it. This type of voyage, to obtain raw materials or enter into other trade, to carry gifts or tribute, was not unusual in Micronesia. The ability of the skilled navigators in determining their courses between islands by means of stars and other natural signs was of particular importance to the peoples of the smaller atolls, whose limited resources made trade with the more sizeable high islands particularly desirable. In some areas this navigational knowledge has not yet been lost. Understandably, a great navigator was held in high esteem.

FANUR AND HAGUR

A legend of two skilful navigators, Fanur of Pulawat and Hagur of Pulap, comes from the central Caroline Islands:

Fanur had designs upon the wife of Hagur. To achieve his ends, he sailed to Pulap and made friends with the other navigator. They would go fishing together and on longer trading trips, guiding their canoe by the stars and sun, the patterns of waves and swells and their knowledge of reefs and shoals. In the course of a trading voyage to the islands of Truk, Fanur acted to fulfil his plans, knocking Hagur overboard. Confidently leaving him to drown, he sailed on to Truk to complete his business, trading for turmeric, perfume and other goods. However, Hagur was not lacking in magical skill and, when a piece of bamboo floated by, he concealed himself inside it and travelled within it back to Pulap. There he revealed himself to his wife when she came to the shore, speaking from the bamboo. But he told her to keep his presence a secret and to behave well to Fanur upon his return.

In due course Fanur came and told of Hagur's accidental

death. He was accepted as the new chief navigator and preparations were made for the feast and ritual connected with the end of a voyage. Hagur instructed his wife to conceal him at the bottom of the food container being made ready for the feast. This she did. When the food bowl was put before Fanur, he first took portions to make offerings to the gods, and then made to offer a portion to his dead 'friend' Hagur, asking to inherit his knowledge. As he reached into the bowl for the morsel of food, the hidden Hagur bit into his hand. Fanur fell dead and Hagur took his place at the feast. It was he who obtained Fanur's knowledge and became the greatest of navigators.

THE ARAWA CANOE

Polynesian legend offers many accounts of the voyages of settlement undertaken by the ancestors in their sailing canoes. Some speak of journeys from an ancestral homeland, Hawaiki or 'Avaiki, and nineteenth-century scholars made many attempts to identify this homeland — islands of Indonesia, even India being suggested, though it was recognized by some that the term 'Havaiki' had also been applied to islands of central Polynesia, later points of departure in the Polynesian expansion. Modern writers have recognized more fully the limitations of historical reconstruction from these oral traditions, and the dangers of biased interpretation. Older ideas of canoes sailing out from Indonesia across the Pacific to the islands of Eastern Polynesia have long been abandoned. The evidence of archaeologists and of the students of the historical development of languages has turned the settlement of the Pacific into a much more gradual process. Proto-Polynesian colonies were established in Tonga (the Friendly Islands) perhaps as early as 1500 BC but New Zealand was not settled until more than 2000 years later, in the last phase of Polynesian expansion. The canoe traditions of New Zealand have been much used in reconstructing the history of its Maori people. Perhaps the most consistent of the legends is that of the Arawa canoe, told by the Arawa people of the central North Island:

A dispute broke out in Hawaiki between Tama-te-kapua and the chief Uenuku which was leading to wider conflict. The Arawa voyaging canoe was constructed and Tama-te-kapua was to be its commander, leaving Hawaiki for good. When the canoe was loaded with cargo and all who were to sail on it were ready, Tama-te-kapua remembered that he had no 'man of knowledge', no one skilled in ritual and navigation, for the Arawa. He therefore abducted the great and knowledgeable Ngatoro-i-rangi and his wife, asking them on board to perform certain ceremonies necessary for the commencement of the voyage and then sailing off with them still aboard.

He also abducted the wife of Ruaeo. He tricked her husband into going ashore to fetch an adze (stone axe) which he claimed to have left in his house. While Ruaeo was gone, the anchor stone was pulled up and the voyage began. Tama-te-kapua took Ruaeo's wife as his own. Her husband, when he realized what had happened, worked a magic which altered the apparent position of the stars, confusing those on board the canoe. Ngatoro-i-rangi, who was now acting as navigator, decided that he would climb up onto the roof of the house or cabin on the deck of the Arawa to see if he could make out the shoreline. However, knowing Tama-te-kapua's interest in women, he was concerned about leaving his wife alone and took the precaution of tying a rope to her hair, holding the other end in his hand as he climbed above. But this did not prevent Tama from interfering with Ngatoro-i-rangi's wife. He untied the rope and fastened it to the canoe's outrigger.

When Ngatoro came down and learned what had happened he was exceedingly angry and worked magic which not only seemed to change the places of the stars in the sky but also called up winds which drove the Arawa towards the place where the sky hangs down upon the ocean, towards the engulfing chasm of the Throat of Parata, which some say was a great whirlpool. The canoe was thrown about and all feared they were lost. Some cried out. Eventually Ngatoro-i-rangi was moved to sympathy by the cries of men, women and children. He went above and worked a charm which calmed the heavens and released the Arawa from her danger.

Their landfall was at Whangaparaoa in Aotea (the Bay of Plenty in the North Island of New Zealand). As they approached land, they saw the pohutukawa trees showing their brilliant red blossom. A lesser chief, Tauninihi was wearing a head-dress of much valued red feathers, kura. Seeing the blossoms, he cried out that the kura of this land was more plentiful than that of Hawaiki and threw the head-dress away, out onto the water. When it was discovered that it was only blossoms they had seen, all the chiefs were much disturbed at the loss of the kura. Later, the head-dress was found at the beach of Mahiti by a man called Mahina, who insisted on keeping it as his own. (Proverbial expressions about Mahina's find are equivalent to 'finders keepers'.) At Whangaparaoa they planted the sweet potato (the most important of the food crops introduced into New Zealand by the Maori.) However, before long they were drawn into an argument with the people of the Tainui canoe, which had also sailed from Hawaiki and had landed nearby. The fighting which they had escaped by leaving their homeland came to the land of Aotea.

VOYAGES FROM HAWAIKI

For many years the Maori canoe legends of this kind were interpreted as showing three periods of voyaging from Hawaiki, which was usually assumed to be somewhere in the Society Islands, perhaps Tahiti, and the arrival of the Arawa canoe was dated to about AD 1350. However, recent investigation has thrown doubt on these conclusions. Even in smaller islands the legends surrounding particular sets of events may be found in several significantly different versions. The canoe legends of the many Maori tribes of New Zealand reveal considerable diversity and complexity in their accounts of ancestral voyages of discovery and settlement. It has been convincingly argued that the widely accepted 'Maori traditions' of three periods of voyaging are in fact rationalizations by European interpreters anxious to create a tidy historical framework.

Archaeology now indicates that New Zealand has been settled by Polynesians since the tenth century, but it also shows a considerable change occurring between the fourteenth and fifteenth centuries — the emergence of the so-called Classical Maori culture with its characteristic tools, weapons and art styles. Could this 'Classical' culture have been spread by population movements within New Zealand? Some experts believe so, and have suggested that the canoe traditions, which seem to belong to this period, may refer to such movements. Hawaiki, in this case, may lie in the north of New Zealand itself.

THE WAR OF TANGI'IA AND TUTAPU

War was certainly not unusual in Polynesia or, for that matter, in a number of areas of Micronesia. (The Gilbert Islanders — now Kiribati — even produced a kind of armour for their warriors, made of plaited vegetable fibre.) Though rank in traditional Polynesian societies was heavily dependent upon descent in a chiefly line, the role of the warrior could also be very important. The tale of the coming of the major tribal ancestors to Rarotonga is one of conflict between chiefly warriors.

A dispute had broken out in Ta'iti between Tangi'ia and his kinsman Tutapu, concerning their relative rank, status and rights to certain food trees or tribute from them. Tutapu conceived an implacable hatred for Tangi'ia and pursued him from island to island, to Mauke, to Atiu, to Aitutaki, to Porapora. He became known as Tutapu-of-the-long-pursuit.

Then Tangi'ia went off to the east, the legend says, to Maketu, and there he met Karika (a chief of 'Avaiki or Manuka) with his war party. Karika saw that Tangi'ia had many men. Afraid of him, he gave his daughter Te Mokoroa-ki-aitu to be Tangi'ia's wife. In recognition Tangi'ia conceded the *au*, a symbol of supreme authority, to Karika. But Tangi'ia's men were unhappy and angry at this and one tore the *au* from his hand and threw it out upon the sea. Karika became angry. Tangi'ia gave him a red feather head-dress in compensation.

Karika said, 'We will go and seek for a land.' Tangi'ia's men were many, he had 200, Karika 140. Said Karika to Tangi'ia, 'You go west, I'll go east.' They sailed away. Then one night Tangi'ia put his hand down into the ocean. It was cold. He said to his men, 'Karika has deceived us, so that we shall die on the great ocean. We will return to the east, towards the sunrise.' Eventually they reached land, and Tangi'ia called it Rarotonga. Karika's deception had led them to the west *(raro)*. The wind that had brought them to land was southerly *(tonga)*, therefore the name Rarotonga was given.

Meanwhile, Tutapu had arrived on the other side of the island. Two of his man told Tangi'ia of his presence. Tangi'ia said to them, 'Return, tell Tutapu for me that there will be peace, the fighting is over.' They went back to Tutapu and told him what Tangi'ia had said. 'Perhaps tomorrow his head will be severed by my club,' he replied.

The next morning Tutapu went to seek Tangi'ia and met him at the place called Tapuae, and was defeated by him there. Karika arrived and joined forces with Tangi'ia in fighting Tutapu, who was completely defeated by them and his corps of warriors broken.

Tangi'ia immediately set off in pursuit of Tutapu to seize him. At Te Atu kiri, Tutapu's neck ornament fell off (this was known as a *ki'iki'i*) and therefore that area is called Ki'iki'i. The fighting was fierce and all Tutapu's warriors were killed.

There followed a lengthy pursuit of Tutapu, during which Tangi'ia's spear once glanced off his back and once struck him in the heel. Eventually Tutapu fled to Ngatangi'ia to save himself by reaching his canoe. Tangi'ia immediately came after him. He fled once more to the mountain, but Tangi'ia overtook him at the pool of Vaikura, killed him, and, pulling out his eyes, placed them in his own mouth. Tangi'ia's gods spoke from above, saying, 'You are a chief who eats hastily, Tangi'ia.' Said Tangi'ia, 'Why should I not eat at once? Until when should I leave it? His pursuit of me has brought him to the night of death. This is that night my gods.' The eyes were offered to the gods above and the body taken down to the shore.

Finally, after the correct formula to remove the sanctity of chieftainship had been found, and the correct firewood gathered, the body was cooked in an earth oven. This act was said to stem from the terrible hatred engendered by the long quarrel.

After these violent beginnings, the legend goes on to become one of construction, as Tangi'ia and Karika build temples or ceremonial centres, establish rituals, and set up chieftainships, some of which survive until this day. It has commonly been stated that Tangi'ia came to Rarotonga from the Society Islands (Ta'iti being Tahiti) whereas Karika came from the Samoan group ('Avaiki being assumed to be Savai'i, or Manuka assumed to be Manu'a) where, it is said, he also appears in genealogies. In fact, as with the New Zealand canoe traditions, these old assumptions may not be as well founded in legend as has been thought. But in this case archaeology seems to give them some support. Most features of traditional Rarotongan culture clearly belonged to central Eastern Polynesia, the cultural region in which lie the Society Islands, Tangi'ia's supposed home, but a number of stone tools found together near Rarotonga's largest settlement, Avarua, belong to a type known from Western Polynesia, in fact from Samoa. It seems very likely that a small number of Samoans came to Rarotonga in the fourteenth century, maybe Karika and his men.

A point worth noting in the Rarotongan legend is its concern with particular places and the giving of place-names, such as Rarotonga and Ki'iki'i. Other sections of the story, not translated here, give accounts of the naming of other natural features on Rarotonga including a harbour and a pool. In some Polynesian legends incidents occur which seem to have been contrived as explanations of local place-names. The need for caution in accepting any one legendary explanation as historical fact is underlined by the case of Whangarei harbour in the north of New Zealand; there are at least six different Maori accounts of the origin of the name 'Whangarei'.

In some cases very real interests were at stake. The idea that an ancestor bestowed a name upon a certain place could serve to underline the special relationship of his descendants with a particular area of land, and help to justify their claims upon it. Legend cannot be assumed to be a neutral reflection upon history. There are several different versions of the story of Tangi'ia, Karika and Tutapu, varying on some important points, particularly those concerning the relative standing of Karika and Tangi'ia. Was the symbol of supremacy really handed over? Who arrived on Rarotonga first? Which of them really killed Tutapu? It must be remembered that Tangi'ia and Karika were founding ancestors for two major lines of chiefs, later to become political and military rivals. The interpretations given to the legend, its significant variations, reflect as much upon the interests of these power blocs in extolling their ancestors, as upon historical realities.

THE DESTRUCTION OF THE LONG-EARS

Another place in Polynesia where legend and archaeology have met, with no very clear conclusion, is the Poike Ditch on Easter Island. Sections of ditch, some 4 metres wide by 3 or more metres deep (13 feet by 10) form a line about 3.2 kilometres (2 miles) long across the base of the Poike Peninsula in the east of the island. An account of their origin is given in a legend which tells of war between a people with long ears, who controlled the island, and a people with short ears who were forced to work in building the *ahu* (large ceremonial stone platforms) near the coast.

The Long-ears ordered the Short-ears to clear stones from the surface of the ground. This they refused to do, saying that they were needed as oven stones and also encouraged growth in their food plants. The enraged Long-ears decided to kill the Short-ears. They built the Poike Ditch and filled it with wood and dry grass, intending to use it as an oven to roast the Short-ears. (In some versions, the original purpose of the ditch is as a line of defence in the warfare.) But a Short-ear woman who was married to a Long-ear man managed to discover their plans and warned her relations. She told them that she would give a signal when the attack was about to come, and that they, the Short-ears, should come up behind the Long-ears as they lit the wood and grass, and force them into their own ovens. That is what they did. As a result of the surprise attack, all but two of the Long-ears were destroyed in the flames. Later these two warriors were adopted by the Short-ears, who were now masters of the island.

This legend has been the object of extraordinary speculation and debate. It has given encouragement to those who believed that Easter Island had been a home to two different population groups − Peruvians and Polynesians, Melanesians and Polynesians, two different groups of Polynesians, or whatever. On this, suffice it to say that the present evidence of archaeology, language and physical type overwhelmingly suggests that the Easter Islanders were nothing other than Eastern Polynesians, and very probably the descendants of a single group of settlers, perhaps from the Marquesas Islands. What of the Poike Ditch? The idea that anyone would build over 3 kilometres (or 2 miles) of ovens is certainly not very plausible, but the idea that the ditch was constructed as a defensive earthwork has received more consideration. Yet, not being a continuous ditch but cut by many causeways, it is not a very convincing form of defence. One suggestion has been that the ditching may have less to do with warfare than with horticulture, providing a sheltered growing area for food crops such as bananas or sugar cane. Parts of the depression may well prove to be natural, a geological feature. One expert has argued that the whole legend may be seen as a local explanation of certain geographical features − the presence of an area devoid of surface rocks (the area in which the Long-ears, who wished the stones to be cleared away, were said to live) and the great trench at Poike. However, archaeological excavation of one part of the ditch showed human activity there in the seventeenth century, the period in which the battle between Long-ears and Short-ears has often been placed.

Some sort of defensive use of the Poike Ditch cannot be ruled out.

When the first European, the navigator Roggeveen, came to Easter Island in 1722 many of the people he saw had long ears, that is they had artifically distended earlobes in which ornaments were worn. Apparently this custom died out slowly, and did not vanish completely until the second half of the nineteenth century. It was towards the end of that century that Easter Island traditions began to be systematically collected. But by that time the continuity of Easter Island culture had been disastrously disrupted by the Peruvian slave-raid of 1862. The population in 1877 was reduced to 110. In the light of these facts, is the legendary distinction between Long-ears and Short-ears a comparatively recent embellishment of an old tradition, made at a time when the significance of the old custom of ear-lobe stretching was no longer fully understood? It seems very possible. Understanding when, and under what circumstances, a legend was collected is most important in assessing what degree of historical content it can be assumed to have.

CHAPTER 43
AUSTRALIA

Legends are on the edge of Australian Aboriginal religious systems. Unlike myths, they are not formally supported by ritual; they are set in the recent past, not in the creative era, and their central characters are living human beings, 'people like us'. (Important myths are sometimes wrongly called legends because they refer to particular localities or are believed to be 'historically true'.) The Aborigines relied on oral, not written transmission. Such material was easily lost in the stress of European settlement, and legends survived only if someone came along to catch them in a more permanent form.

Like myths, legends could spread widely. People mostly stayed within a recognized regional range, but neighbouring groups exchanged gossip and stories at religious gatherings. That always involved changes: in language, in style, in local identity-markers, and in the details that gather around any story-line to make it seem more real to the listeners. Legendary characters were plentiful, but actual stories about them were not. Aboriginal societies emphasized co-operation, not individual achievement. The tabu on uttering a dead person's name in ordinary conversation could last, in different areas, from a few weeks to a few years. Even around the northern coasts, long influenced by outside contact from Indonesia, and through the Torres Strait Islands, stories circulating about famous or notorious persons did not last much beyond their lifetimes.

By the late 1930s Wonggu, the 'Grand Old Man of Caledon Bay' in northeastern Arnhem Land, had a formidable reputation. Actual incidents and rumours were combined and embellished into stories about his quick reaction to slights or opposition; about how he had acquired most of his twenty-odd wives, and who got wounded or killed in the process. By the late 1950s it did not matter that he was too old and weak to fling his spears. Just rattling them was enough to

Ned Kelly in his improvised armour (page 387)

get him his own way, along with the background threat of his large group of sons, who had become part of the legend. For several years after his death people spoke of him cautiously, in whispers. He is still remembered today, even though other events have eroded his importance.

THE STORY OF WURU-NGUNGU'S GRANDFATHER

More co-ordinated narratives developed around rumours or beliefs that had some extraordinary or magical quality. A popular theme was contact with the supernatural world, not in a conventional ritual setting, but as a personal first-hand experience. Many stories tell of human encounters with spirit characters or ghosts. Native doctors, 'powerful' men, were the most likely candidates for this.

One of the most persistent stories comes from the rough escarpment area of western Arnhem Land — 'Mimi country'. Among its oldest cave-paintings are little matchstick figures, Mimi, drawn in blood. They live on eternally in sheltered places among the rocks, and information about them comes from living men who claim to have seen them. The main version is about Joshua Wuru-ngungu's grandfather, who was born in the early 1900s. Wuru-ngungu himself, born in about 1918, told it to R. M. Berndt in 1947 and again on several occasions up to the early 1970s. It is almost identical with what Wuru-ngungu's wife, Dorcas Ngalgin-dali, told me in 1950.

Among the people living in Gurudjmug (said Ngalgin-dali) was my husband's grandfather. He was a margidbu, a native doctor. Early one morning he set off alone to hunt black kangaroo. He climbed high among the rocks, going on and on. At last he speared one. But it was a Mimi's 'dog'; and following the trail of blood he met the Mimi himself, who spoke to him. 'Come home with me, nephew. Two girls are waiting for you. And we've got some other meat cooking for you.' My husband's grandfather was tired, so he agreed to go.

After they had gone a long way, he heard singing. He was afraid. But that Mimi's wife came and embraced him, crying. The other Mimi asked who he was, where he came from. His 'uncle' sent someone for water: 'Quickly, he's thirsty!' But he wouldn't drink it. He wouldn't eat the cooked kangaroo meat either: 'I've got bad toothache.' He wouldn't accept the long basket of wild honey they offered: 'Just hang it up for a while.' He knew that if he took any of these he too would become like a Mimi. Then a didjeridu player and two songmen came over to him and began to sing their special Mimi songs. Three girls stood up to dance. Someone gave him a couple of small chidren to mind, but he didn't take them on his knees properly, 'in case they stay with me forever'. The singing stopped. It was almost dark. Soon they sent two girls over to him. One lay down at each side of him, each with her own small fire.

Everyone slept. He listened: everyone snoring. 'What can I do?' He got up, and found two pandanus-palm stems. He put one in his own sleeping-place, the other sideways under the girls' heads. He had sent 'something', some power to block their ears (and their understanding). He sent darkness for them all, and 'turned the country around' to make it seem different in their minds. Then he took his spear and flew away. The Mimi were angry when they woke up and found him gone. They speared his sleeping-place, spearing him in spirit. His 'uncle' flew up, searching, but couldn't find him; my husband's grandfather had used his spirit-power as a barrier.

When he got home it was late afternoon, and people were weeping for him. His mother and father feared he was dead. They got green leaves, warmed them and put them at his ears, so his ears were opened and he could hear them. He told them what had happened. They all moved away from that place. They wouldn't go hunting again up among those rocks, only to the ordinary bushland and plains.

Ordinary people cannot see Mimi and return home safely. Only a native doctor can do that, and he knows about refusing food and drink and emotional and sexual entanglements (an almost universal folklore motif). But this was told, on every occasion, as a true story of what an actual, identified person did; he went there 'in his own body'. It was not a dream journey, of the kind often reported in traditional Aboriginal accounts.

ABORIGINES AND 'OTHER PEOPLE'

There are similar stories about people visiting the land of the dead, the sky-world, and returning. An example is the legend of Yawalngura (or Yalngura), from Arnhem Land. He went to the land of the dead, the island of Bralgu, where the morning star comes from, voyaging there in his log-canoe. The story recounts his adventures, travelling among various islands, heading eastwards into the Gulf of Carpentaria, toward the source of the morning star. When he reached Bralgu, he accepted three ghost-wives. He finally returned home, ate a good meal, embraced his wife, and died. In other words, he went back to his ghost-wives in Bralgu. It is emphasized that he was a living human being, not a dead man. Because he was human, he could not move successfully between the two dimensions.[1]

On the other hand, there were also stories about people who died and then returned from the land of the dead, and Europeans were often identified as returning Aborigines. An example of 'The White Man as a Ghost' is given by one early writer: 'The best-known and perhaps the most important instance is that of William Buckley, a convict who escaped in the year 1803 from the settlement attempted by Colonel Collins within Port Phillip Bay... After wandering round the shore of the Bay, he was found by some of the

Wudthaurung tribe, carrying a piece of broken spear, which had been placed on the grave of one Murrangurk, by his kindred, according to the tribal custom. Thus he was identified with that man; and, as one returned from the dead, received his name and was adopted by his relatives.'[2]

An alternative view was that Europeans were malignant spirits. The first sight of men on horseback encouraged that view, and later events confirmed it. Even the most hostile creatures in the Aborigines' own environment belonged within a familiar pattern; there was a basis for knowing what to do and what to avoid. Europeans were different and unpredictable.

The 'Macassan' (Indonesian) or Buginese traders who came to the north coast left a better image, at least in retrospect – perhaps as contrasted with Europeans. They certainly made an impact on Arnhem Land culture, especially in the northeast. Stories tell how Aborigines there first encountered them, although they seem to have been coming for several centuries until they were prohibited in the early 1900s.

Northeastern Arnhem Landers have many short legends about shipwrecks and stranded canoes along their coastline, but the Macassan material is arranged in a co-ordinated series, with mortuary-ritual associations. Oral traditions current in the mid-1940s matched quite closely the limited evidence available from other sources such as documents and pottery shards. A few older men had gone with the traders to Macassar, and told almost epic stories of their journey – including, they said, meeting people like themselves on a couple of the islands they visited on the way. Several Aborigines stayed in the Celebes and never returned to Australia. They became 'lost' in the legend of that romantic voyage, and it is only in recent years that their presence there has been verified.

The Japanese pearlers whose fleets came until shortly before the Second World War triggered off another mystery, the legend of Tuckiar (or Dagiar). In 1932 several Japanese, camped on shore, were killed by Aborigines after a quarrel. The suspects were taken to Darwin and tried in 1934. One man, Tuckiar, was sentenced to death; his sentence was commuted later that year, but between Darwin and his home country he 'disappeared' and was not seen again by anyone who had known him. In 1946–47 most of the men who had been involved were still living, and so were Tuckiar's wives and children. Oral accounts of what happened were more immediate and more detailed than they became later on. Like all the Aboriginal reports of the restless years in that region, of police expeditions hunting down suspected killers of Europeans and Japanese, they put a different perspective on incidents and interpretations.

The legend of the lost white women of Arnhem Land was focused on this same area. In 1922 two European women were said to have come ashore from the wreck of the *Douglas Mawson* and been adopted by Aborigines. In 1925 a police party went looking for them. In 1935 a missionary suggested that the cause of the rumours was the arrival of European missionary women and some part-Aboriginal girls at Groote Eylandt mission station. In the late 1940s two sailors tried to join a search expedition they thought was being formed. This was an 'outside' legend, circulating among non-Aborigines who regarded Arnhem Land itself as an exotic, mysterious and legend-prone place.

Publicity helped to develop the Daisy Bates legend in the south. It was unusual enough for a lone female to be wandering about in Australia in the early years of this century (her husband and son receive almost no attention in the legend). It was even more unusual for such a female to show any interest in Aborigines and their welfare, and not seem to mind being physically close to them. She helped the legend along by continuing to wear her high-necked, long-skirted Victorian clothing regardless of the occasion, and by endeavouring to keep her work in the public eye. Twenty years or so after her death in 1951, a television series in several episodes melodramatically presented her as 'Saint Daisy'.

HEROES AND OUTLAWS

Most of the legends about Aborigines in relation to Europeans show them as poor creatures in need of charity and help (a Daisy Bates view), or as gallant helpers on expeditions or in situations of crisis, or as opponents of the European regime. A fourth theme has been present for a long time, but is much more prominent now than before; such opponents are seen as patriots.

A lot of this material has to do with relations between Aborigines and the police, which have always been a sensitive issue. Stories about the police in general (called, for instance, 'those who bind us with chains'), or individual policemen in particular, mostly show them in an unfavourable light, except for comments by Aborigines with personal attachments to particular policemen, as trackers or wives for example. Conversely, accounts of Aborigines saving the lives of Europeans (rescuing them from drowning, or finding water when none seemed available) also tend to develop legendary undertones.

More specifically, heroes and outlaws can be identified together, or contrasted, depending on perspective. One example is the story of 'Pigeon' (Sandimara), an Aboriginal tracker in the Kimberley region of Western Australia in the 1890s. On one patrol he succeeded in capturing a 'notorious outlaw', an Aboriginal who had been spearing cattle. This was a turning point for Pigeon. He listened to his captive's argument, that he should be loyal to other Aborigines and not to Europeans, and certainly not to the police. Pigeon and another tracker then killed the police constable, who was asleep in his camp, and escaped with the guns. They hoped to drive all the Europeans out of the area and consolidate Aboriginal support, but police trackers were generally disliked by Aborigines because they used their position to their own advantage. Nevertheless, Pigeon was now an outlaw (hero) himself. This is underlined in oral narratives about his exploits told by Aborigines in that region today; he was an outlaw *because* he was a hero. In one version he tries to use magical power to prevent bullets from hurting him. In another he is such a skilful bushman that a person can pass quite close without seeing him. And his death by gun-fire, fighting against 'oppression', is taken as symbolizing his heroic effort in the face of overwhelming odds.

In the south of Western Australia, when the first Europeans came up the Swan River in 1827, Yagan was a young man of the Bibelmen (or Bibbulmun) people who owned the land where the city of Perth now stands. He became known to many of the new settlers, took part in several killings as his father and others were killed, and was alternately hero and villain. In 1833, with a price on his head, he was tricked and killed by two young Europeans he had trusted as friends. His head and a section of his back that bore a long scar were cut off, dried, and later sent to England; their present whereabouts is not known. A traveller visiting Perth much later wrote in 1902 about a 'bloodthirsty native called Yagin'. He was shot, she said, by a man 'who afterwards took a large strip of his skin from shoulder to foot, tanned it, and made it into a belt, which he wore for years'. Her account of the shooting does not fit other reports that were closer to it in time, so her 'belt' story may be wrong too.

Perhaps the macabre detail of the smoke-dried head, deprived of mortuary rites, kept some oral traditions about Yagan alive among Aboriginal people of the southwest. According to Alexandra Hasluck, the President of the Legislative Council of Western Australia in an informal discussion of 'who would be considered the most noteworthy West Australian a hundred years hence', nominated Yagan, 'the Wallace of the Age' (referring to the famous thirteenth-century Scottish hero, Sir William Wallace). Hasluck is reluctant to call him a patriot or a hero, as some writers do. Interpreting legends (like myths) always depends on the context and perspective of the interpreter, and this is a clear example.

Yagan's story was revived for the sesquicentenary of the State of Western Australia in 1979. Aborigines and others pressed for a statue of him to be erected in Perth, the capital, and letters and articles in the local press argued the pros and cons. A film, *Yagan,* had already been made about him, with local Aborigines in prominent roles. His story was publicized as a sad reflection of Aboriginal—European relations, past and present.

There were thousands of Pigeons and Yagans throughout the

continent. They remained local heroes or outlaws until something happened to bring one or another into wider prominence with an appropriate legendary aura attached. An excerpt about a New South Wales Aboriginal, Bungaree, from the *Australian Dictionary of Biography* was reprinted in *Aboriginal News* (December 1973), a journal widely circulated among Aboriginal people. He was with Matthew Flinders in 1801–02 in his voyage around Australia, and had other experiences in the far north. Here a European legendary view of an Aboriginal and, by implication, of Aborigines generally, has been taken up by Aborigines themselves. Current Aboriginal concern about land-rights issues and mining developments has led to a refurbishing of legends of the 'hero, *not* outlaw' type. Recognition of shared identity between people of full and part-Aboriginal descent on an Australia-wide basis encourages this trend.

THE WIDER NATIONAL SCENE

The European discovery of Australia was surrounded with legends. One was based on the belief in strange coasts of lodestone that magically pulled passing ships to them. William Dampier, the seventeenth-century English seaman, supposed that early Dutch voyagers called part of the Western Australian coast the 'Land of the Eendracht', or 'indraught' for that reason. Actually, the *Eendracht* was merely the name of the ship in which Dirk Hartog landed in 1616 at the island still known by his name. He left a post there as a landmark, a navigation aid locating the 'New Southland of the Eendracht', but Dampier evidently misunderstood the reference on the Dutch chart. Swift's *Gulliver's Travels* contained a map said to have been copied from Dampier, reinforcing the mystery associated with the great southern continent. James Cook in his voyage of 1768 had instructions to search for the great Terra Australis Incognita, the unknown land of the south.

The legends that have gathered round the journeys of European explorers within the continent are much more numerous. Their stories are kept alive largely through school textbooks, historical studies and official 'revivals' of episodes relating to them. In 1875, for example, Ernest Giles set off with six men and eighteen camels from Adelaide across arid country to Perth. Arriving there in November, after a journey of six months, Giles and his party had a tremendous welcome, the population of Perth being especially fascinated by the camels. In 1979, as part of Western Australia's sesquicentenary celebrations, a team of camels came from Alice Springs to parade solemnly the main streets of Perth as a re-enactment of the scene.

The mysteries and tragedies that surround other explorers make for legends in the more usual sense. The fate of Ludwig Leichhardt is a case in point. He had travelled in the inland and north, as far as Port

Essington. In 1848 he and his party set off from the Darling Downs to cross the continent to Perth. They never arrived. The letter 'L' was found much later, engraved on a tree at the Barcoo River, and nothing more. A. C. Gregory covered large areas in searching for them in 1856 and 1858. Rumours and legends about a 'wild white man' living in western Queensland were current in 1870, and a police expedition went to a water-hole on the Diamentina River, where Aborigines reported that 'a party of white men' had been killed. In 1871 the rumours were revived by a man named Andrew Hume, who said that in 1862 he had seen a European living with Aborigines. In 1873 he said that in the Cooper's Creek area he had met with the same man, who claimed to have been with Leichhardt and that Leichhardt had been killed by other members of his own party. Hume set out to find him again, but he and one of his companions died of thirst. A friend of his took up the story in 1880, and in Sydney that year a reward of £ 1000 was offered for genuine information about the Leichhardt party, to no avail. The legend resurfaces from time to time, but the mystery remains unsolved.

TALES OF GOLD

Gold was discovered in New South Wales in the early 1850s and later in Victoria, with some large finds at Ballarat. Legends about the wealth to be picked up on the Australian goldfields spread beyond Australia and attracted a flood of immigrants. Gold finds in Queensland added to the fever. In Western Australia gold rushes brought irreversible changes to the Kimberley and Pilbara regions in the north, and towns like Kalgoorlie, Coolgardie and Boulder mushroomed. A few 'ghost towns' still dot the landscape, though stories about them are fading except when revived for tourists.

Rumours about gold strikes or nuggets or glittering sands at places named or unnamed, but always just out of reach, were coupled with stories about men who had perished while searching for them, or who had found gold but hidden it and died without revealing its whereabouts. Some of these legends were passed on between individual prospectors and other outback characters. Some circulated sporadically over a larger range of people and a longer time span.

One of the best known of these stories is about a 'lost' gold find known as Lasseter's Reef. Every now and then there are press references to expeditions setting off to search for a cache of gold in arid country northwest of Alice Springs. There is talk of maps and 'new information', but no positive results. Ion Idriess gives a highly romantic account in his book *Lasseter's Last Ride*. Also, in the late 1930s and early '40s in Adelaide, the last old man of the Ngadjuri tribe in the Flinders Range of South Australia, Barney Waria, longed for funds and equipment to get him to the place where he 'knew' the gold was concealed. He had moved about for years in the area around Maree, fossicking (searching) and working, meeting scores of old prospectors and hearing hundreds of tales and fragments of tales that convinced him the legend was true. To C. T. Madigan, however, writing in the 1930s, 'All stories of gold discoveries in the country towards the Western Australian border grew out of one single myth, the myth of Earle's Reef', and 'the whole fabric of the stories of Earle's Reef and Lasseter's Reef' was built up from this. 'Bob B', he says, 'cattleman of the west country, is the present authority on Lasseter's Reef, which is only a newer version of Earle's Reef', and he acted as a guide to it. 'Bob will guide anyone to anywhere'. Madigan knew Earle's son and had read Earle's diary and other documents. He warned, 'As well try to stake the rainbow's end as Lasseter's Reef!' But the legend still lives.

One theme that runs through the earlier gold-mining stories is 'mateship', the ideal of solidarity and co-operation between men. (Women play very minor roles in the stories.) To take one example, in 1979 a life-sized bronze statue was specially made in Perth and set up in the East Kimberley town of Halls Creek to commemorate Russian Jack, 'a legendary gold prospector', shown pushing a sick friend in a wheelbarrow. As reported in *The West Australian,* 'Legend has it that Russian Jack took his friend more than 300 kilometres (over 186 miles) in the wheelbarrow in the early Halls Creek gold rush days.' In the State premier's words, 'the legend of Russian Jack showed the spirit of comradeship that existed in the state's remote areas in early days of hardship.'

THE BUSHRANGERS

Just as important was the theme of rebellion, resistance to formal authority. The iniquitous convict system, basic to the British colonization of Australia, had much to do with this. Convict legends are quite numerous, but for a long time they were always about other people (though families had private legends about their own convict forebears). Escaped convicts loomed large in the first wave of bushrangers, who robbed towns and settlements from refuges in the bush. The second wave came after the early 1860s, when the gold rushes were subsiding and small landholders were at odds with the holders of large estates, the 'squattocracy', and therefore with the police as well. The national song, *Waltzing Matilda,* enshrines this opposition in miniature; a swagman loses his struggle against a 'squatter' and a policeman.

The bushrangers took a more aggressive line. Songs and ballads are the usual medium for their stories, or simply references to places associated with them. 'Kelly country' in Victoria, for instance, was made famous by Ned Kelly. He and his gang robbed banks and small towns until, in the final gun battle with the police in 1880, Kelly was captured, wearing an improvised suit of armour. He was hanged at Melbourne later in the year. A painting by Sidney Nolan publicized him in his armour. A film released in 1970 was expected to make him 'a legend all over the world'. The choice of Mick Jagger to play Ned Kelly raised protests from all over Australia — a sign of concern with him as almost a national symbol. This glamorization of bushrangers overlooks many of the earliest stories of the 'reign of terror' which small armies of them imposed on towns and settlements.

One reason for the development of legends of the outlaw-rebel as hero echoes the Aboriginal 'outlaw as hero' theme. In part, it is a search for something distinctively Australian as a reaction against an imposed identity and control from outside. Colonial ties with Britain, references to Britain as 'home', continuing emphasis on Irish, Scots, English identity, were hard to shake off. Only after the Second World War could Australians be officially 'Australian citizens' with 'Australian nationality'.

THE EUREKA STOCKADE

Attempts to express and shape Australian identity drew upon legends and soon became legendary themselves. 'Legend' here is often used in the sense of 'image'. Vance Palmer wrote of 'a legend of the Australian nineties' in which people from a variety of origins 'had a sudden vision of themselves as a nation'. Russel Ward used the title *The Australian Legend* in contemplating a national 'mystique'.

Then there is the legend of the Eureka Stockade. The trouble was said to have started in October 1854 at Ballarat in Victoria. A rough, drinking shanty, the Eureka Hotel, run by an ex-convict, was burned down by a mob of about 10 000 gold-diggers because a digger had been murdered there, allegedly by the ex-convict himself. Tension about mining licences, hostility to the police, an attack on the diggers by armed troops, culminated in the building of a stockade. The diggers hoisted a blue flag with the white stars of the Southern Cross as a revolutionary symbol. Soldiers and police stormed the stockade. A few of them were killed or injured, about thirty miners died; and the episode was over.

Various accounts of it have survived, but it has been linked with protests and rebels on a wider basis. In 1979, for instance, a gathering of unemployed people used the Eureka flag as their symbol. In 1975 an outdoor amphitheatre in Perth presented for children's entertainment: 'Eureka Stockade, A Children's Environmental Creativity Adventure ... pan for gold (bring old frying pan), make a Eureka flag and recreate a great Australian epic. Help your children understand their democratic history.' This is another example of a legend-myth being shaped in the quest for a national identity. The historical events have become almost irrelevant except in the themes they are taken to symbolize.

Cartoonists and journalists encourage such imagery. Phar Lap, 'Australia's legendary champion race-horse', a stuffed museum-figure in a glass case in Melbourne since early 1930s, is to be moved and 'treated like the folk hero he ought to be'. The gallantry of the Australian and New Zealand Army Corps on the beaches of Gallipoli in 1915 has entered into legend through the efforts of the Returned Soldiers League, accounts that all school-children were obliged to read, and an annual Anzac Day public holiday with a ritual march through the streets of all the major cities.

Legend-enhancers, or builders, or circulators include singers as well as writers. A. B. 'Banjo' Paterson, who wrote down many such songs and bush-ballads, and preserved them for posterity, is often himself called a legendary figure, even a myth-maker. What he put into print in many cases went back into oral circulation again. His versions of *Bold Jack Donahue, The Wild Colonial Boy* and other bushranging ballads became, like his *Waltzing Matilda,* almost the common property of Australians as such. In particular, there is *The Man from Snowy River,* a long poem about a thin young man on a weedy horse who outlasted all his stronger companions in a colt-breaking ride over rough country. Banjo Paterson heard the story from a man called Jack Riley at a cattle station in the Snowy River area. When the poem appeared, Riley was supposed to be the hero, and when he died in 1914 the headstone on his grave said so. Others, however, also claimed to be 'the Man from Snowy River'. Banjo himself said he had created the character and was pleased to find how true to life it was, with so many actual prototypes.

The content of the older European—Australian legends still has living relevance today to many Australians, especially the themes of mateship, dislike of authority, solidarity of the poor against the rich, that run through so much of Australia's early colonial history and spread an aura of 'justice' and 'democracy' over even the most sordid bushranging episodes. The news media and other influences mythologize these legends, and their political aspects tend to predominate; that in itself helps to sustain some continuity in oral tradition among people looking for precedents to support them.

But in trying to find a 'truly Australian' identity, particularly in the face of new migratory waves from Southeast Asia, more people are turning to the *first* Australians. They are using Aborigines and Aboriginal legends to build up a composite picture. Out of this process, encouraged and promoted by the media, new socio-political myths are developing with an emotional flavour much stronger than any of the legends and myths on which they are based.

NOTES

THE FAR EAST

Buddhist Legends in India (pages 28-34)
1 J. J. Jones *The Mahavastu*, 3 vols (London, 1949-56).
2 S. Mukhopadhyaya *The Asokavadana* (New Delhi, 1963).

Tibet (pages 38-44)
1 As related in W. Y. Evans-Weṇtz's rendering of the *Padma-bKa'u-thang-yig* in *The Tibetan Book of the Great Liberation* (London, 1954, 1978, New York, 1968, 1978).

THE MIDDLE EAST

Armenia and Georgia (pages 136-45)
1 Osip Mandelstam *Journey to Armenia*, trans. Clarence Brown (New York, 1933); 3-vol. edn *Collected Works*, Ed. Gleb Struve and Boris Filippov, Introduction by Clarence Brown (New York, 1964-71): *Voyage en Arménie*, trans. Louis Bruzon (Paris, 1973).
2 Prince Ilia Chavchavadze *Gandegili* (The Hermit), (Tbilisi, Georgia, 1883); trans. M. Wardrop (London, 1895). Marjory Wardrop (1869-1909) was the English pioneer of Georgian studies.

Ethiopia (pages 146-151)
1 Yeshaq *Kebra Nagast* (Glory of Kings), trans. from the early fourteenth-century MS by E. A. Wallis Budge (London, 1922, 1932; Boston, Mass., 1922).
2 W. A. Shack and H. M. Marcos *Gods and Heroes: Oral Traditions of the Gurage of Ethiopia* (Oxford and New York, 1974).

THE WEST

Classical Greece and Rome (pages 154-69)
1 Janet Bacon *The Voyage of the Argonauts* (London, 1925; Boston, Mass., n.d.).

Legendary Magicians (pages 268-73)
1 *The Key of Solomon the King (Clavicula Salomonis)*, Ed./trans. S. L. M. Mathers (London, 1889, 1972).

The Gypsies (pages 298-304)
1 F. de Ville *Tziganes, témoins des temps* (Brussels, 1956).
2 K. Bercovici *The Story of the Gypsies* (London, 1929; Detroit, Mich., 1975).
3 Ibid.
4 F. H. Groome *In Gypsy Tents* (Edinburgh, 1880, 1973; Norwood, Pa, n.d.).
5 George Hall *The Gypsy's Parson* (London, 1916).
6 Groome, op. cit.
7 Ibid.

AFRICA AND THE AMERICAS

Africa (pages 308-20)
1 G. Innes *Sunjata: Three Mandinka Versions* (London, 1974).
2 R. M. East *Stories of Old Adamawa* (Farnborough, Hants, 1967 reprint).
3 J. Knappert *Myths and Legends of the Congo* (London, 1971; Atlantic Highlands, N.J., n.d.).

4 Adapted from D. Biebuyck and K. C. Mateene's *The Mwindo Epic* (Berkeley and Los Angeles, Calif., 1969, 1972).
5 T. Mofolo *Chaka: An Historical Romance,* trans. F. H. Dutton (Oxford and New York, 1931, 1967).

Lowland South America (pages 352-360)
1 Walter Roth *An Enquiry into the Animism and Folk-Lore of the Guina Indians,* Bureau of American Ethnology (Washington, D.C., 1915; Norwood, N.J., 1970). Claude Lévi-Strauss *From Honey to Ashes,* trans. J. and D. Weightman (New York, 1973).
2 Curt Nimuendaju *The Tukuna* (Berkeley, Calif., 1952); Claude Lévi-Strauss *The Origin of Table Manners* (London and New York, 1978).

THE PACIFIC

Australia (pages 379-89)
1 R. M. and C. H. Berndt *The World of the First Australians* (Sydney, 1977 reprint).
2 A. W. Howitt *The Native tribes of South-East Australia* (London, 1904).

LIST OF CONTRIBUTORS

Margaret Alexiou, Senior Lecturer in Byzantine & Modern Greek, University of Birmingham (THE BALKANS AND GREECE)

Oriana Baddeley, Department of Art, University of Essex (MIDDLE AMERICA)

Catherine H. Berndt, Lecturer in Anthropology, University of Western Australia (AUSTRALIA)

Gordon Brotherston, Professor of Literature, University of Essex (MIDDLE AMERICA)

Alan Bruford, Archivist, School of Scottish Studies, Edinburgh (SCOTLAND)

Richard Cavendish (ARTHUR AND LEGENDARY BRITAIN; ATLANTIS; LEGENDARY MAGICIANS; MISCELLANEOUS LEGENDARY FIGURES; NEW TESTAMENT FIGURES AND SAINTS)

Anthony Christie, Senior Lecturer in the Art & Archaeology of Southeast Asia, School of Oriental & African Studies, London (BURMA; CHINA; INDONESIA AND MALAYSIA)

Christian Clerk, Department of Anthropology, University College, London (POLYNESIA AND MICRONESIA)

Rosalie David, Assistant Keeper of Archaeology, Manchester Museum (EGYPT)

L. P. Elwell-Sutton, Professor of Persian, University of Edinburgh (THE ISLAMIC WORLD)

John Ferguson, President, Selly Oak Colleges, Birmingham (CLASSICAL GREECE AND ROME)

T. H. Johanna Firbank, formerly Lecturer in Akkadian, School of Oriental & African Studies, London (MESOPOTAMIA)

Brenda Fish, Department of Anthropology, London School of Economics (EL CID; THE NEW WORLD)

John Fox, Professor of French, University of Exeter (ALEXANDER THE GREAT; CHARLEMAGNE LEGENDS; MEDIEVAL TROY LEGENDS)

John R. Hinnells, Senior Lecturer in Comparative Religion, University of Manchester (IRAN)

James H. Howard, Professor of Anthropology, Oklahoma State University (NORTH AMERICAN INDIAN LEGENDS)

Caroline Humphrey, Fellow of King's College, Cambridge (MONGOLIA)

Joanna Overing Kaplan, Lecturer in the Social Anthropology of Latin America, London School of Economics (LOWLAND SOUTH AMERICA)

John D. Kesby, Lecturer in Anthropology, University of Kent (AFRICA)

David M. Lang, Professor of Caucasian Studies, School of Oriental & African Studies, London (ARMENIA AND GEORGIA)

Trevor O. Ling, Professor of Comparative Religion, University of Manchester (INDIAN BUDDHIST LEGENDS)

Erberto F. Lo Bue, Institute of Tibetan Studies, Tring, Hertfordshire (TIBET)

Hyam Maccoby, Librarian, Leo Baeck College, London (JEWISH LEGENDS)

John R. Marr, Lecturer in Tamil, School of Oriental & African Studies, London (HINDU LEGENDS)

Venetia J. Newall, Editor, International Folklore Review, London (UNITED STATES OF AMERICA)

Séamas Ó Catháin, Director, Irish Folklore Institute, University College, Dublin (IRELAND)

Richard Pankhurst, Professor of Economic History, Addis Ababa University, and Librarian, Royal Asiatic Society, London (ETHIOPIA)

Michael Ridley, Keeper of Oriental Art & Archaeology, Russell-Cotes Museum, Bournemouth (JAIN AND SIKH LEGENDS; JAPAN)

Brynley F. Roberts, Professor of Welsh, University College, Swansea (WALES)

M. J. Sallnow, Lecturer in Anthropology, London School of Economics (THE INCAS)

Stewart F. Sanderson, Director, Institute of Dialect and Folk Life Studies, University of Leeds (THE GYPSIES)

Eric J. Sharpe, Professor of Religious Studies, University of Sydney (GERMANIC LEGENDS)

Andrew Strathern, Professor of Anthropology, University College, London (MELANESIA)

Faith C. M. Wigzell, Lecturer in Russian Language & Literature, School of Slavonic & East European Studies, London (RUSSIA)

COMPARATIVE SURVEY OF WORLD LEGENDS

This detailed survey, based on the following twenty-two sections, and keyed to the text pages, shows how the same legendary themes and motifs, with minor variations, appear in many different parts of the world. A fold-out leaf facing page 433 indicates the page location of the different chapters.

1 KINGS AND WARRIORS

i The Ideal King
ii The Wise King
iii The Rich King
iv Conquerors and Warriors
v A Company of Heroes
vi The Pious King
vii Ruling Line with Illustrious Descent

2 HOLY MEN AND WOMEN

i Miraculous Powers
ii Sages and Prophets

3 MAGICIANS AND ARTISTS

i Magicians
ii Enchantresses and Witches
iii Magical Powers and Equipment
iv Physical Strength, Invulnerability
v Artists and Craftsmen

4 EXPLORERS AND WANDERERS

i Travellers
ii A Journey to the Otherworld or Heaven
iii Doomed Wanderers

5 OUTLAWS AND BANDITS

6 CUNNING HEROES, RUSES

i Cunning Heroes
ii Cunning Ruses

7 THE HERO'S BIRTH

i Divine Parentage
ii Animal Parentage
iii Virgin Birth
iv Miraculous Conception
v Portents and Prodigies
vi Humble Origins

8 CHILDHOOD AND UPBRINGING

i A Massacre of Innocents
ii Exposure and Rescue
iii Fostering, Training, Exile

9 THE OUTSIDER

10 BATTLES WITH MONSTERS

11 THE DIFFICULT TASK

12 THE QUEST FOR IMMORTALITY

13 THE HELPFUL ANIMALS

14 HORSE, SWORD, SHIP

i The Hero's Horse
ii A Special Sword or Other Weapon
iii A Special Ship

15 FRIENDSHIP AND LOYALTY

i Fast Friends
ii Loyalty to a King or Lord

16 FAMILY LOYALTY AND CONFLICT

i Parents and Children
ii Step-Parents and Children
iii Brothers and Sisters
iv Incest
v Uncle and Nephew

17 WOMEN, LOVE AND MARRIAGE

i Religious Heroines
ii Protectors of the People
iii The Faithful Wife
iv Feminine Villainy
v Romantic Love

Note: the numbers in brackets refer to text page numbers.

1 KINGS AND WARRIORS

i The Ideal King

A widespread legendary theme is that of the ideal ruler – strong, just, benevolent, keeping good order and caring for his people. Asoka, the great Indian emperor, is an example in both Hindu (25) and Buddhist traditions (34). So are Jamshid in Iran (130), Theseus in Athenian tradition (160), Alexander the Great (233), Attila (Etzel, 177) and King Arthur (236).

Others include Vikramaditya (26), Harsha (26) and Duttabaung (70) in India and Burma; Ge-sar of Ling (38) and Geser Khan (45) in Tibet and Mongolia; Sesostris (85) and Ameni (86) in Egypt; various Muslim rulers including Harun al-Rashid (122); in Iran, Cyrus the Great (125), Gayomard (130) and Faridun (131); Romulus (165); Beowulf (173); Prester John (274) and Peter the Great (296).

ii The Wise King

Another legendary figure is the king who is famed for his wisdom. Examples include Duttabaung (70); Solomon (99, 117, 147); Minos of Crete (154); King Nestor, who typifies the wisdom of old age in the *Iliad* (155); Theseus (160) and the Emperor Maxen (193).

The Russian warrior-hero Ilya of Murom was famed for his wisdom and there are, of course, many examples of wise sages and prophets who were not rulers (Section 2:ii below). The crafty and cunning hero (Section 6) is not the same figure as the wise one.

iii The Rich King

Rulers famed for their fabulous wealth: Duttabaung (70); Solomon (117); Jamshid (130); El Dorado (259) and Prester John (274).

iv Conquerors and Warriors

Alexander the Great is the obvious example of a hero admired as a great conqueror and military genius (163, 230, 283) and in both Jewish (106) and Muslim tradition (116) he is said to have been inspired by God. On the other hand, there are numerous stories which comment unfavourably on his power-hunger and greed (107, 231). Other figures in this category include Chandragupta (26); Vikramaditya (26); Geser Khan and Genghis Khan (45, 47); Gilgamesh (91); Sargon (94): Moses (102); Vakhtang (139); Charlemagne (216) and King Arthur (239), though there are tales

in which he is compared unfavourably with ecclesiastical heroes and
condemned for tyranny and greed (199). There are also Sunjata (310),
Amas (318) and Pachacuti Inca (348).

Some warrior heroes are renowned principally for their prowess as
individual fighting men: Prince Yamato (61), Yoshitsune and Benkei (64);
Rustom (132); Achilles (155, 227), Perseus (161) and Bellerophon (162);
Beowulf (172), Grettir (174) and Sigurd or Siegfried (175); Sir Lachlan
Maclean (204); St George (215); Roland (217); the champions of the
Round Table – such as Lancelot, Guinglain, Gawain, Tristan, Perceval
and Galahad (240-45); the Russian heroes Dobrynya and Alyosha (294);
Mayta Capac (347) and Wonggu (379). Famous legendary outlaws and
bandits (Section 5) fit in here, as do legendary hunters, such as Davy
Crockett and Ethan Allen (336). For warrior-women, see Section 17.

Warrior heroes and heroines may also be national heroes, often those
who lead national resistance to foreign tyranny or invasion. Examples
are the Ranis of Khittur and Jansi in India (27); Samson and King David
in Jewish tradition (97, 98); the heroes of the *Shahname* in Iran (129)
and the *Kebra Nagast* in Ethiopia (147); Arshak, Parnavaz and David of
Sassoun in Armenia and Georgia (138, 139, 143); Theseus in Athens (160);
Aeneas, Brutus and other Roman heroes (164, 167); Cu Chulainn and Finn
MacCool in Ireland (183, 184); Owen Glendower in Wales (197);
Wallace and Robert the Bruce in Scotland (203); in Britain as a whole,
King Arthur (236); in England, Robin Hood, at least in the later tradition
(275), as well as Hereward the Wake and Sir Francis Drake (228, 229);
El Cid in Spain (249); Digenes Akrites, Marko Kraljevic, Kralj Mataz
and Skanderbeg – heroes of the resistance to the Turks in Greece and the
Balkans (284, 286); and Ilya of Murom in Russia (293).

v A Company of Heroes
Some legendary heroes are supported by, or belong to, a group of brave
and loyal companions: Geser Khan and his men (45); the forty-seven
ronin (66); Kuroghli and his brigands (123); the Argonauts (159); Finn
MacCool's men (188); St Brendan and his monks (189); Arthur and his
men in early legends (195) and the knights of the Round Table later on
(240); Charlemagne and his barons (217), Robin Hood and his men (275);
the bandit groups of Balkan and Greek stories (287).

vi The Pious King
Rulers celebrated for their piety include: Asoka in India (34); Duttabaung
and other Burmese kings (70-71); Lalibala in Ethiopia (150) and Numa in
Rome (166).

One motif is that of the king or king's son who renounces the throne
for religion's sake: Chandragupta (26), the Buddha (29, 41), who becomes
Josaphat or Joasaph in Muslim and Christian versions (121, 215), and
Ibrahim (121). On the other hand, in northern Europe admiring stories
were told of how Olav Tryggveson and Olav Haraldsson (18) used the
power of the throne to impose Christianity on their subjects by force.
Similarly in Java, Raden Patah seized the throne to impose Islam on a
Hindu state (77), while Charlemagne (216) and Prester John (274) are
legendary Christian champions against Islam. Sunjata in African legend is
the champion of Islam against evil (310), and so is Modibbo Adama (312).

vii Ruling Line with Illustrious Descent
The kings of Maturai, according to Indian legend, were descended from

a god (17); the Japanese imperial line (61); Javanese dynasties (76, 78); Malay kings descended from Solomon and Alexander the Great (79); the Egyptian Fifth Dynasty descended from the sun-god (84); the Achaemenid line descended from Alexander the Great (116); the Bagratid dynasty claimed descent from David and Solomon (140); an Armenian dynasty descended from Sennacherib (140); Meherr and David of Sassoun descended from the Caliph of Baghdad (143); Ethiopian rulers descended from King Solomon and the Queen of Sheba (147); Roman kings descended from a god (165); British kings descended from Aeneas (237); the chiefs of Saa (368).

2 HOLY MEN AND WOMEN
i Miraculous Powers
One of the most common legendary themes associates miracles with the founders of religions and other religious heroes and heroines. Either they have miraculous powers of their own or miracles occur in their vicinity. Examples come from India (19, 22, 24, 28, 37); Tibet (42); China (56, 60); Japan (66); Burma (69); the Jewish tradition (99, 107); the Muslim tradition (119, 121); the Zoroastrian tradition (134); and the Christian tradition (141, 149, 190, 192, 199, 214, 287).

Miracles are also associated with secular heroes, though far less often, especially with warriors who are champions of one religion against another, such as Charlemagne (219) and El Cid (252).

ii Sages and Prophets
These figures are admired for supernatural wisdom and the ability to divine the future and all sorts of miraculous powers are often credited to them too: Sunan Kalijaga in Java (78); Neferti in Egypt (86); Moses and the great Jewish prophets (99, 105); Muhammad and others in Muslim tradition (114, 116, 120); Zoroaster in Iran (134); Epimenides, Thales, the Seven Sages and Pythagoras in the classical world (163); in Britain, Merlin (200), Taliesin (200) and Thomas the Rhymer (206); and the American rustic sage Johnny Appleseed (334).

3 MAGICIANS AND ARTISTS
i Magicians
Legendary figures held in awe as magicians include: Mpu Barada (77); Dedi (84); King Solomon (105, 270); Mindia (144); Merlin (200, 202, 238, 272); Taliesin (200); Michael Scot (206); Faust (268); also in the European tradition, Gerbert, Roger Bacon, Simon Magus, Zoroaster, Moses, Orpheus, Pythagoras, Apollonius of Tyana and Vergil (270, 272); Kresnik (286); Sumanguru (310); Isanusi (319); Tadodaho (322); Tezcatlipoca (340); Ngatoro (373); Wuru-ngungu's grandfather (380).

The pact with the Devil is a persistent European theme (267, 302); and in Africa see the legends of Sumanguru and Chaka (310, 319).

ii Enchantresses and Witches
Magic wielded by women is frequently connected with female sexuality: Queen Mahendradatta of Bali (74); Queen Dades of Java (76); Queen Makahora (151); Circe (157); Medea (159); Taabe (179); Ceridwen (200); the Witch of Mull (204); the great enchantresses of Arthurian legend, including the Lady of the Lake, Morgan le Fay and Vivien (240, 242, 243, 273). One of the principal roles of these Arthurian figures is to hold a warrior in thrall and prevent him from carrying out his mission in

the world. By contrast Medea in classical legend enables Jason to carry out his mission of recovering the Golden Fleece.

Another motif is that a heroine's nurse or mother is skilled in magic (128, 243).

iii Magical Powers and Equipment

Miracles and marvels are also associated with holy men and women, sages and prophets (Section 2). Besides them, there are other figures – kings and warriors – who cannot be described as magicians, but who are aided by supernatural beings and forces or who wield marvellous powers. Or they may own magical equipment, such as a flying lance, a magic ship, a helmet of invisibility or a magic mirror: Ge-sar of Ling (38); Geser Khan (46); Yoshitsune (64); Duttabaung (70); Sakender (77); Senapati (78); Enmerkar (90); Lugalbanda (91); Gilgamesh (93); Jason (159); Perseus (161); Numa (166); Siegfried (176); Finn MacCool (185); Owen Glendower (197); Prester John (274); Sir Francis Drake (279); Volkh (292); Ilele (314).

Related motifs are those of the helpful animals (Section 13) and the hero's horse, sword and ship (Section 14).

iv Physical Strength, Invulnerability

Another type of magical or marvellous equipment credited to some heroes is preternatural physical strength: Benkei (65); Nga Tinde (72); Samson (97); Antar (123); Rustom (132); Beowulf (172); Grettir (174); Siegfried (177); Cu Chulainn (182); Finn MacCool (185); Llew Llaw Gyffes (193); Wallace (203); St Christopher (214); Lancelot (242); Little John (276); Ilya of Murom (293); Gib Morgan (333); Paul Bunyan (334); Joe Magarac (334); Davy Crockett (335); Mayta Capac (347). This is also a common motif in Greek and Balkan bandit legends (287). Odysseus is not usually put in this category, but the test to succeed him was to bend his bow (158).

Achilles was magically proof against wounds, except at one point, and it was a wound there which killed him (155). The same is true of Siegfried (177), but the two heroes acquired their invulnerability in different ways. There is also the example of Sir Lachlan MacLean, shot through a chink in his armour (204), and both his death and that of Cu Chulainn (184) occurred through the breaking of personal taboos.

v Artists and Craftsmen

The great artists and craftsmen of legend also have a magical mystique. They include Tansen and other musicians of Indian legend and the Indian jester Raman (22-25); Yared in Ethiopia (150); Daedalus, the great inventor and craftsman of classical tradition (154), and Orpheus, the great minstrel (159); Finn MacCool, Taliesin and Thomas the Rhymer as poets and the MacCrimmons as pipers in Celtic legends (185, 200, 206); Hiram Abiff, the martyred architect of Masonic legend (280); and Sadko, the Russian minstrel (295). There are also legends about the skill of the gypsies in music, metalwork and other crafts (300).

4 EXPLORERS AND WANDERERS

i Travellers

Alexander the Great, according to legend, travelled to the ends of the earth and encountered extraordinary marvels and wonders (116, 164, 231). He also explored the heights of the sky and the depths of the sea, as

did King Solomon (271). Other legendary visitors to the bottom of the
sea are Ch'en (54), Sadko (295) and a gypsy hero, Happy Boswell (303).

Odysseus encountered numerous marvels in his wanderings when trying
to find his way home from Troy (157) and the story provided the pattern
for the wanderings of Aeneas (165). St Brendan, the great voyager of
Irish tradition, sailed to the west and found many marvels (189). A
Welsh hero, Prince Madog, sailed to the west and discovered America
(198). Other long journeys into the unknown, replete with marvels, were
undertaken by Gilgamesh (92), Jason and the Argonauts (159) and Brutus
(237), who sailed to Albion and founded the kingdom of Britain. There are
numerous South American legends of lost travellers encountering
supernatural wonders and perils (352-59); Polynesian and Micronesian
legends of voyages, whose heroes are skilful navigators (370-74);
Australian Aboriginal legends of voyages (381); and legends of explorers
in Australia (385). A more prosaic journey was Wenamun's trading voyage (88).

ii A Journey to the Otherworld or Heaven
Some legendary travellers reach mysterious realms outside this world and
return again: Gilgamesh (94); Aeneas (165); Alexander the Great (232);
St Brendan (189); King Arthur (195); Thomas the Rhymer (206);
Yawalngura (381). Some of the adventures of Arthurian knights have a
similar ring, including Guinglain's experiences at the Golden Island and
the Waste City, and Gawain's at the Green Chapel (241, 243), and the
visits of knights to the Grail Castle (244). Both Moses (105) and
Muhammad (119) are recorded to have been to heaven and returned to
earth, and so are the Emperor Lalibala and Yared (149, 150).

iii Doomed Wanderers
These tragic figures are condemned to roam the earth as a punishment:
the Wandering Jew (280); the captain of the *Flying Dutchman* (280); the
entire gypsy race (299). Little Meherr was cursed by his father (144).
Vortigern was pursued by the wrath of heaven for betraying Britain to
the Saxons (194).

5 OUTLAWS AND BANDITS
Outlaws and robbers may be feared or, very often, admired as free spirits
who challenge constituted authority and prey on the oppressors of
ordinary people: Kuroghli and his men (123); Arsena (145); Grettir (175);
Twm Sion Cati (198); the Red-Haired Bandits of Mawddwy (198);
Wallace (203); Robin Hood and his men (275); Hereward the Wake
(278); the Hajduks and Klefts of the Balkans and Greece (287); American
outlaw heroes such as Jesse James, Beanie Short, Billy the Kid and Sam
Bass (329-32); stories of Australian Aborigines as heroic outlaws (383);
and Ned Kelly (387). According to legend, Kuroghli, Arsena, Robin
Hood, Jesse James, Billy the Kid and Sam Bass all took from the rich and
gave to the poor. The first three were also masters of disguise, as were
Twm Sion Cati and Hereward the Wake.

6 CUNNING HEROES, RUSES
i Cunning Heroes
Outlaws and bandits survive largely by cunning and there are other
legendary figures who are admired for their craftiness: Raman the jester
(23); Sivaji (27); sGar-ba (39); Prince Yamato (62); Odysseus (155);

Sisyphus (162); Olav Haraldsson (182); Oedipus cleverly solved the
riddle of the Sphinx (158) and Brutus the riddle of the oracle (167).
Romulus and Augustus quick-wittedly turned an evil omen into a good
one (166, 169). Amleth (Hamlet, 174) craftily feigned madness to gain
revenge.

ii Cunning Ruses
Examples of successful trickery occur frequently in legends, evidently
to be enjoyed for their own sake. Perhaps the most famous ruse of all
is the wooden horse of Troy (156, 227), which has a parallel in an
Egyptian legend about the capture of Joppa (87). Penelope outwits her
suitors by a famous ruse (158). Solomon tricks the Queen of Sheba into
his bed (147) and ruses are also employed to win a woman by Pelops (156)
and Milanion (163). A horse's shoes are turned backwards to baffle
pursuit in stories about Bonnie Prince Charlie and Robert Bruce (186,
203). South American Indians in legend craftily outwit the aggressive
Caribs (359).

 Other examples occur in legends about Ts'ai Hsiang (57); Angrok (76);
Miriam (96); Moses (102); Elhanan (110); Khosrou Parviz (122); Medea
(159); Queen Thyra (179); Daniel O'Connell (186); Owen Glendower
(198); in tales of cruel lairds in Scotland (205); in stories of Sunjata's
sister and Sumanguru (310); Kororomanna (353); Fanur and Hagur (371);
and Tama-te-kapua (373).

7 THE HERO'S BIRTH
There is often something supernatural or miraculous about the conception
and birth of a legendary hero or heroine.

i Divine Parentage
The hero of heroine is the child of a deity: Geser Khan (46); Angrok
(76); Gilgamesh (93); Minos (154); Helen (155); Achilles (155); Theseus
(160); Perseus (161); Evander (164); Aeneas (165); Romulus and Remus
(165); Augustus (169); Cu Chulainn (183); Jesus (209); Marko Kraljevic
(285); Kresnik (286).

 Alexander the Great was reputedly the son of a stranger masquerading
as a god (164). Taliesin was the offspring of a witch (200) and Merlin
was the son of a demon (238).

ii Animal Parentage
Bulagat (49); Bedayi (69); Nga Tinde's sons (73); Alexander the Great
in some versions (230, 283). For legends of babies nourished by animals,
see below, Section 8:ii.

iii Virgin Birth
The Buddha (29); Mahavira (36); Nichiren (67); Zoroaster (134); St
Kentigern (202); Jesus (209); Merlin (272); Dekanawideh (322).

iv Miraculous Conception
The child's conception is in some other way miraculous or extraordinary:
Tatatakai (17); Sankara (19); Tansen (22); Ge-sar of Ling (38); gShen-
rab (41); Padmasambhava (42); Genghis Khan (47); Servius Tullius
(167); Thomas the Rhymer (206); the Virgin Mary (208); King Arthur
(239); Mwindo (316); Mayta Capac (347).

v Portents and Prodigies
In many cases the child's birth is preceded or surrounded by portents

and strange events, or the child is prodigiously gifted, or both. This applies to the founders of religions: the Buddha (29, 41); Mahavira (35); Nanak (37); Muhammad (118); Zoraster (134); Jesus (209). It also applies to great rulers and warrior heroes: Samson (97), Cyrus the Great (126); Rustom (132); Perseus (161); Scipio (168); Augustus (169); Arthur (238); Alexander the Great (283). The same type of story is told of Chaitanya (21); Tansen (23); Benkei (65); Kobodashi (67); Angrok (76); Abraham (115); Antar (123); Ardashir (127); Zal (132); Lalibala (150); Oedipus (158); Daniel O'Connell and Eamon de Valera (183); Owen Glendower (197); the Virgin Mary (208); Brutus (237); Merlin (273); Digenes Akrites (284) and Mwindo (316).

On the other hand, the Russian hero Ilya of Murom (293) was not precocious, but crippled and slow to develop, and Narasimh, a Hindu saint (21), was dumb from birth, hopelessly impractical and held in contempt by his family. Abu Zaid and Antar in Islamic legends (123) both succeed in spite of being crippled and unprepossessing, Chaka despite being a bastard (319).

vi Humble Origins
Some legendary figures make their mark on the world from lowly origins and circumstances: Fan Wen (60); Angrok (76); Antar (123); Ardashir (127); Kava (131); Servius Tullius (167); Robin Hood in the earlier tradition (276); William Tell (278); Pope Joan (279); Ilya of Murom (293); Sadko (295).

8 CHILDHOOD AND UPBRINGING
Recurrent motifs deal with the dangers and trials which beset the hero as a child. Often, attempts are made to kill him. In many stories he is abandoned or exposed to die by his parents, but rescued by others. Legendary heroes and heroines frequently grow up away from their natural homes and families.

i A Massacre of Innocents
A wicked king orders a slaughter of children, but the hero is saved: Moses (96); Abraham (115); Jesus (209).

ii Exposure and Rescue
The hero is abandoned or exposed to die as a baby, but is saved by strangers and sometimes by animals: Bulagat and Genghis Khan were each set adrift on a lake in a cradle (49); T'ang-seng was set adrift on the River Yangtze in a bucket (55); in a Burmese story, two blind princes are set adrift on a river on a raft (69); Sargon was set adrift on a river in a reed basket (94), and so was Moses, on the River Nile (96); Perseus and his mother were pushed out to sea in a box (161); St Cenydd was pushed out to sea in a cradle and was fed by gulls (200); Taliesin was cast into the sea in a skin bag (200): St Kentigern's mother, pregnant with him, was set adrift in an oarless boat (202).

Kabir was abandoned by a river (24); Pao-ssu was exposed as a baby (54); Gilgamesh was thrown off the citadel wall, but saved by an eagle (91); Cyrus the Great was exposed in the hills and, according to one story, was suckled by a bitch (126); Zal was exposed to die, but was brought up by the Simurgh-bird (132); the infant Zoroaster was put in a wolf's den to kill him, but the wolf brought him up and a sheep suckled him (134); Oedipus was exposed in the hills (158); Atalanta was abandoned in the hills and suckled by a bear (162); Romulus and Remus were exposed and suckled by a wolf (165); Mwindo's father tried persistently to kill him as a child (317); Yahuar-Huacac was exposed in the mountains (348).

iii Fostering, Training, Exile

Then there are stories in which the hero loses his father or mother at a very early age, or is sent away to be specially trained, or for some other reason grows up away from his natural home. Sundarar was adopted by a chieftain (19); Tansen was trained by a holy man (23); the Buddha's mother died and he was brought up by a foster-mother (29); T'ang-seng was brought up by a monk (55); Yoshitsune grew up in a monastery (64); Yoritomo grew up in exile (64); Angrok was sent to study with a brahmin (76); Moses grew up in Pharaoh's palace (96); Muhammad's mother died and he was brought up by a foster-mother (119); Abraham grew up hidden in a cave (115); St Gregory the Illuminator grew up in exile (141); Mindia was snatched away by evil spirits (144); Jason grew up in exile (159) and so, in a sense, did Theseus (160); Olav Tryggveson was sold into slavery and trained in youth at a foreign queen's court (181); Finn MacCool's father was killed before his birth and he was brought up secretly in the forest (185); the Virgin Mary was brought up in the Temple (208); Jesus grew up in exile in Egypt (210); Charlemagne, for his own safety, was brought up at a foreign court (221); Arthur was brought up secretly in the country (239); Lancelot's father was killed and he was brought up by the Lady of the Lake in her enchanted palace (242); Guinglain was brought up without a father (241), as was Perceval (245), and Tristan without father or mother (243); Galahad was reared in a nunnery (245); Sunjata grew up in exile (310).

9 THE OUTSIDER

The effect of many of the stories in the preceding section is that the hero comes to his adult sphere of action from the outside, as a stranger. Other examples of this theme are: the Buddha, who is brought up in isolation from the everyday world, which proves to be his sphere of action (29); Sri Tri Buana (79); Pelops (156); Cadmus (158); Evander (164); Aeneas (164); Beowulf (172); Brutus (237).

A similar position occurs in tales of the hero who goes into exile or into hiding and subsequently returns to achieve success or happiness: Rama (16); Sinuhe (85); Muhammad (119); Yared (149); Odysseus (157); Camillus (168); Dietrich (178); Hildebrand (178); Bertha (221); Robert Bruce (203); El Cid (250).

On the other hand, there are stories of exile followed by an unfortunate return: Nga Tinde (72); Jason (159); Coriolanus (168); Bonnie Prince Charlie (186).

10 BATTLES WITH MONSTERS

In another common theme the hero overcomes great powers of evil, dragons, giants or other fearsome monsters: Rama and the demon-king (16); the Buddha and Mara (30); Ge-sar of Ling destroys demons (38); Geser Khan kills the giant tiger (46); Buidung (46); Gilgamesh and monsters (93); David and Goliath (98); Moses and Og (104); Moses and the dangerous angels (106); Faridun and the dragon (131); Rustom kills monsters and demons (133); Odysseus blinds the Cyclops, outwits the Sirens, passes Scylla and Charybdis (157); Cadmus kills a holy snake or dragon (158); Oedipus and the Sphinx (158); Theseus and the Minotaur

(160); Perseus kills monsters (161); Bellerophon and the Chimaera (162); Atalanta and the boar (162); Beowulf as a monster-slayer (172); Grettir the Strong (174); Sigurd or Siegfried and the dragon (176); Dietrich (178); Cu Chulainn (184); King Arthur as a monster-killer (195, 239); St Martha subdues a dragon (211); St George and the dragon (215); Oliver defeats a giant (222); Alexander the Great overwhelms monsters (233, 283); Arthurian knights (241, 243); Kresnik (286); Alyosha and the dragon (291); Dobrynya and the dragon (292); Ilya of Murom and the monster (293).

By contrast, there are a few stories in which the hero is worsted, and sometimes killed, by a monster: Prince Yamato and the Great Serpent (63) (63); Solomon subdues the chief of demons, but later the tables are turned (105, 117); Beowulf is killed by a dragon, though he gives the monster its death-wound (173); Gawain is worsted by the Green Knight (243).

11 THE DIFFICULT TASK
The hero or heroine is set an impossible or hopelessly difficult task to carry out, but succeeds, often with supernatural help: in the cases of Jason (159), Perseus (161) and Bellerophon (162) the task is set in the hope of killing the hero. Other examples are Bedayi (69); Enmerkar (90); Culhwch (195) and Guinglain (241).

12 THE QUEST FOR IMMORTALITY
The adventures of some heroes include a search for the secret of eternal life. Gilgamesh finds the plant of rejuvenation, but a snake steals it (94); Alexander the Great finds the Water of Life, but someone else drinks it (116, 283); the Grail quest in the Arthurian stories is a version of the search for immortality, in which Galahad succeeds (244); Digenes Akrites wrestles with Death, but is defeated (284).

13 THE HELPFUL ANIMALS
Besides the legends of animals rescuing and nourishing infant heroes and heroines (Section 8:ii), there are other tales in which the central character is helped by animals: Rama and the monkeys (16); Ch'en Kuang-jui and the carp (54); Ts'ai Hsiang and the Dragon King (57); Fan Wen and the carp (60); Lugalbanda and the eagle (91); Muhammad (119); Mindia (144); Phrixus and Helle (159); Kororomanna (354). Cimidyue is helped by some animals, but others are unkind to her (354), and the same is true of Perisuat (357). There is also the story of the snake people (366).

Yared was inspired by the example of a worm (149) and Robert Bruce similarly by that of a spider (203). Christian saints in legend frequently have a special rapport with animals which help them (142, 200, 215), and see also the legends of Johnny Appleseed and Mountain Mary in the United States (334). The chief buffalo gave the Ponca people the war dance (324). Warrior heroes often have the aid of a supernatural or special horse (Section 14). Some legendary characters understand the languages of animals and birds: Mindia (144): Siegfried (176); Solomon (270); Happy Boswell (303).

14 HORSE, SWORD, SHIP
i The Hero's Horse
The hero has a special horse, which often has magical powers, the ability to talk or extraordinary swiftness: Antar's horse, Abjar (123); Kuroghli's

wonderful horse, Qirat (124); Rustom's horse, Raksh (133); Little
Meherr's magic horse (144); Cu Chulainn's great horse, the Grey of Macha
(184); Gawain's warhorse, Gringolet (243); Alexander the Great's man-
eating horse, Bucephalus (283); Marko Kraljevic's horse, Sarac (285).
There are also flying horses, Buraq in Muslim tradition (119) and Pegasus
in classical legends (162).

ii A Special Sword or Other Weapon
Two magic swords in the story of Fan Wen (60); Yamato's sword, Cloud
Cluster (63); Angrok's magic kris (76); Antar's sword, Dhami (123);
Faridun's mace (131); Rustom's mace (132); Sigurd's sword, Gram (176);
Siegfried's sword, Balmung (176); Cu Chulainn's weapon, the *gae bolga*
(184); King Arthur's sword, Excalibur (Caledfwlch) (196, 239); Roland's
sword, Durendal (219).

iii A Special Ship
Noah's Ark (100, 136); Jason's ship, Argo (159); Arthur's ship, Prydwen
(196); Prince Madog's ship, Gwennan Gorn (198).

The motif of the fatal ship with black or white sails occurs in the stories
of Theseus (160) and Tristan (244).

15 FRIENDSHIP AND LOYALTY
i Fast Friends
In Japanese tradition, Yoshitsune and Benkei become fast friends after
fighting each other, and they eventually die together (65); Gilgamesh and
Enkidu also become fast friends after fighting each other (93) and so do
Robin Hood and Friar Tuck (277); Roland and Oliver are fast friends
who die together (219); Little John is ready to sacrifice his life for his
friends (277); there are Australian legends of comradeship (387). Gunnar
puts loyalty to his friend, Siegfried, before loyalty to his wife, Brynhild
(176), but on the other hand, caught in a tragic conflict of loyalties, Cu
Chulainn fights and kills his dear friend, Fer Diad (184).

ii Loyalty to a King or Lord
The story of the forty-seven ronin (66); Rustom is the greatest support of
the throne (133); so are Cu Chulainn (183), Finn MacCool (184) and
Lancelot (242); the nine brothers of Queen Milica are loyal to the king to
the death (285); and the Russian bogatyrs are loyal to the weak and
cowardly Prince Vladimir (291); Billy the Kid is said to have been inspired
by the duty to avenge his murdered boss (332).

16 FAMILY LOYALTY AND CONFLICT
Many legends centre on the tensions created by love, jealousy and ambition
within a family, often involving a tragic conflict of loyalties and the duty of
revenge.

i Parents and Children
Raden Patah's loyalty to Islam is stronger than his loyalty to his father
(77); Brutus executes his own sons for treason, putting loyalty to the state
above family loyalty (167), and so does Ivan the Terrible (297);
similarly, Coriolanus is destroyed by his mother to prevent him from
destroying Rome (168); by contrast, Antigone puts family loyalty before
duty to the state (159).

Hildebrand kills his own son, who has insulted him, and then kills
himself (178); Cu Chulainn is driven by his concept of honour to kill his

son (184); the Dane keeps the secret of heather beer to his own death and that of his son (187); Medea kills her sons by Jason, to punish him (160); Theseus, deceived by his wife, fatally curses his son (161); Althaea kills her son, Meleager, to avenge her brothers (162); Sir Lachlan MacLean's foster-mother kills her son for insulting Sir Lachlan's corpse (205); Queen Judon murders one of her sons to avenge the other (238).

Angrok kills the king, whose death is avenged by the king's son, who is himself murdered in revenge (76); Agamemnon has his daughter killed, his wife and her lover murder him in revenge and they in turn are murdered by Orestes, who is driven to the terrible crime of matricide by his duty to avenge his father (157); Amleth (Hamlet) avenges his murdered father by killing his uncle, the murderer (174).

To protect his inheritance, Ham castrates his father, Noah, who curses him (104); Little Meherr is cursed by his father (144); Oedipus kills his father, marries his mother and succeeds to his father's throne (158); Perseus kills his grandfather and succeeds to his throne (162); Theseus comes to his father's throne in somewhat similar circumstances (160); Tullia persuades Tarquin to murder her father and seize his throne (167); Odysseus is killed by his son, by mistake (228); Brutus causes the deaths of both his parents (237); King Lear's daughters try to dispossess him (238); Arthur's son, Mordred, seizes his father's wife and fatally wounds Arthur, who kills him (246); Alexander the Great kills his father (283); Pachacuti Inca seizes power from his father and brother (348).

The grim motif of a man's sons being cooked and served up to him to eat occurs in the stories of Harpagus (126) and Thyestes (156).

For other examples of relationships between parents and children in legend, see Sections 7 and 8 above, on the hero's birth and childhood.

ii Step-Parents and Children

Rama's wicked step-mother (16); Phrixus and Helle's wicked step-mother (159); Phaedra falsely accuses her step-son of rape and he is killed (161); Amleth and his uncle and step-father (174); Roland belittles his step-father, Ganelon, who plots Roland's death in revenge (218).

iii Brothers and Sisters

Examples of family loyalty: Rama's faithful half-brothers (16); Vikramaditya is loyal to his elder brother, who plots against him (216); the loyalty of Nga Tinde's sister (72); the mutual loyalty of Nga Tinde's twin sons (73); Antigone's loyalty to her brother (159); to avenge her brothers, Althaea kills her son (162); Paris avenges his brothers by killing Achilles (227); Hereward the Wake avenges the murder of his younger brother (278); Marko Kraljevic avenges his brother's death (285); Sunjata's sister is loyal to him (310-11); in a Melanesian story the younger brother saves the elder (368).

By contrast, Yamato kills his elder brother in a fit of temper (62); Yoshitsune is hunted down by his jealous brother, Yoritomo (65); Lugalbanda is left for dead by his brothers (90); Abel is killed by his brother, Cain, and avenged by the death of Cain (103); Ramin seduces his brother's wife (128); Faridun's sons are jealous of their younger brother and murder him (132); Rustom is betrayed to his death by his younger brother, but kills him too (133); David of Sassoun kills his half-brother (144); Lalibala's jealous sister tries to murder him (150).

Atreus quarrels with his brother and murders his brother's children (156); the quarrel between the brothers Eteocles and Polynices leads to their deaths (159); Pelias usurps his brother's throne and tries to destroy his brother's son, Jason (159); Medea murders her brother for Jason's sake (159): the quarrel between the brothers Aegyptus and Danaus leads to murder (161); Amulius usurps his brother's throne and tries to kill his sons (165); Romulus kills his twin brother, Remus (166): Feng kills his brother and marries his brother's wife (174); Kriemhild avenges on her brothers the death of her husband, Siegfried (178); to gain the throne, Porrex kills his brother, Ferrex (238); Arthur's sister tries to murder him (240); Alyosha betrays his sworn brother Dobrynya, because he wants Dobrynya's wife (294); Chaka is murdered by his half-brothers (320); Huitzilopochtli persecutes his sister (338); Atahualpa dethrones and murders his half-brother (350).

iv Incest
This is not a common legendary theme, but there are a few examples: Vis and her brother (128); Charlemagne and his sister (221); Arthur and his half-sister (240); Kresnik and his sister (286); Kralj Mataz and his sister (286); Quetzalcoatl and his sister (340).

v Uncle and Nephew
This relationship is sometimes significant, and particularly close, so that it may be all the more shocking if it is violated: Dara and Alexander the Great (116); Pelias and Jason (159); Amulius and Romulus and Remus (165); Feng and Amleth (174); Cu Chulainn is the nephew of the king (183); Roland is Charlemagne's nephew (217); Gawain is Arthur's nephew (242), and so, in the earlier stories, is Mordred (196); Tristan is King Mark's nephew (243); Huitzilopochtli and Copil (338).

Family tensions also arise in relationships between husbands, wives, in-laws and lovers: see the following section.

17 WOMEN, LOVE AND MARRIAGE
Legends come from male-dominated societies and the female characters frequently remain in the background as the mothers or wives of the male ones. However, they are also given more active parts, ranging from the saint to the warrior-woman, or from the faithful wife to the treacherous temptress. For relationships of mothers, daughters and sisters, see the preceding section.

i Religious Heroines
Female saints and women with important religious roles: Antal (21); Mirabai (22); the Buddha's mother (29); St Brigid (191); the Virgin Mary (191, 208) and her mother, Anna (208); Martha and Mary, the three Marys (211); St Catherine of Alexandria (214); St Uncumber (214).

ii Protectors of the People
The aristocratic heroine who self-sacrificingly employs her sex to protect her people: Lady Dzovinar saves her people from destruction by marrying the national enemy (143); Queen Thyra gains peace for her people by feigning love for an enemy (179); Lady Godiva rides naked to free her people from a burdensome tax (278).

iii The Faithful Wife
This theme celebrates married love and feminine fidelity and virtue: Sita, wife of Rama, shares his exile (16); the wife of Ch'en Kuang-jui (54); Iwato-hime (63); Nga Tinde's sister (72); Penelope, wife of Odysseus

(158); Lucretia, the virtuous wife who kills herself after being raped (167); Kriemhild is tricked into betraying her husband, Siegfried, but then avenges him (177, 178); Procla, wife of Pilate, dies with him (212); Alde, betrothed to Roland, falls dead on hearing of his death (219); Queen Bertha (221); Maid Marion shares Robin Hood's outlawry in the forest (277); the wife of Digenes Akrites dies with him (284); the loyal wife in some versions of the 'walled-up wife' story (288).

iv Feminine Villainy

On the other hand, female treachery and faithlessness bulk large in some legends. Delilah betrays Samson to his enemies (98). From a Philistine point of view she would be a heroine, but the story is not told from a Philistine point of view. Ardaban is betrayed by his favourite maiden (127); Helen is false to her husband (155) and Tullia to her father (167); Gertrude marries her husband's murderer (174); Briseida (Cressida) is false to Troilus (226); Guinevere is false to Arthur (236); and Yseult to King Mark (244); Robin Hood is murdered by a treacherous kins-woman (277); Ilele died because of his wife's whims (314-15).

Other evil female figures of legend are the lecherous and murderous Queen Tamar (139); Clytemnestra (157); Phaedra (161); the tyrannical Tanaquil of Rome (166) and the Saxon princess Rowena, who ensnared Vortigern (194). See also La Llorona (345) and the enchantresses and witches listed in Section 3:ii.

v Romantic Love

Some legends focus on the power of romantic love and its usually tragic consequences, for innocent bystanders as well as for the lovers. Lancelot and Guinevere are driven by their passion for each other to betray King Arthur and the result is the destruction of the Round Table and the passing of Arthur's golden age (236, 242, 246). Vis and Ramin, caught in the grip of a force too strong to resist, also cheat and betray those to whom they owe loyalty (128, 129). The same is true of Tristan and Yseult (244) and there are numerous parallels between these two legends, though one ends happily, for the lovers at least, and the other tragically. Grania, betrothed to Finn MacCool, falls in love with one of his men, Dermot, runs away with him and is pursued all across Ireland by Finn, who has his revenge in the end (188).

The seduction of Helen by Paris causes the Trojan War (155, 225), but love crosses the battle-front in the love-triangle of Troilus, Briseida and Diomedes (226) and in the passion of Achilles for Polyxena – he has killed her brother and his love for her leads to his own death (227). Dido, in love with Aeneas, but unable to hold him, kills herself (165). Brunhild, in her hopeless passion for Sigurd, first tries to murder him and then kills herself (176).

Some tales have happier endings: Padmasambhava wins Princess Mandarava and the kingdom (43); Antar wins Abla against all obstacles (123); the Emperor Maxen falls in love with the beautiful Elen in a dream, searches for her and marries her (193); but when a Spanish princess falls in love in a dream with Sir Lachlan MacLean and searches for him she is killed by his wife (204).

There is also the theme of the woman who falls in love with a stranger and for his sake betrays her own family or people: the Ethiopian princess and Moses (102); Medea and Jason, who eventually betrays her in turn (159, 225); Ariadne and Theseus, who abandons her (160).

vi A Woman Captured or Won
The hero carries off a beautiful woman as his wife, often from among his
enemies: Moses and the Ethiopian princess (102); Artashes (138); Paris
and Helen (155): Jason and Medea (159); the Romans carried off the
Sabine women (166); Cu Chulainn carried off Emer and killed her father,
who had plotted his death (184); Digenes Akrites (284); Marko Kraljevic
(285); Tama-te-kapua (373).

King Solomon did not carry off the Queen of Sheba, for she came to
visit him, but the effect was much the same (147). Other heroes celebrated
for success among foreign or enemy womenfolk are Yoshitsune (64);
Samson (98); Theseus (160); Aeneas (165). See also stories of warrior-
women, below.

In a related motif, a woman is won in a contest of skill or strength:
the Buddha's wife (29); Princess Wen Chang in a Tibetan legend (38);
to win Hippodameia, Pelops had to beat her father in a chariot race, the
penalty for failure being death (156); Penelope would yield to whoever
could bend Odysseus's bow, and Odysseus himself won, in disguise (158);
Atalanta could only be won by a man who could outrun her, and the
penalty for failure was death (162); Aeneas fought Turnus in single
combat, and killed him, for the hand of Lavinia (165); Brunhild could only
be won by a man who could outmatch her in athletic contests, and the
penalty for failure was death (177).

vii Warrior-Women
Empress Jingo (63); the Amazons in classical (160-61) and European
legends (255); Amazonian girl bandits in Balkan and Greek legends
(287). There are also the stories in which one of the hero's exploits is to
subdue a formidable Amazon: Theseus and Hippolyte (161); Siegfried and
Brynhild (177); Cu Chulainn and Aife (184); Digenes Akrites and Maximo
(284); Dunay and Nastasya (295).

viii The Abducted Wife
Here, instead of the hero carrying off a woman, his own wife is abducted:
Sita, wife of Rama (16); Ch'en Kuang-jui's wife (54); Helen of Troy
(155); Guinevere, wife of Arthur (196). Penelope, the wife of Odysseus, is
not abducted but is plagued by suitors when her husband in assumed dead
(158), and a similar situation occurs with Dobrynya's wife (294).

18 THE WILD MAN OR FOOL
Enkidu, the wild man of Mesopotamian legend, lives with the animals
(93); Abraham is brought up in ignorance of the world (115); Merlin goes
mad and lives as a wild man in the forest (200); Perceval is brought up in
ignorance of the world (245); the 'wild white man' legend in Australia
(386).

19 POETIC JUSTICE
A frequent ingredient of legends, enjoyed for its own sake, is of the tables
being turned, the biter bit, the operations of poetic justice or poetic irony:
Terami wins the poetry contest (17, 18); in stories about Tansen (23);
Samson turns the tables on his enemies (98); the death of Cain (101); in
the story of Solomon and the chief of demons (150); in a story about Rabbi
Kalonymos (109); Daedalus is shut in his own maze (155); Odysseus turns
the tables on the suitors (158) and Romulus on Remus (166); Hagen, who
murdered Siegfried, is killed with Siegfried's own sword (178); the thirty

pieces of silver paid for betraying Jesus had earlier been paid to protect
him (210); in the legend of the Cross (213); El Cid turns the tables on
Castilian snobbery (251); Vergil turns the tables on Phoebilla (272);
Merlin's magic is turned against him (273); Robin Hood turns the tables on
the Sheriff of Nottingham (277); Peeping Tom is struck blind (279); in the
story of Pope Joan (279); in the story of the Long-ears (277).

20 PROPHECIES AND CURSES
Other popular ingredients of legend are the prophecy that comes true and
the curse which takes effect. For prophecies and portents connected with
the birth of a hero, see Section 7:v.

i Prophetic and Significant Dreams
The Buddha's mother's dream (29); Mahavira's mother's dream (35);
conception of Duke Lao predicted in a dream (53); Hanina's dream
(108); the future greatness of Cyrus foreseen in a dream (126); and of
Ardashir (127); Charlemagne's dream before Rencesvals (218); Brutus's
dream (237); Manoli's dream (289). Aeneas has a vision of the future
greatness of Rome (165).

ii Prophecies and Supernatural Voices
A voice predicts the birth of Ts'ai (56); the Buddha's prophecy (68);
a voice predicts Senapati's kingship (78); Egyptian prophecies (84, 86);
Naram-Sin disregards a prophecy (95); death of Cain prophesied (103);
an angel predicts the building of Gondar (148); prophecies by Laocoon and
Cassandra are disregarded (156); an oracle's prediction about Oedipus
(158); the future of Perseus predicted (161); an oracle's prediction in the
story of Brutus (167); Camillus overhears a prophecy and makes it come
true (168); a wise old king predicts Sigurd's future (176); a mysterious
figure predicts Olav Haraldsson's future (181); the prophetic Stone of
Destiny (189); Merlin's prophecies (200, 202); a voice from heaven in a
legend of the fall of Constantinople (286); Chaka's dying prophecy comes
true (320); Pachacuti Inca's greatness predicted (349).

iii Curses
The smith's curse on Angrok and his line (76); Gilgamesh cursed (92);
Noah's curse on his son (104); Little Meherr cursed by his father (144);
curse on Pelops and his line (156); on Laius and his line (158); Theseus
curses his son (161); curse on Grettir the Strong (175); St Patrick's curses
on Ireland (189); St Columba's curse on Ireland (191); a mother's curse
fulfilled in Wales (198); the Wandering Jew and the *Flying Dutchman*
(280); a curse on gypsies (299); Yahuar-Huacac's curse (348).

21 MYSTERIOUS DEATHS
Just as mystery may surround the birth of a legendary figure, so it may
cling to his death. Instead of dying in the conventional fashion, he may
disappear or be seen still alive after his 'death'. He may be sleeping in a
cave or under a mountain, often with his army round him, waiting for the
moment to return to the world.

i Disappearances and Translations
Antal and Chaitanya each entered a shrine and was never seen again
(21); S. C. Bose was rumoured not to have died (27); Prince Yamato
turned into a white bird (63); Yoshitsune did not die but became
Genghis Khan (65-66); En no Shokaku flew away (67); Elijah was taken

up alive into heaven and has often returned to the world (99); Enoch
was taken up into heaven (100); Nero was rumoured not to have died
(107); Romulus was taken up to heaven (166); Olav Tryggveson was
seen after his death (181); so was Owen Glendower, who did not die but
disappeared (197); King Arthur was taken away to the mysterious Isle of
Avalon (246); Merlin mysteriously disappeared (273); and so did Moses,
Pythagoras, Apollonius of Tyana and Vergil (273); Tsar Alexander I
of Russia was rumoured not to have died, and so were Lord Kitchener, the
family of Tsar Nicholas II, and Adolf Hitler (279-80).

ii Sleeping and Returning Heroes
Frederick Barbarossa (279); King Dan (179); Finn MacCool, Earl
Gerald, Balldearg O'Donnell, Hugh O'Neill and Robert Bruce (185);
King Arthur (196); Owain Lawgoch (197); Thomas the Rhymer (206);
Charlemagne, Owen Glendower, Siegfried, Sir Francis Drake, Sebastian of
Portugal (279); Kralj Mataz (286); the Emperor of Constantinople (286).

22 PLACES
Numerous legends have grown up around places. They account for the
founding of cities, temples, churches, bridges or castles, or they explain
the origins of features of landscape and place-names. Some legends are
concerned with 'lost' or faraway places, real or imaginary.

i Foundation Legends
Quite often, the site of a city or other construction is decided by the
behaviour of an animal: the Shwezigon Pagoda (71); Singapore (79, 80);
Malacca (80); Gondar (148); Debra Tabor (149); Thebes (158); Lavinium
(165); Rome (165); Celtic monasteries (200); Tenochtitlan, now Mexico
City (338).
   There are also tales of gods and other supernatural agencies taking
an important part in the founding and construction: Maturai (17); the
Loyang Bridge (56); Shriksetra (69); the Shwezigon Pagoda (71); Mecca
(114, 115); Lalibala's churches in Ethiopia (150); the old church at
Glastonbury (245); Stonehenge (273); the story of the Virgin of Guadalupe
(341).
   There are also stories of foundation sacrifices (273, 288).

ii Lost and Faraway Places
Many of the lost places have sunk under water, sometimes as a divine
punishment for wickedness: Atlantis (262, 267) is the obvious example, but
there are many others (25, 188, 201).
   Then there are faraway, idyllic places, never-never-lands, islands of
plenty and realms of gold: Avalon (246); Cathay and Cipangu (254);
Amazon territory in the New World (255); El Dorado (259); the garden of
Eden (262); the Fortunate Isles (264); St Brendan's Isle, the Isle of Brazil
and Antillia (264); the Empire of Prester John (275); and Robin Hood's
idyllic greenwood (275); the lost *estufa* of a Pueblo Indian story (326);
the lost marijuana fields of modern American legend (336); the lost city of
Tula (339); Lasseter's Reef and other lost goldfields in Austalia (386).

iii Other Legends of Places
Other examples of topographical legends come from Tibet (43); Mongolia
(48, 50); China (60); Java (78); Jewish tradition (99); Islamic legends
(114); classical tradition (159, 164); Germanic legends (179); Celtic
legends (187, 193, 201, 237); and the Balkans (288).

BIBLIOGRAPHY

THE FAR EAST

INDIA (General)

Basham, A. L. *The Wonder that was India* (London, 1954, 1971; New York, 1959).

Brent, Peter *Godmen of India* (London, 1972; New York, 1973).

Gray, J. E. B. *Indian Tales and Legends* (Oxford, 1961).

Jackson, Robert, Ed. *Perspectives on World Religions* (London, 1978).

Thomas, P. *Epics, Myths and Legends of India* (Bombay, 1961; New York, 1973; London, 1979).

Winternitz, Maurice *A History of Indian Literature* (1927), 3 vols (New Delhi, 1972; New York, 1978).

Hindu Legends

Adigal, Ilango *Shilappadikaram* (The Ankle Bracelet), trans. A. Danielou (New York, 1964; London, 1967).

Kailasapathy, K. *Tamil Heroic Poetry* (Oxford and New York, 1968).

Lannoy, Richard *The Speaking Tree: Study of Indian Culture and Society* (Oxford and New York, 1971, 1974).

Marr, J. R. 'The Periya puranam frieze at Taracuram' (*Bulletin of the School of Oriental & African Studies* Vol. XLII, Part 2, London, 1979).

Rajagopalachari, C. *Mahabharata* (Bombay, 1976); *Ramayana* (Bombay, 1976).

Ramanujan, A. K., Ed. *Speaking of Siva* (London and New York, 1973).

Buddhist Legends

Conze, Edward *Buddhism: Its Essence and Development* (London and New York, 3rd edn 1957, 1974); Ed. *Buddhist Scriptures* (London and New York, 1959, 1969).

Geiger, W. *The Mahavamsa* (Colombo, Sri Lanka, 1950 reprint; London, 1964).

Jones, J. J. *The Mahavastu*, 3 vols (London, 1949-56).

Ling, Trevor *The Buddha* (London, 1973, 1976; New York, 1976).

Mukhopadhyaya, S. *The Asokavadana* (New Delhi, 1963).

Thapar, Romila *Asoka and the Decline of the Mauryas* (London, 1961, 1974).

Thomas, E. J. *The Life of Buddha* (London, 3rd edn 1949, 1975; New York, 1949, 1969); *The History of Buddhist Thought* (London, 2nd edn 1951; New York, 1957, 1963).

Jain and Sikh Legends

Cole, N. Owen and Singh Samba, Piara *The Sikhs* (London and New York, 1978).

Jaini, J. *Outlines of Jainism* (Cambridge, 2nd edn 1940).

McLeod, W. H. *Guru Nanak and the Sikh Religion* (London, 1968; Oxford, 1977).

Williams, R. *Jaina Yoga* (London, 1963).

TIBET

Conze, Edward, Ed. *Buddhist Scriptures* (London and New York, 1959, 1969).

Evans-Wentz, W. Y., Ed. *The Tibetan Book of the Great Liberation* (London, 1954, 1978; New York, 1968, 1978).

Karmay, S. G. *The Treasury of Good Sayings: A Tibetan History of Bon* (London, 1972).

O-rgyan-gling-pa *The Life and Liberation of Padmasambhava*, 2 vols (Emeryville, Calif., 1978).

Stein, R. A. *Tibetan Civilization*, rev. edn trans. J. E. Driver (New York and London, 1972).

MONGOLIA
Bawden, C. R. 'Conversation Between a Sheep, a Goat and an Ox' (*New Orient*, Prague, No. 1, 1966).
Chadwick, Nora K. and Zhirmunsky, Victor *Oral Epics of Central Asia* (Cambridge, Engl. and New York, 1969).
Heissig, Walther *A Lost Civilization: the Mongols Rediscovered* (London, 1966).
Lattimore, O. *Mongol Journeys* (London, 1941, 1947; New York, 1975).

CHINA
Birch, Cyril, *Chinese Myths and Fantasies* (Oxford, 1962).
Christie, Anthony *Chinese Mythology* (London, 1968).
Eberhard, W., trans. *Folktales of China* (London and New York, 1965); *The Local Cultures of South and East China* (Leiden, Netherlands, 1968).
Fitzgerald, C. P. *China: A Short Cultural History* (London, 1935, rev. edn 1962; New York, 1942, 1978).
Werner, E. T. C. *Myths and Legends of China* (London 1922; New York reprint, n.d.).

JAPAN
Aston, W. G. *Nihongi: Chronicles of Japan* (1924), (London, 1956; New York, 1969; Tokyo, 1972).
Chamberlain, B. H. *Ko-ji-ki: Records of Ancient Matters* (Yokohama, Japan, 1883).
Davis, F. Hadland *Myths and Legends of Japan* (London, 1913; New York, 1976).
McAlpine, H. and W. *Japanese Tales and Legends* (London, 1958).
McCullough, Helen Craig *Yoshitsune* (Stanford, Calif., 1966).
Spohr, C. *Gempei, the Civil Wars of Old Japan* (Chicago, 1967).
Turnbull, S. R. *The Samurai* (London and New York, 1977).
Waley, Arthur *The Tale of Genji* (London and New York, 1935).

BURMA
Harvey, G. E. *History of Burma* (London, 1925; New York, 1967).
Htin Aung *Folk Elements in Burmese Buddhism* (Oxford 1962, 1978; Westport, Conn., 1978).
Pe Maung Tin and Luce, G. H. *The Glass Palace Chronicle of the Kings of Burma* (Oxford, 1923; New York, 1976)
Temple, R. C. *The Thirty-Seven Nats* (London, 1906).

INDONESIA AND MALAYSIA
Brown, C. C. *Sejarah Melayu or Malay Annals* (Oxford and New York, 1970).
Covarrubias, M. *The Island of Bali* (New York, 1938).
Holt, Claire *Art in Indonesia* (Ithaca, N.Y., 1967).
Rassers, W. W. *Panji the Culture Hero* (The Hague, 1959).

THE MIDDLE EAST
EGYPT
Erman, A. *The Ancient Egyptians: A Sourcebook of Their Writings,* trans. A. M. Blackman (New York, 1966 reprint).
Gardiner, A. H. *Egypt of the Pharaohs* (Oxford, 1961, 1966; New York, 1966).

Pritchard, J. B., Ed. *Ancient Near Eastern Texts relating to the Old Testament* (Princeton, N.J., 3rd edn 1969).

MESOPOTAMIA
Heidel, Alexander *The Gilgamesh Epic and Old Testament Parallels* (Chicago, 2nd edn 1949, 1963).
Pritchard, J. B., Ed. *Ancient Near Eastern Texts relating to the Old Testament* (Princeton, N.J., 3rd edn 1969).

JEWISH LEGENDS
Bension, Ariel *The Zohar* (London, 1932; Boston, Mass., 1974).
Bin Gorion, M. J., Ed. *Mimekor Yisrael*, 3 vols, trans. I. M. Lask (Bloomington, Ind., 1976).
Braude, William G., Ed./trans. *Pesikta Rabbati*, 2 vols (New Haven, Conn., 1968).
Gaster, Moses, Ed. *The Ma'aseh Book*, 2 vols (Philadelphia, 1934); Ed. *The Exempla of the Rabbis* (New York, rev. edn 1968).
Ginzberg, Louis *The Legends of the Jews*, 7 vols (Philadelphia, 1947, 1956).
Maccoby, Hyam *The Day God Laughed* (London and New York, 1978).

THE ISLAMIC WORLD
al-Din Attar, Farid *Muslim Saints and Mystics*, trans. A. J. Arberry (London, 1966, 1979; New York, 1973).
Boyle, J. A. 'The Alexander Romance in East and West' (*Bulletin of the John Rylands University Library of Manchester* Vol. LX, No. 1, 1977).
Clouston, W. A. *Arabian Poetry for English Readers* (Glasgow, 1881); *A Group of Eastern Romances and Stories* (Glasgow, 1889; Darby, Pa, 1977).
Gibb, E. J. W. *A History of Ottoman Poetry*, 6 vols, especially Vol. 2 (London, 1900-09); Ed. E. G. Browne (London, 1958-65).
Koran, The trans. George Sale (London, 1734). Reprinted many times, still valuable for the wealth of annotations on the legendary background.
Lang, D. M. *The Wisdom of Balahvar* (London, 1958).
Nicholson, Reynold A. *A Literary History of the Arabs* (London, 1907, 1969; New York, 1969).
Pelly, Lewis *The Miracle Play of Hasan and Husain* (1879), (London, 1970).
Rahnema, Zeinolabedin *Payambar: The Messenger*, 3 vols, trans. L. P. Elwell-Sutton (Lahore, W. Pakistan, 1964-66).
Rypka, Jan, Ed. *History of Iranian Literature* (Dordrecht, Netherlands and Hingham, Mass., 1968).
Tales from the Thousand and One Nights 3 vols, trans. E. W. Lane (London 1877); trans. N. J. Dawood (London, 1974).

IRAN
Boyce, M. *Zoroastrians: Their Religious Beliefs and Practices* (London, 1979).
Duchesne-Guillemin, J. *The Religion of Ancient Iran* (Bombay, 1973).
Epic of the Kings, The (*Shahname*) trans. R. Levy (London, 1967, 1973).
Fry, R. N. *The Heritage of Persia* (London, 1976).
Gray, B. *Persian Painting* (Lausanne, 1961; London and New York, 1977).
Herodotus *The Histories*, trans. A. de Sélincourt (London and New York, 1954, 1971).
Visramiani trans. O. Wardrop (London and Mystic, Conn., 1966).

ARMENIA AND GEORGIA
Boyajian, Zabelle *Armenian Legends and Poems* (London, 2nd edn 1958).

Burney, Charles and Lang, D. M. *The Peoples of the Hills* (London, 1971).
Chavchavadze, Prince Ilia *Gandegili* (The Hermit), (Tbilisi, Georgia,
  USSR, 1883); trans M. Wardrop (London, 1895).
Der Nersessian, Sirarpie *The Armenians* (London, 1969).
Kelly, L. *Lermontov, Tragedy in the Caucasus* (London, 1977; New York, 1978).
Lang, D. M. *Armenia, Cradle of Civilization* (London, 2nd edn, 1978);
  The Georgians (London and Boulder, Col., 1966); *Landmarks in Georgian
  Literature* (London, 1966).
Surmelian, L. *Daredevils of Sassoun* (London and Chicago, 1966).

ETHIOPIA

Budge, E. A. Wallis *Book of Saints of the Ethiopian Church* (Cambridge, Engl.,
  1928); *The Queen of Sheba* (London, 1922); *Legends of Our Lady Mary*
  (Oxford, 1933).
Cerulli, E. *The Folk-Literature of the Galla* (Cambridge, Mass., 1922).
Lewis, H. S. *A Galla Monarchy* (Madison and Milwaukee, Wis., 1965).
Pankhurst, E. S. *Ethiopia: A Cultural History* (London, 1955).
Pankhurst, R. K. P. *The Ethiopian Royal Chronicles* (Addis Ababa and
  London, 1967).
Pritchard, J. B., Ed. *Solomon and Sheba* (New York, 1974).
Shack, W. A. and Marcos, H. M. *Gods and Heroes: Oral Traditions of the
  Gurage of Ethiopia* (Oxford and New York, 1974).
Tamrat, Taddesse *Church and State in Ethiopia* (Oxford and New York, 1972).
Ullendorff, E. *The Ethiopians: An Introduction to the Country and People*
  (Oxford and New York, 1973).

THE WEST
CLASSICAL GREECE AND ROME

Carpenter, Rhys *Folk Tale, Fiction and Saga in the Homeric Epics* (Berkeley
  and Los Angeles, Calif., 1946, 1974).
Galinsky, G. K. *Aeneas, Sicily and Rome* (Princeton, N.J., 1969).
Gjerstad, E. *Legends and Facts of Early Roman History* (Lund, Sweden, 1962).
Grant, Michael *Myths of the Greeks and Romans* (London, 1962, 1965;
  New York, 1964); *Roman Myths* (London, 1971; New York, 1972).
Kerenyi, C. *The Heroes of the Greeks* (London, 1959; New York, 1978).
Kirk, G. S. *Myth: Its Meaning and Function in Ancient and Other Cultures*
  Berkeley and Los Angeles, Calif., 1970, 1973); *The Nature of Greek Myths*
  (London, 1974; New York, 1975).
Morford, M. P. O. and Lenardon, R. J. *Classical Mythology* (London and
  New York, 1977).
Rose, H. J. *A Handbook of Greek Mythology* (London, 1958, 1964; New York,
  1959).
Schefold, Karl *Myth and Legend in Early Greek Art*, trans. A. Hicks (London, 1966).
Scherer, M. R. *The Legends of Troy in Art and Literature* (London, 1964).
Ward, A. *The Quest for Theseus* (London, 1970).

GERMANIC LEGENDS

Beowulf trans. D. Wright (London and New York, 1957, 1970).
Elton, O. and Powell, F. York *The First Nine Books of the Danish History of
  Saxo Grammaticus* (London, 1894).
Gordon, R. K., Ed. *Anglo-Saxon Poetry* (London, 1954, 1964, 1976; New
  York, n.d.).

Ker, W. P. *Epic and Romance* (New York, 1957 reprint).
Mackenzie, D. A. *Teutonic Myth and Legend* (London, 1912; Boston, Mass., 1978).
Magnusson, M. and Palsson, Eds/trans. *Njal's Saga* (London and New York, 1960, 1970); Eds/trans. *Laxdaela Saga* (London and New York, 1969).
Niebelungelied, The trans. A. T. Hatto (London and New York, 1965, 1973).
Palsson, H., Ed./trans. *Hrafnkel's Saga* (London and New York, 1971).
Snorri, Sturluson *Heimskringla,* Ed. E. Monen (Cambridge, Engl., 1932).
Undset, S. *Saga of Saints,* trans. E. C. Ramsden (London, 1934; New York, 1968).

IRELAND
Bealoideas, the Journal of the Folklore of Ireland Society, Dublin (since 1926).
Curtin, J. *Tales of the Fairies and of the Ghost World* (1895), (New York, 1970; Dublin, 1974).
Danaher, K., Ed. *Bibliography of Irish Ethnology and Folk Tradition* (Cork, Eire, 1977).
Hyde, D. *Legends of Saints and Sinners* (Dublin, 1915, 1973).
MacNeill, M. *The Festival of Lughnasa* (Oxford, 1962).
Ó Catháin, S. and O'Flanagán, P. *The Living Landscape* (Dublin 1975).
Ó Catháin, S. Ed. *The Bedside Book of Irish Folklore* (Cork, Eire, 1980).
O hEochaidh, S. and others *Fairy Legends from Donegal* (Dublin, 1977).
O Suilleabhain (O'Sullivan), S. *Storytelling in Irish Tradition* (Cork, Eire, 1973); *The Folklore of Ireland* (London, 1974).
O'Sullivan, S. (S. O Suilleabhain), Ed. *Legends from Ireland* (London and Totowa, N. J., 1977).

WALES
Bromwich, Rachel *The Triads of the Island of Britain* (Cardiff, 1979).
Gould, S. Baring and Fish, J. *Lives of the British Saints* (London, 1907).
Jones, D. Parry *Welsh Legends and Folk Lore* (London, 1953).
Jones, Gwyn, Ed. *Welsh Legends and Folk Tales* (Oxford, 1955, 1979; New York, n.d.).
Jones, Thomas, Ed. *The Black Book of Carmarthen* (Oxford, 1967).
Mabinogion, The trans. G. and T. Jones (London, 1974, 1976; New York, 1976).
Rhys, John *Celtic Folklore,* 2 vols (Oxford, 1901; New York and Norwood, N.J. reprints, n.d.).
Styles, Showell *Welsh Walks and Legends* (London, 1972).
Wade-Evans, A. W., Ed. *Vitae et Genealogiae Sanctorum Britanniae* (Latin text and English translation, Cardiff, 1944).

SCOTLAND
Campbell, Lord Archibald, Ed. *Records of Argyll* (Edinburgh, 1885); Ed. *Craignish Tales* (London, 1889; New York reprint, n.d.); Ed. *Clan Traditions* (London, 1895; New York reprint, n.d.).
Child, Francis James *The English and Scottish Popular Ballads* (New York, 1965 reprint).
Macdonald, N., Ed. *The Morrison Manuscripts* (Stornoway, Lewis I., Scotland, 1975).
MacKechnie, John, Ed. *The Dewar Manuscripts,* Vol. 1 (Glasgow, 1964).

MacLellan, Angus *Stories from South Uist,* trans. J. L. Campbell (London, 1961).
Tocher, the Journal of the School of Scottish Studies, Edinburgh (since 1971).

NEW TESTAMENT FIGURES AND SAINTS
Attwater, Donald, Ed. *The Penguin Dictionary of Saints* (London and New York, 1965, 1970).
Farmer, D. H. *The Oxford Dictionary of Saints* (Oxford and New York, 1978, rev. edn 1979).
Horton, Adey *The Child Jesus* (London, 1975).
James, M. R., Ed. *The Apocryphal New Testament* (Oxford, 1924, 1972; New York, 1972).
New Testament Apocrypha, 2 vols, Ed. W. Schneemelcher, trans. R. M. Wilson (London, 1963-64, 1973-74).
Warner, Marina *Alone of All Her Sex : the Myth and the Cult of the Virgin Mary* (London and New York, 1976, 1978).

CHARLEMAGNE LEGENDS
Mandach, A. de, Ed. *La Geste de Charlemagne et de Roland* (Geneva-Paris, 1961).
Moignet, G., Ed. *La Chanson de Roland* (Paris and New York, 1969).
Owen, D. D. R. *The Legend of Roland: A Pageant of the Middle Ages* (London, 1973).
Song of Roland, The trans. D. D. R. Owen (London, 1972).
Whitehead, F., Ed. *La Chanson de Roland* (Oxford, 1942, 1947, 1977; New York, 1977).

MEDIEVAL TROY LEGENDS
Benoît de Sainte-Maure *La Roman de Troie,* 6 vols, Ed. L. Constans (Paris 1904-12; Norwood, N.J. reprint, n.d.).
Konrad von Würzburg *Der trojanische Krieg,* Ed. A. von Keller (Amsterdam, Netherlands, 1965 reprint).
Panton, G. A. and Donaldson, D., Eds. *The Gest Hystoriale of the Destruction of Troy* (1869-73), (Parts 1 & 2 reprint, Millwood, New York, 1968).
Scherer, M. R. *The Legends of Troy in Art and Literature* (London, 1964).
Vallay, C. *Les Légendes du cycle troyen,* 2 vols (Monaco, 1957).

ALEXANDER THE GREAT
Cary, G. *The Medieval Alexander* (Cambridge, Engl. 1967 reprint).
Lambert le Tort and Bernay, Alexandre de *Le Roman d'Alexandre,* 6 vols, Ed. E. C. Armstrong (Princeton, N.J., 1937-76).
Lamprecht *Alexander,* Ed. R. Kinzel (Halle, Germany, 1884).
Ross, D. J. A. *Alexander Historiatus* (London, 1963) ; *Alexander and the Faithless Lady: a Submarine Adventure* (London, 1967) ; *Illustrated Medieval Alexander Books in Germany and the Netherlands* (Cambridge, Engl., 1971).

ARTHUR AND LEGENDARY BRITAIN
Ashe, Geoffrey *King Arthur's Avalon* (London, 1957, 1973) ; *Camelot and the Vision of Albion* (London, 1971, 1975).
Barber, Richard *King Arthur in Legend and History* (Ipswich, Suffolk, 1973; Totowa, N.J., 1974).
Cavendish, Richard *King Arthur and the Grail* (London, 1978; New York, 1979).
Chrétien de Troyes *Arthurian Romances,* trans. W. W. Comfort (London and New York reprint 1955, 1975).

Death of King Arthur, The trans. J. Cable – the Vulgate *Mort Artu* (London and New York, 1971).

Fox, John *A Literary History of France: the Middle Ages* (London and New York, 1974).

Geoffrey of Monmouth *The History of the Kings of Britain,* trans. L. Thorpe (London and New York, 1966).

Gottfried von Strassburg *Tristan,* trans. A. T. Hatto (London and New York, 1960, 1970).

Loomis, R. S., Ed. *Arthurian Literature in the Middle Ages* (Oxford and New York, 1959).

Malory, Sir Thomas *Works,* Ed. E. Vinaver, 3 Vols: the Winchester manuscript (Oxford and New York, rev. edn 1967, 1977).

Quest of the Holy Grail, The trans. P. M. Matarasso (London and New York, 1969).

Sir Gawain and the Green Knight trans. B. Stone (London and New York, 1959, 1970).

Stevens, John *Medieval Romance* (London, 1973; New York, 1974).

Treharne, R. F. *The Glastonbury Legends* (London, 1967).

Vinaver, Eugene *The Rise of Romance* (Oxford and New York, 1971).

Wolfram von Eschenbach *Parsifal,* trans. H. M. Mustard and C. E. Passage (New York, 1961).

EL CID

Lomax, Derek W. *The Reconquest of Spain* (London and New York, 1978).

Mackay, Angus *Spain in the Middle Ages* (London and New York, 1977).

Michael, Ian, Ed. *The Poem of the Cid,* trans. R. Hamilton and J. Ferry (Manchester and New York, 1975).

Smith, Colin, Ed. *Poema de mio Cid* (Oxford, 1972); Ed. *Spanish Ballads* (Oxford, 1964; New York, 1965).

NEW WORLD LEGENDS

Hanson, Earl Parker *South from the Spanish Main* (Washington, D.C., 1967).

Harlow, Vincent T. *Ralegh's Last Voyage* (London, 1932).

Hemming, John *The Search for El Dorado* (London, 1978).

Journal of Christopher Columbus, The trans. C. Jane (London, 1960).

Lee, B. T. and Heaton, H. C., Eds. *The Discovery of the Amazon, according to the Account of Friar Gaspar de Carvajal* (New York, 1934, 1970).

ATLANTIS

Galanapoulos, A. G. and Bacon, E. *Atlantis* (London and Indianapolis, Ind., 1969).

Luce, J. V. *The End of Atlantis* (London, 1969, 1970).

Sprague de Camp, L. *Lost Continents* (New York, 1970, 1975; London, 1971).

Webb, J. 'Atlantis' in *Encyclopedia of the Unexplained,* Ed. Richard Cavendish (London, 1974, 1976).

LEGENDARY MAGICIANS

Butler, E. M. *The Myth of the Magus* (Cambridge, Engl., 1948, 1979).

Cavendish, Richard *A History of Magic* (London, 1977; New York, 1978).

MISCELLANEOUS LEGENDARY FIGURES

Anderson, G. K. *The Legend of the Wandering Jew* (Providence, R.I., 1965, 1970).

Dewar, James *The Unlocked Secret : Freemasonry Examined* (London, 1966, 1972).
Harris, P. Valentine *The Truth about Robin Hood* (Mansfield, Nottingham-shire, 1969, 1978).
Keen, Maurice *The Outlaws of Medieval Legend* (London, 1961, 1977; rev. edn, Toronto, 1978).

THE BALKANS AND GREECE
Cary, G. *The Medieval Alexander* (Cambridge, Engl., 1967 reprint).
Chadwick, H. M. *The Growth of Literature*, Vol. 2 (Cambridge, Engl., 1936, 1968; New York, 1969).
Copeland, F. S. 'Some Aspects of Slovene Folklore' (*Folklore* Vol. LX, London, June 1949).
Dawes, E. A. S. and Baynes, G. *Three Byzantine Saints* (Oxford, 1948; Crestwood, N.Y., 1977).
Hobsbawm, E. J. *Bandits* (London and New York, 1969, 1972).
Lawson, J. C. *Modern Greek Folklore and Ancient Greek Religion* (Cambridge, Engl., 1964 reprint).
Low, D. H. *The Ballads of Marko Kraljevic* (Cambridge, Engl., 1922, 1968; Westwood, Conn., 1968).
Mavrogordato, J. *Digenes Akrites* (Oxford, 1956).
Patterson, R. S. *Romanian Songs and Ballads* (London, 1919).
Subotic, D. *Yugoslav Popular Ballads* (Cambridge, Engl., 1932; Norwood, Pa, n.d.)
Vargyas, L. *Researches into the Medieval History of the Folk Ballad* (Budapest, 1967).

RUSSIA
Chadwick, N. K. *Russian Heroic Poetry* (Cambridge, Engl., 1932; New York, 1964).
Costello, D. P. and Foote, I. P. *Russian Folk Literature* (Oxford 1967).
Magnus, L. A. *The Heroic Ballads of Russia* (London, 1921; Port Washington, N.Y., 1967; Folkestone, Kent, 1968).
Oinas, F. J. and Soudakoff, S. *The Study of Russian Folklore* (The Hague-Paris and Hawthorne, N.Y., 1975).
Sokolov, Y. M. *Russian Folklore*, trans. C. R. Smith (Hatboro, Pa, 1966; Detroit, Mich., 1971).

THE GYPSIES
Bercovici, K. *The Story of the Gypsies* (London, 1929; Detroit, Mich., 1975).
de Ville, F. *Tziganes, témoins des temps* (Brussels, 1956).
Groome, F. H. *In Gypsy Tents* (Edinburgh, 1880, 1973; Norwood, Pa, n.d.).
Hall, George *The Gypsy's Parson* (London, 1916).
Thompson, T. W. Manuscript notebooks in the Romany Collection, Brotherton Library, University of Leeds.

AFRICA AND THE AMERICAS
AFRICA
Biebuyck, D. and Mateene, K. C. *The Mwindo Epic* (Berkeley and Los Angeles, Calif., 1969).
East, R. M. *Stories of Old Adamawa* (Farnborough, Hants, 1967 reprint).
Feierman, S. *The Shambaa Kingdom: A History* (Madison, Wis., 1974).
Finnegan, Ruth H. *Oral Literature in Africa* (Oxford, 1970, 1977).

Innes, G. *Sunjata: Three Mandinka Versions* (London, 1974).
Knappert, J. *Myths and Legends of the Congo* (London, 1971; Atlantic Highlands, N.J., n.d.).
Mofolo, T. *Chaka: An Historical Romance,* trans. F. H. Dutton (Oxford and New York, 1931, 1967).
Niane, D. T. *Sundiate: An Epic of Old Mali,* trans. G. D. Pickett (London, 1965; Atlantic Highlands, N.J., n.d.).
Vansina, J. *Oral Tradition: A study in Historical Methodology,* trans. H. M. Wright (London, 1965, 1973).

THE NORTH AMERICAN INDIANS
Alexander, Hartley Burr *North American Mythology* (Cambridge, Mass., 1916; reprint of 1932 edn, New York, 1964).
Boas, Franz *Kwakiutl Tales* (New York, 1910; New Series, New York, 1935; reprint of 1935 edn, New York, 1969).
Clark, Ella E. *Indian Legends of the Pacific Northwest* (Berkeley and Los Angeles, Calif., 1953, 1960).
McAllester, David P. *Peyote Music* (New York, 1949; Norwood, Pa reprint, n.d.).
Parker, Arthur C. *The Constitution of the Five Nations or the Iroquois Book of the Great Law* (Albany, N.Y., 1916).
Parsons, Elsie Clews *Taos Tales* (New York, 1940; Millwood, N.Y. reprint, n.d.).

THE UNITED STATES OF AMERICA
Boatright, Mody *Folklore of the Oil Industry* (Dallas, 1963).
Botkin, Benjamin *The American People* (London, 1946).
Brunvand, Jan *The Study of American Folklore* (New York, 1968, 1978).
Dorson, Richard *America Begins* (Bloomington, Ind., 1950, 1971; Chicago, 1959; New York, 1972); *Bloodstoppers and Bearwalkers* (Cambridge, Mass., 1952, 1972); *American Folklore* (Chicago, 1959); *Buying the Wind: Regional Folklore in the United States* (Chicago, 1964, 1972); *America in Legend* (New York, 1971; Chicago 1972).
Fry, Gladys-Marie *Night Riders in Black Folk History* (Knoxville, Tenn., 1975).
Settle, William *Jesse James was his Name* (Lincoln, Neb., 1966, 1977).

MIDDLE AMERICA
Bierhorst, J. *Four Masterworks of American Indian Literature* (New York, 1974).
Brotherston, G. *Image of the New World* (London, 1979).
Edmonson, M., Ed. *The Book of Counsel: the Popol Vuh of the Quiche Maya* (New Orleans, 1971).
Hunt, Eva *The Transformation of the Hummingbird* (Ithaca, N.Y., 1977).
Leon-Portilla, M. *The Precolumbian Literatures of Mexico,* trans. Grace Lobanov (Norman, Okla, 1969, 1975).
Paz, O. *Labyrinth of Solitude* (New York, 1962; London, 1967).
Roys, R. L., Ed. *The Book of Chilam Balam of Chumayel* (Norman, Okla, reprint 1967, 1973).
Wolf, E. R. *Sons of the Shaking Earth* (Chicago, 1959, 1962).

THE INCAS
Métraux, Alfred *The History of the Incas,* trans. G. Ordish (New York, 1969).
Sarmiento de Gamboa, Pedro *The History of the Incas,* trans. C. R. Markham (London, 1907).
von Hagen, Victor, Ed. *The Incas of Pedro Cieza de Leon* (Norman, Okla, 1959, 1977).

LOWLAND SOUTH AMERICA

Kaplan, Joanna O. *The Piaroa, a People of the Orinoco Basin* (Oxford and New York, 1975).

Lévi-Strauss, Claude *From Honey to Ashes*, trans. J. and D. Weightman (New York, 1973); *The Origin of Table Manners* (London and New York, 1978).

Murphy, Robert F. *Mundurucu Religion* (Berkeley, Calif., 1963).

Nimuendaju, Curt *The Tukuna* (Berkeley, Clif., 1952).

Wilbert, Johannes *Folk Literature of the Warao Indians* (Berkeley, Calif., 1970).

THE PACIFIC

MELANESIA

Blong, R. J. 'The Krakatoa Myth and the New Guinea Highlands' (*Journal of the Polynesian Society* Vol. LXXXIV, Wellington, N.Z., 1975).

Burridge, K. O. L. *Tangu Traditions* (Oxford and New York reprint 1969, 1972).

Codrington, R. H. *The Melanesians* (Oxford and New York reprint 1969, 1972).

Glasse, R. M. 'Bingi at Tari' (*Journal of the Polynesian Society* Vol. LXXII, Wellington, N.Z., 1963).

Lawrence, P. *Road Belong Cargo* (Melbourne, 1964; Atlantic Highlands, N.J., 1967; Manchester, n.d.).

Poignant, R. *Oceanic Mythology* (London, 1967).

Vicedom, G. F. *Myths and Legends from Mount Hagen,* trans. Andrew Strathern (Port Moresby, Papua, 1977).

Wagner, R. *Lethal Speech, Daribi Myth as Symbolic Obviation* (Ithaca, N.Y., 1978).

Watson, J. B. 'Krakatoa's Echo' (*Journal of the Polynesian Society* Vol. LXXII, Wellington, N.Z., 1963).

POLYNESIA AND MICRONESIA

Alpers, Antony *Maori Myths and Tribal Legends* (Auckland, N.Z., 1964).

Grey, Sir George *Polynesian Mythology and Ancient Traditional History* (1885), Ed. W. W. Bird (Auckland, N.Z., 1974; reprint of 1906 edn, New York, 1976).

Grimble, Sir A. *Migration, Myth and Magic from the Gilbert Islands* (London, 1972).

Lessa, W. A. *Tales from Ulithi Atoll* (Berkeley, Calif., 1961).

Métraux, Alfred *Ethnology of Easter Island* (Honolulu, Hi., 1940).

Mitchell, R. E. *Micronesian Folktales* (Nagoya, Japan, 1973).

Simmons, D. R. *The Great New Zealand Myth* (Wellington, N.Z., 1976, 1978).

AUSTRALIA

Berndt, R. M. and C. H. *Arnhem Land: Its History and Its People* (Melbourne, 1954); *The World of the First Australians* (Sydney, 1977 reprint).

Coleman, P. and Tanner, L. *Cartoons of Australian History* (Melbourne, 1967).

Durack, Mary *Yagan of the Bibbulmun* (Melbourne, 1976 reprint).

Hasluck, Alexandra 'Yagan the Patriot' (*Westerly* 21, University of Western Australia, Nedlands, 1978).

Madigan, C. T. *Central Australia* (Melbourne, 1944 reprint).

Marshall, J. and Drysdale, R. *Journey Among Men* (London, 1962; Melbourne, 1966).

Palmer, Vance *The Legend of the Nineties* (Melbourne, 1966 reprint).
Salter, E. *Daisy Bates* (London, 1963).
Semmler, C. *The Banjo of the Bush: the Life and Times of A. B. Paterson* Brisbane, 1966, 1974); 'A. B. ("Banjo") Paterson, The Man from Snowy River' (in *Australian Poems in Perspective,* Brisbane, 1978).
Wannan, Bill *Legendary Australians* (Adelaide, 1974); *Great Book of Australiana* (Adelaide, omnibus edn 1977).
Ward, Russel *The Australian Legend* (Melbourne, 1958; Oxford, 1967).
Warner, W. L. *A Black Civilization* (New York, 1958 reprint).

INDEX